Linguistic Perspectives on a Variable English Morpheme

"Who would have thought there was so much to say about verbal –s? In this engrossing book Laura Rupp and David Britain tie together an immense body of work from historical linguistics, formal linguistics, functional linguistics and sociolinguistics to propose a coherent and convincing account of the linguistic, social and discourse-pragmatic meanings conveyed by verbal –s. Their remarkable feat points to an entirely new way of thinking about English morphology. This book is essential reading!"

—Prof. Jenny Cheshire, *Department of Linguistics, Queen Mary, University of London, UK*

"This state-of-the-art book on verbal-s is a *tour de force* that will engage scholars interested in novel accounts of the phenomenon's development or who want to understand its morpho-syntax alongside its social and functional versatility in diverse English dialects from East Anglia to the Antipodes. The authors' approach is unique in utilising diachronic, formal, functional and variationist models to address the 'Iconicity Hypothesis', which proves crucial for explaining the spatial and temporal adaptability of verbal –s."

—Prof. Karen Corrigan, *School of English Literature, Language and Linguistics, Newcastle University, UK*

Laura Rupp · David Britain

Linguistic Perspectives on a Variable English Morpheme

Let's talk about –s

palgrave
macmillan

Laura Rupp
Faculty of Humanities
Vrije Universiteit Amsterdam
Amsterdam, The Netherlands

David Britain
Department of English
University of Bern
Bern, Switzerland

ISBN 978-1-4039-3968-5   ISBN 978-1-349-72803-9   (eBook)
https://doi.org/10.1057/978-1-349-72803-9

Library of Congress Control Number: 2019932924

© The Editor(s) (if applicable) and The Author(s), under exclusive licence to Springer Nature Limited 2019
The author(s) has/have asserted their right(s) to be identified as the author(s) of this work in accordance with the Copyright, Designs and Patents Act 1988
This work is subject to copyright. All rights are solely and exclusively licensed by the Publisher, whether the whole or part of the material is concerned, specifically the rights of translation, reprinting, reuse of illustrations, recitation, broadcasting, reproduction on microfilms or in any other physical way, and transmission or information storage and retrieval, electronic adaptation, computer software, or by similar or dissimilar methodology now known or hereafter developed.
The use of general descriptive names, registered names, trademarks, service marks, etc. in this publication does not imply, even in the absence of a specific statement, that such names are exempt from the relevant protective laws and regulations and therefore free for general use.
The publisher, the authors, and the editors are safe to assume that the advice and information in this book are believed to be true and accurate at the date of publication. Neither the publisher nor the authors or the editors give a warranty, express or implied, with respect to the material contained herein or for any errors or omissions that may have been made. The publisher remains neutral with regard to jurisdictional claims in published maps and institutional affiliations.

Cover illustration: Model Matt Stöckli, photographer Dominik Tomasik

This Palgrave Macmillan imprint is published by the registered company Springer Nature Limited
The registered company address is: The Campus, 4 Crinan Street, London, N1 9XW, United Kingdom

Acknowledgements

We would like to thank Danielle Tod and Selina von Allmen for their help in copy-editing the final version of this book, Matt Stöckli for modelling services (!) and Dominik Tomasik for the photo on the front cover. An anonymous reviewer gave us very useful feedback on the final draft. Robert, Sue and our families have demonstrated superhuman patience and stamina during the long long long production of this volume, and for that we are truly truly grateful!

Contents

1	**Introduction**	1
	References	16
2	**Verbal –s**	25
	2.1 Introduction	25
	2.2 Verbal –s	26
	2.3 The History of Verbal –s	27
	2.4 Verbal –s as a Case of Functional Shift	33
	2.4.1 The Northern Subject Rule (NSR)	39
	2.4.2 Other Uses of Verbal –s	72
	2.5 The Iconicity Hypothesis	88
	References	111
3	**Verbal Zero**	129
	3.1 Introduction	129
	3.2 The History of Verbal Zero	131
	3.3 Verbal Zero: East Anglian and African American Vernacular English	133

vii

viii   **Contents**

3.4	Contact and Verbal Zero	140
3.5	A Formal Linguistic Perspective of the East Anglian Subject Rule	150
	References	156

4   Past BE   **165**

4.1	Introduction	165
4.2	Current Patterns of Past BE	166
4.3	The History of Past BE	168
4.4	Dialectological Research on Past BE	172
4.5	Variationist Analyses of Past BE	176
	4.5.1 Preservation of Historical Past BE Forms	177
	4.5.2 Analogical Levelling	179
	4.5.3 Reallocation	183
	4.5.4 Grammatical Conditioning: The Northern and East Anglian Subject Rules	196
4.6	A Formal Linguistic Perspective on Past BE	205
4.7	Past BE from the Perspective of Exaptation and Diagrammatic Iconicity	210
	References	226

5   Verbal –s in Existential *there* Sentences   **237**

5.1	Introduction	237
5.2	Description and Formal Analysis of Existential *there* Sentences	241
5.3	Socio-Historical Linguistic Work on Verbal –s in Existentials	251
	5.3.1 The History of Verbal –s in Existentials	252
	5.3.2 Variationist Studies	254
5.4	Tying Together the Aims of Formal Linguistics and Variationist Studies	260
	5.4.1 Conditioning of Verbal –s by Properties of the Associate-NP	261
	5.4.2 Implications of the Effects of 'Distance', 'Tense' and 'Contraction'	270

5.5 The Grammaticalisation of Existential *there* into a Presentative Sign	273
5.6 Discussion	294
References	310

6 Conclusion — 321
6.1 Verbal –s	321
6.2 Verbal Zero	322
6.3 Past BE	323
6.4 Existentials	323
References	327

References — 329

Index — 365

List of Tables

Table 2.1	The present-tense indicative and subjunctive verb paradigm in the OE West-Saxon dialect from 800	28
Table 2.2	The present tense indicative paradigm in Middle English	29
Table 3.1	Grammatical agreement, ambiguous agreement and anaphoric agreement compared	152
Table 4.1	The geographical distribution of forms of past BE in the Middle English period	169

1

Introduction

Present-day Standard English has little subject-verb agreement morphology. Historically, all verbs were marked for person and/or number in the present and past tense indicative paradigms. This is illustrated by the Middle English data in (1a–b) for the 2nd sing. (*thou*) and the 3rd pl. (*thei*). In the course of the Middle English period, however, most of this agreement marking was lost as a result of the operation of various phonetic changes, the tendency towards the levelling of different forms and the dropping of weak vowels, final –n, and so on (see Fisiak (1968: 90–99) for a detailed overview of the different stages in this development). Currently, in the present tense indicative, the verb is inflected with –s only when the subject is 3rd sing. (compare (2a–c)). As shown in (3a–b), in the past tense, only the verb *to be* has retained distinctive singular and plural forms. By contrast, lexical verbs have a uniform –ed ending across the past tense paradigm (3c–d):

© The Author(s) 2019
L. Rupp and D. Britain, *Linguistic Perspectives on a Variable English Morpheme*,
https://doi.org/10.1057/978-1-349-72803-9_1

1

(1) a. **Thou partest** nat so lightly, by Seint John. (14thC *The Pardoner's Tale*, Chaucer; in Mossé 1952: 98) 'You sha'n't depart so easily, by St John.'[1]

  b. [m]any prophetis and kyngis wolden … heere tho thingis, that ʒe heere, and **thei herden** not. (c1384 *WBible(1)*; in the *Middle English Dictionary*) (2011–2014) '[m]any prophets and kings have desired … to hear the things which you hear, and have not heard them.'[2]

(2) a. **She goes** there all the time, you know. (Clarke 1997: 232)

  b. People says 'yeah but look at your weather, you gets it freezing cold in the winter, **you get_** all the rain.'

  c. **They call_** 'em something like a battlehead or something … (both from Godfrey and Tagliamonte 1999: 89)

(3) a. **She was** here … about three months ago … (Tagliamonte and Smith 1999: 9)

  b. So **you were** all—you were all just bairns. (example from Smith 2000; cited by Adger 2006: 512)

  c. Right away **I called** the children to send a car …

  d. Yes, since **they killed** him. (both from Tagliamonte and Poplack 1993: 179, 192)

It has been noted that many varieties of English demonstrate a use of verb forms that differs from the contemporary Standard English system. In this volume, we will focus on four major non-standard uses: verbal –s, verbal zero, past tense forms of the verb *to be* (past BE) and verbal –s in existential *there* sentences. These uses are illustrated in (4–7) below, respectively. Verbal –s (in (4)) is the use of the suffix –s in contexts that extend beyond the 3rd sing., which in contemporary Standard English is the only grammatical person where –s is permitted. Verbal zero (in (5)) is the opposite: the absence of the –s ending in 3rd sing. contexts.[3] Past BE (in (6)) is variation in the distribution of *was* and *were*; for example, use of *was* in plural contexts where Standard English uses *were*. Verbal –s in existential *there* sentences (in (7)) has been shown to warrant separate treatment (Tagliamonte 1998, amongst others) and involves –s usage with a plural subject.

(4) *Verbal –s*
    The children shouts all the time. (Belfast English; Henry 1995: 20)
(5) *Verbal zero*
    that's **what make** us so cross. (Tristan da Cunha; Schreier 2002: 23)
    Past BE
(6) **We wasna** getting a house at the time. (Buckie; Smith and Tagliamonte 1998: 106)
    Existential there *sentences*
(7) There**'s some pork pieces** left up there too. (New Zealand English; Britain and Sudbury 2002: 218)

We will henceforth use 'verbal –s' as a cover term to refer to these four non-standard usages in varieties of English.[4]

Three questions immediately arise in relation to verbal –s:

1. If verbal –s is not used as an agreement morpheme, what is it?
2. How has verbal –s come to be used for purposes other than for agreement marking?
3. Why is verbal –s used for these other purposes?

Over the past years, these questions have been addressed in research in the fields of language variation and change (henceforth: LVC), where it has received much attention, dialectology (e.g. the *Survey of English Dialects*; Orton and Dieth 1962–1971), historical linguistics (e.g. Holmqvist 1922), and to a lesser extent formal linguistics (e.g. Chomsky 1995) and functional grammar (e.g. Hannay 1985). So have historical linguists demonstrated that in Old English, –s was originally the ending of the 2nd sing. but acquired an extended use across the present indicative paradigm in northern England in the tenth century (Holmqvist 1922: 3–4). LVC-researchers have shown that verbal –s is deployed in a particularly rich variety of ways around the English-speaking world, many of which have roots deep in the history of English. Today, contemporary vernaculars show further uses of verbal –s which add to these historical patterns and compete or coexist with them in an apparent situation of 'layering' (Hopper 1991). Attested functions of verbal –s include: the Northern Subject Rule (NSR; Ihalainen 1994: 221) by which verbal –s may be used with 3rd pl. NP-subjects but not with adjacent pronouns; marking habitual aspect, narrative turns, or polarity; and constructing social identity (Clarke 1997; Rodríguez Louro and Ritz 2014; Schilling-Estes and Wolfram 1994; Cheshire 1982, respectively, and many others whose work we will address here). Formal linguists (like Henry 1995; Mittelstaedt and Parrott 2002; Adger 2006 and others discussed in this volume) have inquired into properties of the language system that play a role in the occurrence of verbal –s.

Whilst a great deal of research has been devoted to documenting and studying verbal –s all around the Anglophone world, there have not been, as Godfrey and Tagliamonte (1999: 88) point out, 'any conclusive or unifying explanations for verbal –s ... This suggests that verbal –s may have been reinterpreted and restructured by speakers in different communities and socio-cultural contexts rather than exhibiting continuity within its source.' While the NSR is frequently presented as the core constraint on verbal –s and has come under the most intense research scrutiny, Montgomery and Fuller (1996) and Cheshire and Ouhalla (1997) have listed at least five other uses. These other patternings of verbal –s have received less attention and to date it is unclear whether they have the same base as the NSR. Throughout the volume, however, we will point to the way in which verbal –s has been systematically deployed to perform particular functions, both linguistic and social. Pulling together the work of several researchers and adding our own perspective, we aim to sketch a theoretical and coherent approach to explaining the diachronic trajectory of the morpheme that has led to its different contemporary manifestations.

Regarding the first research question on the function of verbal –s (*If verbal –s is not used as an agreement morpheme, **what** is it?*), we believe the principal contribution of this study to be our attempt at disentangling the nature of the Northern Subject Rule (NSR). While some have remained somewhat agnostic on the particular way that the NSR distinguishes between NPs and pronouns, thus far, one of the most principled accounts has derived from generative syntax in which pronouns and NPs occupy different positions in the clause structure (Henry 1995; Tortora and Den Dikken 2010; De Haas 2011; see also Börjars and Chapman's 1998 alternative account in the framework of Lexical Functional Grammar). However, as we will show in Chapter 2, it has proven difficult to provide an account that accommodates *both* sub-constraints of the NSR: (1) the Type-of-Subject Constraint, which favours –s in the context of NP-subjects over pronouns, and (2) the Proximity Constraint, which favours –s where the subject is not adjacent to the verb (including pronoun subjects). They have rarely been treated together in the same analysis. We will argue that the NSR is probably best understood as a discourse-pragmatic strategy for entities with low accessibility in the discourse—namely, NPs and distant pronouns—to be signalled by overt marking on the verb (Ariel 1999, 2001). Our discourse-steered approach has been inspired by Givón's (1985: 196–197) 'predictability hierarchy' (that predicts that the less predictable a subject-NP is in the discourse, the more coding material is used to represent it) and Epstein's (1995) discourse perspective on alternative routes in grammaticalisation. Our account is anticipated by Corrigan (1997: 200) who speculated that verbal –s may be 'the default for all persons and numbers in discourse contexts where identification of the non-adjacent subject required greater than usual processing' (see also Clarke's (2014: 90) analysis of the NSR that views the adjacency effect as an 'epiphenomenon deriving largely from cognitive processes', 'rather than constituting an NSR-related grammatical constraint'). The analysis that we propose is situated in Barlow's work on *Agreement as a Discourse Phenomenon* (1992, 1999). Barlow advocates a reconsideration of the nature of agreement relations as primarily belonging to the discourse-pragmatic component of the grammar, rather than to morphosyntax. He points out that theoretical treatments of agreement (in which some identity function maps morphosyntactic agreement features between a subject and a verb) have difficulty handling situations of 'feature discord' or 'feature mismatches' (1999: 191 ff.) (our verbal –s). By contrast, in a discourse-based account of agreement, Barlow maintains, an apparent feature conflict allows for the specification of *extra* rather than conflicting properties, such as animacy, social status, speakers' attitudes, and other information associated with a discourse situation.

Barlow (1999: 193) cites, amongst other examples, data from Turkish where the referent of a plural noun is conceived of as inanimate when it is combined with a singular verb. He postulates that regular subject-verb agreement simply reidentifies the referent, whilst predicates whose features conflict with the features of the subject convey particular conceptions or classifications of intended referents. Thus, following this view, agreement patterns are sensitive to discourse information, and situations in which the features of the subject and the predicate are in conflict 'provide evidence concerning the fundamental nature of the agreement relation' (1999: 191). At a more general level, we take account of Cheshire (2005a, b) who in work on the social embedding of syntactic variants has called for the analysis of syntactic data in their discourse context: 'Speakers use syntactic forms to construct discourse.' (2005a: 503). 'There are many interactional factors, then, that can affect a speaker's choice of construction and that may constrain [syntactic] variation ...' (2005b: 98). Cheshire has argued that syntactic variants should not be 'abstracted from the interactional context in which they occur' (2005b: 87).

We propose that at the heart of the second research question '*How has verbal –s come to be used for purposes other than for agreement marking?*' lies the application of 'functional shift'. In this volume, we will use the term 'functional shift' to refer to the redeployment of an existing linguistic form in a new function. We assume that –s and the past BE forms *was* and *were* may lose their function of marking person and number distinctions where they are generalised across the verb paradigm (Klemola 2000: 329; Pietsch 2005: 180) or no longer have a place/lose their place in the verb paradigm (developments that will be discussed more extensively in later chapters). Subsequently, they can take on other roles: for example, that of signalling relatively inaccessible subjects, marking narrative turns, conveying positive and negative polarity, etc. Cole (2014: 216) has recently argued along similar lines that verbal –s has come to mark the 'cognitively more salient' grammatical distinction of subject type rather than an opaque person-number distinction. In the case of polarity that in some varieties is expressed by a *was/weren't* dichotomy, Schilling-Estes and Wolfram (1994) suggest that 'arguably, the ability to distinguish negatives from positives is functionally far more important than the ability to determine subject person and number – particularly as English sentences have overt subjects' (1994: 290).

The change whereby old grammatical forms may take on new functions has extensively been discussed in the literature and different terms have been proposed to describe it. They are: '(primary) grammaticalization' (Meillet 1912), '(secondary) grammaticalization' (Givón 1991; Traugott 2002), 'exaptation' (Lass 1990, 1997), 'regrammaticalization' (Greenberg 1991), and 'lateral shift' (Joseph 2004). As a general label, we will use the term 'functional shift'. In the course of this volume, we will examine uses of verbal –s against the backdrop of these specific notions of functional shift, whose particular details will be outlined in the following chapters. Specifically, in Chapter 2 we will suggest that verbal –s has undergone 'regrammaticalization'. 'Regrammaticalization' is the 'reinterpretation in a new function' (Greenberg 1991: 301) of an expression at the end of its trajectory of grammaticalisation. Note in relation to verbal –s that it has been demonstrated that verb inflections have frequently grammaticalised from free pronouns (Greenberg 1966; Givón 1976; Siewierska 1999, amongst others). As Cole (2014: 200, Footnote 71) has pointed out, the (primary) grammaticalisation of anaphoric pronouns into agreement morphemes has also been established in the history of English. The 2nd sing. suffix –st is taken to have derived from the reanalysis of an inverted sequence consisting of a verb ending in the suffix –s and the second person pronoun *þu*: verb–s + *þu* > –stu > –st (Campbell 1959: 297, §731). It is this –s(t) morpheme that subsequently generalised across the present tense paradigm and, we assume, turned into a kind of general verbal marker in the final stages of its grammaticalisation trajectory before it took on functions associated with verbal –s. Secondly, we will, in Chapters 2 and 4, suggest that some of the other uses of verbal –s as well as past BE constitute instances of 'exaptation'. Lass (1997: 316) has described 'exaptation' as 'opportunistic: it is a kind of conceptual renovation, as it were, of material that is already there, but either serving some other purpose, or serving no purpose at all.' Amongst the apparent cases of exaptation discussed in this volume are Childs and Van Herk's (2014) fascinating example of the new social meaning that verbal –s has taken on in Newfoundland, Canada, as the more structural role of –s has undergone decline. Lass (1990; in his interpretation of Cheshire's 1982 work on verbal –s in Reading), Godfrey and Tagliamonte (1999), Wright (2001), and Fernández Cuesta (2011) have previously suggested that verbal –s may have been exapted but these proposals have not been worked out in any detail, with the exception of Willis's (2016) work on past BE. Thirdly, we will argue in Chapter 5 that verbal –s in existential *there* sentences has undergone 'secondary' grammaticalisation, along the lines of Traugott (2002). This involves a further development subsequent to the primary grammaticalisation of the locative adverb *there* into existential *there* (Breivik and Swan 2000). We will show that secondary grammaticalisation of existential *there + be* has resulted in the form *there(')s*.[5]

It has been argued that despite the many insights that have come out of studies on functional shifts, we should approach the concepts that they have postulated with some caution. In relation to exaptation, it has been contended that it primarily refers to (just) the *outcome* of a change: 'more a synchronic interpretation of a feature's functionality rather than a hypothesis, or even explanation, of a feature's emergence' (Vermandere and Meul 2016: 281). Joseph (2016) has critically asked whether proposing 'exaptation' as a separate phenomenon is really warranted or whether it is simply a manifestation of more regular and well-understood mechanisms of language change, such as reanalysis and analogy. He concludes that 'ultimately that what matters is that there be available material – marginal or dysfunctional or otherwise – with which speakers can achieve results, i.e. create or extend new forms and serve new communicative uses' (2016: 39).

However, we hope that the functions currently associated with verbal –s may present a window on the nature of functional shifts (in particular, what social and linguistic meanings expressions can potentially acquire). That is, an investigation of verbal –s might enable further refinements of our understanding of the factors that can shape language change. In this context, we will respond to the third research question '***Why*** *has verbal –s come to be used for these other purposes?*' by embracing the possibility that the phenomenon of 'iconization'[6] (Woolard 2008: 438) can motivate and give direction to functional shifts. Fischer (1997)

1 Introduction 9

and De Cuypere (2008) have previously envisaged a role for iconicity in linguistic innovations and language change (especially with respect to word order/syntactic structure). In De Cuypere's (2006: 11) words: '[i]conicity potentially offers an explanation for linguistic structure, either synchronically motivating language use, or diachronically motivating language change ...' [*our translation*].[7] But what is iconicity? The notion of an 'icon', ascribed to the philosopher Peirce (1931–1958), can be understood in contrast to the two other known signs: symbols (which stand in an arbitrary or conventional relationship to the objects or state of affairs they denote) and indexes (which indicate non-referential properties). Following Wescott (1971: 416), an 'icon' is 'a non-arbitrary intentional sign – that is, a designation which bears an intrinsic resemblance to the thing it designates.' Peirce distinguished between 'iconic images' and 'iconic diagrams'. 'Iconic images' 'look like' their referent and occur relatively infrequently in language except in, for example, onomatopoeia (for example *meow*). More relevant for our purposes are 'iconic diagrams', which are based on *relational* similarity (De Cuypere 2008: 115). Haiman, who developed the concept of iconicity in linguistics in his seminal 1980 article on the 'iconicity of grammar' (De Cuypere 2008: 92), defined 'iconic diagrams' as 'a systematic arrangement of signs, none of which necessarily resembles its referent, but whose relationship to each other mirrors the relationships of their referents' (1980: 515). Haiman assumed two subprinciples of diagrammatic iconicity: 'isomorphism' and 'motivation'. By 'isomorphism', there is 'a one-to-one correspondence between the signans [form] and the signatum [meaning/function], whether this be a single word or a grammatical construction' (1980: 515). As McMahon (1994: 86) notes, one example of isomorphism between form and function is that plural number is now usually denoted by one morpheme, –s (*book-books; brother-brothers*), whereas in Old English there were more markers of plurality (*bōc-bēc; brother-bretheren*, in the sense of multiple male siblings). By 'iconic motivation', linguistic expressions reflect a relation between referents in extralinguistic reality. The stock example of iconic motivation that is prevalent in the literature on iconicity is that of sequence, as it is, perhaps somewhat trivially, found in narrative descriptions where the order of narrative clauses mirrors the temporal sequence of the events they describe (Haiman 1980: 516). Another oft-cited example is causative constructions in which the linguistic distance between expressions is perceived to correspond to a greater conceptual distance between their referents; for example, the distance between the causative verb *cause* and the to-infinitive *to fall* in *I caused the tree to fall* makes the activity feel less direct than with the verb *fell* in *I felled the tree* (Haimann 1983: 784). Note also that the isomorphic number distinction that we just cited has been said to be iconically motivated in that plurality in form (N + s = more/larger than N) corresponds to a situation in which there is more that one referent (Fischer 1997: 69).

In this volume, we will suggest that the demise of distinctive person and number marking that triggered the 'functional shift' of –s caused a diagrammatic iconic relationship to be lost/absent, and we will explore whether the subsequently attested uses of verbal –s have restored/implemented such a relationship. In the spirit of Kortmann (1999), we will call this hypothesis THE ICONICITY HYPOTHESIS. It has been shown before that isomorphism may be disrupted—and subsequently reimplemented—by language change (see McMahon 1994: 74 on diachronic developments in the English verb paradigm) and argued that restoration of isomorphism can be a motivating factor in grammaticalisation (see Ramat 1995: 123 on the grammaticalisation of a Latin modal construction into future tense formation in Romance languages). We will assess our Iconity Hypothesis by examining the extent to which the various occurences of verbal –s that we find among varieties of English appear to be of a diagrammatically iconic nature. For example, in Chapter 2 we contemplate that the Reading peer groups of Cheshire (1982) use verbal –s (rather than a standardised form) as an iconically motivated expression of non-standard behaviour. Note in this relation that signs in diagrammatic iconicity can be phonological or grammatical, and that the reflected relationship may be social or denotational. Irvine and Gal (2000: 39–47) have demonstrated an example of diagrammatic iconicity that is phonological and social in their analysis of the use of clicks in Nguni languages in South Africa. What is important to know here is that clicks are not native sounds to speakers of Nguni; they adopted them from Khoi. Irvine and Gal argue that, accordingly, the Nguni appear to have constructed a linguistic ideology in which clicks represent 'foreignness' and are seen as socially emblematic of (the distance felt to) Khoi speakers (2000: 36). In a related development, using clicks has become a means to convey social distance in the special Nguni respect register (2000: 40–45). As Irvine and Gal put it: 'Linguistic features that index social groups or activities appear to be iconic representations of them, as if a linguistic feature somehow depict[s] or display[s] a social group's inherent nature or essence' (2000: 37). An example of grammatical and denotational diagrammatic iconicity has been put forward by Kortmann and Wagner (2005: 3). They posit that the contemporary *was/weren't* pattern in past BE mirrors positive and negative polarity because the two expressions *was* and *weren't* are maximally contrastive (see also Schilling-Estes and Wolfram 1994; Britain 2002).

In our exploration of iconicity as a factor in the outcome of functional shifts that have affected verbal –s, we will take account of concerns about the validity of the notion of 'iconicity' as they have been expressed by, amongst others, McMahon (1994) and Schilling-Estes (2013), and addressed most extensively by De Cuypere (2008). McMahon (1994: 86) notes that 'iconic motivation is a rather more loosely defined concept [than isomorphism LR&DB], embracing widely differing cases where some linguistic form, or set of forms, in some sense mirrors non-linguistic reality' and goes on to say that 'iconicity presents a general tendency in language, but is by no means a law forcing change in a particular direction. [A]t the same time, it seems natural that, given a choice of a number of alternative strategies to resolve a perceptual problem, speakers might select one conforming with such a broad, conceptually-based tendency' (1994: 160). Schilling-Estes cautions that 'we would do well to remember that variants, by their classic definition, can have no social meaning apart from those which they are (initially) *arbitrarily* given by language users, and so variants need not have related meanings across speech communities' (2013: 345). De Cuypere (2008: 1) concurs that it cannot be that similarity between a sign and (our conception of) reality will determine the functioning of a sign because human beings have such natural ability to perceive similarities that either the notion is vacuous or we should only have iconic signs. However, whilst linguists agree that language has a predominantly symbolic character (De Saussure 1915), it has been shown that symbolism and iconicity (as well as indexicality) are not mutually exclusive (for example Eckert 2017: 1200). Levon et al. (2017: 984) have argued that 'standard assumptions about the relationship between linguistic form and perceived meaning' have been challenged by the discovery of 'cross-linguistic exceptions to arbitrary form meaning-pairs' (see for example their discussion of the exploitation of vowel contrasts across languages; see also Kortmann's 1999 typological study of adverbial subordinators). There is some consensus amongst scholars working within the research programme on iconicity that iconic motivation obtains when speakers take up apparent form-meaning correspondences and make them 'work' to convey particular meaning (Irvine and Gal 2000; De Cuypere 2008; Levon et al. 2017 and references therein), a perspective that we will explore for the case of verbal –s.[8]

Next to our major goal of addressing the central research questions: *If verbal –s is not used as an agreement morpheme, what is it? How and why has it come to be used for purposes other than for agreement marking?* this volume has two further aims. First, we will show that the distribution of verbal –s is determined by an interaction of historical, social, structural and discourse-pragmatic factors, and accordingly make the case that LVC-researchers and formal and functional linguists should work together to come to a fuller understanding of the story of verbal –s. Data on verbal –s can also inform and feed back into these disciplines and serve to shed additional light on more general questions in linguistic theorising. For example, formal linguistics can help LVC-research identify grammatical constraints on verbal –s because their theories of subject-verb agreement make predictions as to where verbal –s may or may not occur. It has been a key assumption in variationist linguistics that factors conditioning the use of a variant can be deployed as a diagnostic tool (Poplack and Tagliamonte 1991): 'If two varieties present the same conditioning and direction of effects … then it is highly likely they [have the same grammar LR&DB] and come from the same source variety' (Durham 2013: 60). An apparent similarity in the ranking of constraints has figured prominently, for example, in the ongoing debate as to whether verbal –s occurrences that pertained in post-colonial African American Vernacular English (AAVE) derived from a prior creole or from early British English dialects that were brought to North America (amongst others, Schneider 1983; Bailey et al. 1989; Montgomery et al. 1993; Montgomery and Fuller 1996; Clarke 1997; Singler 1997; Tagliamonte and Smith 2000; Poplack and Tagliamonte 2004; Van Herk and Walker 2005).[9] The strand of research examining this structural interrelatedness of (especially geographically dispersed) language varieties has become known as 'comparative sociolinguistics' (see Tagliamonte 2013). One particularly relevant example of this in the study of verbal –s is Walker's (2007, 2014) comparison of factors influencing two manifestations of verbal –s in existential *there* sentences, *there is* and *there's*, in an attempt to decide whether or not they are of the same kind. Conversely, data from LVC-research on verbal –s are equally useful to issues of importance to grammatical theory. We will show, for example, that these data offer us a way to gain insight into the way in which agreement systems work (cf. for example, the earlier-mentioned possibility of agreement as a discourse phenomenon).

Further, the volume adds new data to the record of verbal –s. We will document a form that is somewhat less well explored: verbal zero, perhaps best known from East Anglia in England and AAVE in the US (Trudgill 1974: 55–56). In this context, we observe and attempt to explain an effect on the use of verbal zero in East Anglia that appears to be the reverse of the Northern Subject Rule (NSR). Recall that by the NSR, NP-subjects promote and pronominal subjects inhibit the occurrence of verbal –s, except when pronouns are separated from the verb. An empirical finding from work by Kingston (2000) and Spurling (2004) has been that in East Anglia, by contrast, NP-subjects are a favouring context for verbal zero and pronominal subjects a favouring context for –s as well as non-standard *was* (Britain 2002). After Britain and Rupp (2005), we will coin this pattern the East Anglian Subject Rule (EASR), and suggest that it may extend into a geographically broader Southern Subject Rule (SSR).

The structure of this volume is as follows. In the following four chapters we address the four categories of verbal –s in English in turn. In each of the chapters, we begin by introducing and providing background to the type of verbal –s under consideration. We then outline any issues that arise, and go on to discuss perspectives from the fields of

LVC and grammatical theory, respectively, before we present our own account that invokes the notions of functional shift and iconicity in language. Finally, we conclude, by foregrounding a number of advances we have made through our investigations of verbal –s and by presenting a unified account of its different structural and functional manifestations. Inevitably, we will have to leave some issues unresolved, and we hope that these may lead to productive discussions and future collaboration between LVC-researchers and formal and functional linguists.

Notes

1. Gloss derived May 2019 from http://www.jsu.edu/depart/english/gates/pardprt.htm.
2. Gloss derived May 2019 from https://www.kingjamesbibleonline.org/Luke-10-24/.
3. In our analysis of verbal –s, we will only consider full verbs because it has been shown that auxiliaries may behave differently. For example, Cheshire (1982) and Clarke (2010) found that in Reading and Newfoundland respectively, speakers use verbal –s only with full verbs, not with auxiliaries, as illustrated for *have* in (8a–b). An added complication is that (in effect, conversely) auxiliaries may sometimes be used without –s in the 3rd sing., as illustrated for the verb *do* in (8c–d). We do think that an investigation of this differential distribution might well generate important evidence for broader theoretical issues at stake, such as the positioning of full verbs and auxiliaries in generative clause structure (see, for example, Ouhalla 1991), but we will not explore these here.

> (8) a. **We has** a muck around in there. (Cheshire 1982: 32)
> b. **They have** been down here once.
> c. **They does** it four or five nights through 'till Christmas. (Clarke 2010: 75)
> d. … you know if **the net don't** tangle too much in the rocks; **it don't** cost the fishermen no money.

4. In the existing literature, other terms have been used to refer to the subject of this study, including, for example, 'non-standard agreement', 'singular agreement', and 'singular concord'. Since, as we envisage, the

non-standard usage of verb forms under consideration here actually embodies *absence of agreement*, we prefer to use the more neutral term 'verbal –s'.

5. Note that it is not the goal of this volume to review and assess the various notions of functional shift in detail. For a fuller survey, see for example Traugott (2004). We have not included in this overview the concept of 'functional renewal' of Brinton and Stein (1995). '[F]unctional renewal' refers to the retention or revival of an existing syntactic form with a new or a renewed function. [...] In essence, functional renewal is the equivalent on the syntatic level of what Lass (1990) calls 'exaptation' ...' (1995: 34). Thus, 'functional renewal' applies to syntactic constructions parallel to the application of 'exaptation' to smaller expressions like morphemes. One core example of functional renewal of linguistic material put forward by Brinton and Stein (1995) is the eighteenth century development of the conclusive perfect construction, which came to express resultative meaning (cf. *I have my paper finished = My paper is in a finished state*; 1995: 34–38). This meaning was previously associated with the perfect construction, which specialised into conveying an activity sense (cf. *I have finished my paper*).

6. Following Irvine (2001: 12, 33), the term 'iconization' is most appropriate to refer to the process leading to iconic expressions/structures and 'iconicity' to the result of that process.

7. '[I]coniciteit [kan] een mogelijke verklaring bieden voor de taalstructuur, hetzij synchroon als mogelijke motivatie van de taalgebruiker, hetzij diachroon als mogelijke verklaring voor de taalverandering die geleid heeft tot de taalstructuur in haar huidige vorm.'

8. We will stick to this general perspective of 'language use' and not engage in the theoretical debate as to whether iconicity has a cognitive-functional basis in that iconic language structures are easier to process or, rather, '[i]conically motivated language is highly consciously created language use in which efficiency is not the primary consideration' (De Cuypere 2008: 193) (for discussion, see, amongst others, Givón 1985; Fischer 2001; De Cuypere 2008: Chapter 6).

9. It has been recognised, though, that despite the historical relationship, the evolution of AAVE has since diverged; particulary in contexts where speakers have been restructuring their ethnolinguistic identities (for example Wolfram and Sellers 1999). This perspective is known as the Neo-Anglicist position (Mallison and Wolfram (2002: 744) and references therein).

References

Adger, D. (2006). Combinatorial variability. *Journal of Linguistics, 42,* 503–530.

Ariel, M. (1999). The development of person agreement markers: From pronouns to higher accessibility markers. In M. Barlow & S. Kemmer (Eds.), *Usage-based models of language* (pp. 197–260). Stanford: CSLI Publications.

Ariel, M. (2001). Accessibility theory: An overview. In T. J. M. Sanders, J. Schilperoord, & W. Spooren (Eds.), *Text representation: Linguistic and psycholinguistic aspects* (pp. 29–87). Amsterdam: John Benjamins.

Bailey, G., Maynor, N., & Cukor-Avila, P. (1989). Variation in subject-verb concord in Early Modern English. *Language Variation and Change, 1,* 285–300.

Barlow, M. (1992). *A situated theory of agreement.* New York: Garland.

Barlow, M. (1999). Agreement as a discourse phenomenon. *Folia Linguistica, 33,* 187–201.

Börjars, K., & Chapman, C. (1998). Agreement and pro-drop in some dialects of English. *Linguistics, 36,* 71–98.

Breivik, L. E., & Swan, T. (2000). The desemanticisation of existential *there* in a synchronic-diachronic perspective. In C. Dalton-Puffer & N. Ritt (Eds.), *Words: Structure, meaning, function: A Festschrift for Dieter Kastovsky* (pp. 19–34). Berlin: Mouton de Gruyter.

Brinton, L., & Stein, D. (1995). Functional renewal. In H. Andersen (Ed.), *Historical linguistics 1993: Selected Papers from the 11th International Conference on Historical Linguistics, Los Angeles, 16–20 August 1993* (pp. 33–47). Amsterdam: John Benjamins.

Britain, D. (2002). Diffusion, levelling, simplification and reallocation in past tense BE in the English Fens. *Journal of Sociolinguistics, 6,* 16–43.

Britain, D., & Rupp, L. (2005). *Subject-verb agreement in English dialects: The East Anglian Subject Rule.* Paper presented at The International Conference on Language Variation in Europe 3, Amsterdam, The Netherlands.

Britain, D., & Sudbury, A. (2002). There's sheep and there's penguins: 'Drift', 'slant' and singular verb forms following existentials in New Zealand and Falkland Island English. In M. Jones & E. Esch (Eds.), *Language change: The interplay of internal, external and extra-linguistic factors* (pp. 209–242). Berlin: Mouton de Gruyter.

Campbell, A. (1959). *Old English grammar.* Oxford: Clarendon Press.

Cheshire, J. (1982). *Variation in an English dialect: A sociolinguistic study.* Cambridge: Cambridge University Press.

Cheshire, J. (2005a). Syntactic variation and beyond: Gender and social class variation in the use of discourse-new markers. *Journal of Sociolinguistics, 9,* 479–508.

Cheshire, J. (2005b). Syntactic variation and spoken language. In L. Cornips & K. Corrigan (Eds.), *Syntax and variation: Reconciling the biological and social* (pp. 81–106). Amsterdam: John Benjamins.

Cheshire, J., & Ouhalla, J. (1997). *Grammatical constraints on variation.* Paper presented at UK Language Variation and Change 1, University of Reading, UK.

Childs, B., & Van Herk, G. (2014). Work that -s! Drag queens, gender, identity, and traditional Newfoundland English. *Journal of Sociolinguistics, 18,* 634–657.

Chomsky, N. (1995). *The minimalist program.* Cambridge, MA: MIT Press.

Clarke, S. (1997). English verbal -s revisited: The evidence from Newfoundland. *American Speech, 72,* 227–259.

Clarke, S. (2010). *Newfoundland and Labrador English.* Edinburgh: Edinburgh University Press.

Clarke, S. (2014). The continuing story of verbal -s: Revisiting the Northern Subject Rule as a diagnostic of historical relationship. In R. T. Cacoullos, N. Dion, & A. Lapierre (Eds.), *Linguistic variation: Confronting fact and theory* (pp. 75–95). London: Routledge.

Cole, M. (2014). *Old Northumbrian verbal morphosyntax and the (Northern) Subject Rule.* Amsterdam: John Benjamins.

Corrigan, K. P. (1997). *The syntax of South Armagh English in its socio-historical perspective* (Doctoral dissertation). University College Dublin, Dublin.

De Cuypere, L. (2006). Iconiciteit in taal: Evolutionarisme en creativiteit. *Studies van de BLK, 1,* 1–12. Retrieved May 2019 from https://sites.uclouvain.be/bkl-cbl/wp-content/uploads/2014/08/cuy2006.pdf.

De Cuypere, L. (2008). *Limiting the iconic: From the metatheoretical foundations to the creative possibilities of iconicity in language.* Amsterdam: John Benjamins.

De Haas, N. K. (2011). *Morphosyntactic variation in Northern English: The Northern Subject Rule, its origins and early history* (Doctoral dissertation). Radboud University, Nijmegen.

De Saussure, F. (1915). *Course in general linguistics.* C. Bally & A. Sechehaye (Eds.) in collaboration with A. Riedlinger (W. Baskin, Trans.). New York: McGraw-Hill Book Company.

Durham, M. (2013). Was/were alternation in Shetland English. *World Englishes, 32,* 108–128.

Eckert, P. (2017). The most perfect of signs: Iconicity in variation. *Linguistics, 55,* 1197–1207.

Epstein, R. (1995). The later stages in the development of the definite article: Evidence from French. In H. Andersen (Ed.), *Historical linguistics 1993: Selected papers from the 11th International Conference on Historical Linguistics, Los Angeles, 16–20 August 1993* (pp. 159–175). Amsterdam: John Benjamins.

Fernández Cuesta, J. (2011). The Northern Subject Rule in first-person-singular contexts in Early Modern English. *Folia Linguistica Historica, 32,* 89–114.

Fischer, O. (1997). Iconicity in language and literature: Language innovation and language change. *Neuphilologische Mitteilungen, 98,* 63–87.

Fischer, O. (2001). The position of the adjective in (Old) English from an iconic perspective. In O. Fischer & M. Nänny (Eds.), *The motivated sign* (pp. 249–276). Amsterdam: John Benjamins.

Fisiak, J. (1968). *A short grammar of Middle English.* Warsaw: Państwowe Wydawnictwo Naukowe.

Givón, T. (1976). Topic, pronoun and grammatical agreement. In C. N. Li (Ed.), *Subject and topic* (pp. 149–188). New York: Academic Press.

Givón, T. (1985). Iconicity, isomorphism and non-arbitrary coding in syntax. In J. Haiman (Ed.), *Iconicity in syntax* (pp. 187–220). Amsterdam: John Benjamins.

Givón, T. (1991). The evolution of dependent clause morpho-syntax in Biblical Hebrew. In E. C. Traugott & B. Heine (Eds.), *Approaches to grammaticalization (Vol. 2): Focus on types of grammatical markers* (pp. 257–310). Amsterdam: John Benjamins.

Godfrey, E., & Tagliamonte, S. (1999). Another piece for the verbal -*s* story: Evidence from Devon in the Southwest of England. *Language Variation and Change, 11,* 87–121.

Greenberg, J. H. (1966). Some universals of grammar with particular reference to the order of meaningful elements. In J. H. Greenberg (Ed.), *Universals of language,* (pp. 73–113). Cambridge, MA: MIT Press.

1 Introduction   19

Greenberg, J. H. (1991). The last stages of grammatical elements: Contractive and expansive desemanticization. In E. C. Traugott & B. Heine (Eds.), *Approaches to grammaticalization (Vol. 1): Theoretical and methodological issues* (pp. 301–314). Amsterdam: John Benjamins.

Haiman, J. (1980). The iconicity of grammar: Isomorphism and motivation. *Language, 56,* 515–540.

Haiman, J. (1983). Iconic and economic motivation. *Language, 59,* 781–819.

Hannay, M. (1985). *English existentials in functional grammar.* Dordrecht: Foris.

Henry, A. (1995). *Belfast English and Standard English: Dialect variation and parameter setting.* Oxford: Oxford University Press.

Holmqvist, E. (1922). *On the history of the English present inflections particularly -t and -s.* Heidelberg: Carl Winter.

Hopper, P. J. (1991). On some principles of grammaticization. In E. C. Traugott & B. Heine (Eds.), *Approaches to grammaticalization (Vol. I): Theoretical and methodological issues* (pp. 17–36). Amsterdam: John Benjamins.

Ihalainen, O. (1994). The dialects of England since 1776. In R. Burchfield (Ed.), *The Cambridge history of the English language (Vol. V): English language in Britain and overseas: Origins and development* (pp. 197–274). Cambridge: Cambridge University Press.

Irvine, J. T. (2001). "Style" as distinctiveness: The culture and ideology of linguistic differentiation. In P. Eckert & J. R. Rickford (Eds.), *Style and sociolinguistic variation* (pp. 21–43). Cambridge: Cambridge University Press.

Irvine, J., & Gal, S. (2000). Language ideology and linguistic differentiation. In P. V. Kroskrity (Ed.), *Regimes of language: Ideologies, polities, and identities* (pp. 35–84). Santa Fe: School of American Research Press.

Joseph, B. D. (2004). Rescuing traditional (historical) linguistics from grammaticalization 'theory'. In O. Fischer, M. Norde, & H. Peridon (Eds.), *Up and down the cline* (pp. 44–71). Amsterdam: John Benjamins.

Joseph, B. D. (2016). Being exacting about exapting: An exaptation omnibus. In F. Van de Velde & M. Norde (Eds.), *Exaptation and language change* (pp. 27–55). Amsterdam: John Benjamins.

Kingston, M. (2000). *Dialects in danger: Rural dialect attrition in the East Anglian county of Suffolk* (MA dissertation). University of Essex, Colchester.

Klemola, J. (2000). The origins of the Northern Subject Rule: A case of early contact? In T. Hildegard (Ed.), *Celtic Englishes II* (pp. 329–346). Heidelberg: Winter.

Kortmann, B. (1999). Iconicity, typology and cognition. In M. Nänny & O. Fischer (Eds.), *Form miming meaning* (pp. 375–392). Amsterdam: John Benjamins.

Kortmann, B., & Wagner, S. (2005). The Freiburg Dialect Project and Corpus. In B. Kortmann, T. Herrman, L. Pietsch, & S. Wagner (Eds.), *A comparative grammar of British English dialects: Agreement, gender, relative clauses* (pp. 1–20). Berlin: Mouton de Gruyter.

Lass, R. (1990). How to do things with junk: Exaptation in language evolution. *Journal of Linguistics, 26,* 79–102.

Lass, R. (1997). *Historical linguistics and language change.* Cambridge: Cambridge University Press.

Levon, E., Maegaard, M., & Pharao, N. (2017). Introduction: Tracing the origin of /s/ variation. *Linguistics, 55,* 979–992.

Mallinson, C., & Wolfram, W. (2002). Dialect accommodation in a bi-ethnic mountain enclave community: More evidence on the development of African American English. *Language in Society, 31,* 743–775.

McMahon, A. M. S. (1994). *Understanding language change.* Cambridge: Cambridge University Press.

Meillet, A. (1912). L'évolution des formes grammaticales. Scientia (Rivista di Scienza) 12, No. 26, 6. In *Linguistique historique et linguistique générale* (pp. 130–148). Paris: Librairie Ancienne Honoré Champion.

Middle English Dictionary. (2011–2014). University of Michigan. Retrieved May 2019 from https://quod.lib.umich.edu/cgi/m/mec/med-idx?egs=all&id=MED20505&type=id.

Mittelstaedt, J., & Parrot, J. (2002). *A distributed morphology account of weren't levelling.* Paper presented at New Ways of Analyzing Variation 31, Stanford University, U.S.

Montgomery, M., & Fuller, J. (1996). What was verbal -*s* in 19th-century African American English? In E. W. Schneider (Ed.), *Focus on the USA* (pp. 211–230). Amsterdam: John Benjamins.

Montgomery, M., Fuller, J., & De Marse, S. (1993). 'The Black Men has wives and Sweet harts [and third person plural -*s*] Jest like the white men': Evidence for verbal -*s* from written documents on 19th-century African American Speech. *Language Variation and Change, 5,* 335–337.

Mossé, F. (1952). *A handbook of Middle English.* Baltimore, MD: John Hopkins University Press.

Orton, H., & Dieth, E. (1962–1971). *Survey of English Dialects.* Leeds: E. J. Arnold.

Ouhalla, J. (1991). *Functional categories and parametric variation*. London: Routledge.

Peirce, C. S. (1931–1958). *Collected papers of Charles Sanders Peirce* (Vols. 1–8). Cambridge, MA: Harvard University Press. [Hartshorne, C., & Weiss, P. (Eds.) 1931–1935 (Vols. 1–6); Burks, A. W. (Ed.) 1958 (Vols. 7–8)].

Pietsch, L. (2005). *"Some do and some doesn't"*: Verbal concord variation in the north of the British Isles. In B. Kortmann, T. Herrman, L. Pietsch, & S. Wagner (Eds.), *A comparative grammar of British English dialects: Agreement, gender, relative clauses* (pp. 125–210). Berlin: Mouton de Gruyter.

Poplack, S., & Tagliamonte, S. (1991). African American English in the diaspora: Evidence from old-line Nova Scotians. *Language Variation and Change, 3*, 301–339.

Poplack, S., & Tagliamonte, S. (2004). Back to the present: Verbal -s in the African American English diaspora. In R. Hickey (Ed.), *Legacies of colonial English: The study of transported dialects* (pp. 203–223). Cambridge: Cambridge University Press.

Ramat, A. G. (1995). Iconicity in grammaticalization processes. In R. Simone (Ed.), *Iconicity in language* (pp. 119–139). Amsterdam: John Benjamins.

Rodríguez Louro, C., & Ritz, M.-E. (2014). Stories down under: Tense variation at the heart of Australian English narratives. *Australian Journal of Linguistics, 34*, 549–565.

Schilling-Estes, N. (2013 [2008]). Investigating stylistic variation. In J. Chambers, P. Trudgill, & N. Schilling-Estes (Eds.), *Handbook of language variation and change* (2nd ed., pp. 327–349). Oxford: Blackwell.

Schilling-Estes, N., & Wolfram, W. (1994). Convergent explanation and alternative regularization patterns: *Were/weren't* levelling in a vernacular English variety. *Language Variation and Change, 6*, 273–302.

Schneider, E. W. (1983). The origin of the verbal -s in Black English. *American Speech, 58*, 99–113.

Schreier, D. (2002). *Terra incognita* in the Anglophone world: Tristan da Cunha, South Atlantic Ocean. *English Word-Wide, 23*, 1–29.

Siewierska, A. (1999). From anaphoric pronoun to grammatical agreement marker: Why objects don't make it. *Folia Linguistica, 33,* 225–251.

Singler, J. V. (1997). The configuration of Liberia's Englishes. *World Englishes, 16*, 205–231.

Smith, J. (2000). *Synchrony and diachrony in the evolution of English: Evidence from Scotland* (Doctoral dissertation). University of York, York.

Smith, J., & Tagliamonte, S. (1998). 'We were *all thegither, I think we* was *all thegither*': *Was* regularization in Buckie English. *World Englishes, 17,* 105–126.

Spurling, J. (2004). *Traditional feature loss in Ipswich: Dialect attrition in the East Anglian county of Suffolk* (BA dissertation). University of Essex, Colchester.

Tagliamonte, S. (1998). *Was/were* variation across the generations: View from the city of York. *Language Variation and Change, 10,* 153–192.

Tagliamonte, S. A. (2013). Comparative sociolinguistics. In J. K. Chambers & N. Schilling (Eds.), *Handbook of language variation and change* (2nd ed., pp. 128–156). Oxford: Wiley-Blackwell.

Tagliamonte, S., & Poplack, S. (1993). The zero-marked verb: Testing the creole hypothesis. *Journal of Pidgin and Creole Languages, 8,* 171–206.

Tagliamonte, S., & Smith, J. (1999). Analogical levelling in Samaná English: The case of *was* and *were. Journal of English Linguistics, 27,* 8–26.

Tagliamonte, S., & Smith, J. (2000). Old *was*, new ecology: Viewing English through the sociolinguistic filter. In S. Poplack (Ed.), *The English history of African American English* (pp. 141–171). Oxford: Blackwell.

Tortora, C., & Den Dikken, M. (2010). Subject agreement variation: Support for the configurational approach. *Lingua, 120,* 1089–1108.

Traugott, E. C. (2002). From etymology to historical pragmatics. In D. Minkova & R. Stockwell (Eds.), *Studies in the history of the English language* (pp. 19–49). Berlin: Mouton de Gruyter.

Traugott, E. C. (2004). Exaptation and grammaticalization. In M. Akimoto (Ed.), *Linguistic studies based on corpora* (pp. 133–156). Tokyo: Hituzi Syobo Publishing.

Trudgill, P. (1974). *The social differentiation of English in Norwich.* Cambridge: Cambridge University Press.

Van Herk, G., & Walker, J. A. (2005). S marks the spot? Regional variation and early African American correspondence. *Language Variation and Change, 17,* 113–131.

Vermandere, D., & Meul, C. (2016). How functionless is junk and how useful is exaptation? Probing the -I/ESC- morpheme. In F. Van de Velde & M. Norde (Eds.), *Exaptation and language change* (pp. 261–285). Amsterdam: John Benjamins.

Walker, J. (2007). "There's bears back there": Plural existentials and vernacular universals in (Quebec) English. *English World-Wide, 28,* 147–166.

Walker, J. (2014). Contrasting patterns of agreement in three communities. In N. Dion, A. Lapierre, & R. Torres Cacoullos (Eds.), *Linguistic variation: Confronting fact and theory* (pp. 7–21). London: Routledge.

Wescott, R. (1971). Linguistic iconism. *Language, 47,* 416–428.

Willis, D. (2016). Exaptation and degrammaticalization within an acquisition-based model of abductive reanalysis. In F. Van de Velde & M. Norde (Eds.), *Exaptation and language change* (pp. 197–225). Amsterdam: John Benjamins.

Wolfram, W., & Sellers, J. (1999). Ethnolinguistic marking of past *be* in Lumbee Vernacular English. *Journal of English Linguistics, 27,* 94–114.

Woolard, K. (2008). Why *dat* now? Linguistic-anthropological solutions to the explanation of sociolinguistic icons and change. *Journal of Sociolinguistics, 12,* 432–452.

Wright, L. (2001). Third-person singular present-tense -*s*, -*th*, and zero, 1575–1648. *American Speech, 76,* 236–258.

2

Verbal –s

2.1 Introduction

The following chapter probes verbal –s. In present-day Standard English, –s is used as an agreement morpheme on verbs with 3rd sing. subjects. In many other varieties of English, however, speakers use –s in different contexts outside the 3rd singular. Previous studies have already provided a great many insights into verbal –s. Historical linguists have traced the origin of verbal –s to Old English. Generative syntacticians have identified syntactic structures where we might expect verbal –s not to function as an agreement morpheme. Variationist studies have identified a range of other uses and ways in which –s has been deployed— according to the so-called Northern Subject Rule and also, for example, as a marker of habituality, narration or vernacular identity. We will tie these findings together in this chapter, exploring *what lies at the heart of the development of verbal –s?* In order to unravel the story of verbal –s, we first delve into its history (Holmqvist 1922; Cole 2014). We then review the case of the Northern Subject Rule. The evidence that the Northern Subject Rule affords leads us to the conclusion that verbal –s may be invoked to signal subjects that have relatively low accessibility

© The Author(s) 2019
L. Rupp and D. Britain, *Linguistic Perspectives on a Variable English Morpheme,*
https://doi.org/10.1057/978-1-349-72803-9_2

25

(Givón 1985; Ariel 1999, 2001), a perspective that has a place in a discourse-situated framework of agreement (Barlow 1992, 1999). It also seems to us that speakers have redeployed –s in a way that restores or implements a diagrammatic iconicity relation (Haiman 1980; McMahon 1994). We will examine to what extent this (what we will term) 'Iconicity Hypothesis' also offers an explanation for the other uses of –s that have been reported on. The processes of functional shift that we hold responsible for the redeployment of –s are regrammaticalisation (Greenberg 1991) and exaptation (from Lass 1990, 1997).

2.2   Verbal –s

Different from what happens in Standard English, English speakers may be found to use the present tense morpheme –s where the subject is other than 3rd singular. We will call this phenomenon 'verbal –s'. Here are some examples that exemplify this use:

(1) a. *1st sing. pronoun*
         I enjoys me, **I likes** me wildlife anything, anything bar computer. (Godfrey and Tagliamonte 1999: 109)
     b. *2nd pronoun*
         You looks like Sarah. (Clarke 1997: 242)
     c. *1st pl. pronoun*
         We buses it down the town. (Cheshire 1982: 43)
     d. *3rd pl. pronoun*
         And **they says** till him 'Well, Mr. Smith, come in on Monday.' (Adger and Smith 2010: 111)
     e. *3rd pl. NP*
         dis (yon) horses pulls weel. (Melchers and Sundkvist 2010: 30)
         And **the women brings** the cooking there … (Jankowski and Tagliamonte 2017: 249)

Verbal –s is a vernacular feature that has been studied in many varieties of English. It has been extensively documented for: many parts of England including the east Midlands (Pietsch 2005); Devon (Godfrey and Tagliamonte 1999); the south-west (Wakelin 1972); Grafton, west Oxfordshire (Wright 2015); Reading (Cheshire 1982); the outer London borough of Redbridge (Levey 2006); the Black Country (Asprey 2007); Lancashire/Greater Manchester (Farnsworth, Shorrocks 1980); Tyneside (Newcastle, Cole 2008; Childs 2011; Buchstaller et al. 2013), Wallsend, Hawick Scots (Childs 2012); Scotland (Edwards and Weltens 1983), including Buckie (Smith 2000); Shetland, one of Britain's 'Northern Isles' (Melchers and Sundkvist 2010: 17); the north and south of Ireland (McCafferty 2003, 2004 and references therein; Beal 1993; Harris 1993; Filppula 1999), including Belfast (Henry 1995) and rural South Armargh (Corrigan 1997); Australia (Rodríguez Louro and Ritz 2014); New Zealand (where it was lost, but survived in existentials; Hay and Schreier 2004); North America, including Newfoundland (Clarke 1997, 1999, 2014; Van Herk et al. 2009; Comeau 2011; Childs and Van Herk 2010, 2014); the Ottawa Valley, Canada (Jankowski and Tagliamonte 2017: 249, though 'extremely rare'); Alabama (Feagin 1979); Ozark (Christian et al. 1988); Ocracoke (Schilling-Estes and Wolfram 1994; Hazen 2000), Roaring Creek (Mallinson and Wolfram 2002) and Hyde County (Wolfram and Thomas 2002), all three in North Carolina; Appalachia (West Virginia, Hackenberg 1973 cited in Feagin 1979; Wolfram and Christian 1976; Montgomery 1989, 1997; Tortora and Den Dikken 2010; Zanuttini and Bernstein 2011); Harrison County, Indiana (José 2007); Smith Island, Maryland (Schilling-Estes and Zimmerman 2000); Brazos Valley, Texas (Bailey et al. 1989); and the Falkland Islands (Sudbury 2001)[1,2].

2.3 The History of Verbal –s

It is a common understanding in variationist linguistics that in order to comprehend the nature and the patterning of contemporary variation in English, we need to examine the situation in earlier stages in the history of the English language (for example Labov 1989). In our contextualisation of verbal –s, we will draw in particular on Holmqvist (1922) and Cole (2014) who have chronicled the historical development of the morpheme.

28   L. Rupp and D. Britain

We begin with Old English (OE). In his important (1922) work on the history of English present tense inflections, Holmqvist reports that in early OE of the eighth century, the OE inflections paralleled the original Germanic endings: 2nd sing. –s, 3rd sing. –þ and –ð, and the plural ending –aþ and –að.[3] According to De Haas (2011: 64), the paradigm had already undergone some syncretism in the plural compared to the 'common Germanic system'. A generalised present-tense indicative and subjunctive paradigm for strong and weak verbs in the southern West Saxon dialect looked like Table 2.1. The verb *trymman* 'strengthen' has been chosen for illustration using the example of Hogg (2012: 45).[4]

Holmqvist (1922: 1) and Cole (2014: 22) note that there are only a few extant records from the eighth and ninth centuries in the early northern Northumbrian dialect (short texts, poems, and runic inscriptions; De Haas 2011: 32; Benskin 2011: 167); however, they suggest that present-tense verb morphology resembled that of the southern dialect. Following Hogg (1992b: 149), the –e ending in the 1st sing. present indicative derived from the subjunctive. Early on the 2nd singular had ended in –s, but later in Old English –st replaced this widely. The final –t in the 2nd singular appears to have arisen from reanalysis of an inverted form in which the 2nd person pronoun *þu* cliticised onto the verb and the intial consonant was reanalysed as part of the verb ending (viz. *þu rides* > **rides þu* > **ridestu* > *þu ridest*). However, the Northumbrian dialect retained –es, as Campbell (1959: 301) has stated: 'Northumbrian has –st rarely'. Lass (1992: 134) notes that of the inflections shown in Table 2.1, three survived into Middle English: –(e)st, –eð and –en, as well as a zero ending –Ø. The developments that led to this situation were the following. At the end of the Old English period, vowels in unstressed syllables were affected by a neutralisation

Table 2.1 The present-tense indicative and subjunctive verb paradigm in the OE West-Saxon dialect from 800

Indicative		Subjunctive	
1st sing.	trymme		
2nd sing.	trymest	singular	trymme
3rd sing.	trymeð		
pl.	trymmað	plural	trymmen

and reduction process (see also Cole 2014: 23–24). Verb endings that were previously differentiated by these vowels could therefore no longer be sustained as separate morphemes, as a result of which the distinction between the 3rd sing. and pl. collapsed into –(e)ð. (The ending of the plural imperative –að, not included in Table 2.1, additionally merged.) The *e* of the ending –est was also subject to syncopation. Furthermore, final –e was lost, leaving the 1st sing. indicative and the singular subjunctive with no ending (next to the imperative singular, which was already endingless). Finally, early (ninth century) loss of final –n led to the decline of a separate inflection for the subjunctive altogether (Hogg 1992a: 305). In addition to this, first in the southern West Saxon dialect, and later in Northumbrian, plural indicative endings were reduced to –e/–Ø when they occurred in inverted structures before the 1st or 2nd pl. pronouns, 'e.g. *wē singaþ* but *singe wē*' (Mitchell and Robinson 2011: 44). Benskin (2011: 159) has called this pattern 'West Saxon' concord. It is thought that the reduced endings in inverted indicatives were copied from the subjunctive because subjunctives regularly occurred with pronoun subjects (2011: 178 ff.). De Haas (2011) and Benskin (2011) attribute the idea to Sweet (1871), and Benskin additionally reports on an alternative, phonological explanation that suggests an even earlier dating than the occurrence of reduced endings in the subjunctive (2011: 160 ff.).

From late Old English into the Middle English period, the verb paradigms of Northumbrian and those of the other dialects further diverged. In Northumbrian, the preserved –(e)s ending in the 2nd sing. was extended to the 3rd sing. and the pl. and eventually into the whole present indicative paradigm including the 1st sing.[5] Lass (1992: 136) calls this the 'innovative' paradigm. Table 2.2 (derived from Fisiak 1968: 97) presents regional verb paradigms in Middle English.

Table 2.2 The present tense indicative paradigm in Middle English

	North	Midlands	South
1st sing.	drinke	drinke	drinke
2nd sing.	drinkes	drinkes(t)	drink(e)st
3rd sing.	drinkes	drinketh/es	drinketh
pl.	drinkes	drinke(n)	drinketh

The most distinctive differences were in the 3rd sing. and pl.: –s was northern, –eth southern and pl. –en was a typical Midlands feature in Middle English.[6] Lass (1992: 138) notes: 'It is well known that for fourteenth-century London speakers [–(e)s] was a northern stereotype: in the Reeve's Tale Chaucer uses it as one of the markers of his northern clerks: they say *ga-s*, *fall-es*, *wagg-es*, *far-es* while the narrator and the non-northern characters say *goo-th*, *mak-eth* etc.'.

Tenth-century northern glosses to three Latin manuscripts attest to the development that caused the variation. The three manuscripts are: the *Lindisfarne Gospels*, the Northumbrian parts of the gloss found in the *Rushworth Gospels* (Rushworth) and the *Durham Ritual*.[7] In these texts, in 3rd sing. and pl. contexts, both the normal OE þ-ending and –s occur. Holmqvist (1922: 2) writes: 'Here, then, we find alternately such forms as findeð, findes in the 3rd sing., and findað, findas in the plur.' Below is an example from Fernández Cuesta (2015: 102) from the *Lindisfarne Gospels* demonstrating the variation between –s and –ð in the 3rd sing. (see also Cole (2014: 24) and De Haas (2011: 67) for illustrating material).

(2) & gif þæt wif **forletas** ðone wer hire & to oðrum onfoas hiu **syngeð** (*Lindisfarne Gospel* Gloss Mk. 10.12)
'And if a woman shall put away her husband and be married to another, committeth adultery.'

Holmqvist, who, like Cole (2014), studied the three glosses, reports that two different theories about the origin of verbal –s have been advanced (1922: 2 ff.). These are: (1) sound change of final –þ to –s, and (2) transfer of –s, by analogy, from the 2nd sing. to the other persons (we refer to his work for references to exponents of these theories). The first theory is dismissed by Holmqvist for, amongst others, the reason that no forms in –s are recorded in the case of nouns ending in –að and –eð (but see Ross 1934 for a rebuttal of these arguments and the idea that the change from [θ] > [s] more readily occurred in particular phonological contexts). Holmqvist argues that we would have expected that sound change had operated blindly across categories, and not selectively to specific grammatical categories (verbs). With respect to the theory of analogical levelling, Holmqvist notes that such a strong influence of the less frequent 2nd person on the much more common 3rd person is somewhat surprising. However, he points out that there was a parallel phenomenon in Old Norse where the 2nd sing. morpheme –r supplanted the 3rd sing. and also invaded the plural. Lass (1992: 136) as well as Hogg (1992b: 151) have ascribed the origin and extension of –s in English to contact with Scandinavian settlers during the Danelaw.[8] Holmqvist counted the relative frequency of occurrence of verb forms ending in –s and –ð and found that –s was decidedly more common (both absolutely and relatively) in the plural than in the 3rd sing. (1922: 9, concrete figures can be found on p. 14 of his study). In the light of this finding, he concludes that the –s of the 2nd sing. must have spread analogically to the 2nd pl. and next to all persons of the plural earlier than to the 3rd sing. (Stein 1986 provides more detail and discussion of the matter.)[9] Following Holmqvist, subsequent details of this development in the north are unknown because no northern texts from the end of the tenth century until the beginning of the fourteenth century have survived. Still, Cole (2014: 216) notes that in the plural, –s will, in turn, have come under the pressure of the ending (–e)/–Ø that was generalised from inverted plural indicatives and present subjunctives to non-inverted indicative clauses.[10] Pietsch (2005: 177) has dated this process to the eleventh–thirteenth centuries.[11,12]

Another innovation that took place in northern Middle English was the transfer of –s to the 1st sing.: 'In the Northern dialect, the –s ending is gradually extended to the 1st person singular of the present indicative' (Mossé 1952: 79, Note Ia), so that 'in this area, the whole paradigm ended in –s' (Wakelin 1972: 119) (see also Mustanoja 1960: 481–482; Lass 1992: 136–137). As we will see, many dialects of present day English may still show –s endings in the plural as well as in the 1st sing. to varying extents. Holmqvist (1922: 49) highlights that the development in the 1st sing. is of a later date. He dates the earliest instance of 1st sing. –s on record to Richard Rolle's *Prose Treatises* (1349). This later dating is supported by De Haas's study of texts in the *Linguistic Atlas of Early Middle English 1150–1350* (LAEME; Laing and Lass 2008–2013), in which she found only one token. Fernández Cuesta

(2011) discovered a few more tokens in her study of LAEME, but in a Goldvarb analysis of a corpus of legal texts from Yorkshire, she has identified the beginning of the Early Modern English period (1450–1490) as showing the highest rates of 1st sing. –s. This 1st sing. use patterned according to the Northern Subject Rule (NSR), a particular constraint on verbal –s that we will address in Sect. 2.4 (cf. for example, *I putt full trust in my wife and **requyres** hir on Goddis be halve* ... (TE 60 1472) 'I put full trust in my wife and require her on God's behalf ...' (2011: 93)). Holmqvist maintains that verbal –s in the 1st sing. was restricted to the context of the NSR. Rodríguez Ledesma (2013) arrives at the same conclusion for Scots in a survey of the *Linguistic Atlas of Older Scots*.

In general, in the Midlands, –s only occurred in the 3rd sing. and was not extended according to northern rules (but see Cole 2014 and McIntosh 1989 for a different perspective on this, which is outlined in Sect. 2.4.1.1). The morpheme progressively spread through the Midlands in the Middle English period (Lass 1992: 136), where it competed with –th. Holmqvist (1922: 50) examined the scope of –s in the Midlands in detail. He did not find any evidence of –s in the twelveth century Midland texts *The Peterborough Chronicle* and *The Orrmulum* (northern Lincolnshire). He also looked at texts from the east and west Midlands from the thirteenth to the fifteenth centuries (1922: 98–99). His conclusion is that at the beginning of the thirteenth century, 3rd sing. –s had not yet spread even to the northernmost part of the east Midlands. Northern west Midland texts showed a tendency to use the new –s ending in the 3rd sing. from the middle or latter part of the fourteenth century. In the central Midlands the dialect was more a mixture between the original –th ending and –s. In the southern part, the 3rd sing. and plural –th forms were maintained the longest, well into the fifteenth century. De Haas (2011: 88) did find a few tokens of plural –s among early Middle English texts from the east- and north-west Midlands in LAEME but they were 'dwarfed' in number by (–e)/–Ø/–n endings and plural –s in the north.

According to Holmqvist (1922: 18), throughout the Middle English period the Northern present tense –s ending did not occur in southern texts. –s did not impose on the plural in the south at all. Rather, Lass (1992: 137) notes that in London texts, the –eth plural began to yield ground to the midland –e(n) that was eventually lost, due to the instability of –e. Hogg (1992b: 151) postulates that the use of –s in the 3rd sing. was not fully established in the southern part of the country until Early Modern English. Holmqvist did not find –s in London texts until the last part of the fifteenth century (1922: 126 ff.) in, for example, the *Cely Papers* (1475–1488). 'In the dialectal area occupied by London and the adjoining countries, to which the *-s* ending was originally quite alien, the forms in *-s* in the 3rd sing. towards the close of the fifteenth century gradually displaced the *-th* forms and became more and more firmly established, primarily in colloquial usage' (1922: 132). From London, usage of –s in the 3rd sing. spread to other districts that were under the influence of the standard dialect. Holmqvist (1922: 185), Stein (1987), and Raumolin-Brunberg (1996: 104–107), in a sample of the *Corpus of Early English Correspondence* (CEEC), have tracked the spread of 3rd sing. –s at the expense of –th across space, grammatical contexts, generations, social strata, literary works and registers in time. Following Kytö (1993), the later stages of the development of the 3rd sing. ending from –th coincided with the beginnings of early American English in the seventeenth century. In a study of early Modern British and American texts in the *Helsinki Corpus*, Kytö found that the rate of change was faster in the colony than back in Britain (1993: 120), contrary to the idea of 'colonial lag' (Görlach 1987) (a delay in language change in the settler variety as compared to the 'home' variety). The developments described in this section stand in marked contrast to the trajectory of development found in the dialect of East Anglia, where a zero suffix was generalised to all subjects, including the 3rd sing. (Trudgill 1974, 1998). The phenomenon of 'verbal zero' is addressed in Chapter 3.

2.4 Verbal –s as a Case of Functional Shift

In the previous section, we saw that in the north of England, –s was generalised from the 2nd sing. across the present-indicative paradigm in early Middle English. It would seem that –s no longer marked a grammatical distinction, leaving it with no clear role. As Klemola (2000: 329, Footnote 2) writes: 'In this type of pattern, where the inflectional marker –*s* has been generalised over the whole paradigm, we cannot describe the –*s* ending as an agreement marker anymore, since it does not serve to signal any information about the characteristics of the subject'[13] (see also Pietsch 2005: 180). However, verbal –s did not give way.[14] As we will see in this chapter, at both earlier times and in contemporary communities, the morpheme has come to be deployed for a variety of different purposes. Among the types of functional shift that have been identified in the literature (see the introduction to this volume again), we think that those of 'regrammaticalization' (Greenberg 1991) and 'exaptation' (Lass 1990, 1997) provide the best perspectives on the new uses of verbal –s. Before we discuss each of these uses in turn in the following sections, we will first outline the notions of 'exaptation' and 'regrammaticalization'.

Both 'regrammaticalization' and 'exaptation' have been associated with the final stages of 'grammaticalization' (Meillet 1912), a phenomenon that we will take up in most detail in Chapter 5. Here we will concentrate on the connection between grammaticalisation and subject-verb agreement. Following Siewierska (1999), most scholars working on agreement take anaphoric pronouns and agreement morphemes to be manifestations of the same token: namely, expressions that identify referents in the discourse. Accordingly, it is commonly assumed that agreement morphemes evolve from anaphoric pronouns. Lehmann (1988: 62) characterises the diachronic relation as follows: '[P]ronouns [signal] that we are dealing – still or already – with a referent also appearing elsewhere in the discourse or in the speech situation. This function of identification or reidentification of a referent and keeping the reference to it constant is also the original function of agreement markers when they develop from pronouns.' In a cross-linguistic investigation of 272 languages, Siewierska found a correlation between reduced phonological substance/a decreasing syntactic independence (from independent pronoun to affix) and loss of referentiality. Since these are core characteristics of grammaticalisation trajectories (Hopper and Traugott 2003: 10–11), the development from pronoun to agreement marker can be seen as a grammaticalisation trajectory. The trajectory is schematised in (3) adapted from Siewierska (1999: 225, 231).

(3) independent pronoun > unstressed pronoun > clitic > affix
   +referential --> -referential[15]

Specifically, when agreement markers first develop from anaphoric pronouns, they initially 'commonly continue to perform an anaphoric function' (1999: 225). At this stage, they are 'anaphoric' agreement markers in that they are in complementary distribution with lexical (pronominal or nominal) subjects. Givón (1976: 151) writes: 'Thus, it is well known that languages with a viable paradigm of subject-verb agreement may anaphorically delete the subject NP without replacing it with an independent pronoun' (think of *pro drop*/null subject languages like Spanish and Italian). Over time, however, this referential function may be lost. Subsequently, at what Siewierska conceives of as the final stage of the grammaticalisation of agreement markers, agreement markers can only co-occur with a referential subject. They will become fully grammatical(ised) to the extent that they completely lose their referentiality and only redundantly express person, number and/or gender; 'redundantly', as these features are now expressed by the subject (Siewierska uses the terms 'anaphoric' and 'grammatical' agreement to distinguish the two types of marking that were postulated by Bresnan and Mchombo 1986). With reference to Campbell (1959: 297, §731), Cole (2014: 200, Footnote 71) points out that the grammaticalisation of an anaphoric pronoun into an agreement morpheme has been observed in the history of English. As we outlined in the previous section, the historical 2nd sing. suffix –st derived from the reanalysis of an inverted sequence consisting of the verb ending –s and the 2nd person pronoun *þu*: verb–s + *þu* > –stu > –st.[16] Siewierska notes that English currently has grammatical agreement.

We now turn to the notion of 'regrammaticalization'. Greenberg (1991: 301) introduced the term 'regrammaticalization' to refer to 'the reinterpretation in a new [grammatical] function' of a morpheme that has become marginal. He illustrates the notion with his earlier work on the development and grammaticalisation of the definite article. When a definite article grammaticalises (Stage III in Greenberg's 1978 cycle), it will be attached to nouns obligatorily and indiscriminately and comes to function 'merely' as a general marker of nominality. One example of this is French, where the definite article is even used in a generic sense, as in *J'aime le fromage* '((In general) I like (*the) cheese'; Harris 1980 cited in Epstein 1995: 162). Regrammaticalization of the definite article occurs when 'since, in fact it exists on virtually all nouns, it becomes a sign of nominality and becomes a productive morpheme with derives nouns from verbs' (Greenberg 1991: 305). Wall and Octavio de Toledo y Huerta (2016: 367) describe Greenberg's notion of regrammaticalization as follows: it 'concern[s] extremely generalized forms … that have therefore lost motivation'.

Next, consider 'exaptation'. In his seminal (1990) paper, Lass introduced the concept of exaptation from biology into the study of language change. Gould and Urba (1982) coined the term in biology where it denotes 'the co-optation during evolution of structures originally developed for other purposes' (Lass 1997: 316). For linguistics, Lass (1990: 81–82) has described the course of exaptation as follows:

> Say a language has a grammatical distinction of some sort, coded by means of morphology. Then say this distinction is jettisoned, PRIOR TO the loss of the morphological material that codes it. This morphology is now, functionally speaking, junk; and there are three things that can in principle be done with it:
>
> (i)   it can be dumped entirely;
> (ii) it can be kept as marginal garbage or nonfunctional/nonexpressive residue (suppletion, 'irregularity');
> (iii) it can be kept, but instead of being relegated as in (ii), it can be used for something else, perhaps just as systematic.
>   […] Option (iii) is linguistic exaptation.

Lass (1990) originally defined linguistic exaptation as the reuse of 'junk': linguistic material with no function. However, the appropriateness of this view was questioned for the reason that linguistic structure is rarely without function (cf. for example Vincent 1995: 435–436) or else we would expect a linguistic item to simply disappear. Lass later acknowledged this criticism and revised his description, admitting that 'useful' features are also commonly exapted: 'Exaptation does not presuppose (biological or semiotic) "emptiness" of the exaptatum'. Rather, exaptation involves 'material that is already there, but either serving some other purpose, or serving no purpose at all' (1997: 318, 316). Other researchers have since attempted to characterise the precise nature of linguistic material that is eligible to undergo exaptation. For example, Willis (2016: 203) speaks of the reuse of 'obsolescent' material, Heine (2003: 168) of 'grammatical forms which have lost most or all of their semantic content', whilst Ramat (1998: 109) has said that '[the] process of functional emptying in most cases is not total, but only partial, in the sense that some features can disappear, while others persist'[17] (see De Cuypere 2005: 17 for an illustrating example from the evolution of progressive aspect in English).

Next to the nature of the exapted material (a non-functional structure becoming functional or existing functional structure acquiring a different function), the other key feature of Lass's definition of exaptation is the 'novelty' of the newly exapted function. '[E]xaptation is "conceptual invention", not extension or levelling or reformulation of paradigms in accordance with a "target" or a "model". In exaptation the "model" itself is what's new' (Lass 1997: 319). Much debate in the literature on exaptation has been centred on the question: what constitutes an innovation? Changes that have been explored as (relatively) new range from an emerging function that was previously non-existent (Joseph 2016: 39), a situation of 'extreme reanalysis' (Willis 2016: 203), a 'leap-like jump' from one function to another (Norde and Van de Velde 2016: 28), a later function that is unrelated or only marginally related to its original use (Lass 1990: 80), a shift in functional priorities (Vermandere and Meul 2016: 269), and change that lacks any apparent motivation on a cognitive or semantic basis (Gardani 2016: 254). In a comparison of exaptation and grammaticalisation, Vincent (1995: 435, Footnote 4) sees exaptation best viewed as an association of an old form and a new function that were 'not [previously] combined in the same linguistic sign' (in contrast, grammaticalization involves both a new form and a new function). Similarly, according to Traugott (2004), in exaptation 'non-decategorialization' and semantic/functional discontinuity occurs, whereas in grammaticalisation, decategorialisation is prototypical, and earlier and later meanings of an expression are different but clearly related within the same semantic domain. De Cuypere (2005) has expressed strong concern that the concept of 'exaptation' loses explanatory power if it is stretched too widely (à la Booij (2010: 211), cited in Vermandere and Meul (2016: 269), who 'strips exaptation to its basics, defining it as the "re-use of morphological markers"' for something different from their original use). Lass has been aware of this concern: 'As presently laid out, the concept of exaptation is not really precise enough; in particular, I do not want to claim that ANY change in the use of linguistic material can be seen as exaptive, which would reduce the concept to triviality' (1990: 82).

Lass (1990: 98) has noted that 'historical junk … may be one of the significant back doors through which structural change gets into systems, by the re-employment for new purposes of idle material'. That is to say that 'exaptation' is an alternative to loss (Norde 2002: 55). McMahon (1994: 172), Traugott (2004: 151), and Narrog (2007) find that exaptation has a natural place at what could otherwise be the end of a trajectory of grammaticalisation. Wall and Octavio de Toledo y Huerta (2016: 314) have proposed to view exaptation as 'a change that does not follow but "breaks out" of an existing or expected course of grammaticalization'. Exaptation hence challenges the 'principle of unidirectionality' (Hopper and Traugott 2003: Chapter 5) that has guided much of the research within the framework of grammaticalisation. As Brinton and Stein (1995) have phrased it: 'Underlying most traditional work in historical linguistics in general have been two basic assumptions. The first assumption is that linguistic change is unidirectional, i.e. non-reversible. It may be retarded, proceed at different speeds during different periods, or get stuck, but it may not be reversed.' The occurrence of counterexamples is recognised by Traugott (2004) albeit that she considers the impact of the challenge to be low. She classifies cases of exaptation as rare and irregular (2004: 151). Joseph (2014: 4) critically notes that no serious attempt has been made at enumerating counterexamples, whilst Narrog (2007) has provided empirical data apparently showing that cases of exaptation are not idiosyncratic and replicated across languages.[18] Hopper and Traugott (2003: 131) appear to allow for a way out when they say that 'a particular grammaticalization process may be, and often is, arrested before it is fully "implemented"'. Wall and Octavio de Toledo y Huerta (2016: 368) offer an alternative view: 'as a matter of fact, syntactic exaptation starts where grammaticalization ends. [...] lying beyond the grammaticalization continuum, this kind of exaptation cannot run counter to it'.

Lass presents several cases of exaptation, the most oft-cited of which is probably the shift in function of adjective morphology in Afrikaans (1990: 88 ff.). In seventeenth century Dutch, adjectives were marked for Case by –e or zero endings depending on the gender of the noun. In Afrikaans, the gender system collapsed, leaving –e without motivation. This situation could have provoked loss; yet quite the opposite happened. The suffix –e was redeployed as a marker of, amongst other things, a category of morphologically complex adjectives (cf. for example *ge-heim-e recepte* 'secret recipes' (1990: 92)).

Summarising, the two notions of 'regrammaticalization' and 'exaptation' refer to the reuse of grammatical structures that have become marginal in the system. In both cases, expressions retain their (the same) grammatical status. We would agree with Von Mengden (2016: 145) that 'the differences between [them] lies in a few details'. What we can make out is that in the case of 'exaptation', the new purpose is a fundamentally novel one.[19] In the next subsections, we will explore historical and contemporary functions of verbal –s that would seem the result of 'regrammaticalization' and 'exaptation'.

2.4.1 The Northern Subject Rule (NSR)

One of the best known recorded uses of verbal –s is the Northern Subject Rule (NSR). By the NSR, use of the morpheme –s is dependent on the category of the subject and the relative distance between the subject and the verb, rather than governed by the subject's person and number features. The term 'northern subject rule' was put forward by Ihalainen (1994: 221).[20] The naming reflects the assumption that the use has historical roots in northern varieties of British English (including northern Midlands dialects and Scots; De Haas 2011: 14; Montgomery 1994). Mustanoja (1960: 481–482) states that this pattern has occurred in present tense verbs in older varieties of Scots and northern England since Middle English times; and that in some dialects the pattern has endured to the present day. He describes the NSR as follows:

> In Northern ME and Middle Scots the conjugation of the verb in the present indicative depends on the nature and position of the subject. If the subject is a personal pronoun immediately preceding or following the verb, the ending is -is (-s) in the 2nd and 3rd person singular; in other persons, singular and plural, there is no ending. Otherwise (i.e. when the personal subject-pronoun is separated from the verb by an intervening word or several words, or when the subject is some other pronoun or a noun) the verb ends in -is (-s) in all persons, singular and plural. (pp. 481–482)

Murray (1873: 211–212) was one of the earliest dialectological studies that reported on this use of verbal –s. Since Montgomery (1994), it has, accordingly, been customary in the literature to see the rule as consisting of two constraints, which we will call: the 'Type-of-Subject Effect' (NP-subjects favour verbal –s over pronouns) and the 'Proximity Effect' (non-adjacent subjects favour verbal –s over subjects that are immediately adjacent to the verb). The effect of subject type and adjacency can be illustrated with the data in (4a–c) from Devon in Godfrey and Tagliamonte (1999: 108–109). The adjacency effect is further illustrated in (4d–g). These examples are from north-east Yorkshire (Cowling 1925: 129, cited in Chapman 1998: 37), Devon again (Poplack and Tagliamonte 2004: 214), Mallinson and Wolfram (2002: 751), and Feagin (1979: 193).

(4) a. **Tractors runs** away. [adjacent NP-subject]
   b. **They sell** tickets so **they know** near enough how many's coming round about. [adjacent PRN-subject]
   c. **You** go off for the day, and **gives** 'em fish and chips on the way home. [distant PRN-subject]
   d. **I** often **tells** him. [intervening adverb]

e. **They** all **plays** duets. 'T is jolly nice, really. [intervening quantifier]
f. **The dogs** in the trucks **barks**. [intervening PP]
g. My **two greatgrandchildren** that **lives** at Oxford **loves** games better than anything. [intervening relative pronoun/clause][21]

Scholars have argued that in the course of the history of the NSR, the scope of the rule has shrunk or changed. In collections of sixteenth and seventeenth century letters, Montgomery (1994) and Rodríguez Ledesma (2017) found the NSR to be still robust in Early Modern Scots to the extent that both subclauses applied almost categorically. However, in a study of early Middle English texts, De Haas (2011) reports that at the time, the second subclause of the NSR showed variation the further the distance to Yorkshire, the core area of the NSR in England: 'Most of the variability is found in the strength of the adjacency condition, which seems absent even in some Northern texts with a strong subject effect' (2011: 22). According to Pietsch (2005: 128), the pattern has become more variable in Modern English dialects (where it occurs), and it is especially favoured in particular syntactic structures. Further, Cole (2014), in a quantitative study of the glosses to the *Lindisfarne Gospels*, and drawing on previous work by McIntosh (1983), has most extensively argued that the NSR is not in fact restricted to the north and occurs with different endings than –s and –Ø. Specifically, the NSR has been attested with –th and –s as early as Old English, and with –en and (–e)/–Ø in the Midlands. Below we will take account of the NSR-matters outlined in this section, as they have been addressed in existing historical, dialectological, contemporary variationist and formal linguistic accounts of the NSR. We will then propose our own account that exploits the discourse properties of nominal and pronominal subjects.

2.4.1.1 Historical Perspectives on the NSR

As Cole (2008: 91) has put it, '[i]t is only by looking into the past that the development of [the NSR] can be accurately assessed in present day varieties'. The NSR has a documented history in northern England and Scotland since the Middle English period. Holmqvist reports: 'In the earliest texts in that dialect which are extant, e.g. *Cursor Mundi*, c. 1300, the tendencies, discernible in Old Northumbrian, towards extension of –s to the plural and the 3rd sing. of the pres. indic. where –ð was the original inflection have been fully carried out, i.e. –s is the only ending in use in the 2nd and 3rd sing. and prevails in the plural, but contrary to the usage in Old Northumbrian, it is used in the plur. only when the verb is not immediately preceded or followed by its proper pronoun' (1922: 49).

De Haas (2011) conducted a quantitative study of present indicative endings in the *Linguistic Atlas of Early Middle English 1150 to 1325* (Laing and Lass 2008–2013) and two other early Middle English texts. She focused on variation between the endings –e/–Ø/–n, verbal –s and –th in the northern dialect area, the bordering areas of the north-west Midlands, and the north-east Midlands. In eleven texts that showed variation between –e/–Ø/–n and –s in the plural, she obtained statistically significant effects for the NSR from a chi-square test in eight texts from the north and the (north-)east Midlands. However, there were differences in the extent of the effect. Whereas the subject condition applied (nearly) categorically in a number of northern and (north-)east Midland texts, the adjacency condition was more variable, even in the north (2011: 95–96). That is, the Proximity effect was not in evidence in some texts which did show the effect on subject type (2011: 100). De Haas summarises: 'it seems to imply that since the pattern was strongest in the northern texts in the corpus, this was probably also the approximate region where the NSR originated; and second, it implies that the subject condition is a more stable and potentially more essential characteristic of the NSR than the adjacency condition.' (2011: 215). She concludes that 'the adjacency condition seems to be most properly analysed as an extra, variable outcome of the distinct syntactic status of pronoun subjects' (2011: 22).[22] However, in Sect. 2.4.1.4 we will suggest that both the Proximity Effect as well as the variability of this effect are accounted for by a discourse-oriented view of the NSR.

Until Cole (2014), it was thought that it was not possible to exactly date the emergence of the NSR because there are no texts from the late tenth until the fourteenth century from which evidence could be gathered. However, in an attempt to uncover any apparent signs of an incipient NSR in Old Northumbrian, Cole (2014) investigated the *Lindisfarne* glosses more closely by applying current multivariate statistical analysis. She found evidence that the NSR was already part of the Northumbrian grammar in Old English, only with different morphological material than the variation between (–e)/–Ø and –s that we know from the present-day NSR: namely, the morphemes –s versus –ð. Recall that this was at a time when in late Old Northumbrian –ð got displaced by the –s ending that was extended from the 2nd sing. to the plural and the 3rd sing. In fact, amongst 3053 tokens with –s or –ð endings, Cole found that in the *Lindisfarne*, the innovative suffix –s was favoured by pronouns and the –ð ending by NPs and contexts in which the pronouns subjects were not adjacent to the verb. The result was statistically significant (2011: 105, 120). (5a–d) presents illustration of this from Cole (2014: 93) and Fernández Cuesta (2015: 107).

(5) a. *1st pl. pronoun* (18/37 tokens of –s (49%))
þæt ue gesegun **we getrymes** ~ quod uidimus testamur (JnGl (Li) 3.11)
'What we have seen we testify'

b. *2nd pl. pronoun* (172/354 tokens of –s (49%))
huu minum uordum **gelefes gie** ~ quomodo meis uerbis credetis (JnGl (Li) 5.47)
'How will you believe my words?'

c. *3rd pl. pronoun* (28/60 tokens of –s (47%))
nedro **hia niomas** ~ serpentes tollent (MkGl (Li) 16.18)
'They will take up serpents'

d. *plural NP* (24/112 tokens of –s (21%))
Nu is ðonne **ða deade gehera ð** stefn sunu godes ... (JNGl (Li) 5.25)
'When the dead will hear the voice of the Son of God ...'

Cole (2014) concludes that while the morphemes may differ, the pattern with –s/–ð is sufficiently similar to the later –Ø/–s pattern to confidently trace the date for the emergence of the NSR to Old Northumbrian. Notably, Cole found a similarly strong effect to exist in 3rd sing. environments, 'with the personal pronoun subject *he* favouring the occurrence of –s significantly more so than singular full NP subjects' (42% vs. 24% –s) (2014: 105–106); a finding that has been replicated in contemporary varieties of English for the morphemes –Ø and –s (see the discussion in Sect. 2.4.1.4). Further, Cole already encountered some tokens of –Ø in all plural pronominal environments (not solely with 1st and 2nd pl. pronoun subjects in the 'West-Saxon concord' contexts of subject-verb inversion). She notes that while alternation between –s and –ð may have been prevalent, –Ø was a 'low-variant form' 'in perfect conformity with the Subject Rule' (2014: 173).

The observation that the pattern of the NSR is independent of current morphological material is commonly attributed to McIntosh (1989) [1983]. He reported the occurrence of variation in the plural between –th (in the context of plural nouns) and the traditional Midland ending –en (in the context of adjacent pronouns) in an area in the east Midlands which includes 'NE Leicestershire, N Northamptonshire, the extreme north of Huntingdonshire, and parts of N Ely and NW Norfolk' (1989: 117; also see his map on p. 120). This area is sandwiched between the region of northern Middle English, where plural –eth gave way to –es, and a southern region, where the Old English plural –(i)aþ was retained longer. McIntosh thinks that the plural use of –th in the east Midlands area does not, however, derive from OE but can be explained as an innovation that was modelled on the NSR paradigm that operated in neighbouring dialects across the border to the north. 'It reflects it … not by introducing the alien morpheme –*es*, but simply by employing … the morpheme –*eth*, familiar already as a third person singular form, for use in the plural as well' (1989: 118). Holmqvist (1922: 148–157) dates this development to the fifteenth and sixteenth centuries: 'The plural form in –*th*, which in ME was at one time completely ousted … by the regular Midland form [–en L&DB] in those dialects out of which Standard English developed, seems to have been revived towards the close of the 15th cent. in the standard language, and becomes comparatively common in the 16th cent. …'. In other words, the speakers in the east

Midlands localised the NSR by deploying –th endings instead of –s with NPs and non-adjacent pronouns. The pattern is illustrated in the ME translation of the *Rosarium Theologie* (McIntosh 1989: 119) and the sixteenth century text *Duke Huon of Burdeux* (Holmqvist 1922: 152):

(6) a. **þei pretende** þam or **feyneþ** (59/20 Caius College Cambridge 354/581).
'They pretend (them) or feign' (translation from De Haas 2011: 79)
b. **the two children resembleth** (12/11)[23]

There have been other variants of the NSR that build on local verb endings. One of them is the plural –n ending, which (as we have seen) has an historical base in the Midlands. However, Fernández Cuesta (2015: 108) presents data from Fernández Cuesta and Rodríguez Ledesma (2007: 126) demonstrating that even in a text from West Riding, Yorkshire, the zero suffix (*we forgyue*) alternates with the –n ending (*þaim þat misdon*) depending on the category and adjacency of the subject, for example:

(7) als **we forgyue þaim** þat **misdon** hus (*Pater Noster*, London British Library Cotton Cleopatra B vi fol 204v, West Riding Yorkshire, thirteenth century)
'As we forgive them that wrong us'

Previously De Haas (2011: 101–102) discovered a north-west Midland NSR dialect in *The Anturs of Arther* from Lancashire where attestations of –n (with pronouns) are found besides –s (with NPs):

(8) a. The dere in the dellun, **Thay droupun** and **daren.**
(*Arthurs IV*, North, ms. 1400–1500 / text 1300–1400)
'The animals in the dells, they droop and tremble'
b. **Thenne byrenes bannes** the tyme.
(*Arthurs IV*, North, ms. 1400–1500 / text 1300–1400)
'The men curse the time'

Thus, data like these demonstrate that the NSR is a more general strategy that is not tied to particular morphemes. As Fernández Cuesta has put it: 'As it diffused southwards, the NSR adopted the morphology of the areas where it spread' (2015: 110; we refer to De Haas (2011: 84–90) for an overview of the endings that were deployed in different regions in early Middle English).

In work on –Ø/verbal –s, it has been somewhat of a contested matter what gave rise to the Type-of-Subject effect (the alternation between NP and pronominal subjects). One view is that it arose when the reduced –Ø endings in inverted indicative constructions with 1st and 2nd pl. pronouns were extended to non-inverted clauses and were also adopted in the 3rd pl. (see Pietsch (2005: 177) for a factor that might have contributed to the latter development). Benskin (2011: 178) notes that such a process will have been facilitated by the displacement of Old English (OE) Verb-Second constructions (that generated X(=any fronted material)–verb–subject orders) by increasingly fixed subject-verb orders in Middle English. Pietsch (2005: 177–178) has postulated that because of the association with (inverted) plural pronouns, reduced endings came to be established as plural *pronoun* endings.[24] The other view is that substratum influence played a role when Anglo-Saxons, speaking Northumbrian, met with Brythonic Celts, who spoke Cumbrian, in the north of England during the OE period (Hamp 1975–1976; Klemola 2000). In Modern Welsh, a descendent of the Cumbrian variety of Brythonic Celtic, the canonical order between the subject and the verb is inverted. Further, it has been observed that Welsh morphology likewise varies between NP-subjects and adjacent pronouns. (9) is an example from Modern Welsh that Adger and Smith (2005: 168) have cited. (9a) and (9b) show that in Welsh, a pronominal plural subject triggers plural inflection on the verb, whereas a plural NP-subject does not but is used with an invariant (3rd sing.) verb form:

(9) a. Gwelodd/Gwelsant   ef/hwy   y car
         saw/saw-3PL   he/they   the car
         'He/They saw the car'
     b. Gwelodd/*Gwelsant   y dyn/dynion   y car
         saw/*saw-3PL   the man/the men the car
         'The man/men saw the car'[25]

According to Siewierska (1999: 228), the pattern arose at a time when agreement morphemes lost their anaphoric/referential function and started co-occurring with overt subjects. In Welsh, however, this has been a partial process to the effect that it only affected pronouns. We will draw on this analysis in our explanation of the conditioning of verbal zero in Chapter 3. We refer to De Haas (2011: Chapter 5) and Benskin (2011) for discussion of the pros and cons of the two views on the emergence of the NSR.

De Haas (2011) has shown that the historical attestation of the Type-of-Subject Effect with (–e)/–Ø vs. –s endings is accounted for by the generative syntactic model of clause structure. In her explanation, she draws on the analysis that Henry (1995) has proposed for the NSR in contemporary Belfast English (see Sect. 2.4.1.3). She points out that research by Van Kemenade (2009) and others has shown that NP- and pronominal subjects occupied different positions in Old English (OE) and early Middle English (ME) clauses: namely, (Spec,TenseP) and a higher subject position that she terms (Spec,FP) (say, what may be (Spec,Agr(eement)P) in contemporary English varieties), respectively. Evidence for the existence of differential subject positions in OE and early ME can be gathered from, amongst other diagnostics, the distribution of subjects in relation to discourse adverbs such as *þa* and *þonne* (both: *then*). De Haas cites research by Van Kemenade (2009) and Fischer et al. (2000) that has demonstrated that in OE texts, NP-subjects either categorically or clearly tend to follow discourse adverbs, while pronominal subjects precede them. The positional difference is shown in the data in (10) below, where the pronoun subject *he* occurs before the adverb *ðonne* ('then') and the NP-subject *se biscep* ('the bishop') after it, respectively (2011: 131–132).

(10) a. Hu mæg **he ðonne** ðæt lof & ðone gilp fleon
           how may he then the praise and the vainglory avoid
           (Cocura, 9.57.18.364)
           'How can he then avoid praise and vainglory…?'
      b. Hu gerades mæg **ðonne se biscep** bruncan ðære hirdelican
           are

how properly may then the bishop enjoy the pastoral dignity (Cocura, 18.133.3.898)
'How, then, can the bishop properly enjoy the pastoral dignity?'

De Haas's corpus study of LAEME texts (*Linguistic Atlas of Early Middle English 1150 to 1325*) confirmed that subject pronouns and subject-NPs had a different distribution relative to adverbs. The difference in placement between the two subject categories was highly significant in all three dialect groups: the north and the east- and west Midlands (2011: 136–148). The two different configurations for the syntax of pronominal and NP-subjects, as proposed by De Haas (2011), are outlined in (11a) and (11b):

(11) a. *Configuration for pronoun subjects*

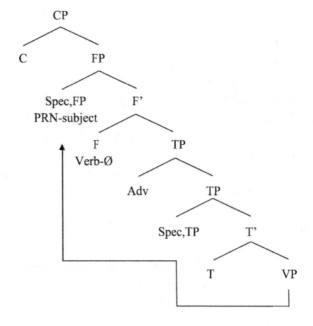

(11) b. *Configuration for NP-subjects*

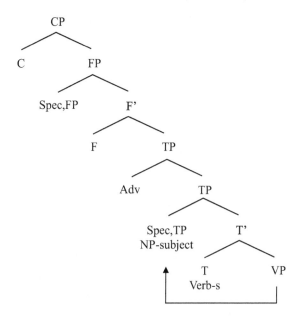

De Haas (2011) assumes that agreement between the subject and the verb must take place within FP. She also assumes that the zero ending is a plural agreement morpheme, whilst –s marks present tense but embodies lack of agreement. On these assumptions, pronouns move across adverbs into (Spec,FP), where they agree with the verb, as illustrated in (11a). By contrast, plural NP-subjects only raise as far as (Spec,TP), as illustrated in (11b).

It is interesting that De Haas (2011) refers to Van Kemenade and Los (2006) and others arguing that in Old English, the position of the subject was actually not so much determined by its syntactic category (viz. pronoun versus NP), but more broadly by discourse properties: the higher subject position (Spec,FP) was for discourse-old entities and the lower subject position (Spec,TP) for discourse-new entities. The point is that entities that are discourse-new are usually full NPs while personal pronouns normally refer back to entities earlier mentioned in the discourse. However, in principle any discourse-old expression could occur in the higher subject position to the left of adverbs in OE.[26] (12) is an example of a pre-adverbial discourse-old NP-subject in the corpus of LAEME texts that De Haas (2011) examined. The example includes the NP-subject *Crist* 'Christ', which, so De Haas argues, has 'a special status in that [it is] always presuppositionally present in religious texts and therefore discourse-old and eligible for placement in (Spec,FP)' (2011: 143–144).

(12) Bot god men sal **crist þan** lede / Til hefenes blis to tak þar mede
      But good men shall Christ then lead / to heaven's bliss to take
      their reward
      (Edincmb f34vb, North, 1300–1325)

We think that it is opportune to explore the possibility of a discourse-driven NSR-system. In the account of the NSR that we propose in Sect. 2.4.1.4, discourse properties are a central explanatory factor.

Cole seems to anticipate an interpretation of the NSR that makes reference to discourse properties. In her view, the NSR is best seen as 'a concord system based on a subject-type distinction, rather than on person/number features'. Such a system would develop 'when covariant forms compete in the same environments' (2014: 4). Cole argues that there is ample evidence that this is a tendency that is attested far beyond the boundaries of the north of England in varieties that are 'separated in time and space' (2014: 85). Recall the historical non-northern varieties that have been discussed in this section; we will also see it in the discussion of the NSR in contemporary varieties in the next section. Cole concludes that the term 'Northern Subject Rule' is a misnomer and finds that it is better replaced by the more neutral term 'Subject Rule' (2014: 1). She (2014: 206) also notes that her analysis compares to the analysis of the innovative use of past BE forms that Schilling-Estes and Wolfram (1994) have observed for the variety of English spoken in Ocracoke (see the discussion in Chapter 4).[27] In this volume, we endeavour to propose a unified account of both these two and other tokens of verbal –s that is embedded in theories of functional shift and iconicity.

We would subscribe to many parts of the analysis provided by Cole (2014). However, we feel that that two fundamental issues are left unresolved. The first is what is meant by 'a concord system based on a subject-type distinction, rather than on person/number features'? Does it mean that it depends on the type of subject whether it agrees with the verb or not? Or does it mean that there are separate agreement morphemes for different types of subject? Or, if it means that agreement morphemes have been remorphologised as markers of type of subject, what is the purpose? Why pronouns and NPs? Secondly, Cole remarks on an 'a predisposition within English for morphological variation and processes of levelling, where they occur, to be conditioned by competing agreement systems, one based on person and number and the other on *subject type and adjacency*' (2014: 156) [our italics]. However, if nothing else is said, the patterning between NPs and non-adjacent pronouns remains rather mysterious. As De Haas (2011: 117) has noted: 'In order to fully understand how and why these patterns arose, we need an account of the syntax and morphology involved that explains the difference between pronoun subjects (Spro) and NP subjects (SNP), including the ways in which they can trigger different inflection, and that also explains why adjacency/non-adjacency would have a variable effect on the inflections, conditioned by subject type.' We will attempt to tackle these issues in Sect. 2.4.1.4, after we have shown how generative syntax has dealt with them. First, however, we will discuss dialectologist and variationist research on the NSR in contemporary English varieties, the findings of which add another piece of the puzzle.[28]

2.4.1.2 Dialectologist and Variationist Studies of the NSR

Reviewing all dialectologist and variationist studies of the NSR would be well beyond the scope of this work.[29] Instead, we will focus on a tendency for the NSR to decline and to get restricted to particular syntactic environments or more or less fixed constructions. Pietsch (2005: 171) has phrased this in terms of 'prototypes'.

Klemola (2000: 331–333) examined 12 questionnaire items from the *Survey of English Dialects* (SED; Orton and Halliday 1962) that could demonstrate the NSR. Among these were IV. 6.2. *Some people have a shed and a wire-netting run at the bottom of their garden in which they … [keep hens]* and III. 10.7 *Bulls … [bellow]*. He concludes that 'the counties representing the North proper (North Humberland, Cumberland, Durham, Westmorland)' follow the Northern Subject Rule more consistently than parts of Yorkshire and the north Midland counties to the south of Yorkshire.[30] Pietsch (2005) additionally consulted the Incidental Material (recorded spontaneous utterances of the SED-informants) and found that in what he calls the 'transition zone' of the NSR (see his Map 7 on p. 163), almost 80% of the recorded tokens of verbal –s occurred in a set of special environments. The corresponding figure for the core northern area was lower but nonetheless amounted to 50%. Pietsch observed similar prototypes in two other corpora: *the Northern Ireland Transcribed Corpus of Speech* from the 1970s (NITCS; Kirk 1991) and Lowland Scottish and northern English data from a preliminary version of the *Freiburg English Dialect Corpus* that was collected between the 1970s and the 1990s (FRED; Kortmann and Wagner 2005). (We refer to Pietsch (2005: 132–133) for details of these corpora.) The two corpora could be studied quantitatively in a Varbrul analysis and the results for the four most strongly favouring environments converged (2005: 162, 171–172). They are listed in (1–4 below). We have added (5) from the literature.

1. *Relative clauses with plural antecedents* ('take verbal –s up to twice as often as other clauses' Pietsch (2005: 168); also cf. for example Feagin (1979: 191), Eisikovits (1991: 248), Clarke (2014: 84), Chapman (1998: 38): 'In the West Riding area of Yorkshire analogical –s has been lost everywhere except in relative clauses', and José 2007: 262).

   (13) a. My **two greatgrandchildren** that **lives** at Oxford **loves** games better than anything. (Anniston, Alabama; Feagin 1979: 193)
   b. Them's **the men** that **does** their work best. (Wright 1892: 156; cited in Chapman 1998: 38)
   c. You get **wee ones** that **screws** things. (Irish English; Harris 1993: 155);

2. *Subjects separated from the verb (including tokens of subject-verb inversion).*

   (14) a. **I** hold both farms in my own hands and **puts** them under Stock and crop myself. (Charles Montgomery, October 10, 1824; in Montgomery and Fuller 1996: 219)

b. With new residents **comes new vehicles** to increase traffic congestions to and from St. John's. (Telegram, August 25, 2012, A17; Clarke 2014: 88)

c. **Has thi taties** comed up yet? (SED: Y7; Pietsch 2005: 166) (note that in contemporary NSR-dialects, verbal –s will occur on auxiliaries in inverted questions);

3. *Clauses with indefinite pronoun subjects such as* some *or* a lot of them.

(15) Now **lot of people wants** to know if … (Appalachia; Montgomery 1989: 258);

4. *The demonstratives* them *and* thae *when dialectally used as subject pronouns.*

(16) **Them's** what they carried. (Farnsworth; Shorrocks 1980: 568)[31];

5. *NPs that are "heavy"* (i.e., plural nouns that are modified by extensive material like 'a sequence of several prepositional phrases' (Bailey, Maynor and Cukor-Avila 1989: 291)–and, as a result, get separated from the verb).

(17) **the fishers of Oregon**, generally **comes** to Cape Juda. (Newfoundland, Dorset; Clarke 2014: 84)[32,33]

The favouring effect of especially relative clauses and interrogatives on the presence of verbal –s was already noticeable in the history of English. Cole (2014: 155) in her account of the NSR in Old Northumbrian, speaks of 'adjacent plural pronouns in contrast to full NP subjects, *relative clauses*, null and non-adjacent pronoun subjects'. The section *Notes to Questionnaire*, from *The Linguistic Atlas of Early Middle English 1150–1350* (LAEME; Laing and Lass 2008–2013) states: 'in northern ME, the pres. ind. pl. takes a consonantal suffix in "-s" when the subject is a noun, *interrogative or relative pronoun*. So "horsis rennys", "qwat lordis feghtis?", "yai yat callis" '('horses run', 'what lords fight', 'they that call' [LR&DB]'. And the dialectologist Joseph

Wright (1905: 296, §435) writes: 'In Sh. & Or.I. Sc. Irel. n.Cy [north country] and most of the north midland dialects all persons, singular and plural, take, **s**, **z**, or **əz** when not immediately preceded or followed by their proper pronoun; that is when the subject is a noun, *an interrogative or relative pronoun*, or when the verb and subject are separated by a clause.' [all our italics] (see also Murray (1873: 211–212) on Scottish English and De Haas (2011: 93–94), who did not, however, observe an effect of inversion in the early Middle English texts that she studied). Clarke (2014: 85 ff.) presents rather an extensive survey showing that verbal –s has been used in these kinds of structures throughout the history of English, even in varieties that do not otherwise show the NSR.

The direction of effect outlined here has been observed in a number of contemporary varieties. One is Tyneside English as spoken in Newcastle. Cole (2008) surveyed the *Newcastle Corpus of Tyneside English* (NECTE; Corrigan et al. 2001–2005) and found that occurrences of the NSR were no longer prevalent but had dropped in this area. The Proximity Effect did not seem to operate anymore whatsoever (the apparent result of a longitudinal development; see Sect. 2.4.1.1 again) while the Type-of-Subject Effect was far less productive (31% of the time in 1969, but only 7.6% in 1994) (2008: 99–100). Furthermore, in an analysis of the Type-of-Subject Effect, Pietsch's (2005) prototypes were found to all constitute a favouring effect in 1994 as compared with 1969, whereas regular NPs no longer contributed to the probability of verbal –s. Thus, Cole's findings on the Newcastle data underline the development that '[particular] subject types [seem] to dominate among the occurrences of verbal –s' (2008: 101).[34]

Godfrey and Tagliamonte (1999: 106) observed the traditional Type-of-Subject Effect (of NPs versus pronouns) in the variety of English spoken in Devon in south-west England. Interestingly, they found the Proximity Effect to hold over NPs (rather than pronouns): thus, non-adjacent plural NPs were more likely to occur with verbal –s than adjacent plural NPs. McCafferty replicated this result in a study of nineteenth century Ulster-Australian emigrant letters published in Fitzpatrick (1994), albeit that the effect there equally held over pronouns (2003: 131), as would be expected. In Sect 2.4.1.4, in which we will present our own account, we will suggest that NP- and pronominal subjects are expected to behave alike regarding the Proximity Effect on a discourse perspective of the NSR. Further, we think that Godfrey and Tagliamonte (1999) were quite right in categorising some of the apparent NSR-subject prototypes that we just discussed under the scope of the Proximity Effect (for example relative clauses, where a relative pronoun intervenes between the subject and the verb, cf. *That's me **two grandsons** that **lives** there* (1999: 109); inversion is another clear candidate). The comparatively low rates of the Proximity Effect that have been reported across studies of the NSR might thus have fallen out higher had this analysis been taken into consideration.

Summarising this section, the situation that has been sketched in the literature is that in contemporary varieties that once had a robust NSR, verbal –s is no longer productive.[35] Rather, its use has become 'fossilized' in particular syntactic environments (Cole 2014: 47) to the extent that certain subjects—relative, inverted, heavy, etc.—favour verbal –s more than others (Pietsch's 2005 'prototypes'). In view of the fact that this use of verbal –s appears to have existed throughout history, we feel the picture that appears to be unfolding is one of continuation of an existing pattern in a more restricted form. Following Jankowski and Tagliamonte (2017), this stage of the NSR provides an excellent opportunity to investigate the traits of 'dialect dissipation'. Schilling-Estes and Wolfram (1999: 487) earlier argued that ongoing processes of dialect obsolescence constitute an oft-overlooked but important source of information on the various trajectories that language change may take. A dissipation course can highlight the way 'in which distinguishing dialect features are lost or drastically eroded' (Schilling-Estes and Wolfram 1999: 487). In an apparent-time study of two sets of data from a dialect in the Ottawa Valley in Canada, Jankowski and Tagliamonte (2017) found, first, that verbal –s had virtually receded to past BE, and second, that while social constraints had neutralised, linguistic constraints endured; in particular, the adjacency condition on NPs (which they take to include relative clauses) (2017: 255–256). They conclude that it is typically features that are historically entrenched that survive: 'forms retreat to a restricted set of fossilized contexts that were once the most favoured locations for the variants in the past' (2017: 268). Building on Jankowski and Tagliamonte's (2017) perspective, and looking at the constructions in which the NSR has survived in contemporary varieties, it appears to us that the NSR too is retained in especially favourable contexts. Before we probe these contexts in Sect. 2.4.1.4, we will first discuss formal linguistic analyses of the NSR.

2.4.1.3 Formal Linguistic Analyses

Formal linguistic treatments of agreement hold the view that agreement relations are situated within the domain of morphosyntax. The subject-verb agreement relation is a dependency relation between a subject and a verb in which an identity function ensures that they have the same morphosyntactic properties. Barlow (1999: 187–189) and Corbett (2006) provide a clear overview of the tenets of subject-verb agreement models in formal linguistic theory. The tenets can be summed up as follows:

(a) there is a *controller* of agreement (a (pro)nominal constituent). The controller is specified for agreement features and determines agreement;
(b) there is an agreement *target* (the verb in the case at hand). The form of the target is determined by agreement;
(c) there is an *agreement relation* that ensures that identical agreement features occur on the agreement target;
(d) there is an *agreement domain* in which agreement should occur.

The form that the agreement relation is assumed to take depends on the constructs of the particular theoretical framework; for example, a feature-copying transformation, a co-indexing relation, a checking procedure or some other kind of morphosyntactic dependency. However, these all boil down to 'some kind of identity function' between the controller and the target (Barlow 1999: 187). In addition to this, there may be:

(e) *agreement conditions*: factors that have an effect on agreement (whether or not agreement in fact occurs).

Corbett (2006: 5) summarises: 'Thus, within a particular domain, a target agrees with a controller in respect of its feature specifications ...; this may be dependent on some other condition being met'.

An inquiry into verbal –s may provide evidence for these tenets or, in contrast, reasons to reconsider them in the light of new evidence. Many formal linguists who have addressed verbal –s assume that it reflects non-agreement and that the source of non-agreement ultimately lies in the properties of the *controller*. In the context of the NSR, this is what we propose regarding the properties of the controller also. However, while in many other accounts the relevant properties are grammatical features like case, person and number, our account posits a central role for *discourse* properties. We will outline some of the existing formal linguistic accounts before turning to our own proposal in Sect. 2.4.1.4.

Generative linguistic accounts can be divided into two types: (1) configurational and (2) feature-based. In configurational accounts there is a central role for agreement domains. They assume that the grammatical properties of the subject determine the particular position that the subject occupies in the clause structure. Configurational accounts take occurrences of verbal –s to be evidence that agreement between the subject and the verb may only be established at certain places in the clause structure (agreement domains), or else, if the subject is not within this domain, subject-verb agreement will not occur. In feature-based accounts, agreement relations have a central role. These accounts see occurrences of verbal –s as evidence for the particular feature specification of constituents. An agreement relation cannot be established when the grammatical features of the subject (controller) do not match those of the verb.

Henry (1995) is one of the earliest configurational accounts of verbal –s that appeals to agreement domains in the syntactic clause structure. Through her account, the occurrence of verbal –s lends support to the idea that the clause structure is split into a number of different 'functional projections'. These are additional phrases in the clause structure in which particular grammatical relations are established, such as AgrP for subject-verb agreement and nominative Case-marking of the subject by the verb (see Pollock 1989 for the original motivation for positing such additional phrases, based on word order differences

58 L. Rupp and D. Britain

between English and French). Henry (1995: 16, 18, 24) reports on verbal –s in Belfast English and terms this singular concord.[36] In accordance with the NSR, verbal –s is used with full NPs but not with pronouns, as shown in (18a–b), except when these have an accusative or 'case-vague' form rather than a nominative form, as is shown in (19a–c). She accordingly assumes that in Belfast English nominativity is relevant for singular concord:

(18) a. **These cars go/goes** very fast.
　　b. *****They goes** very fast.
(19) a. *****We students is** going.
　　b. **Us students is** going.
　　c. **Usuns was** late. / **Themuns has** no idea.

Henry goes on to note that in Belfast English, verbal –s does not occur when an adverb intervenes between the subject and an auxiliary but it is possible when an adverb intervenes between the subject and a lexical verb. She interprets this situation as indicative of there being two different positions available for subjects and verbs in the clause structure in Belfast English: one in a lower TP (Tense Phrase) and one in a higher AgrP.[37] Henry (1995) associates the presence and absence of verbal –s with these two positions, respectively. She assumes that in Belfast English, verbal –s is a pure tense marker and lacks agreement features. Verbal –s therefore occurs in the head T(ense) position of TP. Henry also assumes that subject-verb agreement is correlated with nominative Case-marking and that the 'checking' (or: licensing) of both agreement- and nominative Case-features takes place between the Agr head and the so-called specifier of AgrP. Because of this, nominative pronouns are forced to move to (Spec,AgrP) and therefore they cannot occur with verbal –s, which is in T. NPs, on the other, need only raise as far as the specifier of TP and therefore they can occur with verbal –s. Accusative or 'case-vague' pronouns also stay in (Spec,TP). In this relation, Henry (1995) goes on to note that in Belfast English, verbal –s is impossible in inverted structures like questions. This is shown in (20a–b) below. On her account, the reason is that interrogative structures involve raising of the verb to C via Agr, and this should trigger agreement (p. 16).[38]

(20) a. **The eggs is** cracked.
  b. ***Is the eggs** cracked?

Henry's analysis is illustrated in (21) below:

(21)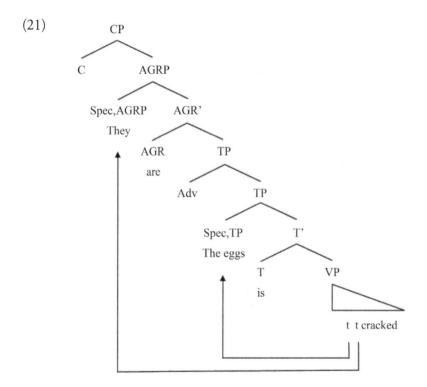

Tortora and Den Dikken (2010) compare the occurrence of verbal –s in Belfast English and Appalachian English. They propose a similar configurational account, citing cross-linguistic evidence from Welsh and Arabic that different subject positions correlate with (non-)agreement (see the references in their study). They (2010) report on a number of differences between Belfast English and Appalachian English regarding the use of verbal –s. They note that in contrast with Belfast English, Appalachian English allows for nominative pronouns to co-occur with verbal –s when they are morphologically complex. Such a complex nominative pronoun is *we'uns*, as in **We'uns is** *planning a picnic* (2010: 1093). They conclude that in Appalachian English there must be yet another, intermediate subject position available that is located in a phrase between AgrP and TP and hosts complex nominative pronouns. The intermediate subject position should be a non-agreeing position and they simply label it Subject Position. They invoke this intermediate subject position additionally to account for more differences between speakers of Belfast and Appalachian English. For example, according to Tortora and Den Dikken (2010), Appalachian English speakers also admit verbal –s with complex coordinated nominative pronouns (as in *It is true that **he and I gets** in a fight some time*; 2010: 1095). Further, verbal –s can occur in interrogatives (as in ***Is them cars** fast?*; 2010: 1099; from Bernstein 2008), which they ascribe to the possibility of the verb inverting to the head position of the intermediate phrase and the subject staying lower. Overall, Henry (1995) and Tortora and Den Dikken (2010) have provided insightful accounts of verbal –s in Belfast English and Appalachian English, and theirs are pioneering studies in considering vernacular data in syntactic theorising. However, it would be interesting to explore if the scope of their analysis extends beyond the Type-of Subject Effect to the Proximity Effect (a similar remark has previously been made by Childs 2012: 324).

Three feature-based accounts of verbal –s that assume a breakdown in agreement relations are those by Börjars and Chapman (1998), Bernstein (2008), and Zanuttini and Bernstein (2011). Börjars and Chapman (1998) provide an analysis within Lexical-Functional Grammar. Central to their analysis is that they take pronouns to be ambiguous items, sitting between arguments and agreement inflections. This idea builds on the diachronic and synchronic connections between the two. Pronouns are commonly seen as the historical source of agreement morphology, and synchronically they both express properties of discourse referents (albeit it that currently in English, agreement morphemes are not referential; see the discussion in Sect. 2.4 again). Thus, Börjars and Chapman (1998) have argued, when the pronoun is adjacent to the verb, the pronoun is essentially the inflection (a clitic-like marker of agreement; Chapman 1998: 39). It is ungrammatical to have agreement double-marked on the verb and therefore pronouns and agreement markers are in complementary distribution; see (22a–b) (1998: 74, 77) to which we have added (c):

(22) a. they go
   b. *they goes
   c. The professors goes

However, when the subject is separated from the verb or coordinated, the pronoun is an argument and the verb gets inflected, as in (23).

(23) **they** often **goes**

Börjars and Chapman (1998) thus assume that the primary context for verbal –s to occur is when the subject and the verb are not adjacent. Pietsch (2005: 188) observes that strictly speaking, this analysis wrongly excludes the occurrences of tokens such as *they often go*. Furthermore, Buchstaller et al. (2013: 107), who, with Henry (1995) assume that verbal –s is a tense ending, critically note that to postulate that separate agreement and tense morphemes cannot co-occur in English is ad hoc, given that this is what happens in French 'in a case like *Nous part-ir-ons*, lit. "1PL-leave-FUT-1PL", meaning "We will leave"'. However, we believe that one of the great advantages of Börjars and Chapman (1998) is that they provide a unified account of the two subcomponents of the NSR. Only, we are not certain whether assuming that pronouns have dual status constitutes a sufficiently principled account. In our own account we will exploit the differential discourse properties of referents that are instigated by nouns and pronouns.

Bernstein (2008) accounts for the occurrence of verbal –s by arguing that while –s marks number in Standard English, verbal –s marks person in several conservative varieties of English in North America and the British Isles (for example Belfast English, Appalachian English). Exploring diachronic evidence, she notes that (as we saw in Sect. 2.3) historically in the south of England, the form –þ (–th) was a 3rd person marker on 3rd person verbs (sing. and pl.). She goes on to point out that, subsequently, –th was generalised as a marker of 3rd person in (pro)nominal expressions; demonstratives (*that, this*), the existential subject (*there*), relative pronouns (*that*), among others, and also in the incipient definite article (*the*). Lastly, the 3rd pl. pronoun, which was a h– form in Old English, shifted to þ– (*they, them*) as a result of contact with Old Norse that was spoken by Danish and Norwegian populations in northern England. At the time when the pronominal þ– was introduced, the form was lost from the verb and replaced by –s, also under the influence of Old Norse. Bernstein (2008) envisages that when person came to be expressed on the pronoun, it was no longer marked on the verb, while –s started to mark number. That is to say that –þ as a marker of 3rd person changed from being a verbal marker to a pronominal marker þ–. She postulates that conservative varieties, in contrast, have continued to use –s for marking person on the verb. In these varieties, therefore, –s does not co-occur with *they*, which already marks person. In subsequent work, Zanuttini and Bernstein (2011), probing Appalachian English, argue that in varieties like Appalachian English that show the NSR, person is the relevant feature to subject-verb agreement. Nouns lack person (they are only 3rd person), therefore verbal –s occurs. In Standard English, on the other hand, number is the relevant feature to subject-verb agreement. Since the noun has number, regular agreement occurs. Returning to Bernstein (2008), her historical analysis provides a great many valuable insights in the development and current nature of agreement markers. We only wonder to what extent the account is compatible with the actual occurrence of verbal –s in the contexts of th– pronouns other than *they*. Recall from the previous section that subject uses of *them* have been earmarked as frequently occurring with verbal –s (viz. **Them's** *only two lessons I didn't like*; NECTE/ Cole 2008: 101), and this is also particularly true of the existential subject *there* as we will see in Chapter 5.

Finally, Pietsch (2005) proposes a usage-based account of verbal –s from Construction Grammar. Construction Grammar postulates that grammars are collections of constructions, which the language user abstracts from actual linguistic events. These constructions are encountered in discourse at different frequencies, and Construction Grammar assumes that the most frequent constructions are the most readily accessible to the language user. Pietsch (2005) explores verbal –s as support for the existence of such prototypical constructions. He finds support in the particular direction that the NSR has taken in contemporary varieties of English, as we outlined in the previous section: 'Certain types of environments, defined in syntactic, lexical, or possibly also semantic terms, are associated with a relative preference for the use of the conservative dialectal option of verbal –s.' (2005: 171). However, an alternative to viewing verbal –s as 'fossilized' or an 'arbitrary propert[y] associated with specific construction types' (2005: 172) is to seek a principled explanation as to why verbal –s should be found in these contexts especially. It is to this challenge that we now turn.

2.4.1.4 An Alternative Account: The Role of Discourse Properties

Research on the NSR might be summarised as follows:

1. When verbal –s was generalised across the present tense paradigm, speakers started to deploy –s to differentiate NP-subjects from pronoun subjects (the Type-of-Subject Effect). Given the grammatical category of NPs, this only applies in the 3rd person.
2. Where pronouns are separated from the verb, they also occur with verbal –s, in the same way as with NP-subjects (the Proximity Effect). This happens across persons.
3. The NSR has occurred in different guises: the most well-known pattern has been traced to Middle English northern dialects and concerns differential use of –s and zero (Ø) in the context of NPs and (adjacent) pronouns, respectively. Other NSR-like patterns that have been attested include –ð versus –s in Old English (Cole 2014) and –th versus –en in the Midlands (McIntosh 1989). This suggests that differentiation between pronoun- and NP-subjects per se is at the essence of the NSR.

Regarding the nature of verbal –s, Buchstaller et al. (2013: 107) have said that 'much recent work on the syntactic-morphological analysis of this system of agreement concurs that the -s on the verb is a non-agreeing form'; namely a present tense affix. They conclude: 'It is thus actually misleading to refer to the -s in a system observing the NSR as "triggered by the NP subject": in such a system the -s form is the unmarked present tense form, and so is not actually triggered by anything as such.' In the context of their analysis, Buchstaller et al. (2013: 107) are right to go on to ask 'what is it about pronouns that make them trigger agreement [with Ø LR&DB] where other NPs don't?'. However, we will argue that NP-subjects in effect do trigger verbal –s because –s has been remorphologised as a marker of particular types of (NP-)subject; a proposal reminiscent of Cole (2014: 4) that the NSR is 'a concord system based on a subject-type distinction, rather than on person/number features'. We envisage that what it is about these subjects that triggers –s is that they have particular discourse properties.

The discourse-oriented approach to the NSR function of verbal –s that we have in mind has been much informed by the discourse-based theory of agreement of Barlow (1992, 1999).[39] Barlow observes that in the framework of formal linguistic theory, subject-verb agreement is treated as an identity relation in which 'the NP and VP must carry the same values for agreement features' (1999: 188). He contends that since such mapping is in effect redundant, especially when an overt subject and the verb occur adjacent, this view has led to the postulation of decontextualised agreement rules. Moreover, most grammatical theories cannot handle non-standard use of agreement morphemes in a principled manner. Barlow argues that they become unworkable when faced with a situation in which the features of the noun are in conflict with the features of the verb, unless some 'special' assumptions are made. He concludes that morphosyntax does not seem the appropriate domain for agreement relations (1999: 195).

Barlow is of the opinion that agreement fits much more naturally (and therefore should be placed) within a discourse domain. He puts forward an account in which agreement morphemes provide information about (properties of) discourse referents. First, in their basic function agreement morphemes can be a tool for the hearer to track or (re)identify an intended referent in the discourse, like anaphoric pronouns (recall the historical relationship between agreement and pronouns outlined in Sect. 2.4). Following Lehmann (1988: 155) an agreement morpheme 'does this by giving information on grammatical properties of its referent and, thus, of the NP representing it if one is around'. Additionally, agreement morphemes can, according to Barlow, be used as a device for the speaker to convey a particular perception of a referent in the discourse. This second role comes to the fore when there is an apparent mismatch between the features of the NP and the VP: the mismatch in effect encodes new or extra information about a referent.

Barlow (1992) explains:

> It is plausible to assume that in the initial stages of introduction of a referent in the discourse it is necessary to provide a clear identification of a discourse referent. If this is the case, it will lead to the specification of the same properties by the agreement morphemes as are indicated by the noun. Once established, however, there is the possibility of either adding new features to indicate new information about the discourse referent or of identifying the primary discourse referent by use of fewer properties than were used initially. (p. 37)

Among the additional properties that Barlow has mentioned are: animacy,[40] social status or distance, speaker attitude and other information associated with a discourse situation (1999: 205). For example, as illustrated in (24), in some Polish dialects, a singular predicative adjective may be combined with a plural pronoun to indicate respect (example from Makarski 1973 cited in Barlow 1999: 193; we refer to the reference provided there):

(24) Wy będziecie chora
YOU-PL WILL-BE.PL ILL-SG
'You will be ill.'

Another example is presented in (25) (1999: 192). Here, Barlow takes the number mismatch to reflect the speaker's construal of the NP as a singular collective.

(25) I think Ways and Means is getting close.

Barlow points out that a discourse perspective is more accepting of agreement mismatches: they are not exceptional but *functional*: 'feature conflicts are due to the specification of extra (rather than conflicting) properties' (1999: 200). In fact, they provide 'evidence concerning the fundamental nature of the agreement relation' (1999: 191) that any theory of agreement should be able to account for. Note also that if agreement is sensitive to information in the discourse, and if morphemes are polysemous and may encode more than one property, we would expect speakers to deploy them variably depending on the particular discourse situation at hand:

> What is important is the fact that agreement is providing information about the nature of referent rather than information about the morphosyntax of the controller. Even in those cases where the relationship is conventional and fixed, the historical source of that relationship is somewhat mysterious unless there is some kind of connection between agreement markers and perceived objects or discourse referents. The classificatory role of agreement is even clearer in situations in which there is some optionality, and speakers are able, to a greater of lesser degree, to choose among alternative agreement patterns in a way that corresponds to differing classifications or perceptions of a discourse referent. (1999: 194)

In a different context, Corbett (1979: 223) has concluded that conflicts of agreement demonstrate that 'agreement is not a discrete phenomenon, rather that some items "agree more" than others'.

In our analysis of the NSR, we would like to build on Barlow's perspective that agreement morphemes have a 'discourse tracking role' (1999: 205) and can provide particular information about a referent. At this juncture, we also draw on Ariel's (1999, 2001) Accessibility Theory. The basic principle behind Ariel's Accessibility Theory is 'that referring expressions instruct the addressee to retrieve a certain piece of Given information from his memory by indicating to him how accessible this piece of information is to him at the current stage of the discourse.' (2001: 29). Note that 'accessible' should be understood as the degree to which a referent has been previously 'activated' in the addressee's memory (Ariel 2001: 61). For a detailed discussion of the notion of 'accessibility', we refer to Epstein (2002) who shows that while there is no doubt that, on many occasions, referents that are construed as 'accessible' constitute 'given' information, there are occurrences of NPs 'whose referents are portrayed (by the speaker) as accessible even though they would normally be viewed as constituting new – rather than given – information' (2002: 346 ff.). One of the central claims of Ariel's Accessibility Theory is that 'the form of referential expressions can be explained by means of accessibility theory: the less accessible a referent is [in terms of processing effort], the more elaborate the referential markers used by the language user' (2001: 27). Ariel postulates that 'elaborateness of form' involves three criteria: informativity (the amount of lexical information); rigidity (the ability to pick a unique referent); and attenuation (phonological size): '[T]he more informative, rigid and unattenuated the expression is, the lower the degree of accessibility it codes, and vice versa, the less informative and rigid and the more attenuated the form is, the higher the accessibility it codes.' (2001: 32). Thus, the idea is that referential expressions have a specialised form (more and less elaborate) for signalling different degrees of accessibility.

From earlier research, Ariel has put forward an accessibility marking scale, which we have adapted below. The scale proceeds from low accessibility markers (which may activate a referent for the first time) to high accessibility markers (which retrieve entities that have already been activated) (2001: 31):

> Full name(+modifier) > long/short definite description > first/last name > distal demonstrative (+modifier or +NP) > proximate demonstrative (+modifier or +NP) > (un)stressed pronoun > cliticised pronoun > verb inflection > zero

Note that the referential expressions on each end of the scale are precisely those that typically do and do not occur with the NSR: noun phrases versus pronouns (the Type-of-Subject Effect), where NPs may be part of larger expressions. Following Epstein's (2002: 345) characterization of definite descriptions, '[a]ccess paths triggered by definite descriptions – markers of low accessibility – are typically [...] complex, insofar as they tend to comprise a larger number of elements, connections and/or mental spaces'.

Ariel makes two further points that appear relevant to our discourse-oriented approach to the NSR. First, she argues that several factors may influence the degree of accessibility; one such factor being *distance*. The measure of accessibility that she has in mind in this relation is the distance between a current mention of a referent and a later mention: 'The larger the distance separating the different mentions of the same mental entity, the lower the degree of accessibility with which the mental representation is entertained' (2001: 33). Arguably, another apparent accessibility measure might be the distance between the subject and the verb upon activation of the predicate. Second, Ariel has argued that it is not only nominal expressions that guide the addressee in the retrieval of an entity: a low degree of accessibility may be heavily marked by double linguistic coding on both a nominal expression as well as on *the verb* (1999: 243) [our italics].

Ariel's proposal that the form-function correlations on accessibility marking scales are not arbitrary (namely, more/less elaborate forms of referring expressions code a low/high degree of accessibility, respectively) would seem to go back to Givón (1985). Givón has ranked various referential expressions along a continuum of degree of 'predictability', where 'predictability' (similarly to 'accessibility') should be understood in the psycholinguistic sense of real-time processing of information in discourse. Since pronouns refer back to an entity already introduced, they appear higher in the predictability hierarchy than nouns. Nouns, in turn, are higher in the hierarchy than modified NPs; that is, NPs containing an adjective or a relative clause, which are associated with discourse entities of low predictability. The hierarchy that Givón (1985: 196–197) assumes goes from the most to the least conscious/predictable material: zero anaphora (for example *pro*-drop) > unstressed pronouns > verb agreement > stressed pronouns (e.g. used for contrast) > full NPs > modified full NPs (e.g. NPs that head relative clauses). He then goes on to argue that 'the less predictable/continuous/accessible a topic is [or] the more *mental effort* is expended in processing a topic-NP (i.e. in establishing its referential identity in discourse), the more *coding material* is used to represent it in a language.' For example, in general, NPs are clearly 'larger' at the code (form) level than pronouns. Givón explains that it is not that information carried by NPs is weightier *per se*, but rather that it is less recoverable in the discourse context and thus weightier for the task of retrieving a referent. He postulates that the relation between form and function shown in the predictability hierarchy derives from an *iconicity meta-principle* in language, which he states as follows: 'All other things being equal, a coded experience is easier to *store*, *retrieve* and *communicate* if the code is maximally isomorphic to the experience' (1985: 189). Reminiscent of this, we will in the remainder of this volume suggest that the NSR and other uses of verbal –s restore a diagrammatic iconic relationship that was lost as a result of the analogical spread of –s across the present tense paradigm. We will take up this matter in the next Sects. 2.4.2 and in 2.5.

Taking the perspective that these frameworks afford together with the facts of the NSR, we would now like to outline our discourse-oriented approach to the NSR, in which we exploit the discourse properties of NPs and pronouns rather than their morphosyntactic features. We propose that –s has undergone regrammaticalisation in the sense of Greenberg (1991: 301): 'the reinterpretation in a new [grammatical] function' of a morpheme that has become marginal. We envisage that by Middle English, in the north, –s had generalised to such an extent that it lost motivation as a present tense subject-verb agreement marker, perhaps reducing to a mere nominal marker. Subsequently, verbal –s got regrammaticalised and came to signal the presence of discourse-weighty, less accessible subjects. Note that in accordance with the concept of 'regrammaticalisation', the former and ensuing function of verbal –s are related: it is still a referential marker that previously encoded person and number features. The account that we put forward bears some resemblance to that of Corrigan (1997: 200) who speculated that verbal –s may be 'the default for all persons and numbers in discourse contexts where identification of the non-adjacent subject required greater than usual processing'.[41] In a similar vein, Clarke (2014: 90) has concluded that the Proximity Effect, 'rather than constituting an NSR-related grammatical constraint, may represent an epiphenomenon deriving largely from cognitive processing'. Our account is also consistent with the finding that discourse-pragmatic factors may influence grammaticalisation trajectories (cf. for example Traugott 1995 on the 'subjectification' of a number of constructions in English and Epstein 1995 on the current role of the zero article in French).

It seems to us that on a discourse-oriented account, the two components of the NSR, which have proven difficult to unite, as well as a number of other facts about the NSR, fall out quite naturally. First, we expect that verbal –s is used with NP-subjects because their referents are relatively inaccessible (this is the Type-of-Subject Effect). Note in this relation that some of the prototypical NSR-subjects that have been identified in the literature (recall Sect. 2.4.1.2[42]) are especially discourse-weighty: in particular, heavy NPs such as NPs modified by relative clauses[43] (in Sect. 2.5, we will return to other subjects that were found to be particularly susceptible to verbal –s, like dialectal demonstrative *them*). Bare/simple pronouns normally do not occur with verbal –s because they are high in the accessibility hierarchy. However, (and this is where the Proximity Effect ties in), where pronominal subjects are separated from the verb, their referent is, we assume, more difficult to retrieve. We agree with Clarke (2014: 90) that such an analysis clarifies the observed 'instability' of the Proximity Effect (discussed in Sect. 2.4.1.1) as adjacency is a relative notion: distant subjects may be more or less accessible depending on their actual distance to the verb.

Second, an account that appeals to discourse properties appears to provide an explanation of some lesser known facts about the NSR and to make new predictions. For example, whilst the Proximity Effect is most familiar in relation to pronoun subjects (because they do not otherwise allow for verbal –s), the Proximity Effect should apply to pronouns and NPs alike: the greater the distance between the subject and the verb, the less accessible the subject and the greater the likelihood of verbal –s occurring. Findings from McCafferty (2003) testify to this expectation. McCafferty conducted a multivariate statistical analysis of a collection of nineteenth century letters from Northern Irish immigrants. He found the Proximity Effect to affect plural subjects in general, not just pronouns; nonadjacent plural NPs were considerably more likely to occur with –s than adjacent plural NPs (2003: 130–131). In a 1718 merchant report from Newfoundland (60 tokens of non-auxiliary verbs in a plural context; see Clarke 1997:

237), Clarke (2014), too, in effect found the Proximity Effect applying to NPs to the extent that verbal –s was favoured by non-adjacent NPs. She comments that this is not 'the classic NSR pattern' (2014: 84–85); however, we think that it may well be a genuine effect that has previously gone unnoticed because studies have associated NPs more with the Type-of-Subject Effect. The Proximity Effect has otherwise only been observed in NPs in the research by Godfrey and Tagliamonte (1999: 106) and Hazen (2000: 135–136) on Devon and Ocracoke English, respectively. Hazen has argued that the finding is evidence that the Proximity Effect is separate from the Type-of-Subject Effect.

Note further that, as we would anticipate, the NSR has additionally been found to operate in 3rd sing. environments, so that 3rd sing. NPs and distant pronouns occur with –s but adjacent pronouns with Ø. This is shown in the examples (26a–b) below. They are from Bailey et al.'s (1989: 294) study of vernacular African and European American English in Texas, and Schneider and Montgomery's (2001: 400) research on the English of plantation overseers in the American South in the nineteenth century, respectively:

(26) a. When **the frost hits** … let's see how **it look** down there.
     b. **it bear** a fine colour and **grows** well.[44]

Summarising, we have proposed a unified account of the Type-of-Subject Effect and the Proximity Effect that believes the relevant distinction between pronouns and NPs to lie in their different discourse properties.[45] NPs, as well as distant subjects, are more discourse-weighty than pronouns in that they are less easily recoverable. Verbal –s is a referential marker that historically expressed 2nd sing. agreement features but now signals inaccessible subjects.

The research literature shows that in addition to the NSR, verbal –s is deployed in a range of other functions in varieties of English in the world. In some cases, –s has acquired alternative grammatical functions (such as that of an aspectual marker); elsewhere the functions appear more discursively or socially motivated (for example to convey narrative effects or in identity construction). We consider these alternative deployments, and the type of functional shift that appears to have given rise to them, in the next section.

2.4.2 Other Uses of Verbal –s

Other factors than the NSR are known to influence the appearance of verbal –s. Both Montgomery and Fuller (1996: 214) and Cheshire and Ouhalla (1997) have listed a number of different uses of verbal –s, to which we add (7) and (8). They are:

1. an agreement marker for 3rd sing. subjects
2. a marker for NP-subjects
3. a marker of distant subjects
4. a form of hypercorrection
5. an aspectual marker
6. a narrative marker
7. a marker of vernacular identity
8. a presentational marker in existential *there* sentences (see Chapter 5)

Use (1) is the Standard English use as a 3rd sing. agreement marker. (2) and (3) are the two components of the Northern Subject Rule, which have been the most studied. Uses (4) and (5) are known as characteristic features of African American Vernacular English (AAVE; for example Poplack and Tagliamonte (1989: 68) and Trudgill (1996: 451) and references therein).[46] However, (5) has also been shown to occur in Britain, in particular in the south-west of England (Wakelin 1972; Clarke 1997; Godfrey and Tagliamonte 1999, among others). In addition to this, two other uses of verbal –s have been reported to exist: (6) a marker in narrative clauses (Myhill and Harris 1986) and (7) one of vernacular identity (Cheshire 1982). The last presentational use, (8) in existentials, will be addressed in Chapter 5. Clarke (2014: 89) concludes that 'verbal –s does not involve a uniform trajectory of diffusion across English varieties separated in time and space' (see Montgomery (1989: 253) for a remark to the same effect), but we will suggest that they all follow from the phenomenon of iconisation that we outline in Sect. 2.5.

2.4.2.1 Verbal –s as a Habitual Marker

Verbal –s has been identified as a marker of the grammatical category of aspect (especially habitual aspect). Clarke (1997, 2014) has explored this use of verbal –s in the vernacular English of Newfoundland, Canada's easternmost province.[47] Following Clarke (1999: 330), the island of Newfoundland was England's first colony in the New World, settled in the sixteenth century. The settlers largely came from two areas: south-west England (Dorset and Devon in particular) and south-east Ireland (see the references cited in her paper). This, together with the fact that it is a relatively isolated area, has led to what Clarke has described as the 'highly conservative' character of Newfoundland English (NFE). Hence, NFE is likely to show traces of the two input varieties, in accordance with the founder effect (Mufwene 1996).

In her investigation of the function of verbal –s in NFE, Clarke (1997, 2014) conducted multivariate analyses of two datasets. One is the Earlier NE-corpus (ENEC) from the 1960s to 1970s. This corpus comprises mostly tape-recorded folktales told by 16 rural male Newfoundlanders born between 1872 and 1905. The other is the later LNEC-corpus from the early 1990s. This corpus holds sociolinguistic interviews with 14 male and 12 female speakers aged 25–35 and 60+ from Burin, representing traditional NFE dialect (Childs and Van Herk: 2010: 82) and providing 981 tokens of verbs in the present tense. Both data sets showed high overall –s usage at rates of 87% in the ENEC (Clarke 2014: 81) and 68% (56% excluding the 3rd singular) in the LNEC (Clarke 1997: 233). Clarke's results show that in contrast to the NSR-dialects that we have looked at thus far, the category of subject does not affect the occurrence of verbal –s in NFE: verbal –s occurs in every grammatical person. Rather, the grammatical category of aspect is a significant factor.

Clarke (1997: 241–242) distinguished between (1) habitual, (2) durative, and (3) punctual aspect, which she describes as follows. 'Habitual' aspect 'represents an iterative event' that has taken place repeatedly prior to the present day and which is expected to keep recurring. A habitual event may be marked by temporal adverbs or conjunctions such as *every time*, *always* or *whenever* (27a–b). 'Durative' aspect concerns continuous events or processes that are extended in time or states that exist continuously (28a–b). 'Punctual' aspect designates 'dynamic events of momentary duration' (hypothetical or otherwise) (29a–b).[48]

(27) a. I always **calls** him Joseph, see.
   b. Dat's where **me and mudder falls out** all de time.
(28) a. **I likes** anything salty.
   b. **You looks** like Sarah.
(29) a. I don't know what I'm doin' yet til **I gets** through to him [i.e., to the doctor, by phone]
   b. Not unless anoder company takes it over or **more students comes** in dere.

Verbal –s was used to designate habitual events most (79%), followed by punctual (66%) and durative events (37%) (1997: 242). Clarke concludes that 'the use of verbal –s remains extremely robust in NVE and seems in little danger of disappearing despite the incursion of standard English' (1997: 250).

The expected founder effect is borne out as the use of verbal –s across subjects has been documented quite extensively for the south-west of England in dialectological work (Wright (1905: 296), Ihalainen (1994: 222), Filppula (1999: 153), and Klemola (2000: 333) on data in the SED; specifically, item VIII.5.1 *They goes to church*; Peitsara 2002). Elworthy (1877: 51) reports that –s is 'common to all persons, in both numbers' in West Somerset, as in (30), which he cites as an example of the 'present habitual' (p. 50):

(30)   **aay, ee** (etc) **digz** dhu græwn. [= I, you (etc) digs the ground]

That verbal –s is used as an aspectual marker in the south-west of England has been confirmed in a later, variationist study of a series of informal conversations with eight elderly speakers in and around Tiverton, a town in rural mid-Devon. Godfrey and Tagliamonte (1999: 89) report that in the local dialect, verbal –s occurs in all environments, irrespective of type and position of the subject, cf. (31a–f).

2 Verbal –s   75

(31) a. Her gives me a hug and a kiss, when **I comes** in and when
        I go. (1ˢᵗ sing.)
      b. People says 'yeah but look at your weather, **you gets** it freez-
        ing cold in the winter, **you get** all the rain.' (2ⁿᵈ sing.)
      c. **He comes** every- three times a week **he come.** (3ʳᵈ sing.)
      d. **We belong** to Senior Citizens, we don't call them Old Age
        Pensioners, **we calls** 'em Senior Citizens. (1ˢᵗ pl.)
      e. **Kiddies come over** … and they'm talking to the animals
        and that. And **the animals looks** down, you know. (3ʳᵈ pl.)
      f. Funny big head he got. They **call** 'em something a battle-
        head or something, they **calls** 'em, don't 'em? (3ʳᵈ pl.)

They investigated the role of several factors and found that aspect
exerted a significant effect on shaping –s usage in Devon, albeit only in
the 3ʳᵈ sing. and in the 1ˢᵗ person. The aspectual distinctions are illustrated in (32a–c) (1999: 105–106).

(32) a. **They** sort of **commutes** to town, to work and back again.
        [habitual]
      b. **She likes** anybody go round to see her 'cos she gets a bit
        lonely, don't she. [continuous]
      c. As long as **I gets** there tomorrow, I don't care. [punctual]

In the 3ʳᵈ sing., habitual contexts favoured –s, continuous contexts
were neutral and punctual aspect disfavoured. The same pattern was
observed in the 3ʳᵈ pl., but it was not selected as significant. Godfrey
and Tagliamonte (1999) postulate that in the 3ʳᵈ pl., the habitual effect
was neutralised by the Northern Subject Rule, which also obtained (see
Sect. 2.4.1.2). We will take note of Godfrey and Tagliamonte's (1999)
findings regarding –s in the 1ˢᵗ person in the section on the narrative use
of –s below.

Speakers of the other input variety to NFE, southern Irish English,
too, have been shown to use verbal –s in an aspectual function. Filppula
(1999: 150) reports that Hume (1878: 25) associated 'the Irish dialect'

with the NSR: '[t]he third person singular of verbs is invariably used, unless when immediately preceded by the pronoun *they*'. Henry (1958: 130–131), however, stated that in Anglo-Irish '*-s* is the common ending of the present pl.'. Filppula surveyed a sample of a corpus of four varieties of southern Irish English (24 largely NORMs interviewed in the late 1970s–early 1980s). These data showed use of verbal –s with nouns as well as personal pronouns, though the rates of the latter were very low. Some illustrations are given in (33) (1999: 154–155):

(33) a. [...] but then, **sons of theirs comes** over here, an odd time has come.
   b. Oh well, only, **they gets** pensions, you know, and I get the old-age pension.
   c. **We keeps** about ten cows that way, you know, and few cattle.

Filppula (1999: 157–159) thinks that southern Irish English shows a mixture of influence from Northern Middle English and Scots (the NSR type of verbal –s) and southern British English (the more extended type of verbal –s) (and perhaps Irish) though he concludes 'All things considered, the evidence for "northern" influence on S-V concord in H[iberno] E[nglish] is stronger than that for "southern"'.[49,50]

A number of more recent analyses of English in Newfoundland have underlined the absence of an NSR effect there in tandem with the occurrence of –s marking across the person and number paradigm. Van Herk et al. (2009), Comeau (2011), and Childs and Van Herk (2010) examined interviews in a contemporary, socially stratified sample of 24–28 residents from Petty Harbour-Maddox Cove (following Childs and Van Herk 2014, henceforth Petty Harbour). Petty Harbour is a town located close to the provincial capital of St John's, which (following an economic upturn in the 1990s) developed from a traditional maritime settlement into a more urbanised community. However, in a data set of over 1090 tokens of non-3rd sing. present tense verbs, the attested rates of verbal –s were, contrary to Clarke, low (8%; Comeau 2011: 35) and 'habituality' was not a significant factor (Van Herk et al. 2009: 91). Instead, they observed a tendency for speakers to favour verbal –s in sentences headed by the adverbials *when, if* or *whenever* where these meant 'every time that X happens, Y happens' (Childs and Van Herk 2010: 87), especially amongst the youngest generation <30 (Comeau 2011: 36). By contrast, other overt expressions of habituality, like the adverb *always* or the PP *at Christmas*, disfavoured, while tokens with no overt adverbial specification yielded a neutral result (Van Herk et al. 2009: 91). The tokens concerned are exemplified in (34a–d) from Van Herk et al. (2009: 90) and Comeau (2011: 32, 35):

(34) *Habitual adverb*
  a. **I always goes** up to Mick's cabin on the weekends.
     Habitual when(ever)-clause
  b. That's **when you gets** into freezing spray at the cold times of year.
     Habitual if-clause
  c. **If you throws** a case of beer, they were only more than happy to help.
     Other
  d. But **people pictures** a Newfie as the dumbest person alive.

Comeau accounts for this change within a generative framework. He suggests that the Newfoundland English grammar of the older generation has an Asp head (which he terms Asp^1) that has an intrinsic feature [HAB]. The grammar of the younger generation, on the other hand, has an Asp^2 head that has a variable feature that must be bound by an operator. The adverbials *when, whenever*, etc., he argues, can function as operators to bind this variable feature. Van Herk et al. (2009: 92) conclude that 'the habitual effect may be more complex and more syntactically constrained than previously thought'. We wonder whether the favouring of habitual –s in *when/whenever/if*-clauses can be seen as part of the development that Pietsch (2005) envisages whereby verbal –s is increasingly becoming associated with particular prototypes (see Sect. 2.4.1.2).

Since the habitual use of verbal –s is related to its original use as a present tense agreement morpheme (both uses belong to the functional domain of verbs),[51] we feel that it is best analysed as an instance

2.4.2.2 Verbal –s as a Narrative Marker

We move now to the case of verbal –s in narrative clauses. Labov (1972: 359–360) described a narrative as 'one method of recapitulating past experience by matching a verbal sequence of [narrative] clauses to the sequence of [narrative] events which (it is inferred) actually occurred. [...] [w]e can define a minimal narrative as a sequence of two clauses which are temporally ordered: that is, a change in their order will result in a change in the temporal sequence of the original semantic interpretation.' In narrative clauses, both past tense verbs and present tense verbs can be used to refer to past events. '[T]he use of the present tense to refer to past events' has come to be known as 'the historical present tense' (Schiffrin 1981: 45). Within a narrative, this particular use of the present tense is seen particularly in 'complicating action clauses', which designate 'an event –a discrete occurrence in time– which is understood to follow the event immediately preceding it, and to precede the event immediately following it' (Schiffrin 1981: 49). Research on narratives agrees that the historical present tense (HP) is not merely a grammatical substitute for the past tense (P). Rather, it is thought that speakers alternating between the two tenses is a meaningful discourse strategy and a means to organise the narrative (see for example the references cited in Levey 2006). It has been a matter of some contention, though, whether (1) it is the use of the HP per se or more specifically the switch between HP and P that is functional, and (2) precisely what considerations motivate switching between different tense forms. Historical-descriptive grammars like Mustanoja (1960: 485–488) have listed a range of purposes of deploying the HP, including indicating 'vivid descriptions of actions and situations and of deep emotions', 'the main action as against subordinate and less important actions', 'the situation at the beginning of a new phase in the narrative', 'when the narrative moves from one person to another' 'the end of a series of events', while the HP is also used with 'verbs of saying ... introducing direct speech'.

2 Verbal –s   79

Wolfson (1979) is a proponent of the functionality of the tense-switch in both directions from HP to P and from P to HP (1979: 172, 174). In a study of 'conversational narratives, tape-recorded in a variety of everyday speech situations' (1979: 170), she has argued against the view that using the HP has a dramatic impact, representing events as if they are actually happening, or as if the narrator were reliving the past event. In her own words, she has been critical of '[t]he point [that] the use of the present tense somehow makes it seem that the events themselves are taking place at the moment of speaking, rather than at some point in the past' (1979: 169). Wolfson has pointed out that narrative clauses in the past tense can have exactly the same impact; therefore, creating a dramatic impact cannot be an inherent semantic property of the historical present tense (1979: 172). In addition to this, she has noted that in English, present tense verbs are not actually used to convey a present-moment action. ('It is ungrammatical in English to reply to a question like *What are you doing?* with the answer *I take a shower* or *I read the newspaper now*'; 1979: 179–180). Wolfson subscribes to the view that switching from one tense to another rather has the structural effect of partitioning off an event 'when the verb represents an action which is at a different level of importance to the story' (1979: 178). That is, 'such a switch is a structural marker of a segmentation of events' (1979: 174). This segmentation is exemplified in (35).

(35) So he **picks up** the agreement—all of a sudden **he looked** at the agreement …

Levey, in a study of 56 narratives of personal experiences collected among 28 preadolescents in 2000–2004 in the outer London borough of Redbridge, concurs that a shift into another tense can frame important episodes within a narrative. Consider the following excerpt from his corpus (2006: 131):

(36) a. I **fell** backwards
     b. and I really **banged** my head on the wall
     c. and my brother, my brother … then I **got** my brother […]
     d. and then he go … he **goes** back out the garden

e. **gets** his scooter
f. and **puts** it right on top of me by an accident

Following Levey, in (36), the simple past is used to foreground a series of events that culminate in the girl's accident, while the HP is used to describe how the girl's brother exacerbated the situation by accidentally placing his scooter on top of her. An account of the HP that it helps separate events would be supported by the fact that there is no tense-switch in *when*-constructions where two component clauses constitute a single event or 'report material which is not sequentially ordered' (Schiffrin 1981: 52). Consider (37) (Wolfson 1979: 174):

(37) When I **got** home, my husband **said** how he had …

However, Schriffin (1981), in a pioneering quantitative variation-ist analysis of narratives (1288 narrative clauses in 73 narratives told by communities in Philadelphia in the late 1970s, p. 45, Footnote 1) has demonstrated that it is only the switch from HP to P that has the structural effect of dividing events (1981: 56). She sticks with the tra-ditional perspective, showing that in her data the HP occurs signifi-cantly more frequently in the progressive form than P and noting that 'the co-occurrence of the HP with the progressive is a way of making a past event sound as if it were occurring at the moment of speaking' (1981: 57). She also reminds us that the present tense is used in other constructions for conveying that reference time is simultaneous with the moment of speaking; for example, sport commentaries, demon-strations of cooking techniques, magic tricks, and so on. We will not directly engage in this debate. Rather, we will present a brief overview of existing studies of the use of verbal –s in narrative clauses, and, taking account of these, conclude that verbal –s might be specialising as a nar-rative marker.

As Myhill and Harris (1986: 26) have pointed out, the way in which vernacular narrative clauses differ from their Standard English counter-parts is that speakers use –s beyond the 3rd sing.; that is, regardless of the person and number of the subject. Given the nature of the narra-tive, the 1st sing. often occurs. Vernacular varieties where verbal –s has been recorded in narratives include: Anniston, Alabama (38a) (Feagin 1979: 188; who notes that most tokens were *I says*), Farnsworth (38b) (Shorrocks 1980: 572; in a study of 54 tape-recorded responses to the SED-questionnaire by NORMs, also including female informants, p. 112 ff.), Ireland (38c) (Harris 1993: 156), Appalachia (38d) (Montgomery 1994: 255–256), Belfast English (38e) (Henry 1995: 18; 'in storytelling contexts'), South Armagh (38f) (Corrigan 1997: Chapter 4), Devon (38g) (Godfrey and Tagliamonte 1999: 107; 'twice as frequent in narrative contexts as in non-narrative contexts' on the note that these contexts were restricted to 1st person and relatively rare), York (38h) (Godfrey and Tagliamonte 1999: 107), St. Helena English (38i) (Wilson and Mesthrie 2004: 1013; cautioning that 'further work needs to be done to establish whether … -*s* fulfils a narrative function here'), the Black Country (38j) (Asprey 2007: 121 citing Higgs 2004 that –s appears 'extremely frequently among all age groups with the verbs *say* and *go*', whilst 'narrative tense' was also evident in her own data), and Newcastle-upon-Tyne (38k) (Cole 2008: 102; 'probably best considered conservative forms').

(38) a. So **I reaches over** and get it.
b. oh **we pulls**.. this pony out of the shafts.. and.. we took it into the yard.
c. And **I goes** down and **gets** him by the neck.
d. **They comes** back, and Scott says he was a-coming over to their house when Lester come back.
e. **The girls goes** and **tells** them.
f. I took a drink of tea, that's what I took, and **I hears** this noise and **I looks** down in the room.
g. So, **I goes** up, **goes** off the road, **goes** down this track, **goes** over this little stone bridge, only a narrow road, uh, track, go over the stone bridge. […] So **I goes** in and **sees** him.
h. **I says**, "Look." **I says**, "Just send them a threatening letter back yourself" and **I says**, "Tell them that we didn't ask for their services."

82   L. Rupp and D. Britain

    i.   And then **we goes** along and we spread out.
    j.   I always [**calls**] it the living room.
    k. So **I gans** into this dance …

Many studies have commented on the frequency of verbal –s in narrative quotative contexts. Schiffrin already showed that the HP is common with direct quotes and verbs of saying (for example *say, tell, yell, go*), claiming that 'they increase the immediacy of an utterance which occurred in the past by allowing the speaker to perform that talk in its original form, as if it were occurring at the present moment.' (1981: 58) (see also Levey 2006: 143–144, 146–147). In the data from FRED and NICTS surveyed by Pietsch, the vast majority of narrative clauses occurred with *says*. He has concluded that 'there is little evidence in the data of the present study that speakers have a productive stylistic rule of using verbal -s as a marker of the historic present as such, over and above the prototypical, idiomatic use of *says* (or its semantic equivalents).' (2005: 146). While numbers were low, Clarke (1997: 247) found a rate of 58% of verbal –s on the verb *say* (11/19) in her study of Newfoundland English. Adger and Smith (2010: 111) say that in Buckie, '-s marking is used to mark a particular narrative/aspectual meaning associated with verbs of communication', as in (39a–b). Childs (2012: 338) reports that 'verbs of communication appear to promote the appearance of –s' in the three communities of Wallsend, Hawick and Newcastle ((39c) is from the NECTE). (See also Buchstaller et al. 2013: 102–103, although they, apparently somewhat counterintuitively, say that 'verbs of communication [we tested *ask* and *say*] *favour the acceptance of the NSR most*' [our italics].)

(39) a. And **they says** till him 'Well, Mr. Smith, come in on Monday.'
      b. Oh aye, a lot of things that **they** never **speaks** about, you ken. 'Oh yes, there are a lot of things that they don't ever speak about, you know.'
      c. So she came down with this huge book, and **I says** "how much is that?"

In their research on (what they term) Black Vernacular English (BVE), Myhill and Harris (1986) were one of the first to characterise the use of verbal –s in narratives as a functional shift. They postulate that this function of verbal –s was an innovation that was made possible by the availability of –s as a morpheme, which to BVE speakers had no transparent function. (40) is an example from Myhill and Harris (1986: 26).

(40) So, Verne was gonna go wif us. [...] So we went to Gino's, **COMES** back.
      So the secon' night, LaV—we said "C'mo, le's—" I **SAY** "Le's go to McDonal's again". So we **GOES** to McDonal' again.

Godfrey and Tagliamonte (1999: 107) point out that 'this patterning is not attested in the historical literature' and therefore, since it 'is attested in many contemporary varieties of British English, it may be a later development in which verbal –s has been reanalysed as a marker for iconically ordered narrative clauses'.[52] Fernández Cuesta (2011: 117) has proposed that the shift is Lass's (1990) 'exaptation', giving rise to a new pattern that has become highly productive across varieties of English. Whether verbal –s in narratives is exaptation or another type of functional shift like regrammaticalisation depends on its precise nature: is it an extension of the regular present tense morpheme (enlivening the narrative, following Schiffrin 1981) or is it a novel narrative marker that fulfils particular pragmatic functions in the story (á la Wolfson 1979)? Henry (1995: 18) has argued that in narratives, verbal –s must be distinguished from the present tense morpheme because there are speakers of Belfast English who accept the NSR verbal –s but not the narrative verbal –s. Wolfson (1979: 179, Footnote 2) has noted that some think that narrative verbal –s 'should be considered as somehow outside the usual tense system' in view of its wider deployment than the 3rd sing. Amongst these researchers is Chapman (1998: 38) who suggests that 'the historic present ... is a special marked tense and not merely the present tense used to refer to the past.'

We feel that research by Rodríguez Louro and Ritz (2014) suggests that narrative verbal –s might be undergoing exaptation. In research on the 'regular' HP, they studied 100 narratives of past personal experience.

The data were collected in Perth in 2011–2012 amongst 38 highly educated male and female speakers aged 12–62. Theirs is one of the first studies to explore the light that sociolinguistic factors (like generational differences) can shed on the choice of the HP in narratives. Rodríguez Louro and Ritz found that the PT constituted by far the highest rate of tense tokens in the complicating action clauses in their sample ($N = 654$): 87% vs. 12% HP. They ascribe this finding to 'the PT [being] renowned for its unmarked function in narrative' (2014: 556) (an observation which they attribute to Fleischmann 1990).[53] The overall frequency of the HP was higher though still lower than the PT in the data of Schiffrin (1981: 51) and Levey (2006: 140): 30% and 32%, respectively. Interestingly, a comparison of the distribution of narrative tenses across two different age cohorts (12–28 and 36–62 year olds) showed that the younger generation favoured the HP over the older generation (16% vs. 6%). Furthermore, analysis of linguistic conditioning showed, amongst other things, that the HP was significantly more likely to be used with the 3rd person and with 'direct speech introducers such as *say*, *go* and *like*' (Rodríguez Louro and Ritz 2014: 558–559). As a matter of fact, one lexical type of quotative verb—namely *be like*—turned out to account for 82% of the data. Rodríguez Louro and Ritz note that Tagliamonte and D'Arcy (2007: 209) previously demonstrated that '*be like* becomes entrenched in the quotative system' (2014: 560). However, the insight that Rodríguez Louro and Ritz have added to our understanding of the restructuring of the quotative system is that the HP becomes the norm. They conclude that 'young speakers combine these two devices [quotative *be like* and the HP LR&DB] to structure their stories'; namely 'the HP can be recruited as an alternative to the PT to signal important speech events or discourse segments as well as changes in protagonists [back to the 3rd sing. LR&DB]' (2014: 561). The following excerpt from their corpus illustrates how tense-switches can be exploited to separate protagonists or demarcate speaker roles (see also Levey 2006: 144 who credits Romaine and Lange 1991). Following Rodríguez Louro and Ritz, 'the first person and the PT introduce information pertaining to the narrator themselves, the third person and the HP introduce material related to entities other than the narrator' (2014: 560):

(41) And so **we were like**, 'Look, really, you can't drive home, like it's just not on, get a taxi'. **He's like**, 'Oh I can leave my car here, I'll get a ticket'. I **was like**, 'Well, because there's like security parking underneath, like we'll put it in the parking spot downstairs, come back in the morning, you know, you can come in' and **he's like**, 'Oh fine'.

Thus, it seems that the HP has been developing into a tool for performing particular pragmatic functions, collocating with quotation and apparently specialising further in a lexical construction with *be like*. It would be interesting to see whether speakers are ever going to use verbal –s in *be like* constructions where the subject is other than *he/she*; for example *they's like* or even *we's like*.[54] If so, we think that the use of narrative verbal –s would be best considered a token of linguistic exaptation, rather than a continuation of marking present tense.

While Pietsch has called the historic present 'a second, apparently quite unrelated pattern [to the NSR LR&DB] involving non-standard verbal -s with pronoun subjects' (2005: 146), we will contemplate in Sect. 2.5 that in both uses, as well as in other uses of verbal –s, speakers have been restoring/implementing diagrammatic iconicity. We will first address one such other use of verbal –s in the next subsection before we turn to the concept of 'iconicity'.

2.4.2.3 Verbal –s as a Marker of Vernacular Social Identity

In his discussion of exaptation, Lass (1990: 99) envisages that speakers can also exapt material to recruit for social purposes.[55] Referring to Cheshire's (1982) study of a variety of English that occurs in Reading, the redeployment Lass specifically had in mind was one of verbal –s turning into 'an indexical marker of vernacularity in some dialects'. Cheshire studied nonstandard morphosyntactic features in the speech of three working-class peer groups who frequented local playgrounds in two neighbourhoods in Reading (18 hours of recorded speech).

The groups consisted of 10 boys, 3 boys and 11 girls, respectively, aged between 9 and 17 years old. Cheshire demonstrated that verbal –s acted 'as [symbol] of adherence to the vernacular culture' in the peer groups (1982: 130) (rather than as a sex marker differentiating the boys and the girls). For example, different degrees of allegiance to the group (peer group status, measured in terms of network ties, p. 87 ff.) correlated strongly with the amount of verbal –s used. In the largest male group, core members used verbal –s 68% in non-3rd sing. environments, while secondary members did so 42% of the time, and the peripheral members 30% (1982: 91). Furthermore, verbal –s was used incrementally according to scores on a 'vernacular culture index' (in the case of the boys, defined on the basis of six indicators including clothing style, toughness, participation in minor criminal activities and job ambitions, p. 97 ff.), with the highest rate being 77% and the lowest 21%. Lastly, Cheshire observed that the peer groups favoured verbal –s on verbs that are used in vernacular culture but do not occur or have a different meaning in Standard English. She labels this 'the vernacular verb constraint' (1982: 42). The frequency of –s ranged from 90–96% on vernacular verbs and 50–66% on regular verbs. Some examples of such verbs are given in (42) below (1982: 43)[56]:

(42) a. **We** fucking **chins** [=hit on the chin] them with bottles.
      b. **I** grabs hold of him and **legs** it [=run away] up Blagdon Hill.
      c. **We buses** it [=go by bus] down the town.
      d. **We bunks** [=play truant] it over here a lot[57,58]

Childs and Van Herk (2014) have more recently reported a similarly social use of verbal –s in Newfoundland. They build on earlier work (Van Herk et al. 2009; Childs and Van Herk 2010), complementing the sociolinguistic interview data collected in Petty Harbour (see Sect. 2.4.2.1) with 451 surveys of usage and awareness of non-standard linguistic features that students at Memorial University have collected since 2008. They also included a 46-minute recording of a gathering of nine members of the local St. John's drag community (Sheppard 2006, 2014: 642, 646). Childs and Van Herk demonstrate how in this urban(ising) area of Newfoundland, over time, verbal –s has evolved from a more general and widespread characteristic of the vernacular into a less common (2014: 640) but nevertheless highly salient label. Traditionally –s is a habitual marker mostly associated with men and rural lifestyles. However, young women have been leading a change whereby –s is lexicalised and combined with a particular set of stative verbs like *know, love* and *hate* (2014: 641–642). In this manner, –s has acquired a social meaning indexing 'young, urban, female, performed, ironic, playful, in-group' (2014: 650). Consequently, Van Herk and Childs show, –s has come to be used, in hyperstylised ways, by the drag community in urban St. John's. As they have put it: '*loves* is "seen in [the] community as a very female thing to say"' (2015: 202). Drag queens have been celebrating the –s form and driving its popularity further along, often in the 1st sing., with or without the pronoun (2014: 646), as in (43):

(43)   Taking pictures of me, too. **Loves**.

Childs and Van Herk (2014: 652) point out that this switch has occurred against a background of the relative obsolescence of –s marking, due to the feature being associated with rurality and low education, and a reappreciation of Newfoundland identity (2014: 637, 645). 'In this way a feature that may have once been undesirable among one generation will transition to being regarded in a positive way by the next. [A]s a result the feature becomes desirable and makes a comeback.' (Childs and Van Herk 2013: 140). They figure that when a feature turns exceedingly rare, it may reach a point at which it is 'noticed, adopted, and adapted' (Van Herk and Childs 2015: 203) and provide a resource that can be worked for identity creation. In the case of verbal –s, a grammatical stereotype of traditional Newfoundland English has transitioned into new contexts where it bears no stigma but carries prestige, meaning 'urbanized local "Newfoundlandy" identity' (2014: 648–650). Childs and Van Herk (2013: 140) think that 'its infrequency increases the "punch" that it carries when used'. They describe this functional shift as 'upcycling' (2014: 635) whereby features are made to do new work (2015: 203). They argue that 'upcycling' should be distinguished from 'recycling' or 'reclaiming' a feature, which is known as a normally male-oriented development. For an example of

88   L. Rupp and D. Britain

'recycling', we refer to Tagliamonte and Roeder (2009: 449, 462) who have argued that Definite Article Reduction, an older feature of the variety of English spoken in York, has been recycled by young male speakers for asserting Yorkshire identity. Another apparent example of 'upcycling' might be the female-led exaptation of past BE in York English that Tagliamonte (1998) has reported on and we will discuss in Chapter 4. In Newfoundland, then, verbal –s has been exapted from a local grammatical dialect feature (what Childs and Van Herk call 'Old -s': the traditional habitual use with non-stative verbs, for example *I goes*) into an enregistered and even commodified stylistic resource indexing stance, persona and identity ('New -s': the s-marking with a stative verb; for example *I loves*) (2014: 643).[59] Accordingly, Childs and Van Herk postulate a distinction between traditional forms that are 'routinely' transmitted across generations and forms that become available for manipulation by speakers as agents in identity performance (2014: 652).

We summarise the findings and thoughts expressed in this chapter thus far. The distribution of –s has changed since it was a 2nd sing. agreement morpheme in Old English. We hold the functional shifts of regrammaticalisation and exaptation responsible for its renaissance. There are currently a number of meanings associated with –s variation: speakers can recruit the morpheme for signalling discourse-heavy subjects, marking habituality and narrative turns, or for identity construction. We will now attempt to explain the direction of the change.

2.5   The Iconicity Hypothesis

Now, how come that verbal –s is used for (particularly) these other purposes? We would like to explore the possibility that the functional shifts of –s have restored or implemented diagrammatic iconicity in the sense of Haiman (1980) (in essence, a similarity relation). After Kortmann (1999), we will call this idea the 'ICONICITY HYPOTHESIS'. Recall that Haiman assumes a distinction between two subtypes of diagrammatic iconicity. One is isomorphism; following De Cuypere (2008: 92), an essentially structuralist *language-internal* principle that invokes a 'tendency to associate a single invariant meaning with each single invariant form' (Haiman 1985: 4).[60] The other is iconic motivation, according to which a relationship between two referents in *extra-linguistic* reality is reflected by a relationship between two linguistic expressions (while the individual expressions and the individual referents themselves do not resemble each other). Thus, diagrammatic iconicity entails that there are relations that are non-arbitrary.

We will start with isomorphism. In the north, due to the generalisation of –s throughout the present tense paradigm in early Middle English, the –s ending was no longer isomorphic signalling (just) 2nd sing. properties of the subject. (Note once more that, different from Henry 1995 and others, we do not assume that –s continued to mark present tense regardless of the neutralisation of person and number contrasts because verbs can be interpreted as present by default in the absence of past tense marking.) As a result, the –s ending did not function as an agreement morpheme anymore and became available for recruitment for other functions. The new deployments of –s include signalling 'discourse-heavy' subjects, the habitual occurrence of events, narrative turns, or vernacular identity. At first sight, it might appear that these multiple uses of –s run counter to the notion of isomorphism, but we would like to suggest that the apparent conflict is, indeed, only apparent. Note first that many communities tend to each deploy (just) one from the set of potential uses of –s. Think, for example, of Clarke's (1997) assertion that the traditional dialect of Newfoundland uses –s as a habitual marker but not according to the NSR. The communities in Devon and Reading studied by Godfrey and Tagliamonte (1999) and Cheshire (1982), respectively, are perhaps the most apparent counterexamples to isomorphism because –s has been reported in two or three linguistic functions there. However, Godfrey and Tagliamonte show that their Devon speakers favoured different uses of –s with different forms: narrative –s with 1st sing., habitual –s with 3rd sing., and the NSR –s with 3rd pl. In fact, many studies that were discussed in Sect. 2.4.2.2 have highlighted the tendency for narrative –s to be associated with the first person singular. Additionally, reports abound that narrative –s is not productive but lexicalised into a separate unanalysable narrative form with the verb *say* (*I says*) (a form now giving way to

'*I'm like*'). In this capacity, it would no longer embody one of the alternative uses of the *morpheme* –s. This leads us to Cheshire's observation that Reading adolescents deploy –s both according to the vernacular verb constraint (see Sect. 2.4.2.3) and the 'following complement constraint' (see Note 58). Since the 'vernacular verb constraint' only concerned 8 vernacular verbs (1982: 43), we would contemplate that (as with narrative –s) vernacular –s verbs have become separate lexical items. What is more, we would agree with Cheshire that in its use with vernacular verbs, –s has the social function of reflecting 'adherence to the vernacular culture' (1982: 130) rather than a grammatical function, leaving just the grammatical 'following complement constraint'. With respect to Reading –s having both a social and a grammatical function, it is worth noting that social variation seems shaped by linguistic conditioning in that social group marking is often performed by using grammatical variables *in a particular linguistic context*. We could adapt Podesva's (2011: 141) description of style for the purposes of the current discussion: social meaning emerges not through the employment of isolated grammatical variables, but through the linguistic ways in which grammatical variables are used. The drag-queens of St. Johns are a perfect illustration of this: they are different from other Newfoundland verbal –s users by deploying it specifically on stative verbs in the first person singular: *loves* (Childs and Van Herk 2014: 646). We believe that such a joint social/grammatical trait constitutes one use of –s. Lastly, it is well-established that grammaticalisation trajectories, like the one that we envisage for verbal –s, show what Hopper (1991) has termed 'layering': an intermediate stage that is characterized by the coexistence of old and new forms/meanings before the old make way for the new. Hopper's principle states: 'Within a broad functional domain, new layers are continually emerging. As it happens, the old layers are not necessarily discarded, but may remain to exist with and interact with the new layers.' (1991: 22). That is to say that as grammaticalising morphemes take on revised functions in the grammar, different 'layers' of the grammaticalisation process appear at a single synchronic point in time. Recall from Sect. 2.4.2.3 that Childs and Van Herk (2014) report on a generational change in the grammatical function of –s among speakers in urban Newfoundland, which they describe in terms of

'Old –s' and 'New –s'. In the context of layering, we'd also take note of the demise of NSR –s and the claim that narrative –s is most likely 'a later development' (Godfrey and Tagliamonte 1999: 107). Chapters 4 and 5 will demonstrate that other forms of verbal –s are associated with different uses again: past BE may, among other things, signal polarity (*was/weren't*) or stances in tag-questions (*weren't it*), and existential *there(')s* the introduction of new information. We will see that some of these forms seem similarly to have undergone lexicalisation and may have a use that has been encroaching on an older one.

To what extent may 'iconic motivation' be a factor implicated in the outcome of functional shift? De Cuypere (2008: 1) has commented that the notion of iconicity has been met with some suspicion. The concern is that we can find similarity anywhere if only we try hard enough and therefore resemblance in itself cannot have any explanatory force. And yet, similarity relations have been reported in the literature many-a-times. Levon et al. (2017), editors of a special volume of *Linguistics* on the social meaning of phonological variants of –s (a subject which we will not address here), say: 'The discovery of sustained cross-linguistic similarity among a diverse group of languages calls [the] assumption of arbitrariness into question, and requires us to consider alternative explanations for the source of convergent perceived meaning.' (2017: 984). Eckert, in the same volume, adds: 'The fact that linguistic signs need to be basically arbitrary does not mean that iconicity cannot play an important role in the construction of signs.' (2017: 1200). And while '[p]honological sociolinguistic variables are pure indexes, as they non-referentially point out distinctions in the social world, many of them … are both indexical and iconic' (2017: 1198). Extrapolating from the literature (amongst others, De Cuypere 2008: 109, 111; Levon et al. 2017 and references therein), there is, for example, evidence that across languages, the contrast between front and back vowels (for example /i/ and /a/ vs. /ɔ/), or the fronting and backing of vowels, iconically correlates with differences in size (for example *petite* vs. *large*). From there, the contrast has been operationalised to convey other informational meaning, such as differences in time (for example *think* vs. *thought*) as well as 'affectively engaged' meanings (Levon et al. 2017: 985), such as personal closeness (for example intimate vs.

distant), positive and negative emotional states (Eckert 2011: 19; citing Silverstein 1994), perceived personal traits (Levon et al. 2017: 989) like 'big' (adults) and 'small' (kids) (2017: 987), and so on. In syntax, spatial, linear differences can mirror conceptual differences (Fischer 2006: 2). For example, in English, we may conceive of a simple past tense sentence (*I felled the tree*) as different from a *to*-infinitive (*I caused* [*the tree to fall*]) in that we feel that in the latter, the tree falling is less directly caused by the action of the speaker concerned. This 'iconicity of distance' (Newmeyer 1992: 761) is also apparent in dative alternation. Thompson and Koide (1987: 402) note that, in contrast to a construction like *Bonnie **taught Ronnie** linguistics*, the recipient (Ronnie) might not have learned anything in *Bonnie **taught** linguistics **to Ronnie***. Similarly, Fischer (2001) argues that the structure of both attributive adjectives, which are part of the noun phrase, and postnominal adjectives, which are separable predicates, is reflected in their meaning: attributive adjectives modify the noun restrictively 'as it were, chang[ing] the noun into a new "compound noun"' (2001: 258), whilst postnominal adjectives provide non-restrictive additional information. Compare, for example, *the responsible man* (= the trustworthy man) to *the man responsible* (= the man who is to blame) (2001: 251). We refer the reader to De Cuypere (2008: 97–98 and 142 ff.) for more examples of the ways in which a distance effect can be created via structure. Following Seiler (1995), it seems uncontroversial that language, in its varied manifestations, is a mixture of the symbolic, the indexical and the iconic. 'Iconicity alternates or coccurs with the indexical-indicative and the symbolic-predicative modes of representation' (1995: 141). Newmeyer (1992: 760–761) assesses a principle of isomorphism as 'essentially correct' though 'in its strongest form … untenable'.

This said, Eckert (2017: 1200) has pointed out that iconicity is not natural; otherwise 'a particular iconic form would always have the same meaning'. Haspelmath (2008: 7) lists many counterexamples to iconicity in areas like plural formation; for example in Welsh the singular (*plu-en* 'feather') can be longer than the plural (*plu* 'feathers'). In response, it has been argued that iconisation may not apply or apply differently because it can be culturally determined or dependent on particular conceptualisations or linguistic ideologies (for example Irvine

2001).[61] Woolard (2008: 439) has more generally argued that 'cultural conceptions of language structure and use inevitably shape and alter that structure' (see also the references in Woolard 2008 on this point). Levon et al. (2017: 987) note: 'It is ... not only the network of sound symbolically linked meanings that are potentially language- and culture specific, but also the interpretation of the iconicity of the form itself'.

De Cuypere has critically remarked that while a number of experimental studies have demonstrated that speakers are very apt at perceiving similarities (2008: 110–113), 'linguistic structures may resemble the reality referred to, but a theoretical reflection about what these results actually bear out appears to have been largely neglected' (2008: 2). Von Mengden (2016: 135), in a different context on grammaticalisation, has said: 'It is, of course, not implausible to assume that change in form and change in function are capable of mutually influencing each other. But as such this is an assumption, not an empirically substantiated statement. The presupposed interaction between form and function therefore needs to be assessed and described in detail prior to building it axiomatically into a diagnostic tool for, or a definition of a type of language change.' There is some consensus amongst scholars working within the research programme on iconicity that for iconic motivation to obtain, '[a] form-meaning association is only the first step' (Levon et al. 2017: 989). Speakers must subsequently operationalise apparent form-meaning correspondences and make them 'work' in practice. That is to say, iconisation is seen as a creative process whereby speakers are agents who add a layer of meaning to denotational meanings or phonemic contrasts (that is, symbolic meanings) at the level of discourse (De Cuypere 2008: 141). As Fischer (2006: 1) has put it, through iconisation 'linguistic structures acquire meaning'. An iconic principle may prompt the speaker to consciously create or select available structural or stylistic options (Newmeyer 1992: 773–775; Fischer and Nänny 1999: xx). De Cuypere (2008: 204) appeals to Coseriu's (1994: xxx) notion of 'sense' here: 'the particular linguistic content which is expressed by means of designation and meaning and which goes beyond designation and meaning in a particular discourse, such as the speaker's attitude, intention or assumption'. For example, he maintains that the to-infinitive *I caused the tree to fall* has the same referential meaning as *I felled*

94   **L. Rupp and D. Britain**

the tree; the 'extra' meaning is the conceptual difference. Drawing on work by Sonesson (1997: 740), De Cuypere (2008: 219) postulates an account of iconic motivation that distinguishes between 'the *possibilities* for iconicity in language' (the 'iconic ground') and 'the *actual use* of iconicity in discourse' (iconicity proper) [our italics] by which associations can be used for meaning-making. Eckert (2012: 97) has similarly spoken of 'iconic potential'. She sees iconisation as a factor in the establishment of second-order indexical fields that speakers can associate with linguistic features and strategically exploit to invoke particular characteristics, take on particular stances, perform ideological moves, [make social meaning; Woolard 2008: 437–438] and so on in situated use. In this relation she has referred to the various qualities that variants of /t/ release and what she calls 'dropping your g's' in, for example, *walkin(g)* can index, such as (hyper)articulateness or the reverse (2012: 96 ff. and references therein).

De Cuypere (2008: 171) admits that 'it is not always easy to prove that a particular linguistic creation is iconically motivated, for it is not always easy to demonstrate that the observed iconic ground conveys extra meaning on the level of discourse. Yet the thrust of what I have been saying … is that such a demonstration of the extra iconic meaning on the level of discourse is to be considered a necessary condition for a linguistic structure to qualify as iconically motivated.' De Cuypere argues that 'real data have to be examined to see whether the iconic ground is creatively deployed in discourse' (2008: 98), and thinks that diachronic research can help establish 'whether iconicity was actually involved in the original innovation which created the construction via language change' (2008: 255) (see also Fischer 1997). What complicates this endeavour is that linguistic innovations may be conventionalised in language change to the extent that they are no longer noticed as iconically motivated but considered part of the symbolic grammar (Fischer and Nänny 1999: xix). Following De Cuypere, though, 'the original iconic ground remains available as the potentiality for iconicity in the discourse' (2008: 174). We are currently not aware of any other distinctive—for example, grammatical—features that can adduce evidence for the putative iconic motivation of verbal –s, similar to the independent morphosyntactic properties that Haiman (1983: 784), Fischer (2001), and Kortmann (1999) have identified in relation to the iconic behaviour of adjectival modification, to-infinitives and adverbial subordinators, respectively. Berretta (1995) has stated that, generally, iconic motivation in morphology is more difficult to argue for than in syntax or phonology:

> At other levels an iconic relationship between sign and reality is much clearer; in some way the structure of the sign reflects a referential feature, or at least a concrete one, as when for example at a lexical level a perceptible element is a source of onomatopoeia; or at the macrosyntactic level, a sequence of events as reported in a text follows the same sequence as the events referred to. In morphology, on the contrary, even if there is a link between sign structure and external world and (especially) the way we perceive it, the conceptual and linguistic mediation is much stronger and the connection between sign and external reality is much less direct. (1995: 198)

Accordingly, the plural –s of nouns, for example, has alternatively been analysed in terms of economy: less frequent expressions are expected to be more marked (Berretta 1995: 198; Haspelmath 2008).

However, we would like to suggest that the iconically motivated meanings of verbal –s that we have in mind build on symbolic (denotational) meaning. Namely, the very occurrence of variation per se is indicative of adding meaning in context. Through the variable, strategic use of an added –s, some *additional* meaning is being attached. Very bluntly, –s signals that more work is being done. Specifically, it seems to us that the various uses of verbal –s may be iconically motivated in the following manner:

- NSR –s: the extra material on the verb signals that subjects are discourse-heavy (difficult to retrieve): NPs (especially in relative clauses) and, more broadly, subjects that are separated from the verb (for example, in inversion)[62];
- Habitual –s: an extended form of the verb codes that an event is recurrent (happens more than once), in contrast to a single event;

- Narrative –s: following Rodríguez Louro and Ritz (2014: 552), narrative –s (the historic present) allows the narrator to indicate that events are to be viewed as (somehow) different 'from other events presented in the PT' [past tense LR&DB]. As Polanyi (1989: 22) has put it, this is 'accomplished by encoding the information ... increased weight in a way which departs from the local norm of the text';
- Identity marking –s: verbal –s iconically reflects vernacular behaviour in the case of the Reading peer groups from Cheshire (1982). As for the Newfoundland drag queens, the active choice of –s is iconically connected to the active and conscious performance of personae that are partly resourced by the indexical meanings that have become associated with the verbal marker. Among these are: traditional, male, rural, 'Newfoundlandy' female, local, urban and even global, as some celebrities are using it 'with a set of arch, diva-ish and perhaps slightly ditzy connotations' (Childs and Van Herk 2014: 650) to refer to themselves in the third person. We could argue that the twisting or volatility of –s usage invokes the performed multifaceted character of drag queens. This perspective ties in with Childs and Van Herk's (2014: 651) view that 'both the local connotations and the global stylistic associations are potentially positive for them. They can position themselves with respect to these associations, or even better, draw on both sets of associations without specifically identifying with either. This ambiguity leaves the interpretation to the listener, and listener collaboration is a major component of performances, especially of dragging'.

For research in the field of language typology, Kortmann (1999) has said: 'If we adopt iconicity as a working hypothesis, that is, if we assume that the structure of language reflects in some way the structure of experience' (p. 375), then 'even if the iconicity hypothesis must be rejected in the first place' […], 'the iconicity hypothesis has given and continues to give us interesting ideas that otherwise would not be followed up' (p. 389). We would assume this for verbal –s. In Chapters 4 and 5, therefore, we will consider other tokens of verbal –s against the notion of diagrammatic iconicity.

Notes

1. Extensive overviews of the literature on verbal –s can be found in Smith and Tagliamonte (1998), Godfrey and Tagliamonte (1999), and Pietsch (2005). See also Wakelin (1972) for the scale of verbal –s in the *Survey of English Dialects* (Orton and Dieth 1962–1971).
2. We will address the occurrence of verbal –s in African American Vernacular English in Chapter 3 in relation to the occurrence of verbal zero there.
3. In their representation of the OE present-indicative voiceless interdental fricative ending [θ], the historical literature/historical manuscripts may be found to either use –ð (which is the spelling in the main Northumbrian monuments (cf. Benskin 2011: 160)), –þ or –th (which were orthographic alternatives in OE). We will adopt the notation deployed by the author concerned. We will use orthographic –th to refer to [θ] in Middle English and Early Modern English.
4. Old English had strong and weak verbs, like Modern English. There were several classes of weak verbs with some phonological differences. However, following Hogg (2012: 48), the present indicative endings of strong and weak verbs were the same. As we will see, the major differences in the present indicative paradigm emerged in early Middle English and they were regional.
5. Following Lass (1992: 96), there are two main types of morphological analogy, extension and levelling. 'Extension is the application of a process outside its original domain … By levelling we mean the ironing out of allomorphy within the paradigm.'. While the generalisation of –s may seem a case of levelling across the present indicative paradigm, later we will see that verbal –s acquired more extended uses.
6. Wakelin (1972: 119–120) reports that the –(e)th ending is to a very limited extent still found in the south-western dialects, as does Wright (1905: 296) for Devon and Somerset, and Elworthy for West Somerset (for example *ee uurnth* (*he runs*): 'The form is still common in our hill-country districts, but throughout the vale of West Somerset it is becoming rare, except with old people' (1877: 51–52). The *Survey of English Dialects* (SED; Orton and Dieth 1962–1971) records *her wear'th the trouwers* from Co [Cornwall] 1 (VI.14.14). However, more recent studies of the south-west do not mention the survival of the –th form today (for example Piercy 2010). The plural ending –(e)n

that was used in the Midland dialects in Middle English was also documented by the SED (for example *we putten* at Db [Derbyshire] 4 (V.2.12)). Wakelin (1972) notes that *The English Dialect Grammar* (Wright 1905: 296) states that this form occurred at least through the first half of the twentieth century in a geographically restricted area, consisting of Lancashire, Cheshire, Derbyshire, Staffordshire, Northamptonshire, Warwickshire, Worcestershire and Herefordshire, especially in the verb *have*. Shorrocks (1980: 568) has characterised it as a 'residual' feature in the dialect of Farnsworth (Greater Manchester country), for example *we wantn*.

7. There are hardly any texts in the Northumbrian dialect from the 8th till about the middle of the tenth century. The glosses of these text editions constitute the first substantial material following the gap in the record. See Cole (2014: 16) for discussion of advantages and shortcomings of working with interlinear glosses, and Chapter 2 in her work for background to the texts. We also refer to the historical studies cited in the current section for details of the manuscripts on which their studies are based.

8. Nevalainen and Raumolin-Brunberg (2000) present yet another, morphophonemic account, while Samuels (1989: 112) has argued that Old Norse also provided the model for the Midland plural form –en.

9. Using modern statistical methodology, Cole (2014: 112) supports the analogical levelling hypothesis but her analysis does not confirm the alleged direction of effect. However, this does not bear on our argument.

10. De Haas (2011: 14) has pointed out that in Middle English, 'the ending corresponding to the –Ø ending was often –e'. –Ø is currently the canonical ending in the 1st and 2nd sing. and pl. in Standard English.

11. Holmqvist (1922: 49–50) notes that from the fifteenth century onwards, –th was revived in the present-indicative 3rd sing. and pl. among northern writers. He thinks that '[e]vidently this change is exclusively due to influence from the standard language' and cites literary works in which the revival can be observed. Moore (2002) has studied the apparent reversal of the process in the Plumpton letters.

12. Cole (2014: Chapter 5) has made a case for there having been additional input to the appearance of (–e)/–Ø in the present indicative.

13. One could argue, as Klemola (2000: 329, Footnote 2) has done, that –s continues to mark present tense, whilst in varieties like Standard

English –s has specialised as a 3rd sing. ending. However, we would agree with Siewierska (1999) that in languages where subjects must be obligatory expressed, agreement morphemes are not (no longer) referential and in effect constitute redundant grammatical elements. Furthermore, if a language has past tense endings, like English, present tense is arguably conveyed by default in the absence of these endings.

14. Cole (2014) has expressed a similar view, only she describes the situation that has given rise to functional shift as one of competition between two forms, or the co-occurrence of two morphological variants (for example –s and –ð). Since she confines her attention to the 'Northern Subject Rule' (NSR) use of verbal –s, we will discuss her view in the section that addresses the NSR.

15. Givón (1976) also thinks that pronouns get re-analysed as agreement morphemes but he suggests that agreement arises via 'topic-shifting constructions'. Topic-shifting constructions are marked constructions in which there is a gap between the first and the second mention of the topic; for example *The man, he came*. Givón envisages that the construction was over-used in an unmarked context. As a result, speakers assigned the construction a more neutral syntax, in which the erstwhile topic was reanalysed as a subject and the anaphoric pronouns as an agreement marker. Schematised:

	Topic-shift (marked)		*Reanalysis (neutral)*	
(44)	a.	The man, he came	b.	The man he-came
	TOP	PRO	SUBJ	AGR

16. According to Benskin (2011: 162, Footnote 14), this is only a 'marginal' case. He points out that while unstressed pronouns have been fused into verbal inflections across many languages, with the exception of –st, this has not otherwise happened in the history of English. However, it is precisely this case that is the centre of our investigation.

17. 'Exaptation' has been the topic of an edited volume entitled *Exaptation and Language Change* (Norde and Van de Velde 2016). We refer to the papers in this volume, as well as De Cuypere (2005), for in-depth theoretical discussion and exhaustive empirical exploration of Lass's notion of 'exaptation'. Here the reader also finds mention of the textbook case of exaptation in biology: feathers (originally thermoregulatory devices) recruited for flight.

18. In this context, Joseph (2004) has postulated the occurrence of what he has dubbed 'lateral shifts'. This is a change in which an expression acquires a new function but no change in grammatical status is occasioned. 'Thus after the change, the element in question is neither more nor less grammatical than before, so it is a "movement", in that change has occurred, but one that goes "laterally" on the cline, not up or down it' (Joseph 2005: 2). The illustration that he provides concerns the use of affixes in Ancient and Modern Greek that have taken on a new role. Norde (2001: 234) calls this 'lateral conversion': 'changes from one category to another on the same level of grammaticality'.

19. Lass (1990: 100) ends with a quote from Konrad Lorenz (1978: 3) to illustrate the notion of 'exaptation', drawing a metaphorical comparison with houses: 'The recognizable historical remains are retained, because the structure can't be entirely torn down and planned anew; this would be quite impossible so long as it was being continually inhabited ... With luck, however, you can redecorate'.

20. The phenomenon has been referred to by other names in the literature. However, unless a different naming reflects an essentially different perspective on the phenomenon, we will not mention it here.

21. José (2007: 264) is right to point out that non-adjacency obtains linearly but not structurally; viz. in (4f) 'the subject could be analyzed not simply as *the dogs*, but as the complex NP [$_{NP}$ *the dogs* [$_{PP}$ *in the trucks*]], which is adjacent to the verb'. Non-linear adjacency is consistent with the processing account of the Proximity Effect that we offer later on.

22. Specifically, De Haas takes the optionality of the Proximity Effect to derive from 'an extra PF condition on morphology', which merges an agreement marker and a verb under adjacency, but 'which may or may not apply' (2011: 195). This allows for the agreement process to take place in non-adjacent contexts, next to the occurrence of verbal –s. She thinks that the relative infrequency of non-adjacent contexts may have led some speakers to not recognize that adjacency is essential to agreement. Clarke (2004: 10) provides a psycholinguistic account, suggesting that verbal –s occurs wherever a speaker 'los[es] track of grammatical agreement as a result of the physical separation of verb and subject head noun'. We will give our own explanation of the Proximity Effect in Sect. 2.4.1.4.

23. Wright also found a (what she terms) *they*-constraint with –th in the seventeenth century *Bridewell Court Minute Books*, which recorded

details of prisoners who were sent from London to Virginia in the
United States. This is illustrated in (45).

(45)   This dotterells howse hathe **two or three wenches** that
       useth there dalie And is there occupied wth sarving men
       and othere and at nighte **they go** to bed in an othere place.
       And **commeth** againe in the mornynge [fo 35, May 1574]
       (Wright 2002: 251)

She found 35 tokens of adjacent *they*, all of which were combined with
Ø, while 35 of 162 3rd pl. NPs were combined with –th (2002: 253).

24. Benskin (2011) allows for the possibility that reduced subjunctive
    forms constituted the direct historical source of the non-inverted indic-
    ative reduced form that specialised as an ending associated with pro-
    nominal subjects. He makes this alternative proposal in light of the fact
    that very few tokens of the 'West Saxon' concord in inverted indica-
    tive clauses have been attested in texts from Old Northumbrian (see the
    references in his work on p. 169). This view receives apparent support
    from the finding that subjunctives tend to occur more frequently with
    pronominal subjects than with NP-subjects (Cole 2014: 179).
25. Following Klemola (2000: 337), the Welsh system is typologically rare,
    but Andrew Spencer (p.c.) tells us that it is a fairly common kind of
    pattern and attested in Modern Hebrew.
26. Diesing (1992) has shown that indefinite NPs may also have a more
    discourse-new or discourse old-interpretation. She has similarly linked
    different semantic interpretations of subjects, like those in (46a–b), to
    different syntactic positions in the clause structure.

(46)   a.   There are **some men** in the garden. [indefinite
            NP=discourse-new]
       b.   **Some men** [=some of the men LR&DB] are in the garden.
            [indefinite NP=discourse-old]

Diesing's work has been heavily drawn upon by accounts of the properties of existential *there* sentences, such as the one by Felser and Rupp
(2001). Existential *there* sentences are known to have two subject

positions; a lower position filled by the associate-NP and a higher position filled by the expletive *there*. See Chapter 5 for extensive discussion of verbal –s in existentials.

27. Cole (2014: 84) cites work by Larsson (1988) that a comparable effect has obtained in the history of Swedish and suggests that we may even be looking at a universal tendency.

28. A number of studies have looked into the continuity of the NSR in the Early Modern English period. Amongst these are: Bailey and Ross (1988; in seventeenth and eighteenth century ship logs written by sailors from the south-west of England who were involved in the slave trade), Bailey et al. (1989; in the fifteenth century *Cely Letters* from London), Schendl (1996; in a selection of Early Modern English texts in the emerging Early Modern English standard variety), Montgomery and Fuller (1996; in nineteenth century letters written by African Americans, plantation overseers and Scotch-Irish immigrants in North and South Carolina), Montgomery (1997; in letters of eighteenth and nineteenth century Ulster immigrants to the U.S., whose NSR-patterns have been preserved in near-categorical use of the NSR in Appalachia), Schneider and Montgomery (2001; in the southern White English of plantation overseers in the nineteenth century), and Moore (2002; in the Early Modern *Plumpton* letter collection).

29. For example, Feagin (1979: 190–191) found the NSR in data from Anniston, Alabama to highly correlate with speakers' class and sex.

30. Like Wright (1905), Wakelin (1972), and Pietsch (2005: 138–140) notes the survival of plural –n in the SED (for example *They think they knowen it* [Ch1]). He more specifically reports that historical alternation between –n and –s is still well-attested in the north-west Midlands, an area 'covering southern Lancashire, Cheshire, Derbyshire, Shropshire and Staffordshire, and reaching also into the south-western corner of Yorkshire'. In a later study of the modern dialect of Bolton in Lancashire, Shorrocks (1999: 114–115) has indicated that –n now recessively alternates with –s according to the NSR. However, he has also observed that –s has come to be deployed as a marker of habituality. We will return to other uses of verbal –s in Sect. 2.4.1.4.

31. Corrigan (1997: Chapter 4) has documented this use with past BE in South Armagh (***Them was** all common in this town in them times*).

32. Following Jantos (2010: 323), who studied subject-verb agreement in the ICE-Jamaica corpus, an alternative explanation is that the verb may be made to agree with the most proximal noun of a complex NP, rather

than with the head of the subject noun phrase, as in *[Preparations for the ceremony]* **is** *now in high gear*.

33. Constructions in which verbal –s is known to be prevalent also include conjoined noun phrases (cf. ***Me and my sister gets*** *in a fight sometimes*; Appalachia, Montgomery 1989: 258) and collective nouns (cf. ***The police is*** *watching you right now*). However, we will not consider this use of verbal –s because it can be explained independently from the NSR. In conjoined noun phrases, the verb may in fact agree with a 3rd sing. second conjunct element and in collective noun phrases, agreement may be semantic depending on whether the referent of the collective noun is conceived of as a group or as a number of individuals (see Cole (2008: 103 ff.) and De Vos 2013 for some discussion). Specifically, in a study of verbal –s in Wallsend (north Tyneside), a traditional NSR-dialect, Childs (2011) found that speakers were significantly more accepting of verbal –s in the context of a conjoined NP when the last conjunct was 3rd sing. rather than 2nd sing. or 3rd pl. (2011: 38–39). Childs's analysis of this result is that verbal –s appearing with conjoined subjects is 3rd sing. –s (an agreement marker), rather than NSR –s. She has concluded that 'verbal *–s* occurrence with conjoined subjects is a generalised phenomenon not characteristic of the NSR' (2011: 46). Corbett (1979) has formalised an account of such alternative agreement forms in an 'agreement hierarchy' that predicts that 'as syntactic distance increases so does the likelihood of semantic agreement'.

34. We refer to Cole (2008: 94) for studies of other contemporary varieties that have replicated the direction of effect. Subsequent reports include Childs (2012) and Buchstaller et al. (2013). In a survey of the perception of verbal –s conducted in Newcastle upon Tyne and the Scottish locality of Hawick, Buchstaller et al. (2013) found that informants did not differentiate at all between adjacent and non-adjacent pronoun subjects (2013: 101) and significantly favoured verbal –s in subject relatives in addition to existential *there* sentences (2013: 104), a phenomenon that we will discuss in Chapter 5. In similar type of research, Childs (2012) has argued that the traditional Pro-(non-complex) NP differentiation is still robust in fact in nearby Wallsend and Hawick Scots in the south-east of Scotland (2012: 334).

35. An exception is Montgomery (1989). He has reported a strong NSR effect on verbal –s in three sets of data from Appalachia in the east of the United States, dating from the 1930s to 1970s (see his work for

details of the sample). He found that verbal –s occurred only marginally with *they* (0.0–0.2%) and envisages that verbal –s 'was once a categorical or near-categorical part of the grammar of AppE' (1989: 259). While Appalachia is known to have preserved older features of English (sometimes anecdotally, see Montgomery 1998), when we more closely look at the breakdown of results (pp. 256–257), they show that verbal –s was in fact most frequent in 'special' constructions like existentials, collective nouns and conjoined NPs, while percentages of other NPs only ranged between 2.5% and 31%. Montgomery endeavoured to establish 'trans-atlantic connections in grammatical patterns' (p. 268), tracing the occurrence of the NSR in Appalachia to Scots-Irish founders, who emigrated from Scotland to North America via Northern Ireland (Ulster) in the early eighteenth century (1989: 229). Mallinson and Wolfram (2002: 750–751) have documented the NSR in Roaring Creek in the Appalachian region of western North Carolina, though levels of verbal –s among their informants (eight European Americans) were receding overall. In a sociolinguistic study of 18 speakers, Hazen (2000) has shown that Ocracoke, an island off the coast of North Carolina, shares Scotch-Irish heritage with Appalachia and demonstrates the classic ancestral NSR pattern albeit at reduced rates and with the difference that verbal –s neither occurred with adjacent or non-adjacent pronouns (p. 133 ff.). The sociohistory of Ocracoke will be discussed in relation to Schilling-Estes and Wolfram's (1994) work on the use of past BE on the island in Chapter 4. José (2007: 262) reports the NSR for Harrison County; an area which is geographically outside Appalachia proper but, he argues, shows *Appalachian-ness* (2007: 274).

36. Earlier studies that have documented the NSR in Ulster speech include Milroy (1981: 12–13).

37. The clause structure that De Haas (2011) postulates in her diachronic analysis of the NSR (shown in Sect. 2.4.1.1) is virtually identical to Henry's (1995) proposition.

38. However, recall from the previous section that many other studies have identified inversion as being particularly favourable towards verbal –s. For example, while inverted environments that could take verbal –s were relatively sparse in the composite corpus that Pietsch (2005) surveyed, the vast majority of them did, and Pietsch concludes that

2 Verbal –s 105

'[i]nverted clauses must therefore be counted as one of the most strongly favouring environments' (2005: 168).

39. Barlow (1992) has formalised his views on the nature of agreement in his Discourse-Linking Theory. We will not consider the details of this theory here.

40. According to Barlow (1999: 192–193), inanimate referents are more likely to show non-standard agreement than animate referents (also see Corbett 1979: 219; Comrie 1979: 325). Apparently contradictory to this is Feagin's (1979: 191–192) finding that white speakers of Alabama English used verbal –s 'largely though not exclusively' with animate subjects. However, Feagin does not provide any statistical evidence, and some of the examples (of animate subjects occurring with verbal –s) that she presents are amenable to an alternative explanation, such as construal of a collective reading or the presence of the singular determiner *a*; for example: *people, a lot of 'em, The Carters*. Examples of inanimate subject occurring with verbal –s as presented by Feagin were: *things, eyes, churches*.

Further, Epstein (2010: 123; see also references therein) states that 'human referents are more likely than animate objects to receive *special grammatical treatment* because people are more highly salient – that is, important – in our experience of the world than things.' [our italics]. Epstein examined the use of the Old English demonstrative *se* in Beowulf, but in the present context of agreement, it is not clear to us whether 'special grammatical treatment' would mean regular or conflicting subject-verb agreement marking. We will leave the matter unresolved, therefore.

41. Rohdenburg (1996) has proposed that the cognitive factor derives from a more general 'complexity principle' (or: transparency principle), which states that 'in the case of more or less explicit grammatical options the more explicit one(s) will tend to be favored in cognitively more complex environments.' (1996: 151). In the context of the NSR, inflected verbs with –s are more explicitly marked than uninflected verbs, while longer subject expressions (for example NPs) are more difficult to process than simple subjects (for example pronouns). Rohdenburg has argued that verbal –s occurs with NPs because 'the more complex the subject becomes the longer it takes to recognize th[e] relationship [between the subject and the verb] and thus to identify the function of the uninflected verb' (1996: 155). We refer to Rohdenburg for other apparent applications of his principle.

In Sect. 2.5, we will propose an alternative principle that intends to also capture uses of verbal –s other than the NSR.

42. Recall from Sect. 2.4.1.2 that many dialects are reported to have been losing the NSR. We speculate that this may be due to contact with varieties that have a standard configuration of –s.

43. We would follow Wright (2002: 260, Footnote 12) in considering modified nouns heavy NPs and light NPs to be 'null subjects, dummy subject *there*, pronoun subjects, unmodified nouns and nouns modified by an article.'

44. The NSR has additionally been attested in the 3rd sing. in historical documents, including the *Cely Letters* from the fifteenth century (Bailey, Maynor and Cukor-Avila 1989) and the Old Northumbrian *Lindesfarne Gospels*, albeit it that the verb endings were different then (Cole 2014: 106). We will address the matter of different endings having been observed for the NSR in Sect. 2.5.

Here we also take note of reports that the NSR may extend to null subjects, making them pattern with NPs, both in Old Northumbrian (Cole 2014: 106) and at a later date (cf. Montgomery's 1994 study of seventeenth century letters, p. 89). The patterning of NPs and null subjects is echoed in Welsh, which Klemola (2000: 337–338) has taken as support for the idea that the NSR emerged in contact with Brythonic Celtic (recall the discussion in Sect. 2.4.1). On our discourse-based account, this is unexpected because null subjects rank high (actually, the highest) on the accessibility scales of Prince (1985) and Ariel (2001). Null subjects are known to be highly accessible where they are retrievable from paradigmatic referential agreement (for example Schütze 1997) or in context (take, for instance, imperative sentences that are canonically directed at the addressee; Rupp 2003). It may be that null subjects are less accessible where they cannot be retrieved in this manner.

45. That the NSR might be a language universal tendency would seem suggested by the fact that the NSR has also been found to hold in the New Englishes in India, Singapore, and Hong Kong, albeit only the Type-of-Subject effect and not the Proximity effect. See Calle-Martín and Romero-Barranco (2017) who surveyed data from the *International Corpus of English*.

46. The deployment of verbal –s has been reported for other English varieties with African roots, including Liberian Settler English (Singler 1997), Samaná English and African Nova Scotian English (Poplack

2 Verbal –s 107

and Tagliamonte 1991: 329). Ellis (1994) has postulated contact with AAVE-speakers as one of the possible sources of the aspectual use of verbal –s that he observed in white southern U.S. writers from the mid nineteenth century, next to the NSR. We refer to Montgomery and Fuller (1996), Walker (2000), and Trüb (2006) for alternative accounts of (the relation between) the aspectual systems of early AAVE and early white southern American English, respectively.

47. A number of other studies have documented apparent occurrences of habitual –s. They include Shorrocks (1980: 570–571) on Farnsworth in north-west England, Macafee (1980: 25) on present-day Scottish English (cited in Montgomery and Fuller 1996: 221), and Cole (2008: 102) on data in the NECTE corpus. Here are examples from these studies, respectively:

(47) a. **We goes** down there regularly, don't we?
      b. Every time, **they goes** away out aw the way tae the road en, and **comes** back empty handit.
      c. **You gets**, you get fellows who like to jump around [change jobs frequently]. (NECTE 1969)

48. According to Clarke (1999: 332), an alternative way for speakers of NFE to convey habitual meaning is to attach verbal –s to the stem *be*, as in (48a–b). This is also a now obsolescent characteristic of the eastern English Fenland (Britain 2015), as in (48c). Clarke (1999: 330) adds that while in the source varieties of NFE the habitual may also be expressed by means of periphrasitic *do*, this does not happen in NFE itself.

(48) a. **It bees** some cold here in winter. (LNEC corpus).
      b. Ususally **I talks** fast and **gets** off because **I bees** embarrassed. (Rural female on St John's, Newfoundland, radio phone-in show, 21/12/92).
      c. He gets **his secretary Delores** what **bes** in there with him to answer the phone, don't he? (Woman, 57, from Wisbech).

49. That the NSR was previously (even) more robust in the south of Ireland is suggested by McCafferty's (2004) study of Fitzpatrick's (1994) set of correspondence letters from Irish-Australian emigrants dated 1805–1906 (71 letters written by 10 males and 10 females). See McCafferty's results on the NSR on pp. 70–72 that show that 'adjacent pronouns never occurred with –s'. McCafferty has argued that rather than having diffused southwards from Ulster-Scots dialects in the north of Ireland, the NSR in Southern Irish English might have been directly imported from speakers from northern England and the north Midlands who settled in the south of Ireland.

50. Sudbury (2001: 73) cites lack of subject-verb concord (*Our fellas has got a little one*) and singular verb forms in existentials with a plural noun (*there's* tapestries *there's* photo's and *there's* penguins) among the morphosyntactic features that are relatively common in Falkland Island English. However, she adds that the frequency of many non-standard morphosyntactic features is very low, and no further details about the features are provided. Elsewhere in her paper Sudbury states that two regions stand out as being especially influential in the peopling of the Falkland Islands; namely Scotland, in particular the Highlands and Western Islands region, and the south-west of England, predominantly Devon and Somerset. It is not clear which of these two regions (or both) is a likely source for the occurrence of verbal –s on the Falkland Islands, and, therefore, what its function may be there.

51. Poplack and Tagliamonte (1989: 76) have argued that analysing verbal –s as a habitual marker is challenged by 'the fact that in many languages, including English, habitual aspect meaning is in some sense *embodied* in the present tense.' (one example of this is Standard English: *That boy always walks to school*). They say 'that there is no straightforward way of *distinguishing* a tense function from an aspectual function of -s, as the two are inextricably linked.' However, recall that we assume that in varieties where –s generalised, it lost its function as a present tense agreement morpheme and present tense is implied by the absence of past tense marking. This allows for the possibility of verbal –s being deployed as a (separate) marker of habitual aspect.

52. Cf. Mustanoja (1960): 'The historical present does not seem to occur in OE, nor in earliest ME' but '[t]here is a spectacular increase in the occurrence of the historical present about the middle of the fourteenth century' (1960: 485–486) [i.e., following the generalisation of –s LR& DB]. Fischer (1992: 242) states that '(t)he use of the non-past in a past

2 Verbal –s   109

time narrative context is a new phenomenon that is first encountered in Late Middle English [texts].' Wright (2003: 47) reports on tokens of narrative –th in the sixteenth century dialect of transportees from London, an area where speakers held on to the 3rd sing. –th suffix longest.

53. In addition to the PT and the HP, the 'historical present perfect' (HPP) may be used in narratives to some extent. See Levey (2006) and Rodríguez Louro and Ritz (2014) for discussion of this use.

54. Alexandra D'Arcy and Sali Tagliamonte (p.c.), who have published extensively on *be like* (cf. for example Tagliamonte and D'Arcy 2007; D'Arcy 2017) say that if a variety has levelling to *be like*, there's no reason why *they's like* and *we's like* wouldn't occur, but in the data that they have been working with, they have not actually seen that happen.

55. Myhill and Harris (1986: 26) previously envisaged that expressions that have lost a transparent function can be assigned either a new linguistic or social function.

56. We noted that many of the vernacular verbs listed by Cheshire are nouns that are used as verbs, an innovative process that is known as 'denominalisation'. In extensive work on this phenomenon, Clark and Clark (1979) have provided a theory of how the meaning of such denominal verbs can be readily figured out: the way in which their sense is perceived depends on the denotation of the verb, the speaker's and listener's mutual knowledge/an awareness of conventions about their use, and the context (the time, place and circumstances) in which they are uttered (o.a. pp. 767–768, 785, 787). In work on noun incorporation, which may also give rise to new verbs, Mithun (1984) has argued that such creative processes commonly denote some institutionalised activity ('an activity recognized in some context', p. 848); for example in Siberian Koryak, '*qoya*- 'reindeer' + -*nm*- 'to kill' --> *qoyanm*- to reindeer slaughter' (p. 847). It seems to us that the vernacular verbs can similarly be understood as denoting institutionalised (namely, peer group) activities.

57. We have not yet accounted for one of the prototypes of the NSR identified by Pietsch (2005) (see Sect. 2.4.1.2): that of verbal –s being favoured with the expressions *them* and *thae*. We think that it may fall out from the 'vernacular usage' of verbal –s that is outlined in this section since they are dialectal forms of the distal demonstrative pronouns (Wright 1905: 297).

58. Cheshire (1982: 39–42) observed another constraint amongst her peer group subjects in Reading involving verb complementation. Namely, when a present tense verb was followed by a tensed clausal complement, –s only occurred on the main verb at a rate of maximally 3% (49a), but when the clausal complement was not tensed, –s occurred more frequently at rates of 48–57% (49b–c).

(49) a. Oh, I **forget** [what the place **is** called].
      b. I **fancies** [**going** over Caversham].
      c. I **wants** [**to kill** animals].

Cheshire has termed this pattern the 'following complement constraint'. In joint work with Jamal Ouhalla, she has postulated an account of the constraint that alludes to conceptual cohesion and information structure. Specifically, Cheshire and Ouhalla (1997) propose that in Reading, verbal –s can function as an overt marker of integration. Therefore, verbal –s appears with non-finite clauses because these are informationally dependent and form one information unit with the main verb (an alternative strategy being using an inclusive prosodic contour). Clearly, this –s should not be interpreted as separating/removing the complement further away from the main clause (see Givón's (1995: 51) Proximity Principle and the discussion of iconicity in complement clause constructions in De Cuypere (2008: 155–157)).

59. Clarke and Hiscock (2009) also demonstrate the identity marking potential of verbal –s in their analysis of a set of lyrics from Gazeebow Unit, a Newfoundland hip hop band. They argue that in lyrics such as (50) below, the band uses traditional 'Old –s' parodically in a projection of a 'skeet image' (p. 257). Namely, they draw upon locally enregistered linguistic markers in order to style a globally congruent and locally responsive performance (2009: 248–249).

(50) **I fights** on da yellow bus.
      Smokin' all da time, den **I commits** da crime.
      [...]
      At d(a) gazebo **we likes** to fight
      [...]
      When **you gets** da new bike come to me for da tips

60. Both Givón (1985: 188) and De Cuypere (2008: 107) have contended that isomorphism is not iconic but presupposes iconicity. However, this does not bear on the concept of isomorphism per se. See De Cuypere (2008: 93, 107, 205) for an alternative interpretation of language-internal iconicity, which, however, does not apply here.

61. Additionally, the exception to plural formation cited here may, rather, be a token of a different category that has been called 'singulative' and is discussed by Nurmio (2017). Nurmio argues that the 'singulative' is related to but separate from the grammatical category number (which has a different suffix). In Welsh, the category of 'singulative' seems to single out a unit. For example, it can individuate a referent from mass nouns and 'collectives' (as with *gwenith* 'wheat'—*gwenithen* 'a grain of weath'—note that similar considerations may apply to the Welsh forms for *feather(s)* that we just discussed). The singulative can also nominalise a noun from an action/verb (for instance *symud-yn* 'a mobile (decoration)' from *symud-* 'move').

62. We are aware that whilst 'there is no denying that in the north proper in Middle English *-s* versus *–el-Ø* tends to be the core syntactically-conditioned pattern', Cole (2014: 38) has shown that the NSR has obtained in the context of variation between other morphemes. This seems unexpected from the perspective of 'THE ICONICITY HYPOTHESIS' that we are entertaining; particularly the application of the NSR to the two variant verb endings –s and –ð in Old English (see the discussion in Sect. 2.4.1.1 again). However, Cole found that this application co-occurred with NSR alternation between –s and –Ø, which was a minority variant. This allows for the possibility that the NSR alternation between –s and –Ø was the original to be iconically motivated and that any other NSR-type patterns, including all the later occurrences, were modelled on it.

References

Adger, D., & Smith, J. (2005). Variation and the minimalist program. In L. Cornips & K. Corrigan (Eds.), *Syntax and variation: Reconciling the biological and the social* (pp. 149–178). Amsterdam: John Benjamins.

Adger, D., & Smith, J. (2010). Variation in agreement: A lexical feature-based approach. *Lingua, 120,* 1109–1134.

Ariel, M. (1999). The development of person agreement markers: From pronouns to higher accessibility markers. In M. Barlow & S. Kemmer (Eds.), *Usage-based models of language* (pp. 197–260). Stanford: CSLI Publications.

Ariel, M. (2001). Accessibility theory: An overview. In T. J. M. Sanders, J. Schilperoord, & W. Spooren (Eds.), *Text representation: Linguistic and psycholinguistic aspects* (pp. 29–87). Amsterdam: John Benjamins.

Asprey, E. (2007). *Black Country English and Black Country identity* (Doctoral dissertation). University of Leeds, Leeds.

Bailey, G., & Ross, G. (1988). The shape of the superstrate: Morphosyntactic features of ship English. *English World-Wide, 9,* 193–212.

Bailey, G., Maynor, N., & Cukor-Avila, P. (1989). Variation in subject-verb concord in Early Modern English. *Language Variation and Change, 1,* 285–300.

Barlow, M. (1992). *A situated theory of agreement.* New York: Garland.

Barlow, M. (1999). Agreement as a discourse phenomenon. *Folia Linguistica, 33,* 187–201.

Beal, J. (1993). The grammar of Tyneside and Northumbrian English. In J. Milroy & L. Milroy (Eds.), *Real English: The grammar of English dialects in the British Isles* (pp. 187–213). London: Longman.

Benskin, M. (2011). Present indicative plural concord in Brittonic and Early English. *Transactions of the Philological Society, 109,* 158–185.

Bernstein, J. (2008). The expression of third person in older and contemporary varieties of English. *English Studies, 89,* 571–586.

Berretta, M. (1995). Morphological markedness in L2 acquisition. In R. Simone (Ed.), *Iconicity in language* (pp. 197–233). Amsterdam: John Benjamins.

Booij, G. (2010). *Construction morphology.* Oxford: Oxford University Press.

Börjars, K., & Chapman, C. (1998). Agreement and pro-drop in some dialects of English. *Linguistics, 36,* 71–98.

Bresnan, J., & Mchombo, S. A. (1986). Grammatical and anaphoric agreement. In A. Farley, P. Farley, & K. McCullough (Eds.), *Proceedings of the Chicago Linguistic Society 22: Papers from the Parasession on Pragmatics and Grammatical Theory* (pp. 741–782). Chicago: Chicago Linguistics Society.

Brinton, L., & Stein, D. (1995). Functional renewal. In H. Andersen (Ed.), *Historical linguistics 1993: Selected Papers from the 11th International Conference on Historical Linguistics, Los Angeles, 16–20 August 1993* (pp. 33–47). Amsterdam: John Benjamins.

Britain, D. (2015). Between North and South: The Fenland. In R. Hickey (Ed.), *Researching Northern English* (pp. 417–435). Amsterdam: John Benjamins.

Buchstaller, I., Corrigan, K. P., Holmberg, A., Honeybone, P., & Maguire, W. (2013). T-to-R and the Northern Subject Rule: Questionnaire-based, spatial, social and structural linguistics. *English Language and Linguistics, 17*, 85–128.

Calle-Martín, J., & Romero-Barranco, J. (2017). Third person present tense markers in some varieties of English. *English World-Wide, 38*, 77–103.

Campbell, A. (1959). *Old English grammar*. Oxford: Clarendon Press.

Chapman, C. (1998). A subject-verb agreement hierarchy: Evidence from analogical change in modern English dialects. In R. M. Hogg & L. van Bergen (Eds.), *Historical linguistics (Vol. 2): Germanic linguistics: Selected papers from the 12th International Conference on Historical Linguistics, Manchester, August 1995* (pp. 35–44). Amsterdam: John Benjamins.

Cheshire, J. (1982). *Variation in an English dialect: A sociolinguistic study*. Cambridge: Cambridge University Press.

Cheshire, J., & Ouhalla, J. (1997). *Grammatical constraints on variation*. Paper presented at UK Language Variation and Change 1, University of Reading, UK.

Childs, C. (2011). *The Northern Subject Rule and coordination: Examining perceptions of verbal -s occurrence in Tyneside English* (BA dissertation). University of Newcastle, Newcastle.

Childs, C. (2012). Verbal -s and the Northern Subject Rule: Spatial variation in linguistic and sociolinguistic constraints. In Á. Pérez, X. Afonso, E. Carrilho, & C. Magro (Eds.), *Proceedings of the International Symposium on Limits and Areas in Dialectology, Lisbon, 2011* (pp. 319–344). Lisboa: Centro de Linguística da Universidade de Lisboa.

Childs, B., & Van Herk, G. (2010). Breaking old habits: Syntactic constraints underlying habitual effects in Newfoundland English. In J. Walker (Ed.), *Aspect in grammatical variation* (pp. 81–93). Amsterdam: John Benjamins.

Childs, B., & Van Herk, G. (2013). Superstars and bit players: Salience and the fate of local dialect features. In A. Barysevich, A. D'Arcy, & D. Heap (Eds.), *Proceedings of Methods XIV: Papers from the Fourteenth International Conference on Methods in Dialectology, 2011* (pp. 139–148). Frankfurt: Peter Lang.

Childs, B., & Van Herk, G. (2014). Work that -s! Drag queens, gender, identity, and traditional Newfoundland English. *Journal of Sociolinguistics, 18*, 634–657.

Christian, D., Wolfram, W., & Dube, N. (1988). *Variation and change in geographically isolated communities: Appalachian English and Ozark English.* Tuscaloosa, AL: American Dialect Society.

Clark, E. V., & Clark, H. H. (1979). When nouns surface as verbs. *Language, 55,* 767–811.

Clarke, S. (1997). English verbal *-s* revisited: The evidence from Newfoundland. *American Speech, 72,* 227–259.

Clarke, S. (1999). Search for origins: Habitual aspect and Newfoundland Vernacular English. *Journal of English Linguistics, 27,* 328–340.

Clarke, S. (2004). Verbal *-s* reconsidered: The subject type constraint as a diagnostic of historical transatlantic relationship. In C. Kay, S. Horobin, & J. Smith (Eds.), *New perspectives on English historical linguistics: Selected papers from 12 ICEHL. Glasgow, 21–26 August 2002 (Vol. I): Syntax and morphology* (pp. 1–14). Amsterdam: John Benjamins.

Clarke, S. (2014). The continuing story of verbal *-s*: Revisiting the Northern Subject Rule as a diagnostic of historical relationship. In R. T. Cacoullos, N. Dion, & A. Lapierre (Eds.), *Linguistic variation: Confronting fact and theory* (pp. 75–95). London: Routledge.

Clarke, S., & Hiscock, P. (2009). Hip-hop in a post-insular community: Hybridity, local language, and authenticity in an online Newfoundland rap group. *Journal of English Linguistics, 37,* 241–261.

Cole, M. (2008). What is the Northern Subject Rule? The resilience of a medieval constraint in Tyneside English. *Journal of the Spanish Society for Medieval Language and Literature, 15,* 91–114.

Cole, M. (2014). *Old Northumbrian verbal morphosyntax and the (Northern) Subject Rule.* Amsterdam: John Benjamins.

Comeau, P. (2011). Verbal *-s* in Vernacular Newfoundland English: A combined variationist and formal account of grammatical change. *University of Pennsylvania Working Papers in Linguistics, 17,* 31–40.

Comrie, B. S. (1979). The animacy hierarchy in Chuckchee. In P. C. Clyne, W. F. Hanks, & C. L. Hofbauer (Eds.), *The elements: A parasession on linguistic units and levels, April 20–21, 1979* (pp. 322–329). Chicago: Chicago Linguistics Society.

Corbett, G. (1979). The agreement hierarchy. *Journal of Linguistics, 15,* 203–224.

Corbett, G. (2006). *Agreement.* Cambridge: Cambridge University Press.

Corrigan, K. P. (1997). *The syntax of South Armagh English in its socio-historical perspective* (Doctoral dissertation). University College Dublin, Dublin.

Corrigan, K. P., Beal, J. C., & Moisl, H. L. (2001–2005). *The Newcastle electronic corpus of Tyneside English.* Newcastle University, UK.

Coseriu, E. (1994). *Textlinguistik: Eine Einführung* (3rd ed., J. Albrecht, Ed.). Tübingen: Francke.

D'Arcy, A. (2017). *Discourse-pragmatic variation and change: Eight hundred years of LIKE.* Amsterdam: John Benjamins.

De Cuypere, L. (2005). Exploring exaptation in language change. *Folia Linguistica Historica, 26,* 13–26.

De Cuypere, L. (2008). *Limiting the iconic: From the metatheoretical foundations to the creative possibilities of iconicity in language.* Amsterdam: John Benjamins.

De Haas, N. K. (2011). *Morphosyntactic variation in Northern English: The Northern Subject Rule, its origins and early history* (Doctoral dissertation). Radboud University, Nijmegen.

De Vos, M. (2013). Homogeneity in subject-verb concord in South African English. *Language Matters: Studies in the Languages of Africa, 44,* 58–77.

Diesing, M. (1992). *Indefinites.* Cambridge, MA.: MIT Press.

Eckert, P. (2011). Where does the social stop? In F. Gregersen, J. K. Parrott, & P. Quist (Eds.), *Language variation—European perspectives III: Selected papers from the 5th International Conference on Language Variation in Europe, Copenhagen, June 5, 2009* (pp. 13–30). Amsterdam: John Benjamins.

Eckert, P. (2012). Three waves of variation study: The emergence of meaning in the study of sociolinguistic variation. *Annual Review of Anthropology, 41,* 87–100.

Eckert, P. (2017). The most perfect of signs: Iconicity in variation. *Linguistics, 55,* 1197–1207.

Edwards, V., & Weltens, B. (1983). Research on non-standard dialects of British English: Progress and prospects. In W. Viereck (Ed.), *Focus on England and Wales* (pp. 97–135). Amsterdam: John Benjamins.

Eisikovits, E. (1991). Variation in subject-verb agreement in inner Sydney English. In J. Cheshire (Ed.), *English around the world: Sociolinguistic perspectives* (pp. 235–256). Cambridge: Cambridge University Press.

Ellis, M. (1994). Literary dialect as linguistic evidence: Subject-verb concord in nineteenth-century literature. *American Speech, 69,* 128–144.

Elworthy, F. T. (1877). *An outline of the grammar of the dialect of West Somerset.* London: Trübner.

Epstein, R. (1995). The later stages in the development of the definite article: Evidence from French. In H. Andersen (Ed.), *Historical linguistics 1993: Selected papers from the 11th International Conference on Historical Linguistics, Los Angeles, 16–20 August 1993* (pp. 159–175). Amsterdam: John Benjamins.

Epstein, R. (2002). The definite article, accessibility, and the construction of discourse referents. *Cognitive Linguistics, 12,* 333–378.

Epstein, R. (2010). The distal demonstrative as discourse marker in Beowulf. *English Language and Linguistics, 15,* 113–135.

Feagin, C. (1979). *Variation and change in Alabama English: A sociolinguistic study of the white community.* Washington, DC: Georgetown University Press.

Felser, C., & Rupp, L. (2001). Expletives as arguments: Germanic existential sentences revisited. *Linguistische Berichte, 187,* 289–324.

Fernández Cuesta, J. (2011). The Northern Subject Rule in first-person-singular contexts in Early Modern English. *Folia Linguistica Historica, 32,* 89–114.

Fernández Cuesta, J. (2015). The history of present indicative morphosyntax from a Northern perspective. In R. Hickey (Ed.), *Researching Northern English* (pp. 90–130). Amsterdam: John Benjamins.

Fernández Cuesta, J., & Rodríguez Ledesma, M. N. (2007). From Old Northumbrian to Northern Middle English: Bridging the divide. In G. Mazzon (Ed.), *Studies in Middle English forms and meanings* (pp. 117–133). Frankfurt: Peter Lang.

Filppula, M. (1999). *The grammar of Irish English: Language in Hibernian style.* London: Routledge.

Fischer, O. (1992). Syntax. In N. Blake (Ed.), *The Cambridge history of the English language (Vol. 2): 1066–1476* (pp. 207–408). Cambridge: Cambridge University Press.

Fischer, O. (1997). Iconicity in language and literature: Language innovation and language change. *Neuphilologische Mitteilungen, 98,* 63–87.

Fischer, O. (2001). The position of the adjective in (Old) English from an iconic perspective. In O. Fischer & M. Nänny (Eds.), *The motivated sign* (pp. 249–276). Amsterdam: John Benjamins.

Fischer, O. (2006). Grammaticalization and iconicity: Two interacting processes. In H. Grabes & W. Viereck (Eds.), *The wider scope of English: Papers in English language and literature from the Bamberg Conference of the International Association of University Professors of English* (pp. 17–42). Frankfurt: Peter Lang.

Fischer, O., & Nänny, M. (1999). Introduction: Iconicity as a creative force in language use. In M. Nänny & O. Fischer (Eds.), *Form miming meaning* (pp. xv–xxxvii). Amsterdam: John Benjamins.

Fischer, O., Van Kemenade, A., Koopman, W., & Van der Wurff, W. (2000). *The syntax of Early English*. Cambridge: Cambridge University Press.

Fisiak, J. (1968). *A short grammar of Middle English*. Warsaw: Państwowe Wydawnictwo Naukowe.

Fitzpatrick, D. (1994). *Oceans of consolation: Personal accounts of Irish migration to Australia*. Ithaca: Cornell University Press.

Gardani, F. (2016). Allogenous exaptation. In M. Norde & F. Van de Velde (Eds.), *Exaptation and language change* (pp. 227–260). Amsterdam: John Benjamins.

Givón, T. (1976). Topic, pronoun and grammatical agreement. In C. N. Li (Ed.), *Subject and topic* (pp. 149–188). New York: Academic Press.

Givón, T. (1985). Iconicity, isomorphism and non-arbitrary coding in syntax. In J. Haiman (Ed.), *Iconicity in syntax* (pp. 187–220). Amsterdam: John Benjamins.

Givón, T. (1995). Isomorphism in the grammatical code: Cognitive and biological considerations. In R. Simone (Ed.), *Iconicity in language* (pp. 47–76). Amsterdam: John Benjamins.

Godfrey, E., & Tagliamonte, S. (1999). Another piece for the verbal -*s* story: Evidence from Devon in the Southwest of England. *Language Variation and Change, 11,* 87–121.

Görlach, M. (1987). Colonial lag? The alleged conservative character of American English and other 'colonial' varieties. *English World-Wide, 8,* 41–60.

Gould, S. J., & Urba, E. S. (1982). Exaptation—A missing term in the science of form. *Paleobiology, 8,* 4–15.

Greenberg, J. H. (1978). How does a language acquire gender markers? In J. H. Greenberg, C. A. Ferguson, & E. A. Moravcsik (Eds.), *Universals of human language (Vol. 3): Word structure* (pp. 47–82). Stanford: Stanford University Press.

Greenberg, J. H. (1991). The last stages of grammatical elements: Contractive and expansive desemanticization. In E. C. Traugott & B. Heine (Eds.), *Approaches to grammaticalization (Vol. 1): Theoretical and methodological issues* (pp. 301–314). Amsterdam: John Benjamins.

Hackenberg, R. G. (1973). *Appalachian English: A sociolinguistic study* (Doctoral dissertation). Georgetown University, Georgetown, DC.

Haiman, J. (1980). The iconicity of grammar: Isomorphism and motivation. *Language, 56,* 515–540.

Haiman, J. (1983). Iconic and economic motivation. *Language, 59,* 781–819.

Haiman, J. (1985). Introduction. In J. Haiman (Ed.), *Iconicity in syntax: Proceedings of a symposium on iconicity in syntax, Stanford, June 24–6, 1983* (pp. 1–10). Amsterdam: John Benjamins.

Hamp, E. (1975–1976). Miscellanea Celtica I, II, III, IV. *Studia Celtica, 10–11,* 54–73.

Harris, J. (1993). The grammar of Irish English. In J. Milroy & L. Milroy (Eds.), *Real English: The grammar of English dialects in the British Isles* (pp. 139–186). London: Longman.

Haspelmath, M. (2008). Frequency versus iconicity in explaining grammatical asymmetries. *Cognitive Linguistics, 19,* 1–33.

Hay, J., & Schreier, D. (2004). Reversing the trajectory of language change: Subject-verb agreement with *be* in New Zealand. *Language Variation and Change, 16,* 209–235.

Hazen, K. (2000). Subject-verb concord in a postinsular dialect: The gradual persistence of dialect patterning. *Journal of English Linguistics, 28,* 127–144.

Heine, B. (2003). On degrammaticalization. In B. J. Blake & K. Burridge (Eds.), *Historical linguistics 2001: Selected papers from the 15th International Conference on Historical Linguistics, Melbourne, 13–17 August 2001* (pp. 163–180). Amsterdam: John Benjamins.

Henry, P. L. (1958). A linguistic survey of Ireland: Preliminary report. *Lochlann, 1,* 49–208.

Henry, A. (1995). *Belfast English and Standard English: Dialect variation and parameter setting.* Oxford: Oxford University Press.

Hogg, R. M. (1992a). *A grammar of Old English (Vol. 1): Phonology.* Oxford: Blackwell.

Hogg, R. M. (1992b). Phonology and morphology. In R. M. Hogg (Ed.), *The Cambridge history of the English language (Vol. I): The beginnings to 1066* (pp. 67–167). Cambridge: Cambridge University Press.

Hogg, R. M. (2012). *An introduction to Old English* (2nd ed.). Edinburgh: Edinburgh University Press.

Holmqvist, E. (1922). *On the history of the English present inflections particularly -t and -s.* Heidelberg: Carl Winter.

Hopper, P. J. (1991). On some principles of grammaticization. In E. C. Traugott & B. Heine (Eds.), *Approaches to grammaticalization (Vol. I): Theoretical and methodological issues* (pp. 17–36). Amsterdam: John Benjamins.

Hopper, P. J., & Traugott, E. C. (2003). *Grammaticalization* (2nd ed.). Cambridge: Cambridge University Press.

Hume, A. (1878). *Remarks on the Irish dialect of the English language.* Liverpool: T. Brakell.

Ihalainen, O. (1994). The dialects of England since 1776. In R. Burchfield (Ed.), *The Cambridge history of the English language (Vol. V): English language in Britain and overseas: Origins and development* (pp. 197–274). Cambridge: Cambridge University Press.

Irvine, J. T. (2001). "Style" as distinctiveness: The culture and ideology of linguistic differentiation. In P. Eckert & J. R. Rickford (Eds.), *Style and sociolinguistic variation* (pp. 21–43). Cambridge: Cambridge University Press.

Jankowski, B. L., & Tagliamonte, S. A. (2017). A lost Canadian dialect: The Ottawa Valley 1975–2013. In T. Säily, A. Nurmi, M. Palander-Collin, & A. Auer (Eds.), *Historical linguistics: A Festschrift for Terttu Nevalainen on the occasion of her 65th birthday* (pp. 239–274). Amsterdam: John Benjamins.

Jantos, S. (2010). Agreement in educated Jamaican English: A corpus-based study of spoken usage in ICE-Jamaica. In H. Dorgeloh & A. Wanner (Eds.), *Syntactic variation and genre* (pp. 305–332). Berlin: Mouton de Gruyter.

José, B. (2007). Appalachian English in Southern Indiana? The evidence from verbal *-s. Language Variation and Change, 19,* 249–280.

Joseph, B. D. (2004). Rescuing traditional (historical) linguistics from grammaticalization 'theory'. In O. Fischer, M. Norde, & H. Peridon (Eds.), *Up and down the cline* (pp. 44–71). Amsterdam: John Benjamins.

Joseph, B. D. (2005). How accommodating of change is grammaticalization? The case of "lateral shifts". *Logos and Language, 6,* 1–7.

Joseph, B. D. (2014). What counts as (an instance of) grammaticalization? *Folia Linguistica, 48,* 361–383.

Joseph, B. D. (2016). Being exacting about exapting: An exaptation omnibus. In F. Van de Velde & M. Norde (Eds.), *Exaptation and language change* (pp. 27–55). Amsterdam: John Benjamins.

Kirk, J. (1991). *Northern Ireland Transcribed Corpus of Speech (Vol. 1) (with S. West and S. Gibson): Textfile.* Colchester: Economic and Social Research Council Data Archive, University of Essex, Colchester.

Klemola, J. (2000). The origins of the Northern Subject Rule: A case of early contact? In T. Hildegard (Ed.), *Celtic Englishes II* (pp. 329–346). Heidelberg: Winter.

Kortmann, B. (1999). Iconicity, typology and cognition. In M. Nänny & O. Fischer (Eds.), *Form miming meaning* (pp. 375–392). Amsterdam: John Benjamins.

Kortmann, B., & Wagner, S. (2005). The Freiburg Dialect Project and Corpus. In B. Kortmann, T. Herrman, L. Pietsch, & S. Wagner (Eds.), *A comparative grammar of British English dialects: Agreement, gender, relative clauses* (pp. 1–20). Berlin: Mouton de Gruyter.

Kytö, M. (1993). Third-person present singular verb inflection in Early British and American English. *Language Variation and Change, 5,* 113–139.

Labov, W. (1972). *Language in the inner city: Studies in the Black English vernacular.* Philadelphia: University of Pennsylvania Press.

Labov, W. (1989). The child as linguistic historian. *Language Variation and Change, 1,* 85–97.

Laing, M., & Lass, R. (2008–2013). *A linguistic atlas of Early Middle English 1150–1325* (Version 2.1). Retrieved May 2019 from http://www.lel.ed.ac.uk/ihd/laeme2/laeme2.html.

Larsson, K. (1988). *Den plural verbböjninge i äldre svenska.* Uppsala: Institutionen för Nordiska Språk vid Uppsala Universitet.

Lass, R. (1990). How to do things with junk: Exaptation in language evolution. *Journal of Linguistics, 26,* 79–102.

Lass, R. (1992). Phonology and morphology. In N. Blake (Ed.), *The Cambridge history of the English language (Vol. 3): 1476–1776* (pp. 23–155). Cambridge: Cambridge University Press.

Lass, R. (1997). *Historical linguistics and language change.* Cambridge: Cambridge University Press.

Lehmann, C. (1988). On the function of agreement. In M. Barlow & C. A. Ferguson (Eds.), *Agreement in natural language: Approaches, theories and descriptions* (pp. 55–65). Stanford: Center for the Study of Language and Information.

Levey, S. (2006). Tense variation in preadolescent narratives. *Journal of English Linguistics, 34,* 126–152.

Levon, E., Maegaard, M., & Pharao, N. (2017). Introduction: Tracing the origin of /s/ variation. *Linguistics, 55,* 979–992.

Lorenz, K. (1978). *Vergleichende Verhaltensforschung: Grundlagen der Ethologie.* Wien: Springer.

Macafee, C. (1980). *Nonstandard Scots grammar* (Unpublished typescript).

Mallinson, C., & Wolfram, W. (2002). Dialect accommodation in a bi-ethnic mountain enclave community: More evidence on the development of African American English. *Language in Society, 31,* 743–775.

McCafferty, K. (2003). The Northern Subject Rule in Ulster: How Scots, how English? *Language Variation and Change, 15,* 105–139.

McCafferty, K. (2004). '[T]hunder storms is very dangese in this country they come in less than a minnits notice ...': The Northern Subject Rule in Southern Irish English. *English World-Wide, 25,* 51–79.

McIntosh, A. (1989). Present indicative plural forms in the later Middle English of the North Midlands. In A. McIntosh, M. L. Samuels, & M. Laing (Eds.), *Middle English dialectology: Essays on some principles and problems* (pp. 116–122). Aberdeen: Aberdeen University Press. [This paper appeared in 1983 in D. Gray & E. G. Stanley (Eds.), *Middle English studies: Presented to Norman Davis on his seventieth birthday* (pp. 235–244). Oxford: Oxford University Press.]

McMahon, A. M. S. (1994). *Understanding language change.* Cambridge: Cambridge University Press.

Meillet, A. (1912). L'évolution des formes grammaticales. Scientia (Rivista di Scienza) 12, No. 26, 6. In *Linguistique historique et linguistique générale* (pp. 130–148). Paris: Librairie Ancienne Honoré Champion.

Melchers, G., & Sundkvist, P. (2010). Shetland and Orkney. In D. Schreier, P. Trudgill, E. W. Schneider, & J. P. Williams (Eds.), *The lesser-known varieties of English* (pp. 17–34). Cambridge: Cambridge University Press.

Milroy, J. (1981). *Regional accents of English: Belfast.* Belfast: Blackstaff Press.

Mithun, M. (1984). The evolution of noun incorporation. *Language, 60,* 847–894.

Montgomery, M. (1989). Exploring the roots of Appalachian English. *English World-Wide, 10,* 227–278.

Montgomery, M. (1994). The evolution of verb concord in Scots. In A. Fenton & D. McDonald (Eds.), *Studies in Scots and Gaelic: Proceedings of the Third International Conference on the Languages of Scotland* (pp. 81–95). Edinburgh: Canongate.

Montgomery, M. (1997). Making transatlantic connections between varieties of English: The case of the plural verbal *-s. Journal of English Linguistics, 25,* 122–141.

Montgomery, M. (1998). In the Appalachians they speak like Shakespeare. In L. Bauer & P. Trudgill (Eds.), *Language myths* (pp. 66–76). London: Penguin Books.

Montgomery, M., & Fuller, J. (1996). What was verbal *-s* in 19th-century African American English? In E. W. Schneider (Ed.), *Focus on the USA* (pp. 211–230). Amsterdam: John Benjamins.

Moore, C. (2002). Writing good Southerne: Local and supralocal norms in the Plumpton letter collection. *Language Variation and Change, 14,* 1–17.

Mossé, F. (1952). *A handbook of Middle English.* Baltimore, MD: John Hopkins University Press.

Mufwene, S. S. (1996). The founder principle in creole genesis. *Diachronica, 13,* 83–134.

Murray, J. (1873). *The dialect of the Southern Counties of Scotland: Its pronunciation, grammar and historical relations.* London: Asher.

Mustanoja, T. F. (1960). *A Middle English syntax (Part I): Parts of speech.* Helsinki: Société Néophilologique.

Myhill, J., & Harris, W. (1986). The use of the verbal -*s* inflection in BEV. In D. Sankoff (Ed.), *Diversity and diachrony: Papers from the Twelfth Annual Conference on New Ways of Analyzing Variation* (pp. 25–32). Amsterdam: John Benjamins.

Narrog, H. (2007). Exaptation, grammaticalization, and reanalysis. *California Linguistic Notes, 23,* 1–27.

Nevalainen, T., & Raumolin-Brunberg, H. (2000). The third-person singular -(E)S and -(E)TH revisited: The morphophonemic hypothesis. In C. Dalton-Puffer & N. Ritt (Eds.), *Words: Structure, meaning and function: A Festschrift for Dieter Kastovsky* (pp. 235–248). Berlin: Mouton de Gruyter.

Newmeyer, F. J. (1992). Iconicity and generative grammar. *Language, 68,* 756–796.

Norde, M. (2001). Deflexion as a counterdirectional factor in grammatical change. *Language Sciences, 23,* 231–264.

Norde, M. (2002). The final stages of grammaticalization: Affixhood and beyond. In I. Wischer & G. Diewald (Eds.), *New reflections on grammaticalization* (pp. 45–65). Amsterdam: John Benjamins.

Norde, M., & Van de Velde, F. (Eds.). (2016). *Exaptation and language change.* Amsterdam: John Benjamins.

Nurmio, S. (2017). Collective nouns in Welsh: A noun category or a plural allomorph. *Transactions of the Philological Society, 115,* 58–78.

Orton, H., & Halliday, W. J. (1962). *Survey of English Dialects (B): The basic material (Vols. 1.1 and 1.2): The six Northern counties and the Isle of Man.* Leeds: E. J. Arnold.

Peitsara, K. (2002). Verbal -*s* in Devonshire: The Helsinki dialect corpus evidence. In H. Raumolin-Brunberg & T. Nevalainen (Eds.), *Variation past and present: VARIENG studies on English for Terttu Nevalainen* (pp. 211–230). Helsinki: Société néophilologique.

Piercy, C. (2010). *One /a/ or two? The phonetics, phonology and sociolinguistics of change in the TRAP and BATH vowels in the Southwest of England* (Doctoral dissertation). University of Essex, Colchester.

Pietsch, L. (2005). *"Some do and some doesn't"*: Verbal concord variation in the north of the British Isles. In B. Kortmann, T. Herrman, L. Pietsch, & S. Wagner (Eds.), *A comparative grammar of British English dialects: Agreement, gender, relative clauses* (pp. 125–210). Berlin: Mouton de Gruyter.

Podesva, R. J. (2011). The California vowel shift and gay identity. *American Speech, 86,* 32–51.

Polanyi, L. (1989). *Telling the American story: A structural and cultural analysis of conversational story telling.* Cambridge, MA: MIT Press.

Pollock, J.-Y. (1989). Verb movement, universal grammar, and the structure of IP. *Linguistic Inquiry, 20,* 365–424.

Poplack, S., & Tagliamonte, S. (1989). There's no tense like the present: Verbal -s inflection in Early Black English. *Language Variation and Change, 1,* 47–84.

Poplack, S., & Tagliamonte, S. (1991). African American English in the diaspora: Evidence from old-line Nova Scotians. *Language Variation and Change, 3,* 301–339.

Poplack, S., & Tagliamonte, S. (2004). Back to the present: Verbal -s in the African American English diaspora. In R. Hickey (Ed.), *Legacies of colonial English: The study of transported dialects* (pp. 203–223). Cambridge: Cambridge University Press.

Prince, E. F. (1985). Fancy syntax and 'shared knowledge'. *Journal of Pragmatics, 9,* 65–81.

Ramat, A. G. (1998). Testing the boundaries of grammaticalization. In A. G. Ramat & P. J. Hopper (Eds.), *The limits of grammaticalization* (pp. 107–127). Amsterdam: John Benjamins.

Raumolin-Brunberg, H. (1996). Apparent time. In T. Nevalainen & H. Raumolin-Brunberg (Eds.), *Sociolinguistics and language history: Studies based on the Corpus of Early English Correspondence* (pp. 93–109). Amsterdam: Rodopi.

Rodríguez Ledesma, M. N. (2013). The Northern Subject Rule in first-person singular contexts in fourteenth-fifteenth-century Scots. *Folia Linguistica Historica, 34,* 149–172.

Rodríguez Ledesma, M. N. (2017). The Northern Subject Rule in the Breadalbane Collection. *English Studies, 98,* 802–824.

Rodríguez Louro, C., & Ritz, M.-E. (2014). Stories down under: Tense variation at the heart of Australian English narratives. *Australian Journal of Linguistics, 34,* 549–565.

Rohdenburg, G. (1996). Cognitive complexity and increased grammatical explicitness in English. *Cognitive Linguistics, 7,* 149–182.

Ross, A. S. C. (1934). A theory of emendation. *Speculum, 9,* 179–189.

Rupp, L. (2003). *The syntax of imperatives in English and Germanic: Word order variation in the minimalist framework.* Basingstoke: Palgrave Macmillan.

Samuels, M. L. (1989). The great Scandinavian belt. In A. McIntosh, M. L. Samuels, & M. Laing (Eds.), *Middle English dialectology: Essays on some principles and problems* (pp. 106–115). Aberdeen: Aberdeen University Press.

Schendl, H. (1996). Text types and code-switching in medieval and Early Modern English. *Vienna English Working Papers, 5,* 50–62.

Schiffrin, D. (1981). Tense variation in narrative. *Language, 57,* 45–62.

Schilling-Estes, N., & Wolfram, W. (1994). Convergent explanation and alternative regularization patterns: *Were/weren't* levelling in a vernacular English variety. *Language Variation and Change, 6,* 273–302.

Schilling-Estes, N., & Wolfram, W. (1999). Alternative models of dialect death: Dissipation vs. contraction. *Language, 75,* 486–521.

Schilling-Estes, N., & Zimmerman, L. (2000). *On the progress of morphological change:* Was/weren't *leveling in Smith Island English.* Paper presented at the Linguistic Society of America Annual Meeting, Chicago, IL.

Schneider, E. W., & Montgomery, M. (2001). On the trail of early nonstandard grammar: An electronic corpus of Southern U.S. antebellum overseers' letters. *American Speech, 76,* 388–410.

Schütze, C. (1997). *INFL in child and adult language: Agreement, case and licensing* (Doctoral dissertation). Massachusetts Institute of Technology, Cambridge, MA.

Seiler, H. (1995). Iconicity between indicativity and predicativity. In R. Simone (Ed.), *Iconicity in language* (pp. 141–151). Amsterdam: John Benjamins.

Sheppard, M. (2006). *Madonna—Loves: Gay speech in Newfoundland, Canada* (Unpublished Course Paper). Memorial University of Newfoundland, St John's.

Shorrocks, G. (1980). *A grammar of the dialect of Farnsworth and District (Greater Manchester, formerly Lancashire)* (Doctoral dissertation). University of Sheffield, Sheffield.

Shorrocks, G. (1999). *A grammar of the dialect of the Bolton area (Part II): Morphology and syntax.* Frankfurt: Peter Lang.

Siewierska, A. (1999). From anaphoric pronoun to grammatical agreement marker: Why objects don't make it. *Folia Linguistica, 33,* 225–251.

Silverstein, M. (1994). "Relative motivation" in denotational and indexical sound symbolism of Wasco-Wishram Chinookan. In L. Hinton, J. Nichols, & J. J. Ohala (Eds.), *Sound symbolism* (pp. 40–60). Cambridge: Cambridge University Press.

Singler, J. V. (1997). The configuration of Liberia's Englishes. *World Englishes, 16,* 205–231.

Smith, J. (2000). *Synchrony and diachrony in the evolution of English: Evidence from Scotland* (Doctoral dissertation). University of York, York.

Smith, J., & Tagliamonte, S. (1998). 'We were *all thegither, I think we* was *all thegither*': Was regularization in Buckie English. *World Englishes, 17,* 105–126.

Sonesson, G. (1997). The ecological foundations of iconicity. In I. Rauch & G. F. Carr (Eds.), *Semiotics around the world: Synthesis in diversity. Proceedings of the Fifth International Congress of IASS, Berkeley, June 12–18, 1994* (pp. 739–774). Berlin: Mouton de Gruyter.

Stein, D. (1986). Old English Northumbrian verb inflection revisited. In D. Kastovsky & A. Szwedek (Eds.), *Linguistics across historical and geographical boundaries (Vol. 1): Linguistic theory and historical linguistics* (pp. 637–650). Berlin: Mouton de Gruyter.

Stein, D. (1987). At the crossroads of philology, linguistics and semiotics: Notes on the replacement of *th* by *s* in the third person singular in English. *English Studies, 5,* 406–431.

Sudbury, A. (2001). Falkland Island English: A southern hemisphere variety? *English World-Wide, 22,* 55–80.

Sweet, H. (1871). *King Alfred's West Saxon version of Gregory's pastoral care.* Early English Text Society. London: Trübner.

Tagliamonte, S. (1998). *Was/were* variation across the generations: View from the city of York. *Language Variation and Change, 10,* 153–192.

Tagliamonte, S. A., & D'Arcy, A. (2007). Frequency and variation in the community grammar: Tracking a new change through the generations. *Language Variation and Change, 19,* 119–217.

Tagliamonte, S. A., & Roeder, R. (2009). Variation in the English definite article: Socio-historical linguistics in t'speech community. *Journal of Sociolinguistics, 13,* 435–471.

Thompson, S. A., & Koide, Y. (1987). Iconicity and 'indirect objects' in English. *Journal of Pragmatics, 11,* 399–406.

Tortora, C., & Den Dikken, M. (2010). Subject agreement variation: Support for the configurational approach. *Lingua, 120,* 1089–1108.

Traugott, E. C. (1995). Subjectification in grammaticalization. In D. Stein & S. Wright (Eds.), *Subjectivity and subjectivisation in language* (pp. 31–54). Cambridge: Cambridge University Press.

Traugott, E. C. (2004). Exaptation and grammaticalization. In M. Akimoto (Ed.), *Linguistic studies based on corpora* (pp. 133–156). Tokyo: Hituzi Syobo Publishing.

Trüb, R. (2006). Nonstandard verbal paradigms in earlier white southern American English. *American Speech, 81,* 250–265.

Trudgill, P. (1974). *The social differentiation of English in Norwich.* Cambridge: Cambridge University Press.

Trudgill, P. (1996). Language contact and inherent variability: The absence of hypercorrection in East Anglian present-tense verb forms. In J. Klemola, M. Kytö, & M. Risannen (Eds.), *Speech past and present: Studies in English dialectology in memory of Ossi Ihalainen* (pp. 412–425). Frankfurt: Peter Lang.

Trudgill, P. (1998). Third person singular zero: African-American English, East Anglian dialects and Spanish persecution in the Low Countries. *Folia Linguistica Historica, 18,* 139–148.

Van Herk, G., & Childs, B. (2015). Active retirees: The persistence of obsolescent features. In R. Torres Cacoullos, N. Dion, & A. Lapierre (Eds.), *Linguistic variation: Confronting fact and theory* (pp. 193–207). London: Routledge.

Van Herk, G., Childs, B., & Thorburn, J. (2009). Identity marking and affiliation in an urbanizing Newfoundland community. In W. Cichocki (Ed.), *Papers from the 31st Annual Meeting of the Atlantic Province Linguistic Association* (pp. 85–94). Fredericton: University of New Brunswick.

Van Kemenade, A. (2009). Discourse relations and word order change. In R. Hinterhölzl & S. Petrova (Eds.), *Information structure and language change* (pp. 91–120). Berlin: Mouton de Gruyter.

Van Kemenade, A., & Los, B. (2006). Discourse adverbs and clausal syntax in the history of English. In A. van Kemenade & B. Los (Eds.), *The handbook of the history of English* (pp. 224–248). London: Blackwell.

Vermandere, D., & Meul, C. (2016). How functionless is junk and how useful is exaptation? Probing the -I/ESC- morpheme. In F. Van de Velde & M. Norde (Eds.), *Exaptation and language change* (pp. 261–285). Amsterdam: John Benjamins.

Vincent, N. (1995). Exaptation and grammaticalization. In H. Andersen (Ed.), *Historical linguistics 1993: Selected Papers from the 11th International Conference on Historical Linguistics, Los Angeles, 16–20 August 1993* (pp. 433–448). Amsterdam: John Benjamins.

Von Mengden, F. (2016). Functional changes and (meta-)linguistic evolution. In M. Norde & F. Van de Velde (Eds.), *Exaptation and language change* (pp. 121–162). Amsterdam: John Benjamins.

Wakelin, M. F. (1972). *English dialects: An introduction.* London: Athlone Press.

Walker, J. (2000). *Present accounted for: Prosody and aspect in Early African American English* (Doctoral dissertation). University of Ottawa.

Wall, A., & Octavio de Toledo y Huerta, A. S. (2016). Exploring and recycling: Topichood and the evolution of Ibero-romance articles. In M. Norde & F. Van de Velde (Eds.), *Exaptation and language change* (pp. 341–376). Amsterdam: John Benjamins.

Willis, D. (2016). Exaptation and degrammaticalization within an acquisition-based model of abductive reanalysis. In F. Van de Velde & M. Norde (Eds.), *Exaptation and language change* (pp. 197–225). Amsterdam: John Benjamins.

Wilson, S., & Mesthrie, R. (2004). St. Helena English: Morphology and syntax. In B. Kortmann & E. W. Schneider (with K. Burridge, R. Mesthrie & C. Upton) (Eds.), *A handbook of varieties of English (Vol. 2): Morphology and syntax* (pp. 1006–1015). Berlin: Mouton de Gruyter.

Wolfram, W., & Christian, D. (1976). *Appalachian speech.* Arlington: Center for Applied Linguistics.

Wolfram, W., & Thomas, E. (2002). *The development of African American English.* Oxford: Blackwell.

Wolfson, N. (1979). The conversational historical present alternation. *Language, 55,* 168–182.

Woolard, K. (2008). Why *dat* now? Linguistic-anthropological solutions to the explanation of sociolinguistic icons and change. *Journal of Sociolinguistics, 12,* 432–452.

Wright, J. (1892). *A grammar of the dialect of Windhill in the West Riding of Yorkshire.* London: Trübner.

Wright, J. (1905). *English dialect grammar.* Oxford: Clarendon Press.

Wright, L. (2002). Third person plural present tense markers in London prisoners' depositions, 1562–1623. *American Speech, 77,* 242–263.

Wright, L. (2003). Eight grammatical features of southern United States speech present in early modern London prison narratives. In S. Nagle & S. Sanders (Eds.), *English in the Southern United States* (pp. 36–63). Cambridge: Cambridge University Press.

Wright, L. (2015). Some more on the history of present-tense -*s*, do and zero: West Oxfordshire, 1837. *Journal of Historical Sociolinguistics, 1,* 111–130.

Zanuttini, R., & Bernstein, J. B. (2011). Micro-comparative syntax in English verbal agreement. In S. Lima, K. Mullin, & B. Smith (Eds.), *NELS 39: Proceedings of the 39th Annual Meeting of the North East Linguistic Society* (Vol. 2, pp. 839–854). Amherst: GSLA, University of Massachusetts.

3

Verbal Zero

3.1 Introduction

Verbal zero is the opposite of verbal –s: the 3rd sing. morpheme on present tense verbs is absent. The verbal zero we consider here only applies to 3rd sing. contexts: after the pronouns *he/she/it/that* or a singular NP.[1] It has acquired fame through both Trudgill's (1974) early study of Norwich in eastern England, and through its widespread use in African American Vernacular English (for example Labov et al. 1968; Shuy et al. 1967; Fasold 1972; Wolfram 1974; Poplack and Tagliamonte 2001; Wolfram 2004), Samaná (Poplack and Tagliamonte 1989: 62 ff.), Nova Scotia (Poplack and Tagliamonte 1991: 324 ff.), and Beech Bottom (Mallinson and Wolfram 2002: 753). It has also been found, for example, in some insular contact varieties of English, such as Tristan da Cunha (Schreier 2003), St Helena (Schreier 2008: 187), Jamaican English (Jantos 2009), Afro-Bahamanian English (Reaser 2010: 168) and Bequia English (Walker and Meyerhoff 2015: 135); in many of the L2 or 'New

© The Author(s) 2019
L. Rupp and D. Britain, *Linguistic Perspectives on a Variable English Morpheme*,
https://doi.org/10.1057/978-1-349-72803-9_3

Englishes' (Szmrecsanyi and Kortmann 2009a, b, c), such as the English varieties spoken in (South) Africa (for example the collection of articles in De Klerk 1996), Singaporean English (Wee 2004: 1059, colloquially; Wee and Ansaldo 2004: 65–66, 'number agreement is sporadic'; Deterding 2007: 46, exceptionally among educated speakers), Ghanaian English (Asante 2012) and Palauan English (Britain and Matsumoto 2015: 331), and in the use of English as a Lingua Franca (Seidlhofer 2004: 220; Dewey 2006: 82–91, 137–140). Here we present a variety of examples from the literature:

(1) a. **She look** jest wholly be'tiful, she do. **That** fairly **seem** to set my heart a-fire. (Charles Benham's *Essex Ballads* 1895) (East Anglia; Trudgill 1996: 413)
   b. **She sing** real good. (Tristan da Cunha; Schreier 2010a: 254)
   c. And sometimes **she go** in the evening and **come** up in the morning. (Samaná English; Poplack and Tagliamonte 1989: 49)
   d. **The rural dweller** also **lack** access to good drinking water and basic health care centres. (Ghanaian English; Asante 2012: 213)
   e. and after i i have the same result as as **another person who: who make** these mistakes. (English as a Lingua Franca; Dewey 2006: 89)

We begin our discussion of verbal zero by briefly returning to the history of verbal marking that we began in Chapter 1 to situate the presence, role and development of zero. We then examine possibly the two most well-known and well-studied sites of verbal zero—East Anglian English in England and contemporary African American Vernacular English (AAVE) in the United States (albeit that we cannot review the sizable literature on AAVE). As we will see, language and dialect contact are often invoked to explain the presence of verbal zero. We identify, at least in a number of relevant varieties, a novel constraint pattern on the variable use of verbal zero—we label it the East Anglian Subject Rule—and, finally, we consider a formal linguistic approach to the understanding of the rule.

3 Verbal Zero 131

3.2 The History of Verbal Zero

Present tense 3rd sing. zero does not seem to have been prevalent in the history of English. Kytö (1993: 118) reports a rate as low as 2% in the Early Modern British English section of the *Helsinki Corpus* (1500–1710; for example *Y^r sister desir ye same to you and to the L^a Cicelea*), which she attributes to the use of the form in other paradigms (zero had a role in, for example, the present 3rd sing. subjunctive and the imminent present plural indicative). However, Wakelin (1977: 119) asserts that '[i]n the south, the *-eth* ending was sometimes lost in ME, without being replaced by an *-s* ending; thus giving a verbal form with no ending at all.' He finds zero in the *Survey of English Dialects* (SED) in the south-west (So 13, W 2, Co 5/7, Do 1) (VI.14.14 *She wears the breeches*; Orton and Wakelin (1967: 770–772) and East Anglia (Nf, Sf, north Ess) (1977: 120). Earlier Wright (1905: 297) spoke of –s being 'often dropped, especially in the South Midlands, eastern and southern dialects'. Wright (2015: 117) extracted some tokens of zero from the sound recordings of the SED in the south-west; for example, *when **the sun get** out in the day* (Slimbridge, Gloucestershire) and *oh ah **this go** right to Yeovil there* (Merriott, Somerset). Godfrey and Tagliamonte (1999: 91) state that '[t]his form, although not the most prominent of the variants, is much more widely attested than is commonly assumed', albeit that within Britain zero seems restricted to the south of England.

The idea that 'the verb stem resulted from the loss of *-þ*, with no replacement by *-s*' (Godfrey and Tagliamonte 1999: 91) is consistent with the historical documentation on verbal zero. Holmqvist (1922: 136) notes: 'To judge from my own text material, the uninflected form does not seem to be older than the 15th c., and it was confined, originally to East Angl. Dialects.' This timing corresponds to the time at which –s spread from the north and encroached on –th in the 3rd sing. in more southern parts of the country (recall the discussion in Sect. 2.2). Additionally, Holmqvist (1922: 134) finds that '[t]he uninflected form of the 3rd sing. is comparatively well instanced' in the *Cely Papers* (1475–1488) from the hand of London merchants. Wright (2003: 47) has also documented a few tokens of zero from London in the late sixteenth century *Bridewell Court Minute Books* (150,000 words). Accordingly, at the time of the change in 3rd sing. marking, alongside variation between –s and –th, there was alternation with zero, as shown in (2):

(2) a. **Man knowe** not who schal be his eyr [Norfolk; c1440 *The Macro Plays: The Castle of Perseverance*, 105] (Holmqvist 1922: 106)

b. & Badde Aungyl, **man** to hym **taketh** [Norfolk; c1440 *The Macro Plays: The Castle of Perseverance*, 97] (Holmqvist 1922: 106)

c. **thy father remembers** his loue to the ...: **thy brother remember** his louingest loue to the ... I had thought to haue written to mr Roberts this time, but **this sudene Iornye of this mesinger affordethe** me not so much time. [Norfolk, Katherine Paston 1626, *PastonK*, 90] (Nevalainen and Raumolin-Brunberg 2003: 179)

d. **my lorde of Send Johnys send** to me for tyyngs every weke for the weche **my lorde takyt** ... [London; c1475–1488 Richard Cely, *The Cely Papers*, 31 (p. 32)] (Holmqvist 1922: 134)

Exploring the role of traditional dialects in the formation of (what they call) Black Vernacular English, Bailey and Ross (1988) examined ship logs kept by sailors from the south-west of England from the seventeenth and eighteenth centuries and found unmarked 3rd sing. forms, as in:

(3) a. heare I found **the compass Vary** from ye No Towards ye E ... (Sloane 1833, 1669)

b. the place affords all sort [sic] of Provision and likewise **cinnamon which cost** them not above 1 penny ... (Sloane 3672A, 1683) (1988: 199)

Wright (2015) has provided an interesting account of the occurrence of 3rd sing. zero in the south-west. She examined tokens of zero in diary entries by William Tayler, a servant born in 1807 in Grafton in west Oxfordshire. She points out that in an analysis of the SED which was compiled three generations later, Klemola (1996) plotted in the south-west an eastern 'periphrastic *do*'-using area (e.g. *the boys do walk*) and a western 'generalised –s'-using area (e.g. *the boys walks*) (see Klemola's 1996: 53 map reprinted in Wright 2015: 115). The two areas showed very little overlap; though in an analysis of a subset of the *Freiburg Corpus of English Dialects (FRED-s)*, De Both (2019: 24–26) has shown that the features of periphrastic *do* and generalised –s seem to have been used in different grammatical functions: the first for marking habitual aspect and the second for marking punctual aspect. Drawing on Elworthy (1886: xlvi), Klemola interpreted this pattern as illustration of the encroachment of generalised –s on the once more prominent use of periphrastic *do*. In the SED, Grafton is located in the generalised –s area. However, the diary entries examined by Wright show a mix of two different forms in the 3rd sing.: an –s form (e.g. *the boy walks*), and a zero form (e.g. *the boy walk*) (21%; 44/212 tokens). These are some examples from Wright (2015: 120–121):

(4) a. March 24 the weather **continues** very cold
     b. September 8 The weather **continue** so very wet
     c. February 27 the parson **say** he Christened 87 Children at the Church where he does duty
     d. April 5 o no **says** she

Wright speculates that when periphrastic *do* receded, –s did not take over straight away. She envisages that the dropping of *do* will initially have resulted in an apparently 'empty slot' (2015: 216–217): viz. *the boy does walk –> the boy (does) walk –> the boy Ø walk_*.

Whatever the precise origin of historically attested 3rd sing. zeros, they all seem to have derived from contact. As we will see, contact arguments have also been proposed to account for other, past and present, occurrences of verbal zero.

3.3   Verbal Zero: East Anglian and African American Vernacular English

We begin by looking at verbal zero in its most salient heartlands of East Anglia in England, and African American Vernacular English in North America, before moving beyond. The Traditional Dialects of

East Anglia in England have long been known to lack 3rd sing. present tense –s. Ellis (1889) reported verbal zero not only in Norfolk (1889: 261, 263, 273), Suffolk (1889: 261, 280, 285, 286, 288) and non-Fenland Cambridgeshire (1889: 249), but also Essex (1889: 222, 224) and Hertfordshire (1889: 197). Kökeritz (1932) additionally notes 3rd sing. zero for east Suffolk. We examined the transcripts of his recordings of these Suffolk speakers and found that two thirds of all tokens of 3rd sing. present tense verb forms showed zero marking. In the *Survey of English Dialects* (SED; Orton and Tilling 1971: 1238), zero marking is found in Norfolk, Suffolk and the far north of Essex. In a footnote to his Norwich study, Trudgill (1974: 56) says that W. N. Francis, in his field-notes for the SED, states that in the Blickling locality of North Norfolk 'the third-person marker is completely lacking', and gives 'She wear' as an example. He also stated: 'This is standard in youngest speakers.' Vasko (2009) suggests that verbal zero is more geographically widespread than claimed, for example, in Trudgill (2001: 6). She looked at data from interviews conducted in the 1970s by Finnish field-workers with 44 older speakers from 26 localities throughout southern Cambridgeshire and 52 speakers from 20 localities in north-east Cambridgeshire.[2] She finds 29% verbal zero in 469 3rd sing. tokens in south Cambridgeshire—see for example (5) below—and 15% verbal zero in 94 relevant tokens in the south of north-east Cambridgeshire.[3]

(5) a. **He make- he make** some good sausages.
     b. **He come** from Girton. Not very far, is it?

She does not report zero for the far north of the county, confirming Britain's (2001, 2015) finding that zero is not attested in those parts of the Cambridgeshire and Norfolk Fenland that are located in the infrastructural hinterland of the consistently –s using Cambridgeshire town of Wisbech.

Trudgill's (1974) research on Norwich was the first to consider the social embedding of verbal zero. He surveyed 60 informants, in formal and casual speech styles, across five different social classes and seven age groups from 10 to 70+. He found that the percentage of verbal zero fell as formality increased. He also found social differentiation to the extent that working-class speakers used over 70% verbal zero in both formal and informal speech styles, the lower middle class used no verbal zero at all in formal speech styles and around 30% in casual conversation, while the upper middle class speakers used no verbal zero whatsoever (1974: 61–62). He concluded therefore that verbal zero is significant as an indicator of social class (1974: 57).

It has become clear, however, that verbal zero is declining in use in East Anglia, both in terms of its geographical distribution and its frequency in those places that retain it. The zero form survives to some extent in the more modern dialects of the northern and central parts of the region, as in the urban dialects of Norwich, Great Yarmouth and Ipswich, but a number of recent studies have highlighted the degree to which verbal zero is in decline. Kingston (2000), for example, examined urban Sudbury and the nearby rural village of Glemsford in west Suffolk. She finds that while her older speakers use verbal zero in almost two thirds of cases, her teenage speakers use it barely 6% of the time. Similarly, Spurling (2004) shows a decline in the large Suffolk urban centre of Ipswich from 79% among the older speakers to 24% among the young, and Potter (2018: 140) finds that in east Suffolk verbal zero has virtually disappeared among his young speakers (used overall just 4.9% of the time). In a survey of recent analyses of these and other East Anglian locations such as Swaffham and Gorleston in Norfolk, Britain (2014) shows that verbal zero is declining fast, and especially in the *rural* locations that have been more significantly affected by counter-urbanising migration flows from south-east England. Furthermore, the mobile phone-crowdsourced English Dialect App (Leemann et al. 2018) data also show rapid decline of verbal zero across apparent time in East Anglia (Britain 2016).

There has been relatively little investigation of the linguistic constraints on the variability of verbal zero. Recently, researchers examining East Anglian English have tentatively identified a constraint that appears to be the opposite of the Northern Subject Rule (NSR). We (Britain and Rupp 2005) have therefore termed the constraint the East Anglian Subject Rule (EASR). By this rule, 3rd sing. –s is used more with 3rd sing. pronouns than with singular NPs. Note that this constraint does *not* concern the 3rd plural. The first to identify an EASR pattern for present tense zero was Kingston (2000) in her work on Glemsford in rural Suffolk. She found –s marking was used 63% of the time after pronouns, but only 45% after NPs (2000: 48). So, for example, 'he likes playing cricket' would be more likely than 'the boy likes playing cricket'. Spurling (2004: 36) later also looked at subject type in urban Ipswich in Suffolk. While the results were not statistically significant, they showed that speakers use the –s form 55% of the time when the subject of the verb was a pronoun and 49% when the subject was an NP. Most recently, Potter (2018: 140, 144) found a statistically significant difference between –s marking after pronouns (86%) and after NPs (80%) in his multilocality research in Ipswich, Woodbridge and Wickham Market in east Suffolk. Whilst the constraint on verbal zero has only been identified in these three studies by Kingston, Spurling and Potter, it also applies, as we will see in the next chapter, to *was/were* variation (past BE). Verbal zero is, however, as we just saw, undergoing rather rapid decline, and so evidence of the EASR in verbal zero varieties such as East Anglia may be short-lived. An empirical analysis of verbal zero in a much larger dataset of East Anglian English that we are currently analysing will hopefully clarify the power of this constraint.

Further, Kingston (2000) finds, perhaps unusually, that habituals are *less* likely to be marked with –s than stative and durative verbs. Vasko (2009) makes a similar claim for Cambridgeshire, saying that verbal zero is found when the present tense of a verb is used to refer to 'an action or state at the moment of speaking, or to an habitual action, or to express an occurrence in the near future'.[4] Here are some examples from her data:

(6) a. (He's a poor old fellow.) **He** never **go** to bed. **He** always **sit** in the chair. **He walk** with his head nearly on the ground.
    b. **He come** to dinner every day[5].

The zero variant would also be typical, Vasko (2009) claims, of 'vivid expressions of past events'. (7) is an example.

(7) **A fellow come**, just **draw** up that glass door and **look** through that, you know, them in 'em cla-, them three and four class. **He see** anybody a bit wrong, **he** just **step** in there. **Treat** them out.

Note that this behaviour in habitual and narrative contexts seems exactly the opposite of what has been observed in verbal –s varieties (as we outlined in Chapter 2). These findings, however, await a more detailed analysis and further verification from other varieties of East Anglian English. We would speculate that in contrast to verbal –s dialects, where it appears that –s is no longer used to mark agreement, in EASR-dialects, verbal –s is not deployed in other functions because it has been specialising as a 3rd sing. morpheme.

Verbal zero is also a salient characteristic of African American Vernacular English, and one that has been examined closely from the very earliest days of sociolinguistic approaches to language variation. Labov et al. (1968: 164), for example, in their study of the T-Birds, Aces, Cobras and Jets in New York showed such high levels of verbal zero that they concluded that 'there is no underlying third singular –s in NNE' (non-standard Negro English—1968: ii). Labov (1998: 146) later reiterates this point: 'a large body of research on the G[eneral] E[nglish] system of AAVE indicates that subject-verb agreement is marginal [...] there appears to be no special mark on the third singular, so that the –s which often appears is inserted variably, as a morphological entry associated with superposed dialects. A ... common generalization across systems is therefore [that] AAVE shows no subject verb agreement except for present-tense finite *be*'.

We recognise that –s marking in AAVE was once more prominent. Work on this has been carried out through the study of early AAVE and other ambient North American varieties of English in historical documents and old letters, such as the nineteenth century African American English writings of freed slaves in the *WPA Ex-Slave Narratives* (Schneider 1983), the black vernacular of rural Texas in the American South (Bailey and Maynor 1987; Bailey et al. 1989), letters

138 L. Rupp and D. Britain

written by semi-literate African-American Freedman between 1861 and 1867, shortly after emancipation (Montgomery et al. 1993), nineteenth century African American letters from the Carolinas (the *Freedman Bureau Letters*; Montgomery and Fuller 1996), and the *OREAAC* corpus of letters written by semiliterate African Americans who settled in Liberia between 1834 and 1866 (Van Herk and Walker 2005). Schneider (1983: 103), for example, found rather robust –s usage of 72% with 3rd sing. subjects, and argued that the occurrence of –s in AAVE might have been variable but not irregular. Another source of important information has been recordings of African Americans whose ancestors migrated to remote areas in the late eighteenth and early nineteenth centuries and who are, therefore, thought to speak a form of early Black English. Among these are enclave communities in the African American diaspora like Samaná in the Dominican Republic (Poplack and Tagliamonte 1989) and Nova Scotia in Canada (Poplack and Tagliamonte 1991).

These forms of AAVE have also been found to show verbal –s in contexts other than 3rd sing., and patternings in accordance with the Northern Subject Rule (NSR). Montgomery and Fuller (1996), for example, found 63% verbal –s with plural NP-subjects and only 8% with *they* in African American letters, as compared to 78% NP and 3% *they* in letters by White Overseers, and 54% NP and 0% *they* in Scotch-Irish immigrant writings (1996: 217). This is illustrated in (8):

(8) a. **the doctors visits** them about three times a week
     b. **the** [they] **ponish** them

This finding has been replicated many a time (for example Poplack and Tagliamonte 1991: 330; Wolfram and Thomas 2002: 83–89; Van Herk and Walker 2005). Studies such as these have been used to argue that –s in AAVE at that time was systematic and had a British source, given that this systematicity appears to mirror a number of traditional dialects from the British Isles (see for example Poplack and Tagliamonte 2004, who compare Samaná and Devon English).

The situation today, however, appears to be different. Wolfram (2004: 122) states that 'Practically all studies of urban ... and rural AAVE ... have documented the current-day pattern of 3rd sg. –*s* absence ... The incidence of 3rd sg. –*s* absence is so high for younger AAVE speakers in some sociolinguistic studies of core vernacular adolescents—reaching levels of 75–100% for some speakers—that it has prompted several researchers to speculate that contemporary urban "AAVE has no concord rule for verbal –*s*" (Fasold 1972: 146).' Schneider (1983: 107) has posited that 'this relatively recent tendency' is a hypercorrected plural zero that emerged under the influence of standardisation, while Poplack and Tagliamonte state, 'the disappearance of –*s* from contemporary AAVE must be seen as a spectacular development, yet to be explained' (2001: 204). Cukor-Avila (2003: 85) has situated it in the context of the 'divergence hypothesis', 'the question of whether AAVE is currently diverging or becoming more different from white vernacular dialects in the US' (Rickford 1998: 154 and references therein) in the (neutral) sense that AAVE is developing in a different way. She demonstrates how 3rd sing. zero has risen at the expense of an NSR-use of verbal –*s* across generations of AAVE-speakers in Springville in apparent time. Bailey and Manor (1989: 14–15) have ascribed the linguistic divergence to 'the most significant demographic process that has affected the United States since its original settlement': the large-scale migration of black speakers out of the rural south into metropolitan centres, especially in the north, that took place in the twentieth century[6] (we refer to their work for discussion of theoretical and methodological issues in the 'divergence controversy').

Verbal zero has also played a role in the debate about the origins of AAVE. Some researchers think that the earliest (and most basilectal forms) of AAVE failed to acquire subject-verb agreement, while others maintain that this feature in AAVE may have its roots in British, and possibly East Anglian sources. As Trudgill (1998: 139) put it: 'East Anglian dialects of English English had their brief moment of international academic glory in the 1960s and 1970s when the big sociolinguistic issue was the historical origins of American Nonstandard Negro English, as it was then called.' In their research on AAVE in

Hyde County, North Carolina, Wolfram and Thomas (2002: 87) find robust levels of verbal zero across apparent time. However, they consider it implausible that AAVE speakers in Hyde County acquired it from European Americans there, because there is no evidence of 3rd sing. absence, historically or in contemporary data, being prevalent amongst the European American population in the region (2002: 84). Wright (2003: 37) envisages (following Holm 1991: 233–234) that the feature occurring in early traditional British dialects as well as in creole may have had a reinforcing effect: 'the convergence of both is more often a satisfactory explanation, not because it is a tactic to placate everyone, but simply because it reflects what is known about the way languages mix'. Wright (2003: 61) has in fact proposed that zero has been exapted in AAVE. She argues that 3rd sing. zero had a British source, noting that in Old English, zero used to mark the subjunctive mood. When zero subsequently invaded the indicative paradigm, it could no longer contrastively mark the subjunctive. Wright has postulated that whilst British dialects have since abandoned 3rd sing. zero (except, perhaps, in East Anglia, providing an alternative explanation of the occurrence of zero there to Trudgill 1998), zero now serves as 'an indexical marker of AAVE in many US communities' (see also Bucholtz 1999; Cutler 1999; Bucholtz and Lopez 2011).

3.4 Contact and Verbal Zero

Whatever the origins of verbal zero in African American Vernacular English, we can be certain that contact—whether language or dialect contact—has played a significant role in its genesis. Contact has indeed often been proposed as an explanation for the emergence of verbal zero more generally. For example, Trudgill (1998, reprinted in 2001) has explored it as a factor that contributed to the occurrence of verbal zero in Norwich, as we will see later.

We begin our exploration of the role of contact with a series of research papers by Szmrecsanyi and Kortmann (2009a, b, c) on a typological approach to morphosyntactic variation. For the purpose of the *Handbook of varieties of English* (Kortmann et al. 2004), they collected data from a questionnaire survey that inquired into 76 morphosyntactic features in over 40 English varieties, including a number of features having to do with subject-verb agreement. They argue that they '[c]rucially, demonstrate that variety type (L1, L2, or P/C) and not, for example, geographical distance or proximity, is the best predictor of a given variety's location relative to … dimensions ['of varying complexity and simplicity levels'] (2009c: 64). They categorised four types of English variety: low-contact L1 vernaculars (for example the north of England, East Anglia), high-contact L1 varieties (for example AAVE), L2 varieties (for example New Englishes) and English-based pidgins and creoles. Utilising a number of quantitative analysis techniques (2009b: 1643), they find, perhaps not unexpectedly, that low-contact L1 varieties most frequently show 'ornamental rules' that complexify the morphosyntactic system 'without providing a clearly identifiable communicative or functional bonus' (2009c: 68). They cite the NSR as an example of such a rule (though in Chapter 2 we have argued that verbal –s has a particular discourse function). They consider features of 'relative' simplicity (2009c: 69) to be, among others, features that may be given up in the process of second language acquisition. Amongst these is 'avoidance of agreement by morphological means, for instance, third person singular -s' (2009c: 70). While pidgins and creoles had the highest score by far, they found that L2 varieties of English did not, as one might have expected, score significantly higher on these L2 features than the L1 varieties, especially the high-contact L1's (2009c: 71). Briefly zooming in on the distribution of particular varieties, they demonstrate that their analysis in fact plots the L1 varieties Earlier African American English and Urban African American English 'on the periphery of the L1 cluster and in relative proximity to the L2 and pidgin/creole groups'. They suggest that the positioning of AAVE perfectly reflects its ambiguous nature (2009b: 1652). Overall, Szmrecsanyi and Kortmann's analysis highlights that degrees of contact is a salient determinant of morphosyntactic similarity clustering. We now turn to Trudgill's contention that the 3rd sing. zero of the L1 variety spoken in East Anglia emerged from language contact also, before we discuss a number of occurrences of verbal zero in well-known contact varieties: extraterritorial, L2 and, more recently, English as a Lingua Franca (ELF).

142   L. Rupp and D. Britain

Trudgill (1998) begins his analysis of zero in East Anglia by noting that languages that do not mark the 3rd sing. have frequently experienced language contact. In earlier work on linguistic and social factors in outcomes of language contact, he has argued that high-contact varieties are characterised by, by and large, processes of simplification (Trudgill 1989: 227–228) which he (crediting Thomason and Kaufman 1988: 27) ascribes to the practice of imperfect language learning by adults and post-adolescents (Trudgill 1992: 197). Turning to the specific case of Norwich, Trudgill (1998) proposes a contact-based argument to account for the use of verbal zero there. In the late sixteenth century, the Spanish rulers of the Low Countries began a period of persecution of local Protestants, and a good number of Dutch, Flemish and Walloon refugees fled to England, especially from 1567 onwards when the Duke of Alba intensified the suppression. They settled in different places including Sandwich (Kent), London and Colchester, with the largest group of refugees ending up in Norwich. Trudgill (1998: 143) claims that by 1579, 37% of the population of Norwich, which at that time was 16,236, were native speakers of Dutch or French. He goes on to point out that the arrival of (what were known at the time as) the 'Strangers' (1998: 144) happened at more a less the same time as the change from the old –th to the new –s morpheme to mark the 3rd sing., which had been spreading from the north and the Midlands. As we mentioned in Sect. 3.1, historical studies have shown that during this period of transition, speakers, to some extent, also used a zero form. Nevalainen et al. (2001: 194), for example, show that some of the Norfolk speakers in their *Corpus of Early English Correspondence* have very high rates of verbal zero. Trudgill (1998) believes that the zero form would have been adopted by the Strangers through contact-induced simplification—in this case their failure as second language speakers to master the 'highly marked', 'non-natural verbal marking system of English', a 'typological oddity' (1998: 144).

The eventual victory of zero in Norwich, is, Trudgill proposes, down to a 'perfect storm' of circumstances: zero was in a three-way competition with <u>both</u> the older –th form <u>and</u> the newer –s form. 'That is, these immigrants arrived *exactly* at the time when the present-tense verb system of verbs in English was in a state of flux in Norwich, with considerable variability between *-th* and *-s* forms. In other words, at any other time in history, competition between minority non-native -Ø forms and majority native forms with third-person marking would *not* have led to the replacement of native by non-native forms. In the late sixteenth century, however, competition was not between zero and a single native form. On the contrary, competition was between -Ø and *–th* and *-s*. It was, that is, a much more equal struggle, as it were, and one in which the non-native form had the advantage of linguistic naturalness and simplicity.' (2013: 20).

As Trudgill notes, the zero form is not confined to Norwich, though has long been most widespread there, and is stereotypically associated most with Norfolk. Just as Norwich (much more influential as a city then than now) would have been a particularly important urban centre diffusing the new zero form, other urban centres in East Anglia also received Strangers. Colchester had around 1300 Dutch residents between 1580 and 1620—one seventh of the total population (Joby 2015: 36), and Sperling (1896) specifically mentions Sudbury in Suffolk as home to many Flemish weavers during this period. Joby also reports Dutch communities in Great Yarmouth, King's Lynn and Thetford in Norfolk, Ipswich in Suffolk, Halstead and Canvey Island in Essex, as well as in the Fens, where the Dutch contributed heavily towards the reclamation effort in the seventeenth century. Heard (1970: 112, in Joby 2015: 133) suggests that many Strangers who first settled in Colchester soon moved on to smaller towns in Suffolk and Essex. Diffusion from the main urban centres would have additionally been supported by migration, therefore.

Joby (2014) questions some elements of Trudgill's argument. He presents evidence that verbal zero may have been well established in eastern England *before* the arrival of the Strangers from the Low Countries (2014: 145). He finds it in texts from before their arrival, and also in the texts of literate scribes and writers outside of Norwich just after the Strangers began to arrive, but too soon for their linguistic innovations to have spread to the literate and to writers well outside of the city. In an earlier study, Holmqvist (1922: 105–108) cites the first few tokens of zero in East Anglia from Norfolk plays of the fifteenth century (for example *I wot not who is his name, for **he** hym not **knowe**; The Macro Plays: The Castle of Perseverance* c.1440: 104) (1922: 106). He asserts that 3rd sing. zero was formed by analogy, seeing that 'the 3rd sing. of the present indicative, from late ME time onwards, has been the only verb form distinguished by a personal ending.' (1922: 137). Joby also disputes Trudgill's argument that –s was a serious competitor to –th and zero when the Strangers arrived, showing that it only began to increase in use well into the seventeenth century (2014: 146, see also 2017). This position equally finds support from Holmqvist (1922), who from an analysis of texts by Norfolk writers concludes that –th still 'preponderates very much over *-s*' in the dialect of Norfolk in the fourteenth century and into the greater part of the fifteenth century (1922: 64–67, 108). In the *Corpus of Early English Correspondence* (CEEC; c.1410–1681), Nevalainen and Raumolin-Brunberg (2003) find that in East Anglia '-TH persisted into the early decades of the seventeenth century' (2003: 178–179). Joby appears to propose a two-stage evolution; firstly, competition between –th and zero (and he points out that –th had the disadvantage of having an interdental fricative alien to both the French and Dutch of the Strangers), and then, later, a three-way competition between zero, a slowly declining –th, and a gradually increasing –s.

Vasko (2009) identified verbal zero in Cambridgeshire as most frequent in the east near the border with Suffolk and north Essex. She attributes this to language contact, with Norfolk and Suffolk speakers whose own dialect was marked with zero, though provides no evidence of such contact. She admits another contact-based explanation; namely, she envisages that the zero form might have already existed in Cambridgeshire before the seventeenth century as a result of contact with Scandinavian settlers in the Danelaw era. Verbal zero would have survived because, she claims, Cambridgeshire was in relative isolation before the drainage of Fens, which began in the seventeenth century but was not completed until the nineteenth century.

Britain (1997b, 2001, 2015) proposes contact explanations for why verbal zero is not present in much of the East Anglian Fenland. Although a number of migrants came to the Fens from the Low Countries as marshland drainage workers, the post-reclamation Fens saw considerable in-migration from outside—from the variably zero-using east, but also from the categorically –s using west and south—and this led to the emergence of a number of contact features in the Fens—an interdialectal realisation of /ʌ/ as neither western [ʊ] nor eastern and southern [ʌ] but an intermediate [ɤ], the reallocation of /ai/, using western [ɑː~ɑɪ] forms before voiced consonants and eastern [əɪ] forms before voiceless, to fossilise an allophonic split (Britain 1997a), and the levelling away of minority forms in the post-reclamation dialect mix, such as eastern 3rd person zero.

Moving beyond the British Isles, we can explore the role of contact in the development of verbal zero further by considering Schreier's (2002, 2003, 2010a) research on the English of Tristan da Cunha, a small volcanic island located in the South Atlantic Ocean. Schreier (2003) has been able to pinpoint the occurrence of verbal zero there by investigating the demographic history of the island. When Tristan da Cunha was first colonised at the beginning of the nineteenth century, there was no indigenous population. The community of Tristan da Cunha has never been large (200–300 inhabitants), and contact with other communities, especially between the mid nineteenth and mid twentieth centuries was extremely limited. The varieties of English spoken by the first residents were especially influential, then, in shaping the eventual development of Tristan da Cunha English (TdCE). These varieties included the British and American dialects of colonisers from various parts of England (the south-west, east London, Sussex, Yorkshire, Humberside), the Scottish Lowlands, New Bedford, and Massachusetts. A second factor in the formation of TdCE has been language contact with English, Dutch, Danish, Italian and quite plausibly Afrikaans speaking migrants. Additionally, a group of women from 'nearby' St Helena came to live on the island in 1827. They spoke Saint Helenian English, an English-based creole (2003: 117–120). TdCE, then, constitutes a prime example of dialect mixture, contact dynamics, and new-dialect formation.

Schreier focussed on 12 TdCE speakers who were born between 1906 and 1934 on the assumption that their speech would provide a window on the early formation period and incipient linguistic norms (cf. Trudgill's 1986 model of new-dialect formation). These speakers had no –s suffixation at all with non-3rd sing. subjects. Moreover, 3rd sing. marking was marginal: only 3% of all subjects received –s marking (2003: 121). Schreier points out that there is a two-way scenario for the emergence of this zero marking: it could have derived from the input of speakers from the south-west of England, where (as outlined in Sect. 3.1) verbal zero has been documented, or have its origins in contact-induced processes that occurred in the early mixture situation. The two residents from the south-west did not stay on Tristan da Cunha very long, however. Also, none of the original settlers came from East Anglia. Schreier (2003: 124) hence concludes that verbal zero in Tristan da Cunha does not qualify as a direct transplant from British dialects or a British founder effect. While TdCE verbal zero could have evolved from the interlanguage of non-anglophone settlers (namely, simplification as a result of L2 language learning processes), Schreier thinks that it is best explained by language contact with St Helenian English (StHE; 2003: 126). He assumes that the St Helenian women acquired a regularised (zero) present tense paradigm before they cross-migrated to Tristan, noting that StHE would have been prone to creolisation following the arrival of African and Asian slaves on St Helena, and seeing that creoles typically have no tense marking (see the cited references on pp. 124 and 126 in his study). StHE today certainly appears to be a verbal zero variety. According to Schreier, there is a 'very strong tendency to avoid morphological tense marking (i.e. lack of –s or –ed marking)' (2010b: 242), therefore 'third person singular present tense is very often zero' (2008: 187).

Thus, 3rd person zero was probably brought to Tristan da Cunha from St Helena. Schreier discusses a number of factors that may have played a role in the selection and survival of verbal zero in TdCE. One of these is the sociodemographic set-up of the community (2003: 126). Schreier suggests that '3rd zero may have been favoured by the fact that the British systems were non-congruent, which was likely to result in complexity and confusion, in a sense resembling the situation with –*eth* and –*s* in sixteenth century Norwich' (2003: 127) (recall the discussion in Sect. 3.3). The impact of StHE would have normalised non-marking, levelling out British patterns and leading to the stabilisation of a regularised present tense concord system. The creole variety that the St Helenian women spoke should have been especially influential because of their child-rearing (and consequently language socialisation) role in the community. Added to this, there was no formal education on the island in the nineteenth century or much interaction with the outside world for some time, and therefore no pressure or influence of a standard variety (2003: 127).

A number of studies of L2-varieties have also explicitly referred to language contact in their descriptions of verbal zero. For example, Bowerman (2004) reports on variation in the use of –s and zero in 'Broad White' South African English and says that contact with Afrikaans may be responsible because Afrikaans has almost no agreement. He notes that the variation may alternatively go back to the English of the settlers of South Africa. Examples from his data include (9) and (10) (2004: 956):

(9)   **He like** to read.
(10) **Does you** go to school?

Watermeyer (1996) addresses Afrikaans English. Influence of Afrikaans seems a likely explanation for the occurrence of verbal zero here; however, she points out that it is not the case that zero has generalised across the paradigm. Rather, zero is used in the singular and –s in the plural. Watermeyer (1996) cites McCormick (1989: 292) that it is possible that speakers 'overgeneralize the plural marking rule for nouns and put the final -s on the verb with plural subjects' while 'by analogy, the word-final -s in constructions with a third person singular subject is omitted' (1996: 114). This would in fact appear an instance of diagrammatic iconicity (both isomorphism and iconic motivation in that –s is used for marking plural: N + N = N–s).

Asante (2012) examined 150 written essays by Ghanaian students and graduates in two tertiary institutions. In the essays, she found that –s was frequently left out with 3rd sing. verbs (55.9%), but –s was used in the context of plural subjects (26.9%). The examples in (11–12) illustrate (pp. 213, 216–217):

(11) a. **The rural dweller** also **lack** access to good drinking water and basic health care centres.
   b. **Ghana** like any other developing country **owe** its rapid development to the university where students are subjected to disciplines purported at rapid development.
(12) a. **The universities** also **serves** as an avenue for the recruitment of school teachers who are the key to qualitative educational change.
   b. The pulp cavity contains **the blood vessels which nourishes** the tooth.

Asante (2012) advances the possibility that verbal –s was introduced in Ghana through Scottish missionaries who operated mission churches and schools between 1917 and 1970. However, in her data verbal –s did not seem to be constrained by any particular 'northern' rule like the NSR. Instead, she embraces the idea of transfer from Akan, one of the major indigenous languages in Ghana. She points out that Akan has no agreement marking, except in contexts where a semantic distinction can be made between individuated (referring to individuals within a group) and non-individuated plural reference (a group as an undifferentiated whole). (This is apparently similar to the phenomenon of collective nouns in British English; for example *The committee has/have decided.*) Individuating plural subjects agree with the verb and plurality is indicated by reduplication of the verb stem or by verbs denoting plural number (a notionally plural verb). Here is an example (2012: 210–211):

(13) a. mmaa no ada.
   women (non-individuated) the sleep
   'The women are asleep.'
(13) b. mmaa no adeda.
   women (individuated) the sleep-sleep
   'The women are asleep.'

Asante (2012) suggests that in Ghanaian English –s might in fact be used as a *singular* verb with non-individuated NPs (an interesting token of diagrammatic iconicity). This apparent usage is illustrated in (14) (p. 217):

(14) **Universities** also **serves** an idealistic function. It is symbolic of the aspirations of the people.

She demonstrates, therefore, not only how contact has produced an essentially verbal zero variety, but also how, through contact with the substrate language, verbal –s is emerging systematically in this dialect.

Finally, 'dropping the third person present tense –s' (Seidlhofer 2004: 220) has also been identified as one of the defining characteristics of the use of English as a Lingua Franca (ELF). (15a–b) give some examples from Dewey (2006: 86):

(15) a. and er **the stage involve** er working and also studying ... erm it's good job.

   b. yeah exactly because you don't have the same – the same values really of **somebody who grow up** in a family place...

Dewey (2006) collected a variety of data from 55 participants speaking 17 different first languages at two institutions of higher education in London (approx. 60,000 transcribed words of spoken discourse). 3rd sing. zero was particularly frequent in the data (108 tokens from 211 singular lexical verbs); however, Dewey observed that the use of zero significantly declined in interactions with native speakers (2006: 83, 85). Dewey thinks that ELF-users may leave out 3rd sing. –s because it has become communicatively redundant: contemporary English is (for the most part) a non-pro drop language and information about the referent is provided by the subject (cf. Siewierska's 1999 notion of 'grammatical agreement', discussed in Chapter 1 and below). Jenkins (2011: 929) has gone further to argue that since ELF involves 'a situation of accelerated language contact, it is leading to accelerated language change and, in many respects, is simply speeding up regularisation processes that are already underway albeit more slowly in L1 English varieties.'. Dewey concludes that 3rd sing. zero is 'entirely to be expected in ELF settings, where language contact is not only considerably extensive, but also a constitutive factor in any occurrence of interaction' (2006: 138).

3.5 A Formal Linguistic Perspective of the East Anglian Subject Rule

We end this chapter by attempting a structural account of the East Anglian Subject Rule (EASR). The situation that has obtained in East Anglia is the reverse of that in verbal –s dialects. In such dialects, –s appears to have lost its function as an agreement morpheme and, through a functional shift, acquired different, apparently iconically motivated, functions beyond the 3rd singular. In East Anglia, on the other hand, –s is gradually being adopted as a 3rd sing. agreement marker. Note, in this relation, that Trudgill (1996: 415) has reported a total absence of hypercorrect present tense –s forms.[7] The rise of 3rd sing. –s in East Anglian English appears to have derived from dialect contact with speakers of dialects that have 3rd sing. –s.[8] We would, therefore, expect the two different tokens of –s, verbal –s and 3rd sing. –s, to be constrained in different ways. According to the NSR, which we have interpreted in terms of discourse properties, in NSR-type dialects verbal –s co-occurs with NPs at higher rates than with more accessible pronouns, unless the pronoun is separated from the verb. In East-Anglia-type dialects and by the EASR, the 3rd sing. agreement marker –s is more frequent with 3rd sing. pronouns than with singular NPs.

We believe that an explanation for the EASR is likely to be found in the close relation between pronouns and agreement marking. This relationship bears out in ways that we will first outline. Recall from Sect. 2.3 in Chapter 2 that it is commonly assumed that agreement morphemes derive from pronouns (the 2nd sing. morpheme –st being the prime example of this in English). Potentially, both pronouns and agreement morphemes can, therefore, evoke referents in the discourse by means of person, number, and gender features (anaphoric agreement). However, the agreement morpheme may lose its potential as a referring expression. The verb then obligatorily takes a subject and only expresses agreement with the subject redundantly. In Bresnan and Mchombo's (1987) terms, the morpheme has turned into a 'pure' grammatical agreement marker. These two situations (grammatical agreement and anaphoric agreement) are indicated in the left-and right-most columns in Table 3.1 which has been adapted from Corbett (2003: 169).

Standard English has grammatical agreement but Siewierska (1999: 238) points out that otherwise languages in which agreement morphemes are pure 'redundant' agreement markers actually form a minority (only 1% from the 272 languages that she surveyed). As indicated in Table 3.1, next to anaphoric and grammatical agreement there is an intermediate situation which Bresnan and Mchombo (1986: 287) have described as follows: 'One stage in the historical evolution of a grammatical agreement marker ... appears to be a *partial* loss of referentiality, allowing the same morpheme to be used ambiguously for grammatical and anaphoric agreement' [*our italics*]. In the literature, such morphemes are known as 'pronominal affixes'. Siewierska (1999) has called it 'ambiguous' agreement. Ambiguous agreement markers occur both in the presence and absence of a pronominal or NP-argument. Bresnan and Mchombo (1987) have argued that where arguments are not expressed (for example, in Table 3.1, the subject in the Italian example and the object in the example from Tuscarora, a native Indian language), the pronominal affix has the status of an incorporated pronoun. To the extent that nominal expressions (like the NP 'the hunters' in the example from Chicheŵa in Table 3.1) occur with incorporated pronouns at all, they are analysed as dislocated topics outside the VP showing anaphoric agreement with the pronoun. On the other hand, when the pronominal affix has no independent pronoun status but tends towards a marker of grammatical agreement, it will be doubled by a(nother) pronoun. Bresnan and Moshi (1990: 151) demonstrate this with data from another Bantu language, Kichaga, in which object markers and independent pronouns obligatorily co-occur. Following Sadler (2003), Welsh also has this pronoun-doubling property. As shown in Table 3.1 and (16) below, in Welsh, pronominal subjects co-occur with agreement but other subjects appear in what she calls the 'unmarked 3S form' (2003: 87). Recall from the discussion of the NSR in Chapter 2 that Siewierska (1999) has analysed this pattern in Welsh as a partial realisation of grammatical agreement and that it has motivated some researchers studying the NSR to posit a Welsh connection.

Table 3.1 Grammatical agreement, ambiguous agreement and anaphoric agreement compared

	Grammatical agreement	Ambiguous agreement		Anaphoric agreement
referential properties	non-argument			argument
linguistic element	'pure' (redundant) agreement marker	pronominal affix		free pronoun
morphology	inflectional form			free form
syntax	obligatory subject (pronoun, NP)	no pronoun, potential left-dislocated NP	pronoun doubling	cross-clausal antecedent
exemplification	**He/My father** watch-**es**. (Mithun 2003: 236–237)	Cant-**a**. sing-3.SG 'He/she is singing.' (Italian: Corbett 2003: 194) wahrakyétkaht wa?-hrak-etkaht-? *factual*-3SG.*agent*/1SG.*patient*-chase-*perfective* 'He chased me.' (Tuscarora; Mithun 1999: 190) Njûchi zi-ná-wá-lum-a alenje Bees SM-*past*-OM-bite-*indic* hunters 'The bees bit them, the hunters.' (Chicheŵa; Bresnan and Mchombo 1987: 746)	**Daeth** y dynion. Came-3SG the men 'The men came.' **Daethan** (nhw). Came-3PL (they) 'They came.' (Welsh; Sadler 2003: 87)	**John**ᵢ sat down. Corbett (2003: 194) **He**ᵢ looked tired.

3 Verbal Zero   153

(16) a. Daeth y dynion.
Came-3SG the men
'The men came.'
b. Daethan (nhw).
Came-3PL (they)
'They came.'

Other apparent evidence for a close relation between pronouns and agreement comes from English data discussed in Den Dikken (2001 and references therein). For example, he reports that in American English dialects from the north-east of the United States, pronoun-subjects of *wh*-relative clauses trigger agreement on the verb, whereas NPs need not show subject-verb agreement. The contrast is illustrated in (17–18) (2001: 20).

(17) a. the people who **he thinks** are in the garden.
b. *the people who **he think** are in the garden.
(18) a. the people who **Clark thinks** are in the garden.
b. %the people who **Clark think** are in the garden.

Furthermore, as Corbett (2003: 177) points out, cross-linguistically there are more agreement features marked on pronouns than on NPs (for example gender in English). He also points out that while the set of pronouns is restricted, there is a vast number of different NPs (2003: 175–176), some of which, we note, can participate in a different kind of agreement than grammatical agreement (for example semantic agreement in *The committee has/have decided*). Den Dikken (2001: 19) states that '[p]ronouns often behave differently from full noun phrases – and typically, when differences between pronouns and full noun phrases present themselves, the pronoun raises to its feature-checking position(s) overtly while the full noun phrase procrastinates' [that is, the NP does not move in the syntax LR&DB].

In the light of these cross-linguistic findings on the relationship between pronouns and marking agreement, we would speculate that EASR-dialects show ambiguous agreement of the pronoun-doubling type.

While these dialects currently seem to be moving towards the same grammatical agreement as that of Standard English, at present –s may be a kind of pronominal affix and therefore East Anglian dialects demonstrate a favouring of –s with pronominal subjects. We assume a configuration à la Henry (1995) (see Chapter 2) where pronouns occur in an AgrP in order to double –s. In contrast, NP subjects remain in VP or in some intermediate phrase that we have labelled XP in (20).

(20)

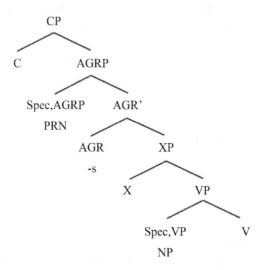

Formal syntactic frameworks would appear particularly useful to analyse morphosyntactic variants that look clearly purely grammatical, like the morphosyntactic variation generated by the EASR (but seemingly unlike the NSR). In Chapter 4 we will consider the application of the EASR to past BE.

Notes

1. In our discussions of verbal zero here, we recognise that there is a degree of overlap with varieties which, for whatever reason, variably can apply –s across the verbal paradigm. In some of the varieties discussed in the

previous chapter, –s occurs with 1st and 2nd persons, but it is nevertheless possible for zero to occasionally occur in 3rd sing. contexts (for example Godfrey and Tagliamonte 1999: 106). We distinguish these varieties not in terms of where verbal –s and verbal zero can and cannot occur, but rather in terms of whether or not they have an underlying subject-verb agreement system. In our view, the varieties presented in the previous chapter may have had such an underlying system, but those outlined in this chapter do/did not. Some of the varieties discussed in this chapter appear to be acquiring such a system, but we would like to suggest, following Labov (1998: 146), that this is the result of contact with superordinate or standard dialects.

2. Retrieved January 2018 from http://www.helsinki.fi/varieng/CoRD/corpora/Dialects/cambridgeshire.html.

3. Retrieved January 2018 from http://www.helsinki.fi/varieng/series/volumes/04/articleC_zero_suffix.html.

4. Retrieved January 2018 from http://www.helsinki.fi/varieng/series/volumes/04/articleC_zero_suffix.html.

5. Retrieved January 2018 from http://www.helsinki.fi/varieng/series/volumes/04/chapter3_1.html#section3.1.1.2.

6. One of the focal points in this discussion has been the way in which twentieth century AAVE has been developing towards a common urban norm; one which shows both the recession of early AAVE features and innovations which it did not have at earlier stages and are not present in white vernaculars. One apparent example of this is 'habitual *be*' as in *Sometimes they be playing games* (see Wolfram 2004: 127 and references in Wolfram 2004: 114, 118–119). Rural communities, on the other hand, are more regularly seen to retain features that are embedded historically through contact with English dialects and have endured in the contemporary local AAVE variety. These communities either align themselves more closely with European Americans or have been found to (re) shape the features in a subtle way in the construction of distinct ethnolinguistic entities (for example Wolfram and Sellers 1999; Wolfram and Thomas 2002; Mallinson and Wolfram 2002).

7. Trudgill has argued that there is no hypercorrection because as a result of the language contact situation in which 3rd sing. –s and zero mixed, the morphemes were reallocated as social and stylistic markers (1996: 422–423). He thinks that this is the reason why the two morphemes survived for so long. However, he was not aware of the EASR then.

8. Britain (2014) argues that one significant cause of this contact is sustained counterurbanisation over the past 80 years from London and the south-east (–s using areas) into East Anglia, combined with an accelerating general demographic churn.

References

Asante, M. (2012). Variation in subject-verb concord in Ghanaian English. *World Englishes, 31,* 208–225.

Bailey, G., & Maynor, N. (1987). Decreolization. *Language in Society, 16,* 449–474.

Bailey, G., & Maynor, N. (1989). The divergence controversy. *American Speech, 64,* 12–39.

Bailey, G., Maynor, N., & Cukor-Avila, P. (1989). Variation in subject-verb concord in Early Modern English. *Language Variation and Change, 1,* 285–300.

Bailey, G., & Ross, G. (1988). The shape of the superstrate: Morphosyntactic features of ship English. *English World-Wide, 9,* 193–212.

Bowerman, S. (2004). White South African English. In R. Mesthrie (Ed.), *Varieties of English (Vol. 4): Africa, South and South-East Asia* (pp. 472–487). Berlin: Mouton de Gruyter.

Bresnan, J., & Mchombo, S. A. (1986). Grammatical and anaphoric agreement. In A. Farley, P. Farley, & K. McCullough (Eds.), *Proceedings of the Chicago Linguistic Society 22: Papers from the Parasession on Pragmatics and Grammatical Theory* (pp. 741–782). Chicago: Chicago Linguistics Society.

Bresnan, J., & Mchombo, S. A. (1987). Topic, pronoun, and agreement in Chicheŵa. *Language, 63,* 741–782.

Bresnan, J., & Moshi, L. (1990). Object asymmetries in comparative Bantu syntax. *Linguistic Inquiry, 2,* 147–185.

Britain, D. (1997a). Dialect contact and phonological reallocation: 'Canadian Raising' in the English Fens. *Language in Society, 26,* 15–46.

Britain, D. (1997b). Dialect contact, focusing and phonological rule complexity: The koineisation of Fenland English. *Special Issue of University of Pennsylvania Working Papers in Linguistics, 4,* 141–170.

Britain, D. (2001). Welcome to East Anglia! Two major dialect 'boundaries' in the Fens. In P. Trudgill & J. Fisiak (Eds.), *East Anglian English* (pp. 217–242). Woodbridge: Boydell and Brewer.

Britain, D. (2014). *Linguistic diffusion and the social heterogeneity of space and mobility*. Paper presented at the 3rd International Society for the Linguistics of English conference, Universität Zürich, Switzerland.

Britain, D. (2015). Between North and South: The Fenland. In R. Hickey (Ed.), *Researching Northern English* (pp. 417–435). Amsterdam: John Benjamins.

Britain, D. (2016). *Up, app and away? Social dialectology and the use of smartphone technology as a data collection strategy*. Paper presented at the Sociolinguistics Symposium 21, Universidad de Murcia, Spain.

Britain, D., & Matsumoto, K. (2015). Palauan English. In J. Williams, E. W. Schneider, P. Trudgill, & D. Schreier (Eds.), *Further studies in the lesser known varieties of English* (pp. 305–343). Cambridge: Cambridge University Press.

Britain, D., & Rupp, L. (2005). *Subject-verb agreement in English dialects: The East Anglian Subject Rule*. Paper presented at The International Conference on Language Variation in Europe 3, Amsterdam, The Netherlands.

Bucholtz, M. (1999). You da man: Narrating the racial other in the production of white masculinity. *Journal of Sociolinguistics, 3*, 443–460.

Bucholtz, M., & Lopez, Q. (2011). Performing blackness, forming whiteness: Linguistic minstrelsy in Hollywood film. *Journal of Sociolinguistics, 15*, 680–706.

Corbett, G. (2003). Agreement: The range of the phenomenon and the principles of the Surrey database of agreement. *Transactions of the Philological Society, 101*, 155–202.

Cukor-Avila, P. (2003). The complex grammatical history of African-American and white vernaculars in the South. In S. Nagle & S. Sanders (Eds.), *English in the Southern United States* (pp. 82–105). Cambridge: Cambridge University Press.

Cutler, C. (1999). Yorkville crossing: White teens, hip hop and African American English. *Journal of Sociolinguistics, 4*, 428–442.

De Both, F. (2019). Nonstandard periphrastic DO and verbal -*s* in the south west of England. *Journal of Historical Sociolinguistics, 5*, 1–35. https://doi.org/10.1515/jhsl-2018-0006.

De Klerk, V. (1996). *Focus on South Africa*. Amsterdam: John Benjamins.

Den Dikken, M. (2001). "Pluringals", pronouns and quirky agreement. *The Linguistic Review, 18*, 19–41.

Deterding, D. (2007). *Singapore English*. Edinburgh: Edinburgh University Press.

Dewey, M. (2006). *English as a Lingua Franca: An empirical study of innovation in lexis and grammar* (Doctoral dissertation). King's College London, London.

Ellis, A. (1889). *On Early English pronunciation (Part V)*. London: Truebner.

Elworthy, F. T. (1886). *The West Somerset word book: A glossary of dialectal and archaic words and phrases used in the West of Somerset and East Devon.* London: Trübner.

Fasold, R. (1972). *Tense marking in Black English.* Arlington: Center for Applied Linguistics.

Godfrey, E., & Tagliamonte, S. (1999). Another piece for the verbal -*s* story: Evidence from Devon in the Southwest of England. *Language Variation and Change, 11,* 87–121.

Henry, A. (1995). *Belfast English and Standard English: Dialect variation and parameter setting.* Oxford: Oxford University Press.

Holm, J. (1991). The Atlantic Creoles and the languages of the ex-slave recordings. In G. Bailey, N. Maynor, & P. Cukor-Avila (Eds.), *The emergence of Black English: Text and commentary* (pp. 231–248). Amsterdam: John Benjamins.

Holmqvist, E. (1922). *On the history of the English present inflections particularly -t and -s.* Heidelberg: Carl Winter.

Jantos, S. (2009). *Agreement in educated Jamaican English: A corpus investigation of ICE-Jamaica* (Doctoral dissertation). Albert-Ludwigs-Universität, Freiburg.

Jenkins, J. (2011). Accommodating (to) ELF in the international university. *Journal of Pragmatics, 43,* 926–936.

Joby, C. (2014). Third-person singular zero in the Norfolk dialect: A re-assessment. *Folia Linguistica, 35,* 135–172.

Joby, C. (2015). *The Dutch language in Britain (1550–1702): A social history of the use of Dutch in Early Modern Britain.* Leiden: E. J. Brill.

Kingston, M. (2000). *Dialects in danger: Rural dialect attrition in the East Anglian county of Suffolk* (MA dissertation). University of Essex, Colchester.

Klemola, J. (1996). *Non-standard periphrastic DO: A study in variation and change* (Doctoral dissertation). University of Essex, Colchester.

Kökeritz, H. (1932). *The phonology of the Suffolk dialect.* Uppsala: Aktibolag.

Kortmann, B., Schneider, E. W., Burridge, K., Mesthrie, R., & Upton, C. (Eds.). (2004). *A handbook of varieties of English.* Berlin: Mouton de Gruyter.

Kytö, M. (1993). Third-person present singular verb inflection in early British and American English. *Language Variation and Change, 5,* 113–139.

Labov, W. (1998). Co-existent systems in African-American Vernacular English. In S. Mufwene, J. Rickford, G. Bailey, & J. Baugh (Eds.), *African*

American English: Structure, history and use (pp. 110–153). London: Routledge.

Labov, W., Cohen, P., Robins, C., & Lewis, J. (1968). *A study of the non-standard English of Negro and Puerto Rican speakers in New York City: Cooperative research report 3288* (Vols. I–II). Philadelphia, PA: U.S. Regional Survey (Linguistics Laboratory, University of Philadelphia).

Leemann, A., Kolly, M.-J., & Britain, D. (2018). The English Dialects App: The creation of a crowdsourced dialect corpus. *Ampersand, 5,* 1–17.

Mallinson, C., & Wolfram, W. (2002). Dialect accommodation in a bi-ethnic mountain enclave community: More evidence on the development of African American English. *Language in Society, 31,* 743–775.

McCormick, K. (1989). *English and Afrikaans in district six: A sociolinguistic study* (Doctoral dissertation). University of Cape Town, Cape Town.

Mithun, M. (1999). *The languages of native North America.* Cambridge: Cambridge University Press.

Mithun, M. (2003). Pronouns and agreement: The information status of pronominal affixes. *Transactions of the Philological Society, 101,* 235–278.

Montgomery, M., & Fuller, J. (1996). What was verbal *-s* in 19th-century African American English? In E. W. Schneider (Ed.), *Focus on the USA* (pp. 211–230). Amsterdam: John Benjamins.

Montgomery, M., Fuller, J., & De Marse, S. (1993). 'The Black Men has wives and Sweet harts [and third person plural *-s*] Jest like the white men': Evidence for verbal *-s* from written documents on 19th-century African American Speech. *Language Variation and Change, 5,* 335–357.

Nevalainen, T., & Raumolin-Brunberg, H. (2003). *Historical sociolinguistics: Language change in Tudor and Stuart England.* Harlow: Pearson Education.

Nevalainen, T., Raumolin-Brunberg, H., & Trudgill, P. (2001). Chapters in the social history of East Anglian English: The case of the third-person singular. In J. Fisiak & P. Trudgill (Eds.), *East Anglian English* (pp. 187–204). Woodbridge: Boydell and Brewer.

Orton, H., & Tilling, P. M. (1971). *Survey of English Dialects (B): The basic material (Vols. 3.1 and 3.3): The East Midland counties and East Anglia.* London: E. J. Arnold.

Orton, H., & Wakelin, M. F. (1967). *Survey of English Dialects (B): The basic material (Vol. 4:2): The Southern counties.* Leeds: E. J. Arnold.

Poplack, S., & Tagliamonte, S. (1989). There's no tense like the present: Verbal *-s* inflection in early Black English. *Language Variation and Change, 1,* 47–84.

Poplack, S., & Tagliamonte, S. (1991). African American English in the diaspora: Evidence from old-line Nova Scotians. *Language Variation and Change, 3,* 301–339.

Poplack, S., & Tagliamonte, S. (2001). *African American English in the diaspora: Tense and aspect.* Malden, MA: Blackwell.

Poplack, S., & Tagliamonte, S. (2004). Back to the present: Verbal -s in the African American English diaspora. In R. Hickey (Ed.), *Legacies of colonial English: The study of transported dialects* (pp. 203–223). Cambridge: Cambridge University Press.

Potter, R. (2018). *A variationist multilocality study of unstressed vowels and verbal -s marking in the peripheral dialect of East Suffolk* (Doctoral dissertation). University of Essex, Colchester.

Reaser, J. (2010). Bahamian English. In D. Schreier, P. Trudgill, E. W. Schneider, & J. Williams (Eds.), *The lesser-known varieties of English* (pp. 158–170). Cambridge: Cambridge University Press.

Rickford, J. R. (1998). The creole origins of African American Vernacular English: Evidence from copula absence. In S. S. Mufwene, J. R. Rickford, G. Bailey, & J. Bough (Eds.), *African American English: Structure, history and usage* (pp. 154–200). London: Routledge.

Sadler, L. (2003). Coordination and asymmetric agreement in Welsh. In M. Butt & T. Holloway King (Eds.), *Nominals: Inside and out* (pp. 85–118). Stanford: CSLI Publications.

Schneider, E. W. (1983). The origin of the verbal -s in Black English. *American Speech, 58,* 99–113.

Schreier, D. (2002). *Terra incognita* in the Anglophone world: Tristan da Cunha, South Atlantic Ocean. *English Word-Wide, 23,* 1–29.

Schreier, D. (2003). Tracing the history of dialect transportation on post-colonial English: The case of 3rd person singular zero on Tristan da Cunha. *Folia Linguistica Historica, XXIII,* 115–131.

Schreier, D. (2008). *St Helenian English: Origins, evolution and variation.* Amsterdam: John Benjamins.

Schreier, D. (2010a). Tristan da Cunha English. In D. Schreier, P. Trudgill, E. W. Schneider, & J. Williams (Eds.), *The lesser-known varieties of English* (pp. 245–260). Cambridge: Cambridge University Press.

Schreier, D. (2010b). St Helenian English. In D. Schreier, P. Trudgill, E. W. Schneider, & J. Williams (Eds.), *The lesser-known varieties of English* (pp. 224–244). Cambridge: Cambridge University Press.

Seidlhofer, B. (2004). Research perspectives on teaching English as a lingua franca. *Annual Review of Applied Linguistics, 24*, 209–239.

Shuy, R., Wolfram, W., & Riley, W. (1967). *Linguistic correlates of social stratification in Detroit speech* (USOE Final Report, 6-1347).

Siewierska, A. (1999). From anaphoric pronoun to grammatical agreement marker: Why objects don't make it. *Folia Linguistica, 33*, 225–251.

Sperling, C. (1896). *A short history of the borough of Sudbury in the county of Suffolk compiled from materials collected by W. H. Hudson.* Marten: Sudbury.

Spurling, J. (2004). *Traditional feature loss in Ipswich: Dialect attrition in the East Anglian county of Suffolk* (BA dissertation). University of Essex, Colchester.

Szmrecsanyi, B., & Kortmann, B. (2009a). Vernacular universals and angloversals in a typological perspective. In M. Filppula, J. Klemola, & H. Paulasto (Eds.), *Vernacular universals and language contacts: Evidence from varieties of English and beyond* (pp. 33–53). London: Routledge.

Szmrecsanyi, B., & Kortmann, B. (2009b). The morphosyntax of varieties of English worldwide: A quantitative perspective. *Lingua, 119*, 1643–1663.

Szmrecsanyi, B., & Kortmann, B. (2009c). Between simplification and complexification: Non-standard varieties of English around the world. In G. Sampson, D. Gil, & P. Trudgill (Eds.), *Language complexity as an evolving variable* (pp. 64–79). Oxford: Oxford University Press.

Thomason, S. G., & Kaufman, T. (1988). *Language contact, creolization and genetic linguistics.* Berkeley, CA: University of California.

Trudgill, P. (1974). *The social differentiation of English in Norwich.* Cambridge: Cambridge University Press.

Trudgill, P. (1986). *Dialects in contact.* Oxford: Blackwell.

Trudgill, P. (1989). Contact and isolation in linguistic change. In L. Breivik & E. Jahr (Eds.), *Language change: Contributions to the study of its causes* (pp. 227–238). Berlin: Mouton de Gruyter.

Trudgill, P. (1992). Dialect typology and social structure. In E. H. Jahr (Ed.), *Language contact: Theoretical and empirical structures* (pp. 195–212). Berlin: Mouton de Gruyter.

Trudgill, P. (1996). Language contact and inherent variability: The absence of hypercorrection in East Anglian present-tense verb forms. In J. Klemola, M. Kytö, & M. Risannen (Eds.), *Speech past and present: Studies in English dialectology in memory of Ossi Ihalainen* (pp. 412–425). Frankfurt: Peter Lang.

Trudgill, P. (1998). Third person singular zero: African-American English, East Anglian dialects and Spanish persecution in the low countries. *Folia Linguistica Historica, 18*, 139–148.

Trudgill, P. (2001). Modern East Anglia as a dialect area. In J. Fisiak & P. Trudgill (Eds.), *East Anglian English* (pp. 1–12). Woodbridge: Boydell and Brewer.

Trudgill, P. (2013). The role of Dutch in the development of East Anglian English. *Taal en Tongval, 65,* 11–22.

Van Herk, G., & Walker, J. A. (2005). S marks the spot? Regional variation and early African American correspondence. *Language Variation and Change, 17,* 113–131.

Vasko, A.-L. (2009). Zero suffix with the third-person singular of the simple present. In A.-L. Vasko (Ed.), *Studies in variation, contacts and change in English (Vol. 4): Cambridgeshire dialect grammar.* Retrieved January 2018 from http://www.helsinki.fi/varieng/journal/volumes/04.

Wakelin, M. F. (1977). *English dialects: An introduction* (2nd Rev. ed.). London: Athlone Press.

Walker, J., & Meyerhoff, M. (2015). Bequia English. In J. Williams, E. W. Schneider, D. Schreier, & P. Trudgill (Eds.), *Further studies in the lesser-known varieties of English* (pp. 128–143). Cambridge: Cambridge University Press.

Watermeyer, S. (1996). Afrikaans English. In V. de Klerk (Ed.), *Focus on South Africa* (pp. 99–124). Amsterdam: John Benjamins.

Wee, L. (2004). Singapore English: Morphology and syntax. In B. Kortmann & E. W. Schneider (with K. Burridge, R. Mesthrie, & C. Upton) (Eds.), *A handbook of varieties of English (Vol. 2): Morphology and syntax* (pp. 1058–1072). Berlin: Mouton de Gruyter.

Wee, L., & Ansaldo, U. (2004). Nouns and noun phrases. In L. Lim (Ed.), *Singapore English: A grammatical description* (pp. 57–74). Amsterdam: John Benjamins.

Wolfram, W. (1974). The relationship of Southern White speech to vernacular Black English. *Language, 50,* 498–527.

Wolfram, W. (2004). The grammar of urban African American Vernacular English. In B. Kortmann & E. W. Schneider (with K. Burridge, R. Mesthrie, & C. Upton) (Eds.), *Handbook of varieties of English (Vol. 2): Morphology and syntax* (pp. 111–132). Berlin: Mouton de Gruyter.

Wolfram, W., & Sellers, J. (1999). Ethnolinguistic marking of past *be* in Lumbee Vernacular English. *Journal of English Linguistics, 27,* 94–114.

Wolfram, W., & Thomas, E. (2002). *The development of African American English.* Oxford: Blackwell.

Wright, J. (1905). *English dialect grammar.* Oxford: Clarendon Press.

Wright, L. (2003). Eight grammatical features of southern United States speech present in early modern London prison narratives. In S. Nagle & S. Sanders (Eds.), *English in the Southern United States* (pp. 36–63). Cambridge: Cambridge University Press.

Wright, L. (2015). Some more on the history of present-tense -*s*, do and zero: West Oxfordshire, 1837. *Journal of Historical Sociolinguistics, 1,* 111–130.

4

Past BE

4.1   Introduction

This chapter examines another type of verbal –s; namely, variable deployments of the lexical items *was* and *were*. Following common practice in the variationist literature, we will henceforth refer to this phenomenon as *past BE*. We will begin by introducing the three most frequently attested current patterns of past BE: use of *was* in contexts where Standard English prescribes the form *were*, use of *were* in contexts where Standard English prescribes the form *was*, and a hybrid *was/weren't* system. In order to contextualise these patterns, we present a brief outline of the history of past BE as it has been documented in the literature and we go on to consider dialectologists' findings of the distribution of past BE in traditional and contemporary dialects. As Schreier (2002b: 71) has pointed out: 'past BE regularization has not advanced at the same rate in the varieties where it has been documented, and there is a significant degree of variability in its directionality'. Our main purpose in this chapter, therefore, is *to examine the different paths that past BE has followed and to explore the factors that shape the course that past BE has been taking.* In this context, we will first examine variationist

© The Author(s) 2019   **165**
L. Rupp and D. Britain, *Linguistic Perspectives on a Variable English Morpheme*,
https://doi.org/10.1057/978-1-349-72803-9_4

analyses of attested patterns of past BE. These variationist analyses have assumed, amongst other factors, a role for the preservation of historical past BE forms in contexts of isolation, ongoing processes of analogical levelling, grammatical conditioning by the Northern Subject Rule and the East Anglian Subject Rule (we refer the reader to our presentation of the latter rule in the discussion of verbal zero in Chapter 3), and a course of 'refunctionalisation' that has resulted in an innovative polarity effect promoting *was* in positive clauses and *weren't* in negative clauses. We subsequently show that theoretical accounts of past BE can complement variationist analyses by shedding light on language-internal mechanisms that structure past BE. We then present our own account that envisages a scenario similar to that for verbal –s: when not or no longer deployed for agreement marking, the allomorphs of past BE may undergo a functional shift and come to serve a different grammatical role. We will suggest that the emergent past BE patterns also have a basis in diagrammatic iconicity and seem to fit Lass's (1990, 1997) 'exaptation' view of functional shift best, tying in aspects of earlier analyses of past BE (Schilling-Estes and Wolfram 1994; Kortmann and Wagner 2005; Willis 2016).[1,2]

4.2 Current Patterns of Past BE

Many vernacular varieties of English that have been subject to research show variation in the realisation of past BE. In variationist studies, the occurrence of non-standard past BE has been documented in, for example, England, including London (Levey 2007; Cheshire and Fox 2009); the Fens (Britain 2002); Cambridgeshire (Vasko 2010); Reading (Cheshire 1982); Birmingham (Khan 2007); Bolton (Moore 2011); Yorkshire (Petyt 1985; Tagliamonte 1998; Richards 2010); Tyneside (Beal 2004; Cole 2008); Scotland (Edwards and Weltens 1983), including Buckie (Smith 2000; Smith and Tagliamonte 1998; Adger and Smith 2010) and the Shetlands (Durham 2013); rural South Armagh (Corrigan 1997); a number of rural and urban communities in the UK (discussed in the comparative study of Tagliamonte 2009); Australia

(Eisikovits 1991; Malcolm 1996); New Zealand (Bauer 1994; Hay and Schreier 2004); Palmerston Island in the Cook Islands (Hendery 2016); Tristan da Cunha (Schreier 2002a, b); the Falkland Islands (Sudbury 2001; Britain and Sudbury 2013); Canada (Meechan and Foley 1994), including Newfoundland (Clarke 1997); Guysborough Village in Nova Scotia (Tagliamonte and Smith 2000); the Ottawa Valley (Jankowski and Tagliamonte 2017); and the United States, including Alabama (Feagin 1979); and Smith Island, Maryland (Schilling-Estes and Zimmerman 2000; Mittelstaedt and Parrot 2002); Ocracoke (Schilling-Estes and Wolfram 1994; Hazen 2000); Robeson County (Wolfram and Sellers 1999; Williams 2007); Roaring Creek (Mallinson and Wolfram 2002); Hyde County (Wolfram and Thomas 2002); Roanoke Island (Carpenter 2004), all in North Carolina; Appalachia and Ozark (Wolfram and Christian 1976; Christian et al. 1988); 'Wilson County', Kentucky (Greene 2010); Harrison County, Indiana (José 2007); 'Southern White American Vernacular English' (Trüb 2006); Cajun English of south Louisiana (Dubois and Horvath 2003) and the Rocky Mountains (Antieau 2011). It is also recognised as 'integral and robust' (Wolfram 2004: 123) within urban African American Vernacular English across North America.

In Standard English, the past tense paradigm for *be* today is the only one that is structured according to person/number: *was* is used with 1st and 3rd sing. subjects and *were* with all other persons. Previous studies have found three prevailing non-standard patterns across contemporary varieties of English:

1. Extensive regularisation to *was* (variable use of tokens of *was* across the entire past tense paradigm, regardless of person and number);
2. Regularisation to *were* as the most frequent pattern observed (variable use of *were*, irrespective of person and number); and
3. A mixed *was/weren't* system along polarity lines in which there is a tendency to generalise *was* to all positive contexts (including standard *was* contexts) and to generalise *weren't* to all negative contexts (including standard *were* contexts), the first of which may be less advanced (Britain 2002).[3]

168   L. Rupp and D. Britain

Following Anderwald (2001), (1) and (2) seem relatively straightforward simplifications whereas (3) a more intricate reconfiguration. Examples of the three nonstandard past BE patterns are shown below for illustration, respectively.

(1) **The Argie soldiers was** living in the peat shed. (Falkland Islands; Britain and Sudbury 2013: 672)
(2) **My Dad were** up there. (York; Tagliamonte 1998: 155)
(3) **It weren't** Calais, but it **was** something like that. (English Fens)
(4) **You was** talking to Eric the other day, Ray, **weren't you?** (English Fens).[4]

Britain (2002: 22) has observed that the *Survey of English Dialects* (Orton and Tilling 1971; e.g. 1187–1189) showed not only the existence of a range of past BE systems around the country in the mid-twentieth century, but also a wide variety of variant pronunciations of these forms (see also Forsström 1948).

4.3   The History of Past BE

In order to be able to interpret contemporary past BE data, it is important to take account of the diachronic context (cf. for example Tagliamonte 1998). To what extent can patterns of variation in past BE be traced back and understood from the historical record?

Historically, forms of past BE were not distributed across the verb paradigm precisely in accordance with present-day prescriptive rules. The work of historical linguists shows that past BE has been variable from the early history of English, in particular showing different attestations of *was* (Forsström 1948; Brunner 1963). With respect to the Middle English period, we know more about *geographical* variation in past BE than any social dimension. Table 4.1 is from Mossé (1952: 84) and presents the past BE paradigm in Middle English according to geographical area.

As shown in Table 4.1, the variation was found specifically in the 2nd sing. and the plural: speakers in the south used *were* but speakers

4 Past BE 169

Table 4.1 The geographical distribution of forms of past BE in the Middle English period

	North	West Midlands	East Midlands	South
1st sing.	was, wes	was	was	was
2nd sing.	was, wes	wǭre	wēre/wast	wēōre
3rd sing.	was, wes	was	was	was
pl.	wēr, wār(e), wes	wǭren	wēre(n)	wēōre, wǣre

in the north used *was*. Forsström (1948: 203) claims that the use of *was* in this context was 'a characteristic feature of the Northern dialect'. The illustrating examples in (5a–b) are from northern texts of the Middle English period (Tagliamonte and Smith 2000: 153, cited from Forsström 1948):

(5) a. **Was þou** not at me riȝt now? (*Cursor Mundi* ca. 1300: 3727)
'Were you not with me just now?'
b. When **þou was** bowne with a brande my body to shende. (*The Wars of Alexander* ca. 1450: 870)
'When you were ready with a sword to injure my body.'

Forsström (1948: 203) adds: 'The sg. form is particularly common in relative clauses and in the phrase *there was* followed by a plural subject. It is very seldom instanced immediately preceded or followed by a personal pronoun.' Her last remark suggests that the Northern Subject Rule (NSR), which we discussed in relation to verbal –s in Chapter 2, similarly operated on past BE. Tagliamonte and Smith (2000: 154) quote Murray (1873), who detailed the NSR, as stating that past BE was included in the NSR:

When the subject is a noun, adjective, interrogative, or relative pronoun, or when the verb and subject are separated by a clause, the verb takes the termination -s in all persons. [...] [t]he analogs of the other verbs, in which a form identical with the 3rd pers. sing. was used in the plural in the absence of the pronoun, led to the use of *es, is,* in like cases for *ar, er,*

170   L. Rupp and D. Britain

though only as an alternative form: in the same way *was*, *wes*, intruded upon *wer*, *war*, in the past tense. (pp. 211–213)

Smith and Tagliamonte (1998: 110) cite the examples in (6a–c) from Murray (1873: 213) to illustrate.

(6) a. I am a commelyng toward þe, And pilgrym as alle **my faders was**. (Hampole, c. 1400)
     b. ... and there to be hangitt be þe heid, ay quhill **thay were** deid ... (*Annals of Hawick*, c. 1400: 215–305)
     c. **They** [toke shyppynge and sayled to Dover and] **was** there by noone. (c. 1523–5 Ld Berners, *Frois* III 357)

As indicated in Table 4.1, the form *was* also occurred in the 2nd sing. in the Midlands. Forsström (1948), who studied a range of Middle English texts from different dialect areas, found that:

> [T]he normal East Midland form is *were* except in the northern part of the area, where *was* seems to have been used, sometimes even as the majority form. It is the Northern 2sg form that has penetrated southwards. (p. 116)

> The South-West Midlands use only *were*, whereas the North-West as regularly has *was*. [...] [t]he central part of the West-Midland district seems to have been a transition area. Audelay has both tokens of *were* and *was*. (p. 163)

Tagliamonte and Smith (2000) note that the southward spread is demonstrated by the great number of examples of *was* with plural nouns from the sixteenth and seventeenth centuries in Visser (1970: 71–72). Brunner (1963: 185) also mentions non-standard use of *was* for the north and the Midlands, but only in the 2nd sing., not in the plural.[5]

Nevalainen's (2006) work on the *Corpus of Early English Correspondence* (CEEC) provides detail of the subsequent historical trajectory of variation in past BE. She studied past BE in texts from four sites (London, the Court, the north, East Anglia) and four periods (1440–1519, 1520–1579, 1580–1639, and 1640–1681). She found a gradual decline in the use of *was* with plural subjects from 11% to 5% between the fifteenth and seventeenth centuries. However, in the north, rates of *was* still peaked in the first two sub-periods at levels exceeding 40%. The CEEC data show evidence of the NSR at the time: *was* does not readily occur with pronouns, but it does in, for example, relatives, as illustrated in (7) (2006: 364):

(7) **all other fermholdes of mine** which **was** not lett before [...] (1523 HPERCY 93)

In the third sub-period 1580–1639, the north also favoured *was* in comparison with the other regions, but only just. The last sub-period 1640–1681 no longer showed any significant regional differences. This development went hand-in-hand with a change in effect of subject type: both plural NPs and pronouns now disfavoured the use of *was* and only the plural subject of existential *there* sentences favoured. We will return to the case of existentials in Chapter 5.

Returning to Middle English, Forsström (1948) notes that in the north, the plural forms *ware, were* were sometimes extended into the singular, the opposite of the tendency to use singular *was* with a plural subject. She contemplates an effect of the preterite subjunctive [which had *were* throughout the paradigm at the time LR&DB]. The following example illustrates (1948: 202):

(8) And as **it ware** aboute þe XI houre of þe day, þare began so grete a wynde to blawe ... (Prose A 76/12)

For Early Modern English, Nevalainen (2006: 360) mentions that 'the pattern of *were* used with a singular subject does occur in the affirmative'. This is demonstrated by (9) from the CEEC:

(9) Mr Hatten youre neighbour, who taried to speke with some of the same clarkes (for **owne of them were** then at home); (1545 JJOHNSON 400)

She did not find tokens of *weren't* generalisation in negatives; in the CEEC data, the form *weren't* only occurred with plural subjects and singular *you*.

Summarising, the incidence of non-standard *was* in the historical record shows that there is a historical precedent. In earlier periods in the history of the English language, use of non-standard *was* in the 2nd sing. and pl. was a regular feature of the north and to some extent found in neighbouring regions. However, application of the NSR in the 3rd pl., as well as overall rates of non-standard *was* decreased over time, except in existential *there* sentences. Apart from occasional use in the north, there are no reports of *were*-generalisation, while non-standard *weren't* seems to have been totally absent. We can glean more information regarding further developments in past BE from late nineteenth and twentieth century dialectological studies that have mapped the regional distribution of past BE patterns. They are discussed in the next section.

4.4 Dialectological Research on Past BE

In apparent accordance with the historical record, Wolfram and Sellers (1999: 94) stated that in comparison to *was*-generalisation, '[l]eveling to *were* … appears to be a minority leveling option attested in selected regions of England … and some eastern coastal regions of the United States'. While it seems they meant to say that, unlike *was*-levelling, *were*-levelling does not occur as an innovation (but only in and under the influence of traditionally *were*-levelling dialects, pp. 109–110), their statement has been qualified somewhat by Anderwald (2001: 2–3) and Moore (2011: 347). Occurrences of generalised *were* can be extrapolated from the first systematic dialectological survey conducted by Ellis (1889). Britain (2002: 21) shows that Ellis reported *was*-generalisation for the south-west and south-east (Enfield in the south-east, west Somerset, Norwich, Southwold in Suffolk) and *were*-generalisation for the north Midlands, the north-west and parts of Yorkshire. Generalised *were* was also sporadically found across a wider area of England (Bedford in the east Midlands, Pakenham in Suffolk, Chapel-en-le-Frith in Derbyshire, Skipton in Yorkshire).

Trudgill (2008) has argued against the perception that *was*-generalisation is the majority variant, drawing on Klemola's (2006) analysis of the tape recordings of casual conversations with informants in the *Survey of English Dialects* (SED; Orton and Dieth 1962–1971), too. He maintains that *were*-generalisation has been:

> the non-standard norm in a very large and well-defined area starting in Lancashire and Yorkshire in the north of England and extending through the central Midlands as far south as Bedfordshire. The other counties included in the area are Derbyshire, Staffordshire, Nottinghamshire, Leicestershire, Rutland, Northamptonshire, Cambridgeshire, and Huntingdonshire. *Were*-levelling is also very common in another contiguous area in the southwest of England that covers Somerset, Wiltshire, and Dorset. (2008: 349)

Trudgill additionally envisages that (what he terms) r-generalisation was more widely distributed across England than it is today. He notes, for example, that while the local dialect of Norfolk nowadays has generalised *was*, Forby ([1830] 1969: 141) writes with respect to the early nineteenth century Norfolk dialect of 'our constant use of *war* for *was*' (Trudgill 2008: 350). Trudgill considers this plausible as Norfolk borders Cambridgeshire, part of the r-area that Klemola (2006) postulated on the basis of the SED tape recordings. Trudgill assumes that generalised –s spread from the Home Counties and other areas in the south-east to formerly r-generalisation areas and outwards to colonial territories. He concludes that the occurrence of –s generalisation in the far north of England must have been a separate development [namely, a remainder from earlier periods in the history of English; see Sect. 4.3 LR&DB].

In his diachronic study, Trudgill offers a pan-Germanic perspective, showing that the /s/~/r/ alternation that we (still) observe in present-day Standard English (*was/were*) resulted from a series of Germanic sound changes that applied to the verb *wesan*. One is Verner's Law, which led to /s/~/z/ alternation through the voicing of voiceless fricatives. The other concerned a sound change called 'rhotacism' (McMahon 1994: 74), which 'turned [z] into [r] in certain contexts'. The pattern survives in a number of Germanic dialects, such as present-day Standard English and also contemporary Dutch that has preserved a mixed /s/~/r/ paradigm (*was/waren*). In the majority of Germanic languages, however, it has been levelled out over the past millennium. Importantly, Trudgill demonstrates that the generalisation can go either way and does not especially favour either the s-forms or the r-forms. For example, the far north and the south-east of England, North America, the Southern Hemisphere, and Afrikaans have all settled for –s (*was*), while Continental Scandinavian languages (*var*), and Standard German (*war/waren*) have gone the route of –r. Schreier (2002b) has contrasted the levelling to *were* in traditional British English dialects with transplanted (post)colonial varieties of English, which show a trend towards *was* as a pivot form.[6]

Other surveys corroborate the distribution of past BE in England as outlined by Trudgill (2008). Pietsch (2005) consulted SED survey data from northern dialects (the basic- and the incidental Material in Orton and Dieth 1962–1971). He found that speakers in the central north (the four northernmost counties of Cumberland, Northumberland, Westmorland and Durham) mostly used *was/were* according to the standard past BE paradigm except where the Northern Subject Rule admitted a generalised form of *was* (2005: 150; see Sect. 4.5.4 for further discussion of the NSR in relation to past BE). In contrast, non-standard *were* was used in 'a compact area centring around southern Lancashire, south-western Yorkshire ... and Derbyshire' in the north-west Midlands. In this connection, he notes that work by Shorrocks (1999) has shown the occurrence of generalised *were* in Bolton in the 1970–1980s. Pietsch adds that '[i]n a broad transitional belt from th[e *were-*]area into the central north, covering northern Lancashire and the north-eastern half of Yorkshire, singular *were* forms are also occasionally recorded but less frequent.' In Cheshire et al's. (1989) *Survey of British Dialect Grammar* amongst 87 schools around Britain, non-standard *were* was 'frequently reported' (next to non-standard *was*) in the north-west, Yorkshire and Humberside, and in the Midlands, as well as being present, but at lower levels, in the south (1989: 201).

Anderwald (2001) obtained a somewhat different result from the late twentieth century *British National Corpus* (BNC). In positive clauses, generalised *were* occurred significantly less frequently than generalised *was* (6.7% vs. 12.2% overall, respectively) (2001: 5). In 60% of the 18 dialect areas that she distinguished, generalised *was* dominated in positive contexts, particularly in East Anglia (41%) and an area from the mid south-west to the north-east (2001: 5). The result seems a corollary of the association of *were*-generalisation with negative sentences, to which we now turn.

Anderwald (2001) observed the greatest generalisation effect in negative clauses (24% vs. 8% in positive clauses). Furthermore, in the majority of areas that could be tested, *weren't* generalisation was favoured over *wasn't*-generalisation. Anderwald (2001) lists four areas as demonstrating a preference for *were(n't)* in both positive and negative clauses: London, the south Midlands, the central north and the north-east. Only speakers in the north-west Midlands generalised both *was* as well as *wasn't*. 58% of the dialect areas in Anderwald's study showed a mixed pattern of generalisation to *was* in positive clauses and *weren't* in negative clauses (2001: 10–12). She concludes that '*wasn't* is clearly not a favoured generalization strategy' (2001: 6).[7] Cheshire and Fox (2009) think that the mixed pattern is a relatively recent use in the history of vernacular English. They point out that Nevalainen (2006: 360) found no difference in negative contexts between the use of *was* and *were* in the regional component of the *Corpus of Early English Correspondence*, which covers the period from 1410 to 1681 (albeit that negative forms of past BE are not very frequent in the data) (see Sect. 4.3). However, the studies by Anderwald (2001) and Pietsch (2005) suggest that in Britain the mixed pattern is, at least currently, quite widespread. According to Pietsch (2005: 151), '[t]his effect is discernible in all parts of the *SED* data except the central north and those parts of the NW Midlands and lower north where *were* levelling is predominant in all environments.' The *Survey of British Dialect Grammar* (Cheshire et al. 1989: 201) reported very frequent use of non-standard *weren't*. 10 schools scattered across the country reported *weren't* but not *were*, confirming that *were* levelling may be restricted to negative contexts. The mixed *was/weren't* pattern was, for example, documented in four schools in the city of Birmingham (West Midlands). At these schools, there were no reports of non-standard *were* in positive contexts, but 50% of all negative contexts were reported as being *weren't*—for example '*Mary weren't singing*'—whilst levelling to *was* in positive plural contexts amounted to 75%. However, the numbers were very small and later, in data from sociolinguistic interviews with Birmingham speakers, Khan (2007) found much lower levels of both non-standard *was* in positive contexts, and non-standard *weren't* in negative contexts.

Findings from the dialectological literature may be summarised as follows: *was*-generalisation, a historically well-attested dialect feature of the north of England, appears to be robust in many parts of Britain. *Were*-generalisation was quite widespread in the nineteenth and twentieth centuries but frequencies seem to have dropped. Nonetheless, *were*-generalisation continues to be found in the form of *weren't* in a mixed *was/weren't* system; a relatively new pattern that has been spreading, both over time and in space.[8] By contrast, extension of *was*-generalisation to *wasn't* in negative contexts is—in comparison—rare.[9] In the following sections, we consider how more small-scale and in-depth variationist studies as well as formal linguistic accounts have contributed insights to our understanding of the development of different past BE patterns, since these are able to provide us with more precise detail on the linguistic embedding of variation.

4.5 Variationist Analyses of Past BE

Among the factors that variationist studies have identified as shaping past BE patterns are:

1. the preservation of past BE forms long attested in the historical record, especially northern *you was*;

4 Past BE 177

2. an ongoing operation of analogical levelling that extends *was* or *were* across the paradigm by analogy with other verbs that show no singular/plural distinction;
3. 'reallocation'—a process whereby locally available variants are put to new purposes, evolving, for example, new social or linguistic functions (Trudgill 1986; Britain 2002; Britain and Trudgill 2005: 183). We discuss new distributions of *was/were* to two specific functional domains: firstly, the domain of polarity (*was/weren't*); and secondly, a particular favouring of *were(n't)* in clause final tags;
4. grammatical conditioning by the Northern Subject Rule (NSR), a constraint which also has a long history and which favours *was* in the context of plural NP and nonadjacent (including pronominal) subjects; or grammatical conditioning by the East Anglian Subject Rule (EASR; from Chapter 3) that imposes the reverse conditioning effect.

We now look at each in turn.

4.5.1 Preservation of Historical Past BE Forms

One well-established claim about variation is that communities that live separated from surrounding populations for an extended period of time tend to preserve features typical of earlier stages in the history of their variety. In their research into diaspora communities of African American English, Walker and Van Herk (2003: 366) have put it this way: 'Because of their isolation from other varieties of English, mainstream or otherwise, they have not participated in changes that have taken place in the time since the communities were founded.' Jennifer Smith (2000) has argued along these lines in her account of non-standard *was* in Buckie. Buckie is a small town situated on the coast of north-east Scotland that has had a stable population of around 8000. It is a close-knit community largely reliant on the fishing industry. Given its location and the nature of the local economy, residents have restricted levels of contact with outsiders and have remained relatively isolated from mainstream (linguistic) developments up to the present day. Smith's sample

178   L. Rupp and D. Britain

consisted of eight speakers ranging from 76–83 years. The overall rates of non-standard *was* amounted to 58%. *You* showed very high rates of non-standard *was* (91%), even higher than existential *there*. There were also high rates of *was* with 3rd pl. NPs (81%) and in 1st pl. contexts (73% non-standard *was*) (although actually only *you* and *there* favoured *was* in a variable rule analysis). In sharp contrast, Buckie speakers showed categorical use of standard *were* with the 3rd pl. pronoun *they*. The examples below are from Buckie (Smith and Tagliamonte 1998: 106, 110; Adger and Smith 2005: 154; 2010: 1110; Adger 2006: 513):

(10) a. Aye, I thocht **you was** a scuba diver.
      b. My mother died four year a-fore **we was** married.
      c. **The mothers was** roaring at ye coming in.
      d. **They were** wild as anything.
      e. There **was other ones**, coopers again.

Smith (2000) suggests that the most relevant perspective on the patterning of past BE in Buckie is one of a historical BE paradigm having persisted in a contemporary variety of English. Specifically, she argues that the use of *was* in the 2nd sing. is likely to be a retention since northern dialects have been reported to have shown *you was* historically (Försstrom 1948; see also Table 4.1 from Mossé 1952). In a similar way, the NSR constraint that already operated in Middle English, differentiating between pronouns and full NPs, is preserved in the categorical use of *were* with *they* versus the use of *was* with plural NPs. The relative pronoun *that* also favours non-standard *was* in Buckie (Smith and Tagliamonte 1998: 120), apparently continuing a tendency from Middle English for relative clauses to favour levelling to *was* (Forsström 1948: 207) under the Proximity Effect of the NSR. Smith and Tagliamonte (1998) think that the use of non-standard *was* with *we*, by contrast, is a later development and not a continuation of a historical pattern. They refer to Forsström (1948) who has demonstrated that historically the use with *we* has been very rare.

4.5.2 Analogical Levelling

We move on to the factor of analogical levelling, a form of language change that extends *was* or *were* beyond its original scope in the paradigm. Following McMahon (1994: 74), 'analogical levelling can be thought of as a natural tendency in language to implement an association of one form with one meaning', thus implementing/restoring isomorphism, one of the core components of diagrammatic iconicity (Chapter 1). In the case of past BE, the historical sound changes that we discussed earlier in this chapter (Verner's Law and rhotacism in Germanic) led to an opaque situation in which two different forms, *was* and *were*, both mark past tense. Selecting one allomorph and extending it across the past BE paradigm levels out the /s/~/r/ variation. Fries (1940) has stated that levelling of the past BE paradigm is a continuation (or extension) of a system-wide loss in English where no other verb retains a singular/plural distinction in the past tense. In the context of *was*-based levelling, he writes: 'This use of *was* is a carrying through of the levelling to a single form which affected all the preterits of strong verbs in early Modern English. As a matter of fact, the verb *to be* with its preterit singular *was* and preterit plural *were* is the only verb left out of more than a hundred that had, up to the time of Shakespeare, distinct forms for singular and plural in the past tense' (1940: 52). In the context of analogical levelling, Hock (1986: 168) commented: '[alternations] which do not seem to signal (important) differences in meaning ... tend to be eliminated'. Accordingly, it can be argued that like verbal –s, the resulting levelled past BE form no longer (redundantly) marks agreement with the subject, but only past tense, while person and number features are encoded on the subject.

Hock (1986: Chapter 10) and McMahon (1994) discuss work by both Kuryłowicz (1949) and Mańczak (1958, 1980) who have postulated that there are apparent laws and tendencies guiding the directionality of analogical change. Among these are the rules that 'basic' forms and/or frequent forms (what Kuryłowicz (1949: 23) calls the *sphère d'emploi* 'sphere of usage' provision) function as the pivot of levelling. They have frequently been invoked to motivate the perception that

180   L. Rupp and D. Britain

analogical levelling readily proceeds in the direction of 3rd sing. forms (that is, *was*). Hock, however, reports that cross-linguistic evidence for the basicness of the category of 3rd sing. is actually meagre, while McMahon (1994) has argued that it is notoriously difficult to define a 'basic' form. She maintains that there is nothing to suggest that we will be able to predict when analogy will occur, 'or what pathways it can follow when it does operate': 'even the most regular types of analogy do not lend themselves to prediction, since they never seem to be obligatory, but represent only one possible reaction to a particular situation' (1994: 76). Hock (1986) highlights Verner's Law in this connection, which derived /r/- from the earlier /s/-forms in Germanic, with some Germanic languages like German subsequently levelling these /r/-forms rather than /s/.[10] Hock (1986) notes that while basicness may not make a particular form suitable as the basis or pivot for levelling, there is good evidence that frequent usage seems to enable forms to resist analogical change more than other vocabulary (see, for example, Bybee and Hopper 2001: 17 for more extensive discussion). Together with the factor of normative pressure, this may have played a role in the retention of the *was/were* alternation in Standard English.

As areas where *was*-levelling is underway, Beal (2004, with reference to Beal and Corrigan 2000) and Anderwald (2004) report Tyneside in the north-east of England and the south-east (London and the so-called Home Countries surrounding it), respectively. Recall from Sect. 4.3 that non-standard *was* in the north is historical *was* and subject to the NSR. The *Newcastle Electronic Corpus of Tyneside English* (NECTE; Corrigan et al. 2001–2005) shows that the NSR continued to constrain the use of non-standard *was*, inhibiting *was*-levelling (Cole 2008: 109). This is illustrated by data like *I worked with **these women** which I thought **was** old then … to me **they were** old* [NECTE 1994] (Cole 2008: 103). Currently, however, according to Beal (2004), the more usual past BE pattern is for speakers in Tyneside to use *was* throughout the paradigm, even with the pronouns *we, you, they*; a pattern that the NSR would/ should normally prohibit. For the south-east, Anderwald (2004) finds in the *Freiburg English Dialect Corpus* (FRED), next to occurrences of *was* with plural NPs, almost categorical use of *was* in the context of the pronouns *we, you* and *they*. This is illustrated with the examples (11a–d) below (2004: 182–183). Negative examples were few in the FRED corpus but where they occurred the levelled form was *wasn't* rather than *weren't*.

(11) a. **We was** never without food.
      b. So **you was** a week on labour, a week off.
      c. They lost their mother when **they was** boys.
      d. And that was when **the first aeroplanes was** built, over at Eastchurch.

Feagin (1979) also assumes that *was*-generalisation in the English of Anniston, Alabama, is an instance of current analogical levelling. Her reasoning is that informants in her study showed very high rates of *was* (especially in the working-class category, ranging from 48.9% up to 98.1%, p. 202) but did not make a distinction between using levelled *was* with pronouns or with NPs, which one would expect if the NSR applied (only females in the urban working class used less *was* with *they*). Here are some examples (1979: 204):

(12) a. **Was you** a majorette?
      b. **We was** in an ideal place for it.
      c. And **all the student teachers** that **was** comin'out to Wellborn were scared to, 'cause they might get cut up, you know!
      d. **They 'uz** all born in Georgie – Mama and my daddy, both.
      e. There **was about twenty somethin' boys** [...]

Verbal –s, by contrast, while less widespread and apparently on its way out, did show reflexes of the NSR. With *we, you* and *they* as subjects, the standard zero ending was categorical. With NP-subjects, the figures amounted to 1% for the Upper Class, 31.9% for the urban Working Class, and 58% for the rural Working Class informants of Feagin's study (1979: 187 ff.). In the variety of English spoken in Harrison County, Indiana, José (2007: 260–262) has similarly found the NSR to hold except for past BE: the use of verbal –s is restricted to 3rd pl. NPs, but past BE (levelled *was*) is used with various personal pronouns.

This patterning corroborates the idea that the NSR with past BE, where it occurs, is (only) derivative of the NSR with verbal –s, a perspective that will be discussed in Sect. 4.5.4.

While determining the direction of analogical levelling has proven difficult, variationist researchers have identified factors that may affect the rate at which analogical levelling progresses. Schreier (2002a, b) presents the English variety spoken in Tristan da Cunha (TdCE) in the South Atlantic as one of the first varieties in which levelling of *was* has nearly gone to completion, which he ascribes to the distinctive settlement history of the island. Overall levelling values are extremely high compared to other varieties; in fact, nearly categorical; viz. 2nd sing. *you* 88.9%; 1st pl. *we* 97.7%; 2nd pl. *you* 100%; NP pl. 94.9%; 3rd pl. *they* 90.2%; and existential pl. 96.3%; reaching a total amount of 93.8%. Here are some examples of the TdCE fully levelled *was* system (2002b: 83–84):

(13) a. **You was** fishin' all the time in them days.
   b. **We was** invited to the crew's bar an' all.
   c. "Where **you ALL was?**", he said.
   d. **The cow's horns was** quite wide.
   e. One day **they was** out campin'.
   f. At that time **it was** no gas stoves.

Schreier (2002b) concludes that this extensive *was*-generalisation in TdCE is an innovation. He notes that while some of the founders of the community came from areas for which *was*-levelling has been reported, the scope of the influence has been difficult to establish. Instead, Schreier assumes that *was*-levelling furthered and accelerated as a result of contact dynamics, given that the island was settled by a diverse population with different linguistic backgrounds (recall from Chapter 3 that TdCE also shows absence of 3rd sing. –s). He also assumes that the regularised past BE paradigm has been sustained by external factors; such as immobility, a long period of being virtually cut off and thus far removed from the influence of other speakers, close-knit networks and the absence of normative pressure of the standard variety from institutionalised education. Schreier points out that quasi-categorical levelling to *was* has also been reported for similarly comparatively isolated and immobile communities that are quite removed from the effects of prescriptive norms. Among these are the enclaves Beech Bottom and Roaring Creek in the mountains of western North Carolina, where Mallinson and Wolfram (2002) investigated both European and African American speakers. Their data demonstrated levelling to *was* at rates between 76.5 and 100% for speakers across all age groups and both ethnicities, regardless of subject type (2002: 756).

Peter Trudgill (1989: 228) maintains that, conversely, the rate of levelling may be intensified in high-contact communities. He argues that high-contact communities tend to reduce morphological complexity, thereby producing simpler systems, because they come into contact with so many different usage norms that it can become impossible to assign functions (whether grammatical or social) to all of them. His view receives support from Cheshire et al.'s (1989: 201) finding that *was*-generalisation is frequent in urban centres.[11]

4.5.3 Reallocation

A further constellation of past BE is the use of *was* alongside *weren't.* Here we see an alternative, perhaps more complex twofold levelling process, resulting in "'remorphologization" [whereby the two *was* and *were*] allomorphs of past BE come to be used to distinguish positives from negatives, rather than to mark person-number distinctions, as they do in Standard English' (Schilling-Estes and Wolfram 1994: 289). That is, speakers deploy *was* and *were* as markers of polarity; specifically, *was* in affirmative clauses and the form *weren't* in negative clauses. In general this mixed pattern seems to occur in varieties that once had a fully levelled *were* system. As we will see, some varieties have a system where the extension to *weren't* is restricted to clause-final tags.

Schilling-Estes and Wolfram (1994) were among the first to observe the pattern, on Ocracoke—one of the most remote islands on the Outer Banks, a chain of islands off the coast of North Carolina. Ocracoke has around 6000 residents; only recently have tourists started to visit the island after a period of long-term insularity (for further details of the socio-demographic history of Ocracoke, see Schilling-Estes and Wolfram

1994). Schilling-Estes and Wolfram held interviews with 45 residents, aged 10 to 82. They assume that past BE levelling in Ocracoke has been pivoting on the *were* allomorph. This is because they observed *were*-generalisation in the speech of their oldest informants. The examples in (14) (from Schilling-Estes and Wolfram 1994: 280) illustrate that *were* is found with subjects of all persons and both numbers:

(14) a. **I were** afraid I was going to miss something.
      b. Yeah, what was that **you were** talking about the other day?
      c. **We were** married about six, seven years before we got this house.
      d. **The neighborhood** she was in **were** just like the old Germans.
      e. **There were** always something going on.

In subsequent research (Wolfram and Schilling-Estes 2003a: 210–211), they point out that *were*-generalisation exists but is relatively rare among American dialects—in current research it has only been documented in a few places along the mid-Atlantic coast of the United States. The more common pattern is for past BE to be regularised to *was*, as in *we was home* or *you wasn't there*. In work from 2005, Wolfram and Schilling-Estes suggest that *were*-regularisation as it occurs in the United States is a founder effect from south-west England (referring to evidence provided by the *Survey of English Dialects* of Orton and Dieth 1962–1971) and developed into a regional feature of coastal varieties (2005: 184–185). While the *Linguistic Atlas of the Middle and South Atlantic States* suggests that *were*-levelling might have been a little less confined, Wolfram and Schilling-Estes (2003a: 212–213) think that it has always been a minority variant in the historical development of American English.

In Ocracoke, *were*-generalisation is no longer common in positive sentences, however. Schilling-Estes and Wolfram (1994: 285) only found 1% *were*-levelling amongst older- and middle-aged speakers and conclude that this use has relic status. Nowadays negative clauses are a more productive context; here they observed rates of nearly 50% levelling to the negative form *weren't*. Examples of this are shown in (15) (1994: 280):

4 Past BE 185

(15) a. I called them and told them **I weren't** going to work that summer.
b. I came to see you yesterday, but **you weren't** home.
c. **My father weren't** here.
d. **It weren't** me and it **weren't** Linda.
e. **We weren't** really interested in learning.
f. Y'all was supposed to go talk to them, **weren't you?**
g. They'd just let them out; **they weren't** wild.

The strength of *weren't* levelling in the negative in Ocracoke, they point out, is highlighted by the fact that speakers use *weren't* even in existential *there* sentences, as in *There weren't a hurricane*. This occurred in both the singular (61.1%) and the plural (71.4%). It is noteworthy because existentials otherwise have the highest incidence of *was* across varieties of English world-wide (1994: 283, 285). Next to *weren't* levelling, all the informants showed [in effect, innovative LR&DB] levelling to (non-standard) *was* in positive sentences, though levels were relatively low (21.6%) as compared with other vernacular varieties in the United States (for example Feagin (1979: 202) reported over 90% *was*-generalisation among her older rural Alabama working-class speakers). Schilling-Estes and Wolfram (1994) envisage that the emergence of *was* in the English of Ocracoke is due to a combination of factors: influence of the standard English paradigm, contact with surrounding *was*-levelling varieties on the U.S. mainland as a result of increasing tourism on the island, and a by-product of the correlation of *were(n't)*-regularisation with negative clauses. Schilling-Estes (2002), who observed increasingly high *was/weren't* levels in the more northerly situated community of Smith Island, thinks that the innovative mixture may have made its way into coastal sites via men's external contacts in, for example, the fishing trade (2002: 71–73).

However, in a context in which Ocracoke appears to be moving towards a *was/weren't* polarity system, cross-generational analysis showed that rates of non-standard *was* had in fact dropped among the younger speakers: 9.4% contra 16.2% among middle-aged speakers (1994: 287).[12] That is, while the youngest speakers would have been expected to show the most advanced stage of this reorganisation of past BE, using a system in which *was*-levelling is only deployed in positive sentences and levelling to *weren't* confined to negative clauses, the regularisation pattern began by previous generations has not been fully realised: levelling to *was* is even declining at the same time that levelling to *weren't* is further intensifying. Britain (2002) has confirmed that *weren't*-levelling and *was*-levelling may follow two distinct trajectories. In a study of speakers in the Fens in the United Kingdom, levelling to *weren't* in negative contexts (88.4%) exceeded that of *was* in positive contexts (62.8%) (2002: 27, 29). Thus, levelling to *weren't* can exist independently of the restructuring of *was* (as the positive variant in a *was/weren't* system). Wolfram and Schilling-Estes (2003a: 223) remark that this is somewhat surprising as 'the unique association of levelling to *was* with positive forms while levelling to *weren't* with negative forms would seem like a natural symmetry'.[13] Schilling-Estes and Wolfram (1994: 294) present several explanations as to why there has not been 'ideal' categorical *was/weren't* levelling in Ocracoke: (1) *were* has been the traditional pivot for past BE levelling, whereas the non-standard *was* form is more recent; (2) *was(n't)*- regularisation is far more stigmatised than the use of *weren't* (which in fact, so Schilling-Estes and Wolfram assert, has been assigned symbolic meaning as an indicator of island identity); and, as will be outlined below, (3) *weren't* has a parallel in other negative verb forms.

Schilling-Estes and Wolfram (1994) make the important observation that in their Ocracoke data, negative past BE-levelling only occurred in the form *weren't* but not as *were not* (viz. **She **were not** on the boat yesterday*; 1994: 281). In this relation, they go on to note that there is a clear precedent for the occurrence of polarity dichotomies of the type *was/weren't*. Cheshire (1981: 366) pointed out that several verbs already had two different forms in earlier periods in the history of the English language: one with a short vowel used in positive sentences and one with a long vowel used in negative sentences. Some of these distinctions have been retained, such as *can* [kæn] and *can't* [kɑːnt] in southern England. Other negative verb forms that show a phonetic shift in the stem are no longer neatly decomposable (Wolfram and Sellers 1999: 100) and cannot be related to their positive counterparts by regular phonological rules anymore. Examples of such pairs are *will* and *won't* and *am/is/are* and *ain't*.[14] Schilling-Estes and Wolfram (1994) report that in the Ocracoke data, occurrences of *ain't* represent 95% of all bound negative forms in the present tense, making it the present tense equivalent of past tense *weren't*.[15] In view of this, they think that *ain't* has served as a basis for levelling to *weren't* by analogical extension. Schilling-Estes and Wolfram (1994) hence group *weren't* with other negative allomorphs and find that their view is strengthened by Zwicky and Pullum's (1983) syntactic analysis of negative *n't*-constituents. Zwicky and Pullum consider *n't*-constituents to be lexical units (*weren't*). They reject the possibility that they derive from independent negation (*not*) through a process of cliticization. One of the arguments that Zwicky and Pullum (1983) put forward in support of their analysis is that uncontracted negative forms (for example *can not*) can convey a meaning that uncontracted forms (for example *can't*) lack. For illustration, in (16a), the Christian can be saved yet not attend church, but attend and still not be saved in (16b) (1983: 509). Note here that Zwicky and Pullum crucially assume that there is only one uncontracted form *not*, which can function as either sentence or constituent negation (1983: 512).

(16) a. A good Christian can not attend church and still be saved.
b. A good Christian can't attend church and still be saved.

In the framework of the Minimalist Program (Chomsky 1995), it is natural to assume that *weren't* is directly inserted into T(ense) (or NEG for that matter) (as illustrated in (17a)), instead of a form that is derived from movement from a lower node into NEG (as illustrated in (17b)), where *not* could attach to *were*. Note that this analysis emerges from the minimalist assumption that lexical items are fully inflected in the lexicon and only check their grammatical features in the syntax. It also rules out the occurrence of non-standard *were not*.

(17) a.   b.

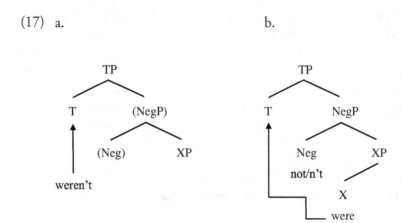

In research on the use of non-standard *weren't* on Smith Island, Maryland, Mittelstaedt and Parrott (2002) offer a comparable account within the theoretical framework of Distributed Morphology (DM; Halle and Marantz 1993; see also Parrott 2007). Following Mittelstaedt and Parrott, DM postulates an additional, distinct level of representation, Morphological Structure (MS), located between the level of syntax and morphology. The syntactic computations deliver bundles of morphosyntactic features, called terminal nodes, to MS where they are subject to further morphological operations. The final morphological operation, termed Vocabulary Insertion, inserts phonological features that are available in a set of Vocabulary Entries (VE). As illustrated in (18a), in Standard English, the negation node is distinct from the node containing the agreement features. Therefore, the VE's for *were* and *not* will be inserted separately. Mittelstaedt and Parrott assume that in the variety of English spoken on Smith Island, by contrast, a particular morphological operation of 'Fusion' blends the phonological features of the tense and negation nodes. Hence, a single VE, namely *weren't*, is inserted into the resulting node. This is illustrated in (18b):

(18) a.   b.

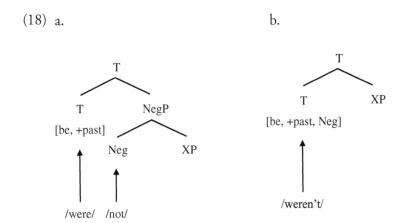

This again captures the lack of *were*-levelling in the context of *not*: *not* is inserted only when the negation has not undergone Fusion. Mittelstaedt and Parrot (2002) point out that this would also explain why *weren't*-levelling can proceed without *were*-levelling. From the perspective of DM, *weren't*-levelling is not a process affecting agreement features, but rather a process affecting the morphological realisation of negation. Therefore, *weren't*-levelling does not cause (or require) any concurrent levelling in the agreement paradigm. By the same token, we expect *was*-levelling not to be impacted in *was/weren't* varieties, as Schilling-Estes and Wolfram (1994) and Britain (2002) have shown. Finally, Mittelstaedt and Parrott (2002) raise the relevant question of whether 'the new *weren't* VE [is] made necessary by the Fusion operation, or [whether] Fusion takes place in order to provide an insertion terminal for the new VE?' (2002: 9). By the end of this chapter it will have become clear that we assume the latter scenario, as we will go on to suggest that the use of the form *weren't* has independent iconic motivation. A second argument concerns the analogical relationship with *ain't* (Schilling-Estes and Wolfram 1994: 290), a fused form that is not analysable as two component parts (*ai not*).

190 L. Rupp and D. Britain

In the United Kingdom, Cheshire (1982) had, in fact, already observed the *was/weren't* pattern in the speech of teenagers in the town of Reading. She found that levelling to non-standard *was* reached 83%—even higher among core members of the group. Further, while levels of nonstandard *were* were very low in positive sentences (ranging from 1 to 4%), in negative sentences they amounted to approximately 40% overall (the group of the Orts Road boys exceeded 50%). This finding led her to suggest that negation is marked rather than grammatical person: 'In Reading English it is negation that is marked, though marking is variable: when the verb is negated, there is an increase of *weren't*, with all subjects, and when the verb is not negated, the form "was" tends to occur with all subjects' (1982: 45).

In his study of the Fens (situated between East Anglia and the Midlands), Britain (2002) has described a situation very similar to that of Schilling-Estes and Wolfram's (1994) Ocracoke: the gradual replacement of a long-standing characteristically levelled *were*-system by a twentieth century *was/weren't* pattern that gets increasingly entrenched. His sample consisted of two groups of older speakers (born between 1925 and 1945) and younger speakers (born between 1960 and 1975) in Norfolk, Fenland, (east) Cambridgeshire and the South Holland district of south-east Lincolnshire. In addition to his own sample of 80 speakers, he studied recordings of eleven over 70-year-old Fenland speakers born around the turn of the twentieth century that were held in a local museum. He found robust levelling to *were* in contexts of standard *was* in the oldest informants. By contrast, young people in the Fens born after 1960 showed high levelling to *was* (91%) (at the expense of non-standard *were*), and almost exclusively used *weren't* in negative contexts (96%).

As Britain (2002) notes, there is evidence from previous research to suggest that *were*-generalisation has been a robust feature of the Fenland variety for well over a century. The dialectologist Ellis (1889) did not focus on morphological variation, but demonstrates, amongst other things, that in parts of the east Midlands (slightly to the west of the Fens) and in East Anglia (to the east of the Fens), non-standard *were* occurred in positive clauses in the nineteenth century. (19a–b) are examples from the county of Bedford (bordering the Cambridgeshire Fens) and (19c) is from East Anglia (1889: 207 and 273, respectively):

(19) a. **It were** so queer.
  b. **The kettle were** a-boiling.
  c. As **I were** a-saying.

More support derives from Kökeritz (1932: 214) who provides transcriptions of a number of early recordings of Suffolk dialect (to the immediate south-east of the Fens). These include examples of levelling to *were*; for example *he were* [wɛːɾ] *a-whinnocking*. Evidence is also provided by Ojanen's (n.d.) study from the 1970s of 18 speakers aged 70–94 from 14 Cambridgeshire villages. In the north, mainly in northwest Cambridgeshire, Ojanen attested levels of *were* at over 90% and there were speakers who used no non-standard tokens of *was* at all. This northern area was split off from an area of *was*-speakers, which covered roughly the north-eastern, south-eastern and south-western parts of Cambridgeshire. These are examples of a *were*- and *was*-speaker from Ojanen (n.d: 5, 8), respectively:

(20) a. Well, I'm please(d) to see you Ernie. I– I knowed you were about ... **He were** a good horse.
  b. I was a horsekeeper ... Times are different now'n what **they was** then.

Negative contexts showed a dominance of *weren't* regardless of the levelling orientation of the speaker; thus, both *was/weren't* and *were/weren't* occurred, and overall levelling to *weren't* reached 86.5%.[16]

Vasko (2010) is a more extensive, later study by the same researcher with a greater scope this time including the far north of Cambridgeshire. The number of informants was larger, too: 50 speakers from 26 localities in southern Cambridgeshire and 52 speakers from 20 localities in northern Cambridgeshire (historically the Isle of Ely).[17] Overall she found that geographical boundaries are now more fuzzy than in her earlier research: levelled *were* occurred in the south-western part of Cambridgeshire, and levelled *was* notably in three regions: the south-east, east and far north. Vasko subscribes to other dialectological work that Cambridgeshire can be characterised as a transitional area, from the east to the west as well as from the south to the north, and suggests that the current predominance of *was* in the region is most likely the result of the spread of this variant from south-east England. In view of Ojanen's (n.d.) data, which showed that *was/weren't* was dominant in the southernmost parts of Cambridgeshire but *were/weren't* further north, Britain (2002) likewise assumes that *was* has been diffusing northwards from the south across the Fens. He notes that the Fens have come under the increasing influence of London and other varieties from the south-east of England as a result of which the older *were* forms are now disappearing. However, similar to what Schilling-Estes and Wolfram (1994) have argued for Ocracoke in relation to mainstream U.S. varieties, in the Fens this has not led to an entire attrition of the traditional dialect form in favour of a fully levelled *was/wasn't* system. Instead, the historical availability of the *were*-variant has allowed Fenland English to focus on a system of the *was/weren't* kind and to shift from a *were/weren't* to a *was/weren't* dialect of English within three generation of speakers, as the apparent time data suggest.

Cheshire and Fox (2009) have recently found comparable patterns to those of the Fens in London. They studied past BE in a sample of elderly and adolescent speakers in multi-cultural Inner London and a parallel sample of predominantly white Outer London speakers. Different from the traditional dialect of the Fens, the south-east of England has been categorised as a *was*-levelling area (Ellis 1889) and, correspondingly, Cheshire and Fox (2009) found no evidence of levelling to *were* in affirmative contexts, only levelling to *was*. Nevertheless, they report differences between elderly speakers and adolescents in Outer London that are much like those documented in the Fens, demonstrating that dialect levelling to a mixed *was/weren't* system is also advancing there. The rates of non-standard *weren't* were higher in Outer London than in Inner London and higher among adolescents than among the elderly (Inner London adolescents: 41%; Inner London elderly: 17%; Outer London adolescents 69%; Outer London elderly

14%—the latter only used the form in tags) (2009: 22). Regarding levelled *was*, the use of non-standard *was* by the Outer London adolescents was considerably higher (58%) than that of the elderly speakers (19.2%) and in fact compared to the Inner London elderly speakers (who showed 51.5% use of non-standard *was*) (2009: 14). Cheshire and Fox observe that increasing *was*-levelling across apparent time is expected in the development of a *was/weren't* pattern (viz. Schilling-Estes and Wolfram 1994), and postulate that the pattern appears to demonstrate convergence towards a south-eastern norm. Levey (2007: 43–44) also found a mixed system amongst groups of preadolescents in the London area, though it was less advanced than in the Fens. The group consisted of 48 children aged 7–11 from a multicultural school in the outer east London borough of Redbridge. They showed levelling to *was* in contexts of standard *were* at 55% and *weren't* in contexts of standard *wasn't* at 37%.

In addition to the research discussed in this section, Tagliamonte (2009: 121) has reported the *was/weren't* pattern for Tiverton, a rural community in the south-west of England, (possibly) the small town of Wheatley Hill in the north-east, and Culleybacky in County Antrim in Northern Ireland. The pattern has also been observed by Wolfram and Thomas (2002) among European Americans and elderly African American speakers in Hyde Country, North Carolina. (Younger African Americans, on the other hand, appeared to have turned to 'a more generalized version of *was* regularization in both negatives and positives – the common pattern for AAVE elsewhere' (2002: 75), hence, showing an advanced state of levelling of *was* in the past tense paradigm of the verb *be*). Wolfram and Sellers (1999) contend that Native American Lumbee Indians have configured *weren't* in their own way, namely, with 1st sing. subjects (*I weren't*). They have interpreted this use as an apparent act of identity vis-á-vis two other ethnolinguistic groups who live in the same locale and show more generalised *weren't* (1999: 110).

The varieties that we have examined above show the reallocation of *weren't* across the entire negative past BE paradigm. In some other dialects, *weren't* has similarly been reallocated, but it is restricted to a specific domain, namely clause final tags. In some cases, the appearance of

194   L. Rupp and D. Britain

non-standard *weren't* in tags appears to be an innovation. In others it derives from a previously *were-weren't* paradigm.

Moore (2011) studied the urban centre of Bolton in north-west England as an example of an area where a levelled *were*-system has traditionally existed but now appears to be in some decline: Bolton has relatively low levels of non-standard *were* in positive sentences, yet markedly higher levels of non-standard *weren't*.[18] If existentials are excluded, she found 17.5% non-standard *were* but 44.2% non-standard *weren't* in 1st and 3rd sing. contexts among 12–15 year-old adolescents (calculated from results presented in Moore (2003: 72–73). There was no real evidence of levelled *was*, except in existentials, which confirms the apparent distinctiveness of these constructions (we will return to this at length in Chapter 5). Moore points out that Bolton speakers are by no means socio-geographically isolated, so why have they nonetheless stuck to their admittedly low levels of *were*-levelling? Inquiring into linguistic factors that favour and disfavour non-standard *were*, she concludes that non-standard *were* maintenance is best explained 'by the combined effect of an established correlation between non-standard *were* and local social structures and ongoing revitalization of the form in contemporary forms of social practice' (2011: 347). Specifically, she found, amongst other things, that non-standard *were* was favoured by one of the adolescent communities of practice that she examined, 'The Townies', who engaged most in practices associated with localness. Further, non-standard *were* appeared to have acquired a specialised use in tag-questions in Bolton, as demonstrated by the fact that occurrences of non-standard *were* in this construction (90%) outranked all other uses (2011: 356).

This result resonates with Tagliamonte's (1998) research on past BE in York, another northern city, in a study of four generations of 40 men and 40 women. Interestingly, note that unlike Bolton, York English has no historically levelled *were*. The *Survey of English Dialects* (Orton and Dieth 1962–1971) situated the city of York in a non-standard *was* area, close to an isogloss distinguishing it from an area with non-standard *were*. That is to say that Tagliamonte observed a relatively new phenomenon of *were* levelling in York that was, however, 'very highly circumscribed. It is used predominantly with negative tag questions with *it*'. Young women in particular turned out to be spearheading this specialised use of non-standard *weren't it* (1998: 179). A similar pattern obtained in Cheshire and Fox's London study mentioned earlier. They retrieved high rates of non-standard *weren't* in tags in their adolescent sample, ranging from 63% to categorical usage, virtually all of which occurred with *it* as the subject[19] (2009: 26).

Tagliamonte (1998) suggests that we may see a broader trend toward invariant tag usage in contemporary British English. Indeed, Cheshire and Fox (2009: 25) envisage that 'the frequent collocation of *weren't* and *it* in tags [...] is resulting in an invariant *weren't it* form that functions as a single unanalyzable unit rather than as a decomposable form that shows agreement with a verb and subject of the preceding clause'. While *weren't*-tags in Bolton differed from tags in York and London in that they did not favour *it*, in all three communities, tag questions showed *weren't* regardless of the form of the verb in the matrix clause (see 21a–d).[20]

(21) a. So this was like um November, **weren't it**? (Tagliamonte 1998: 164)
 b. oh yeah cos I stopped burning **weren't it**. (Cheshire and Fox 2009: 25)
 c. and it's about ten questions as well **weren't it**.
 d. that's not good **weren't it**.

Thus, it seems that in Bolton, non-standard *weren't* is being 'revitalised', with tags remaining a healthy context for *weren't*. In York, meanwhile, non-standard *weren't* has been advancing, making particular headway through the route of tag-questions. In these past BE paradigms, therefore, negative tags are the locus of linguistic (re)structuring. (The situation in London is somewhat different in that adolescents, while using *weren't*-tags up to categorical levels, use non-standard *weren't* beyond tags in other contexts.) In this relation, Moore (2011) has pointed out that several studies (Traugott 2001; Schilling-Estes 2004; Woolard 2008; among others) have shown that usage of local features tends to be intensified in discursively weighty contexts. Accordingly, she postulates that tag-questions are likely to show up in a linguistically salient form because of their pragmatic salience. In other words, rather

196 L. Rupp and D. Britain

than speakers simply moving toward a contemporary *was/weren't* pattern, they may submit to a more universal tendency for pragmatically salient constructions to become correlated with marked linguistic behaviour. We will return to this perspective in Sect. 4.6 when we present our account of past BE that invokes the notion of iconicity.

4.5.4 Grammatical Conditioning: The Northern and East Anglian Subject Rules

In Chapters 2 and 3, we explored the application of the Northern Subject Rule (NSR) to verbal –s and that of the East Anglian Subject Rule (EASR) to the emergent use of –s in varieties that traditionally had verbal zero. In this section, we explore to what extent the NSR and the EASR condition variation in past BE.

We recall from earlier parts of this chapter that historical grammars and work by Murray (1873) have established that the NSR has conditioned the occurrence of historical ('northern') non-standard *was* from the Middle English period onwards. Montgomery (1994) demonstrates continuation of the NSR to the effect that he found it to be an important constraint on both verbal –s and past BE in written documents of Scots English and Scots-Irish (Ulster) English from the fourteenth to the seventeenth century. The data in (22) from Montgomery (1994) (cited in Hazen 2000: 131) show a plural NP co-occurring with *was* in a relative clause:

(22) ***the grite offrandis*** *that **was** offrit be riche opulent men*
      the great offerings that was offered by rich opulent men

Pietsch (2005: 149–150), however, reminds us that verbal –s and past BE have undergone separate diachronic trajectories with respect to the NSR. He argues that verbal –s constitutes an older, conservative form that was extended from the singular to the plural, and came to be conditioned by the NSR at the time when the (now standard) zero plural forms were introduced in Middle English. The form *was*, by contrast, is truly singular in origin and *were* the concurrent plural form; *was* was only later extended to those plural uses admitted by the NSR by way of analogy with verbal –s. This implies that the NSR should not occur with past BE where it does not occur with verbal –s. Pietsch (2005) goes on to argue that while *was* joined the NSR late, it has been retaining the NSR longest, so that in some current varieties *was* tends to be the only verb to sustain reflexes of the 'northern' pattern. A case in point is the rural dialect enclave of the Ottawa Valley (Canada) studied by Jankowski and Tagliamonte (2017). In a trend study with two samples of speakers born between 1884–1928 and 1917–1969, they found that verbal –s (as in *The hens roosts* upstairs ...) had declined to a rate of under 1% (2017: 249). However, the long-attested constraint of the NSR still imposed on past BE: occurrences of *was* were influenced by the degree of adjacency between the subject and the verb (cf. ... *three of them* get a hold on the buggy and ah *was* holding it there) and they only marginally occurred with *they* (2017: 250, 252, 255).

Studies of past BE in contemporary varieties demonstrate that the NSR is operative in Reading (Cheshire 1982), Ocracoke (Schilling-Estes and Wolfram 1994), rural South Armagh (Corrigan 1997), York (Tagliamonte 1998), the English of Native American Lumbee Indians and Anglo-Americans in Robeson County, North Carolina (Wolfram and Sellers 1999: 102, 107), Buckie (Smith 2000; briefly addressed in Sect. 4.5.1 in this volume), Nova Scotian Vernacular English in Guysborough Village, Canada (Tagliamonte and Smith 2000: 160),[21] Smith Island, Maryland (Schilling-Estes and Zimmerman 2000: 6), Hyde County (Wolfram and Thomas 2002: 75–76), and the diverse set of localities studied by Tagliamonte (2009: 114–115). Tagliamonte (1998) has shown that in York English, a historical northern *was*-dialect, use of non-standard *was* is, however, on the wane. She did find high rates of levelling to non-standard *was* in existentials (66%) (which is the focus of Chapter 5), but elsewhere rates were low—around 6%; *you* 12%, *we* 9%, *they* 3% and NP plural 7% (1998: 180). Thus, to the extent that non-standard *was* continues to be used in non-existentials at all, speakers use *was* more frequently in the context of plural NPs than with *they*. Tagliamonte thinks that in York English, this NSR-type favouring of plural NP-subjects over *they*, as well as the higher rates of non-standard *was* in the context of 2nd sing. *you,* is a retention from earlier stages in the history of English (see Sect. 4.3 again). York, therefore, seems to present a typical example of Hopper's (1991) 'layering' where an old use of past BE (the NSR) is on its way out but still co-exists with more extended (existentials) and new uses (*weren't* in tags).

Corrigan (1997) asserts that in rural South Armagh (Northern Ireland), the NSR appears to have remained relatively robust, as it could clearly been seen to operate in transcripts of recorded narratives told by male and female speakers born between 1942 and 1974 (52, 185 words). This is illustrated in (23a–b) (1997: Chapter 4).

(23) a. Peter was tellin' of a woman down the North that come to the door while **they were** churnin'.
          *They was....
      b. **The goats was** a complete crook from start to finish.

She ascribes the occurrence of the NSR in South Armagh to language contact with northern English dialects going back to the Plantations, and asks why the NSR should have persisted in South Armagh English contra other dialects that have turned from NSR- into *was*-levelling varieties. In an interesting account of this tenacity of the NSR, she sees a role for Irish substrate influence. Corrigan proposes that the reason why *was* has generalised from NPs to pronouns in many other varieties lies in the loss of morphological marking on pronouns in the history of English. In this sense, pronouns have become more like NPs over time; think, for example, of the loss of case and number distinctions on the 2nd person pronoun. In Irish, on the other hand, pronouns make more morphological distinctions. Alluding to Henry's (1995) configurational account of the NSR (which we discussed in Chapter 2), Corrigan also contemplates that in South Armagh English, the NSR may be a syntactic reflex of Irish VSO order, but she does not develop this idea.

Ocracoke speakers show evidence of the NSR, too. Schilling-Estes and Wolfram (1994: 283) state the following constraint hierarchy for levelled *was*: plural existential *there* 67.9% > NP plural 34.5% > *you* (pl.) 16.7% > they 7.5%, > we 5.9% > you (sing.) 0%. They note that this pattern of *was*-levelling aligns itself with a broader NSR-constraint

4 Past BE 199

on verbal –s in Ocracoke English. Hazen (2000) has recorded verbal –s as a feature of the English spoken on Ocracoke in the 1990s. In a comparative analysis of the historical written Scots-Irish English data of Montgomery (1994) (see Hazen 2000 for details) and data from 18 speakers of contemporary Ocracoke English collected between 1993 and 1995 by the staff of the North Carolina Language and Life Project, Hazen (2000) concludes that Ocracoke verbal –s is of Scots ancestry and was transmitted by Scots-Irish speakers who came to North America.

Probing past BE patterns has also been instrumental in the historical reconstruction of African American Vernacular English (AAVE). Subsequent to two British-U.S. wars, large numbers of African Loyalists and ex-slaves migrated from the United States and populated a range of scattered locations, including Liberia (Singler 1997), Samaná in the Dominican Republic (Poplack and Tagliamonte 1989; Tagliamonte and Smith 1999), Nova Scotia (one of the maritime provinces on the east coast of Canada; Poplack and Tagliamonte 1991), and Sierra Leone (Montgomery 1999). Following Tagliamonte and Smith (2000), because many of these communities were geographically peripheral and/or socio-politically isolated, they can be expected to have preserved a prototype of early AAVE. Tagliamonte and Smith (2000) investigated speakers of African ancestry in the enclaves of North Preston and Guysborough in Nova Scotia. They found favouring of *was* in the 2nd sing. and observation of the NSR (2000: 160). Taking account of Mufwene's (1996) 'founder principle', and drawing a parallel with Buckie, Tagliamonte and Smith argue that this result is best understood as the retention of transplanted northern English features, lending support to the dialectologist (rather than the Creole–) position on the origins of AAVE. Other historically isolated communities for which the NSR has been reported are Robeson County (Wolfram and Sellers 1999: 107) and Hyde County (Wolfram and Thomas 2002: 75–76); however, Mallinson and Wolfram (2002: 751) did not attest it in Beech Bottom.

By contrast, Britain (2002: 32) seems to have observed the *reverse* effect for past BE in the Fens. Overall, there were quite high rates of levelled *was*—overall 62.5%—and speakers showed a constraint order of plural existential *there was* 81% > *you was* 72% > *we was* 67%, > *they was* 54% > plural NP-subject *was* 48% (while singular subjects were used with standard *was* over 90% of the time).[22] This Pro>NP effect is the greatest among the youngest speakers in the corpus, suggesting it is an innovative development, a result that we will address below. It is worth remembering at this point Kingston's (2000) finding regarding 3rd sing. present tense –s marking in the traditionally verbal zero county of Suffolk in England that we presented in Chapter 3. Recall that her informants favoured 3rd sing. –s with pronouns (63%) over full noun phrase subjects (45%). We called this 'reverse NSR pattern' the East Anglian Subject Rule (EASR). In Kingston's (2000) data, the EASR applied to verbal –s only in the 3rd sing. (*he/she/it* vs. singular NP)— recall that in traditional verbal zero areas of East Anglia –s is not used with persons other than 3rd sing. (Trudgill 1996). However, in the case of past BE in the Fens, the EASR applies to the 3rd pl. (where 3rd sing. is the standard *was* context). In trying to understand this pattern, we need to consider a number of factors:

1. Britain (2002) and Wolfram and Schilling-Estes (2005) make complementary observations that are significant for an analysis of the application of the EASR to past BE. Wolfram and Schilling-Estes (2005) comment that varieties that first developed the mixed *was/weren't* system previously were *were*-levelling varieties (to *were/weren't*); hence, as Britain (2002: 31) points out, the change in progress towards a *was/weren't* system *particularly lies in the levelling of 'was'*. He showed that middle-aged and younger speakers in the Fens had much higher levels of non-standard *was* than the oldest speakers (who maintained a good deal of non-standard positive *were*);
2. In a fully levelled *was/weren't* variety, where *was* signals positive polarity, we expect *was* to occur in positive contexts regardless of person or subject type (cf. Schilling-Estes and Wolfram 1994). This expectation is borne out. The Fenland data show a clear reordering of the constraint hierarchy with respect to the effect of type of subject (pronoun vs. NP). The oldest age cohort shows a (what appears to be) slight NSR effect (NPs 0.539 > Pronouns 0.487, $p < 0.001$—the overall hierarchy[23] is: You > We > 3rd pl. NPs > 3rd pl. pronouns).

In contrast, the middle age cohort shows no effect at all (Pronouns 0.501 > NPs 0.499—the overall hierarchy is: You > We > 3rd pl. pronouns > 3rd pl. NPs);

3. Perhaps unexpectedly, the youngest group shows a very clear preference for *was* after pronouns rather than NPs, namely the EASR (Pronouns 0.586, NPs 0.287, *p* < 0.001—the overall hierarchy is: We > You > 3rd pl. pronouns > 3rd pl. NPs). With respect to past BE, then, the Fens appear to be undergoing 'real', structural linguistic change, since we are witnessing the overturning of a major linguistic constraint hierarchy in the grammar.

Vasko (2010) examined past BE in the part of Cambridgeshire just to the south of the Fens (and consequently nearer to the south-east of England). While she found slightly higher rates of non-standard *was* in southern Cambridgeshire as compared to the northern part of the county, the constraint ranking was the same—the percentages for the south amounted to: plural existential 59.2% > *you* 56.7% > *we* 47.9% > *they* 37.9% > plural NP 33.3% (2010: 290). Thus, like Britain (2002), overall Vasko found more non-standard *was* with *they* as well as with other plural pronouns.

We also consider Cheshire and Fox's (2009) London data where, generally, levels of *was*-levelling were quite high. These were the constraint rankings for the four groups of speakers: Inner London elderly: *you* 92.9% > 3rd pl. NP 53.1% > *we* 46.3% > *they* 42.6%; Inner London adolescents: *you* 61.5% > *we* 51.8% > 3rd pl. NP 34.6% > *they* 29.4%; Outer London elderly: *we* > 39.4% > *they* 10.8% > 3rd pl. NP 8.3% > *you* 0%; Outer London adolescents: *you* 82.6% > *we* 45.2% > *they* 45.2% > 3rd pl. NP 27.8% (2009: 14). As in the Fens, non-standard *was* in the context of the plural pronouns *we* and especially *you* (except for the outer London elderly speakers) showed high rates of levelling. Cheshire and Fox (2009) contemplate that the heightened rates of *was* in the context of *you* might be inspired by a desire to (re) install a structural distinction between the 2nd sing. (*you was*) and plural (*you were*) (see Note 5). Further, it can be seen in the figures just cited that Cheshire and Fox (2009) observed an NSR-effect for the inner London speakers but an EASR-effect for those in outer London.

The inner London elderly and adolescents used non-standard *was* more frequently with NPs than with *they* (53.1% NP vs. 42.6% *they* and 34.6% NP vs. 29.4% *they*, respectively). The outer London speakers showed, conversely, higher frequencies with *they* than with NPs (8.3% NP vs. 10.6% *they* in the elderly speakers and 27.8% NP vs. 45.2% *they* in the adolescents). The EASR also seems to be operative in Levey's (2007) London preadolescent corpus, as the rate of levelling to non-standard *was* with 3rd pl. pronouns outstripped levelling to non-standard *was* with plural noun phrases. Here the constraint hierarchy was: *we* 63% > *you* 57% > *they* 55% > and plural NP 41% (2007: 58).

We have additional evidence of the EASR from data collected in other varieties in southern England, specifically from Basildon and Brentwood in south Essex to the north-east of London. Sue Fox collected data among lower working class boys in Basildon, while Sue Baker recorded upper middle class women in Brentwood, just 10 miles away.[24] Despite their extremely distinct social profiles, the constraint hierarchies for the two groups fell out the same, as shown in Figure 4.1. Finally, we are aware of one other variety that demonstrates the EASR pattern, namely Sydney in Australia. Eisikovits (1991: 252) found the following ranking: *you* > *we* > *they* > NP. Arguably this is not surprising, given the roots of Anglophone settlement to Australia in the south of England in the nineteenth century (Britain 2008).

Thus, the EASR appears a fairly robust constraint across varieties of English in southern England and varieties that have derived from these (for this reason, it might be recoined the Southern Subject Rule (SSR)). Additional research is certainly necessary to define the geographical scope of this factor. But how can the emergence of *was*-levelling in a traditionally *were/weren't* variety like that of the Fens be explained? Britain (2002) suggests that the spread of *was*-levelling in the Fens may have been invoked by analogy with the presence of –s on regular present tense verbs.[25] Note that in conversational speech, the traditional vernacular variant of past BE in both the singular and plural in this area was [wə] (and not [wɒz] or [wɜː], which are citation forms) (see Orton and Tilling 1971: 1300; Britain 2002: 22; Ahava 2010). Conversational *was*

4 Past BE   203

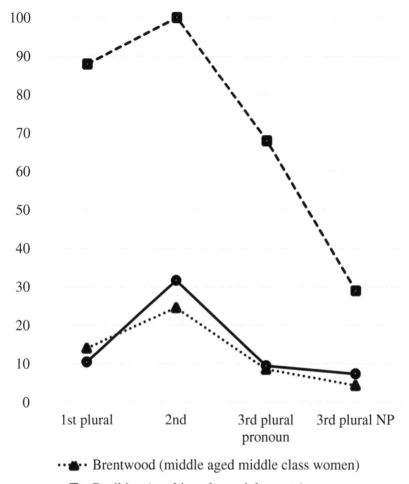

Fig. 4.1 Use of *was* in contexts of standard *were* in Basildon and Brentwood, Essex (England), and Inner Sydney (Australia)

forms – that is [wəz] – can, therefore, be seen as attaching morphological –s to a [wə] verb stem, in just the same way as it operates in the 3rd sing. present tense system for main verbs. Even in past BE, then,

East Anglia once had, essentially, verbal zero, just as it does in ordinary present tense verbs. It is important to point out, to support the analogy argument, that this 'verbal –s', among the older traditional *were/weren't* users of past BE in the Fens, was more common in 3rd sing. contexts than elsewhere (Britain 2002: 32)—in other words, *he/she/it was* occurs more frequently than *I was* (and more frequently than in any other subject context). Note that this is where one would 'expect' –s as an emergent agreement marker.

It seems reasonable to conclude, then, that in a variety that traditionally had *were/weren't* generalisation, *was* entered the system (replacing [wə]) presumably as analogical subject-verb agreement, before *was* was generalised across other persons as it came to indicate positive polarity. From this perspective, the appearance of the EASR amongst the youngest speakers in the Fens data is perplexing. The emergence of a *was/weren't* system, a sign that *was* functions as a marker of positive polarity, and clearly evident among the middle-age group in the Fens data, understandably was accompanied by similar rates of *was* use after both nouns and pronouns. So why are the Fenland youngsters now deploying a Pro>NP subject constraint if the function of *was* is to act as a marker of polarity? Recall from the discussion in Chapter 3 that there is independent crosslinguistic evidence that suggests that subject-verb agreement is more likely to occur with pronouns than with NPs. Accordingly, the EASR (favouring pronouns) should occur in systems where –s has been introduced to mark agreement. In this context, we would like to speculate that the advent of the EASR shaping *was* variability as a more general Pro>NP constraint is the same type of Subject Rule (distinguishing pronominal and NP-subjects) as Cole (2014) has proposed for the NSR, lending apparent support to this analysis. Recognising that more theoretical and empirical investigation is needed of the nature the EASR, we are currently analysing a large corpus of East Anglian data in which we can examine the emergence of –s and a *was/weren't* system in the same speakers. This will hopefully shed further light on the robustness and scope of the EASR and help us understand why it arises in the first place.

4.6   A Formal Linguistic Perspective on Past BE

Research in generative syntax has engaged with variationist linguistics in collaborative work by Adger and Smith (2005, 2010). Looking at Smith's (2000) Buckie data as a case study, Adger (2006) attempts to demonstrate that variation is not only determined by extra-grammatical factors but also localised, in part, in the grammar itself. His analysis is embedded within the framework of the Minimalist Program. He exploits one of the central tenets guiding the program that lexical items (for example concrete nouns, verbs) are comprised of sets of grammatical features that they 'check' or 'match up' with functional categories (for example Tense, C(omplementizer)) in the clause structure.[26] Accordingly, Adger proposes a lexicalist, feature-based approach to verbal –s, in which variability derives from the possibility that verbs, and the functional categories verbs they check with, may be underspecified for agreement features. He calls this approach 'Combinatorial Variability'.

Following a number of other researchers, Adger (2006; see references therein) assumes that pronouns have three types of features: [singular: ±] [participant: ±] and [author: ±]. The feature [singular: ±] marks the number of the pronoun. The feature [participant: ±] marks whether the pronoun refers to a participant in the speech act (the speaker or the addressee) or not (a third party); and finally, the feature [author: ±] distinguishes between the author and the addressee. Thus, for example, the pronouns *you*, *he*, and *they* bear the following feature specifications (where the pronoun is only specified for [author: ±] when it carries the feature [participant: +]):

(24)   a.   you (sing.)   [singular: +, participant: +, author -]
       b.   he   [singular: +, participant: -]
       c.   they   [singular: -, participant: -]

On this account, the sentence in (25) is ill-formed in Standard English because the number feature on the pronoun *he* and the verb do not 'check' (match up): *he* has the feature [+singular], whereas *were* has a feature [-singular].

(25) *He were there

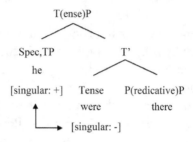

Adger's key assumption of underspecification entails that verbs and functional categories like Tense may bear just one single agreement feature.[27] By means of a particular algorithm, the precise details of which need not concern us here, a Buckie speaker will construct the following minimal feature specification for past BE (2006: 521):[28]

(26) [*u*singular: +] was
      [*u*singular: -] were
      [*u*participant: +] was
      [*u*author-] were
      [*u*author+] was

Postulating minimal feature specification accounts for, amongst other things, Smith's (2000) finding that in Buckie, the 2nd sing. pronoun *you* occurs with non-standard *was*. Adger explains that when Tense is underspecified as the feature [*u*author: -], speakers will use *you* (sing.) with *were*, but when Tense is only specified for the feature [*u*singular: +], *you* (sing.) can be used with non-standard *was*. The variation that is thus generated is illustrated by a comparison of the (a) and (b) examples of (27) from Adger and Smith (2005: 156).

(27) a. He says 'I thocht **you were** a diver or somethin'.'
b. 'Aye, I thocht **you was** a scuba diver.'
c. **They were** aie sort o' pickin' on me, like.
d. **They were** still like partying hard.

Adger (2006) argues that the system of Combinatorial Variability enables us to capture this variability as well as the occurrence of categoricity in Buckie. He points out that in an analysis that treats functional categories as underspecified, the feature that the pronoun *they* will check with the verb in Tense is either [singular -] or [author -]. Since both of these features spell out as *were*, the result will be *were* categorically (cf. (27c–d)).

Adger and Smith (2010) show that in addition to past BE patterns, the approach also accounts for the NSR effect on verbal –s in Buckie. By the NSR, speakers variably use verbal –s with plural NP-subjects to the exclusion of the 3rd pl. pronoun *they*. They cite the data in (28) (2010: 1110, 1114):

(28) a. **What bairns walk** any distance?
b. When **they go** back, **the teachers asks** them to write something and they send them till's.
c. *When **they gets** home. (Buckie judgement)

They suggest the minimal specification for agreement features in regular verbs to be as in (29) (2010: 1125):

(29) [singular: +, participant: -] third singular –s
[singular: -] plural –Ø
[participant: +] plural –Ø
[pronominal: -] verbal –s

Here, the crux lies in the presence or absence of the feature [pronominal: -]. In the case of *they*, the verb in Tense can only be underspecified as [singular: -], resulting in 100% plural –Ø inflection. In the case of a plural NP-subject (for example *the men*), by contrast, underspecification can be [singular: -] or [pronominal: -], predicting a variability of 50% plural –Ø inflection and 50% verbal –s. In their account of the absence of the NSR effect in Standard English, Adger and Smith (2010) propose that the feature [pronominal: ±] is completely absent from the inventory of grammatical features in Standard English.

The model of Combinatorial Variability, then, identifies feature specification as the source of two types of variability that are available in the grammar. One is underspecification of features on functional categories; this gives rise to the variable use of a variant along the lines of the Labovian concept of the 'linguistic variable' (viz. Buckie *you was/were*; *the men walk/walks*; *they walk/*walks*). The other is variation in the feature specification of functional categories. This gives rise to differential usage of a variant among dialects; variation that in generative syntax is conventionally known as 'parametric variation' (compare Buckie *the men walk(s)* to Standard English *the men walk(*s)*). Adger and Smith (2005: 11) highlight that Combinatorial Variability reconciles these two types of variability in one, integral part of the grammar, rather than having to posit additional systems and mechanisms. Specifically, previous treatments of variation have postulated variable rules in the syntax (for example Labov 1969 in the variationist paradigm), assumed the co-existence of multiple grammars (for example Kroch 1989 in historical syntax) or introduced parametric options in the clause structure that invoke different licensing positions for subjects (for example Henry 1995 within the generative framework; see Chapter 1 again), respectively (Adger 2006: 505, 528).

Adger (2006) goes on to argue that the model of Combinatorial Variability does not merely accommodate variability, but also generates variants in a way that predicts the frequency of occurrence of a variant. This is because, in the way that the system is set up, it is possible to have a number of routes to a variant, so that one output will be found more often (with a higher probability) than the other. Adger and Smith (2010: 1112) claim that 'this system makes a rather good prediction about [the statistical variance of *was/were*]'. For example, Smith's (2000) Buckie informants showed rates of 69% of *was* with the 2nd sing. *you* (2010: 1113). As (30) demonstrates, for *you* (sing.), there are, indeed, two ways in which the grammar can output the variant *was*, but only one way to output the variant *were*, depending on the particular feature that the verb will bear:

(30) *you* (sing.)
      [*u*singular: +] was, [*u*participant: +] was, [*u*author-] were

That is to say, the model predicts that we should find *was* twice as often (0.66× times) than *were* (0.33× times), if nothing else is affecting the choice.

Adger (2006) admits that while the model predicts rudimentary probability distributions, higher frequencies of one or the other variant may in fact occur. He assumes that this boils down to pressures pertaining to language use, such as social factors (for example issues of social identity, speaker age) and processing factors (for example the recency of a variant; 2006: 506), neither of which belong to the grammatical system proper. Such factors may all have impact on which variant is ultimately chosen. He envisages that when a variant ends up having a very low frequency altogether, children, in the acquisition process, may come to analyse the variant's low frequency as non-occurrence, and that this will in turn lead to change.

Adger and Smith (2005) summarise as follows: 'we would like to emphasize that our purpose ... has [been] to highlight the usefulness of drawing a distinction between (i) the mechanism which admits variability in an essentially invariant (minimalist) syntactic system, part of I-language, and (ii) factors which may be related to individuals' biologically constrained capacities to use language (for example processing, prosodic or information structure theoretic factors) or to the (possibly tacit) desire of individuals to conform to, or to rebel against, their communities' impositions' (2005: 173). Theirs is very valuable work that gains insight into and teases out the particular contributions of grammar (grammatical features) and use (psycholinguistic processes and sociolinguistic factors) to the occurrence of variability. Both forces must be taken into account since each can govern how variation eventually manifests itself. Combinatorial Variability also neatly accounts for the current pattern of variation that exists in Buckie. Still, as Adger and Smith (2010) also note, the Buckie system is not the only past BE system. Buckie speakers show a split in the use of non-standard *was* by subject type (with the inclusion of singular *you* and the categorical exclusion of *they*). As we have seen in the present chapter, other varieties admit variability throughout the past BE paradigm, or have a different pivot for levelling. Assuming the possibility of different feature specifications may well capture this variation, but we should be mindful of potential circularity in this kind of theorising. However, while the model of Combinatorial Variability is not intended to capture extra-grammatical factors, Adger and Smith assume that psycholinguistic and sociolinguistic influences may interfere with the predicted pattern. In the next section we will explore whether two such apparent further factors, 'exaptation' and 'iconicity', may play a role in the appearance of particular past BE patterns.

4.7 Past BE from the Perspective of Exaptation and Diagrammatic Iconicity

We first summarise what we have established in this chapter thus far. In Sect. 4.5.2 we noted that the historical processes of Verner's Law and rhotacism gave rise to *was/were* alternation in past BE. However, in English, number marking is arguably redundant because number is expressed by the grammatical subject, leaving two different morphs— *was* and *were*—to mark past tense. We found that varieties of English have redeployed forms of past BE in the following ways:

1. Speakers may recruit non-standard *was* according to the Northern Subject Rule (NSR; Murray 1873). Pietsch (2005) has argued that the NSR-effect on past BE was modelled on verbal –s. There may be slight differences in the subject rankings that have been observed, but overall they are robust: *they* disfavours non-standard *was*, and plural NPs are most likely to favour (following existential *there*, which we will probe in Chapter 5). Varieties that show NSR-conditioning of

non-standard *was* are often British varieties from Scotland and northern England in which the pattern has existed as far back as Middle English (Buckie: Smith 2000), or U.S. varieties that acquired the NSR as a result of migrations from these areas (Ocracoke: Schilling-Estes and Wolfram 1994).

2. Other varieties have been developing a generalised *was*-paradigm (for example Alabama; Feagin 1979), which may have gone to (near-) completion, disposing of *were*. *Was*-generalisation is a manifestation of analogical levelling. The operation of analogical levelling is commonly taken to dispose of 'superfluous' morphological material that has arisen from independent language change, as happened to the Old English verb *wesan*. As a result of the loss of number marking in the preterit of lexical verbs, *was*-generalisation provides for *was* to analogically mark past tense in the context of both singular and plural subjects. It has also been observed in communities that are—both geographically and psychologically—far removed from the influence of an imposing standard (for example Tristan da Cunha: Schreier 2002a, b). Full *was*-generalisation is not grammatically constrained and occurs in the context of all subjects; that is, with pronouns and NPs alike.

3. It seems that in varieties that used to level in the direction of *were*, the traditional pattern is fading away. In response, some varieties have completely reorganised the past BE paradigm to the effect that the two allomorphs of past BE, rather than marking the features of person/number, are deployed as markers of polarity, with *was* being used in positive sentences and *weren't* in negative sentences (Ocracoke: Schilling-Estes and Wolfram 1994; the Fens: Britain 2002). In other varieties, reallocation of non-standard *weren't* has been confined to the more specific context of negative clause-final tags (Bolton: Moore 2011). Even varieties that traditionally have no *were*-levelling have been reconfiguring their past BE paradigms in one of these ways (polarity in London English: Cheshire and Fox 2009; clause-final negative tags in York English: Tagliamonte 1998). In view of the fact that negative past BE is only attested in the form *weren't* (*were not is unattested), it has been postulated that *weren't* is one lexical item rather than a form that arises from merging *were* and

not in the syntax, and a similar claim has been made for the invariant tag *weren't it* (Schilling-Estes and Wolfram 1994; Cheshire and Fox 2009). This view falls out naturally from formal linguistic analyses of the nature of the English negation markers *n't/not* and non-standard *weren't* (Zwicky and Pullum 1983; Mittelstaedt and Parrot 2002). The *was/weren't* and *weren't it* patterns are relatively recent phenomena. The former has been ascribed to analogical extension (Schilling-Estes and Wolfram 1994), paralleling other verbs that have different forms in positive and negative sentences (for example *will* and *won't*, and *am/is/are* and *ain't*). Varieties on their way to a fully *was/weren't* system show emergent high levels of both non-standard *weren't* in negative clauses and non-standard *was* across apparent time, irrespective of the type of subject; thus, with plural pronouns and NPs alike (cf. e.g. the middle-age cohort of Britain's 2002 speakers in the Fens).

4. Across East Anglia and the south-east of England more generally (and places settled from this region), non-standard *was* has come to be constrained by the East Anglian Subject Rule (EASR). By this rule, speakers use –s (in the case of past BE, therefore, *was*) more with pronouns than with NPs (English in the Fens: Britain 2002; Cambridgeshire: Vasko 2010; Basildon and Brentwood in Essex: Britain and Rupp, 2005; London: Levey 2007; Cheshire and Fox 2009; and Sydney, Australia: Eisikovits 1991). These varieties all show a consistent subject constraint ranking, with *was* more likely after *you* > *we* > *they* > plural NP—the opposite to the NSR. For the concrete case of East Anglia, we have suggested that the EASR-conditioning of the use of *was* has arisen by analogy with the EASR-conditioning of –s that obtains there. First, we noted that the traditional vernacular stem of past BE in East Anglia was [wə], apparently on a par with verbal zero in ordinary present tense verbs. Forms realised as [wəz] (versus [wə]) can therefore be seen as the application of –s to a verb stem. Second, recall from Chapter 3 that speakers in East Anglia deploy –s exclusively (but variably) in contexts of 3rd sing. subjects (Trudgill 1996) because –s constitutes agreement in places that have traditionally verbal zero. Recall also that cross-linguistically, subject-verb agreement more frequently occurs in the context of pronouns than in the context of subject-NPs.

Correspondingly, *was* was more common in 3rd sing. contexts among the older traditional *were/weren't* users in the Fens than in any other subject position (Britain 2002: 32). The younger speakers appear to have developed a more general PRO>NP constraint on past BE, which includes plural subjects and looks like the Subject Rule that Cole (2014) has proposed for the NSR.

5. Finally, another type of pattern involves a continued historical use of *was* that occurred in dialects in the north of England. At the time, the 2nd person singular pronoun *you* occasioned relatively high rates of non-standard *was* (Forsström 1948; Smith and Tagliamonte 1998 for Buckie). Contemporary varieties that show this use of non-standard *was* preserve a number distinction in the 2nd person: *you* (sing.) *was, you* (pl.) *were* (Pyles and Algeo 2005). Alternative strategies involve the retention of historical 2nd person pronouns (for example *thou*) or the introduction of new ones (for example plural *y'all, youse*).

This overview shows that past BE variability can restore isomorphism, imposing a bi-unique relationship between form and function (cf. e.g. *was*-generalisation for uniform past tense marking; or *was* for positive polarity and *weren't* for negative polarity). And yet it may proceed in different directions and get realised in a range of different ways. The actual realisation of past BE in a particular variety will depend on an interplay of factors. Schilling-Estes and Wolfram (1994: 274–275) say just this:

> [U]nderstanding the processes that [lead to particular past BE patterns and] mechanisms that guide continued maintenance of and changes to [these patterns] calls for more than a single comparison of items within a linguistically defined paradigmatic set and a single underlying principle that guides the leveling process. Instead, we argue, a true understanding of the mechanisms of analogical leveling must appeal to the synergistic intersection of linguistic, psycholinguistic, and sociolinguistic processes.
>
> These processes are linguistic in that there is internal, systemic pressure to level forms within paradigmatic sets. Furthermore, language form and language function may interact with the natural tendency toward leveling in the reconfiguration of a paradigm. At the same time, leveling is

guided by psycholinguistic processes: factors of perception and saliency must be invoked in explaining the directions analogical leveling may take. [S]ocial mechanisms also must be considered as we seek to understand how innovative regularization patterns become accepted and maintained in the speech community.

Additionally, redundant forms (e.g. plural *were*) may not be lost but instead gain other uses (e.g. in invariant *weren't* tags), with shifts in meaning, and old and new forms may co-occur (cf. e.g. the innovative *weren't* tags and the disappearing NSR in York; Tagliamonte 1998) in a transitional stage of 'layering' (Hopper 1991).

Before we explore to what extent the concept of 'iconic motivation' may be one of the extra-linguistic factors governing the nature of particular past BE patterns, we will first address the mechanism that seems to have given rise to these patterns. We already discussed the emergence of the NSR, and *was*-generalisation clearly derives from analogical levelling, but what about the *was/weren't* system? Along with Willis (2016), we would like to suggest that it is best conceived of in terms of the functional shift known as exaptation (Lass 1990, 1997) that we extensively discussed in Chapter 2. 'Exaptation' appears reminiscent of Trudgill's (1986) notion of 'reallocation' that he introduced in the context of dialect contact and dialect mixture and Britain (2002) and Britain and Trudgill (2005) have applied to *was/weren't* levelling in the Fens. In their words, 'reallocation' is a process whereby 'variants in the mixture which were originally from different regional dialects may avoid extinction by acquiring sociolinguistic or other functional roles in the outcome of the mixture. [...] This reallocation ... can either be *socio-stylistic*, where ingredient forms to the dialect mix take on different roles as markers of social status, or *structural*, where [variants] are repositioned to serve linguistic functions' (2005: 184, 205) [our emphasis]. Regarding the concrete path that 'reallocation' takes, Britain (2002) has remarked that 'a reallocation analysis of past BE in the Fens would require ... that there are good reasons why the forms [*was* in affirmative contexts and *weren't* in the negative LR&DB] are linguistically constrained in the way they are' (2002: 36). We would like to suggest that the past BE forms *was* and *weren't* might have undergone both social and linguistic exaptation and that the particular social and linguistic functions that they have taken on are iconically motivated.

First, how exactly does 'exaptation' relate to the case of past BE? Willis (2016: 213) notes that the general demise of number marking in the past tense on English verbs left the category of number as an obsolescent morphosyntactic category, being only expressed on one verb (past BE).[29] He argues that past BE demonstrates the two major scenarios of dealing with obsolescent morphology. An example of the first strategy (abandoning a morph altogether) is *was*-generalisation: varieties level *was* across the paradigm at the expense of *were* (viz. Feagin 1979 for Alabama; Schreier 2002b for Tristan da Cunha; and other varieties discussed in Sect. 4.5.2). The second strategy (of 'exapting' a morph for some other linguistic or social purpose) is shown by *was/weren't* varieties. In these varieties, the forms *was* and *weren't* have come to be deployed for conveying polarity distinctions (as well as, in the case of *weren't*, conveying stances in tag-questions). Note that, in line with current thinking about 'exaptation', these new uses of existing past BE forms are not immediately related to their former function of marking number. Willis (2016) observes that the shift in function of past BE only fits the broader notion of exaptation of Lass (1997) that it is not limited to 'junk', as past BE forms clearly continue to signal past tense.

In an assessment of the applicability of exaptation to past BE, we take note of critical remarks that exaptation is merely a statement about a particular outcome of grammatical change. Similar to his critique regarding the concept of 'grammaticalisation', Joseph (2016: 38) does not see 'exaptation' 'as a fundamentally different kind of grammatical change from what might be thought of as more "garden variety" sorts of change by reanalysis and/or analogical extension'. Narrog (2007), Gardani (2016: 228) and others have also taken the position that reuse is achieved via reanalysis, the core mechanism of grammatical change. Vermandere and Meul (2016: 281) add that exaptation 'concerns more a synchronic interpretation of a feature's functionality rather than a hypothesis, or even explanation, of a feature's emergence' and as such does not advance our insights into language change. Along this line of thinking, one can ask whether 'exaptation' really needs to be invoked for the case of past BE since reallocation of *was/weren't* as polarity markers naturally derives from the analogical extension on the model of other verbs that have distinct positive and negative forms, as Schilling-Estes and Wolfram (1994) have argued (see Sect. 4.5.3).

One possible reanalysis-type account of the advent of *was/weren't* as morphemes signalling polarity perhaps derives from Croft's (2000) notion of 'hypoanalysis'. In 'hypoanalysis', 'the listener reanalyses a contextual semantic/pragmatic property as an inherent property of the syntactic unit. In the reanalysis, the inherent property of the context … is then attributed to the syntactic unit, and so the syntactic unit in question gains a new meaning or function' (2000: 126). As a development demonstrating 'hypoanalysis', he draws attention to the rise of the German umlaut, which was previously discussed by Lass (1990: 98–99) in an examination of the degree of predictability of exaptation. In various West Germanic dialects, a suffixal /i/, which marked plural, triggered the fronting (umlaut) of back vowels in root syllables: 'so OHG *gast* "guest", MHG *gast-gest-e*, Modern German *Gast-Gäste*, etc.' (Lass 1990: 98). As a result of the many plural contexts in which it occurred, the umlaut was reinterpreted, by 'hypoanalysis' according to Croft, as inherently signalling the plural (2000: 128). Thus, the German umlaut started out as an assimilative phonological process and then assumed a morphological, plural function. Subsequently, in German, other nouns that historically used a different pluralisation strategy began to use the umlaut strategy as well; 'e.g. *Baum* "tree"; pl. *Bäume*, OHG *boum/boum-e*' (Lass 1990: 98). It seems conceivable that, in a similar way, speakers have built a new grammatical *was/weren't* system on the basis of contextual properties of past BE. Specifically, the potential of *were* to act as a host for the clitic *n't* may have been reanalysed as an inherent property (viz. *were/n't* → *weren't*) such that it was conventionalised and *weren't* acquired the use as a negative polarity marker.

Joseph (2016) has in fact called for an end to the debate about the specifics of exaptation, suggesting that:

> Whether it is 'junk' (as in Lass's original characterization) or not, I argue, is immaterial to the speaker; all that matters is for there to be some motivation, i.e. the availability of a model – often a very localized one – upon which an analogical change can be based or a basis for a reinterpretation

or the like. Moreover, whether it represents a wholly new function or just some other sort of innovation, is likewise deemed here to be immaterial; what matters is the demonstration that speakers can employ existing restricted material in novel ways. (p. 41) […] … having available material is what matters, not the status of the material. (p. 47)

Gardani (2016) has offered a somewhat different perspective arguing that while it is clear that 'exaptation' has no explanatory status comparable to primary mechanisms of change like 'reanalysis' and 'analogy', it is nonetheless a useful descriptive term because it provides valuable insights into 'what functions are targeted by speakers in a process of change' and 'also what structural properties the elements selected to carry on a new function (that is, the exapted elements) have' (2016: 228, 254).

Furthermore, it would seem that the reallocation of non-standard *weren't* to the more specific context of negative clause-final tags is less amenable to an analysis in terms of canonical analogical extension that derives novel polarity verb pairs from older ones. In this more confined instance of the *was/weren't* mechanism, *weren't* may be used for another purpose than the grammatical function of marking negation. Tag-questions can serve multiple pragmatic roles, from requesting information/confirmation, softening the force of an utterance, facilitating discourse or indicating stance (for example Moore and Podesva 2009: 452 and many others).[30] Back in 1981 already, Cheshire demonstrated that speakers can express certain social meanings in tag-questions by virtue of using a particular linguistic variant (where Moore and Podesva 2009: 448 define 'social meaning' as 'the stances and personal characteristics indexed through the deployment of linguistic forms in interaction'). In a sample of vernacular speech of three adolescent peer groups in working class Reading, Cheshire found that the form *in't* (as opposed to *ain't*) was considerably more frequent in tags than elsewhere, and a number of other scholars have found the same since (for example Anderwald 2002; Amos et al. 2007). Importantly, Cheshire demonstrated, both quantitatively and qualitatively, how the use of *in't* in tags functioned to bring about speakers' (aggressive) stances towards their addressees (1981: 375–376). Moore and Podesva (2009) have gone on to investigate the impact of the grammatical content of tags, such as non-standard morphosyntax, on communicating social meaning, drawing on data from Moore's (2003) ethnographic study of 40 female students in four communities of practice at a high school in Bolton. They demonstrate how tag-questions are variably deployed in discourse to signal speaker stances, styles as well as associations with particular social groups. For example, the 'Townies' used non-standard *weren't* in clause-final tags to enact a rebellious stance 'constructed in opposition to the school and the linguistic norms it enforces' (viz. *Right, I was proper fucked up for some strange reason at her house, **weren't[?] I?**) (2009: 470–471).

Having established that there may well be a role to play for exaptation in past BE, we think that as with verbal –s, 'iconic motivation' is one of the extra-linguistic factors that can give direction to particular new uses. Regarding the remorphologisation of the two past BE allomorphs *was* and *weren't*, we note that Schilling-Estes and Wolfram (1994) arguably anticipated an account that invokes 'iconic motivation'. They first seek to explain why *was* and *weren't* have been recycled in the way they have been; that is, from allomorphs marking number to expressions of positive and negative polarity:

> Arguably, the ability to distinguish negatives from positives is functionally far more important than the ability to determine subject person and number – particularly as English sentences typically have overt subjects. (1994: 290)

> Compare Kuryłowicz's fifth "law" governing analogical change, which Hock (1986: 227) stated thus: "In order to re-establish a distinction of central significance, the language gives up a distinction of marginal significance." Of course, as Hock pointed out, exactly what constitutes "more" or "less" marginal is by no means readily determinable, although it seems intuitively satisfying to view positive/negative polarity as a more crucial distinction than subject person and/or number. (1994: 299, Footnote 8)

They go on to comment on the apparent motive for speakers to use two different allomorphs to mark the polarity contrast:

> Leveling toward the remorphologization of past *be* along positive/negative lines makes explanatory sense in terms of the need to maintain the transparency of the critical distinction between positives and negatives (Lightfoot 1979). When the morphologically and phonologically

4 Past BE 219

independent negative marker *not* is transformed into the phonologically dependent *-n't* clitic, the negativity it denotes becomes less transparent. [...] [M]ore transparent markers of negation arise as a functional need to distinguish clearly negative and positive propositions. (1994: 289)

Schilling-Estes and Wolfram (1994) appeal to the influence of psycholinguistic processes, in particular, the effect of perceptual saliency, as bearing on the development of the *was/weren't* pattern.[31] The polarity system, indeed, appears iconically *motivated*: two maximally different morphemes symmetrically reflect two maximally contrastive situations. Kortmann and Wagner have in fact characterised it as 'a prime example of iconicity' (2005: 3).[32]

And what is the nature of the relationship between the form *weren't* and tag-questions? Recall that a number of studies (for example Tagliamonte 1998; Moore 2011) have found that *weren't* is more frequent in clause-final tags than elsewhere. Further, in clause-final tags, *weren't* may convey a stance such as 'aggression' or 'rebelliousness' (Moore and Podesva 2009), just like *ain't*, the non-standard present-tense equivalent of *weren't*, or other secondary contracted forms such as *in't* (Cheshire 1981). Exploiting work by Errington (1985) and Traugott (2004), Woolard (2008) has argued that especially in such 'pragmatically salient' expressions as tags, prevalent norms of use tend get strategically manipulated in order to convey social messages. 'Pragmatically salient' expressions can be understood as indexing 'subjective interactional stances' (rather than directly indexing social identity). Woolard explains that rather than addressing the question 'Who am I?', pragmatically salient expressions answer the question 'How am I feeling about this?' (2008: 444). Pragmatically salient expressions, therefore, 'are recognized by speakers as more crucial linguistic mediators of social relations' (2008: 438) and hearers will tend to attend closely to socially significant details of the linguistic forms that are used. As examples of pragmatically salient expressions, Woolard mentions 'intensifiers' and 'discourse markers' such as *obviously* and *actually*. Because of speakers' awareness of the potential of strategically using pragmatically salient expressions, they tend to be subject to relatively rapid change (see for example Ito and Tagliamonte 2003 on the versatility of the meaning and use of intensifiers). Silverstein (1979: 206–207) has called such strategic use 'creative indexicality'. This perception fits well with current variationist approaches to stylistic variation. As Schilling-Estes (2008) has pointed out, in traditional sociolinguistics, language variation was seen as reflecting relatively static social group membership. However, informed by ethnographic studies, variationists have increasingly recognised that language variation is more dynamic, unfolding in the discourse and constituting a key resource for individuals to not only shape and reshape social identities, but also to 'convey more immediate interactional meanings, to enact particular stances toward interlocutors and toward the talk at hand' (2013: 328; see also Eckert's 2008 concept of 'indexical field').

The preference of *weren't* forms in tags, then, can be seen as another form of iconic reallocation, one where a salient but minority variant is deployed in discursively 'weighty' contexts and which gains part of its functional force from its structural distinctiveness from forms used in other less pragmatically prominent contexts. Cheshire's functional analysis of *in't* in Reading and the approach we take here to *weren't* show remarkable parallels. Both forms are 'fused', non-standard, positionally constrained, and pragmatically highly salient in the discourse.

Notes

1. There is extensive documentation on past BE, but we will limit the discussion to studies which are of particular relevance to the present investigation.
2. Hay and Schreier (2004) conclude from the literature that the paradigm of present *be* is more robust than that of past *be*, noting that variation in the present *be* paradigm is geographically restricted and only infrequently reported. For example, Eisikovits (1991) reports that, with the exception of existentials, 40 adolescents in Inner Sydney showed very low frequencies of non-standard *present be* (3.95%). Interestingly, such non-standard tokens only occurred in interrogatives, coordinated noun phrases and relative clauses (for example *They try to help me,* **the kids that's** *with me* (1991: 248)). Note that these are structures that

have been identified as canonical Northern Subject Rule configurations (see Chapter 2). However, for reasons of sparseness of data, we will confine the discussion to past BE here.

3. Tagliamonte (2009: 120–121) has in fact reported a fourth pattern; a tendency for *wasn't* in negative and *were* in affirmative clauses. She cites rural Maryport (Lancashire in England), Cumnock (Scotland), Portavogie (Northern Ireland) and two African Nova Scotia locales in Canada (North Preston and Guysborough Enclave) as showing the pattern, for example ***They was nae*** *supposed to get onything, but* ***they were*** *very good to them here* (Portavogie). However, she does not discuss it in depth.

4. Right across the English-speaking world, *was* is also favoured in existential *there* sentences with plural subjects. This effect is related to the favouring of *is/'s* in present-tense existentials. Smith and Tagliamonte (1998: 10) note that this has been a widely documented feature of existential constructions as far back as Old English, and a frequent pattern in Middle English. We address verbal –s in existential *there* sentences separately in Chapter 5.

5. According to Pyles and Algeo (2005: 140), in a later development in the sixteenth century, speakers of southern dialects in fact started using *you was* for the singular and *you were* for the plural. One explanation for this development put forward by Petyt (1985: 237) is that *you was* restored a number distinction in the 2nd person that was lost when the 2nd sing. pronoun *thou* had disappeared. Strang (1970: 140) reports that the distinction was common during the sixteenth to eighteenth centuries, but 'abolished' in the nineteenth century under the pressure of purists. A number of present-day varieties of English now distinguish between singular and plural *you* by invoking various supplementary strategies. These include the use of an alternative form for the 2nd pl., such as *youse* (for example in Ireland, northern England, parts of Scotland, Australia and New Zealand), *you-uns* (Southern Irish, Scots English, Appalachia), *you all* or *y'all* (the south of the U.S.), *you lot* (British), and the common *you guys*. In a survey across 87 schools in the UK conducted between 1986 and 1989, Cheshire et al. (1989: 201) found, in addition to the forms just mentioned, tokens showing the retention of the historical singular form *thou*. They make the interesting observation that the use of distinctive 2nd sing. and pl. pronouns correlated with low rates of non-standard *was*.

222   L. Rupp and D. Britain

6. We refer the reader to Trudgill's (2008) work for interesting details and references to studies that have demonstrated that the direction of levelling is unpredictable and does not seem to be determined by markedness or frequency.

7. Wolfram and Sellers (1999: 109) consider 'the lowered incidence of *was* leveling with negatives' a direct by-product of *weren't* regularisation. However, negative contexts have actually been found to exert an effect on the realisation of *was* in Buckie (Tagliamonte and Smith 2000), Harrison County, Indiana, where 'plural verbal -*s* was found to occur nearly twice as often in negative clauses (32.9% (27/82)) than in affirmative clauses (16.6% (242/1456))' (José 2007: 265), Wincanton in Somerset (Tagliamonte 2009: 120), as well as a number of varieties of English spoken by descendants of freed African American ex-slaves who settled in the Dominican Republic and Nova Scotia in the late eighteenth and early nineteenth centuries (Samaná English; Tagliamonte and Smith (1999: 15) and North Preston and Guysborough Enclave; Tagliamonte and Smith (2000: 160)). To the knowledge of Tagliamonte and Smith (2000: 157), negation was not previously reported as influencing the occurrence of *was* either in the historical literature or in the contemporary dialect literature. Here are some examples:

(31) a. **You wasn't** allowed to use their toilets. (North Preston)
      b. **They wasn't** in no comas. (North Preston)

In Wincanton, Harrison County, and Samaná, however, the constraint was only weak (Tagliamonte 2009: 121) or not significant, respectively, as an effect of 'the extremely sparse data in the negative context' (José 2007: 265) and 'the small number of negative contexts' (Tagliamonte and Smith 1999: 15).

8. Despite the spread, generalisation to *was/weren't* is currently still restricted to areas in England and the historically isolated, mid-Atlantic coastal region of the United States, as Wolfram and Schilling-Estes (2003b: 211) have pointed out, and has as yet not been observed in other varieties of English in the world.

9. See Note 3 for the occurrence of a *were/wasn't* pattern.

10. We refer back here to Trudgill's (2008) discussion of the /s/~/r/ alternation in Germanic, presented in Sect. 4.3.

4   Past BE   **223**

11. Few studies have reported analogical levelling to positive *were* (as Richards 2010 has noted), and we are not aware of any showing an apparent time *increase* towards ever higher levels of *were*.

12. In later research, Wolfram and Schilling-Estes (2003b) compared the situation that obtains on Ocracoke to three other insular communities in the eastern coastal region of the United States. We refer to their study for the details of their findings, which included advanced levels of *weren't* from the oldest to the youngest generation of speakers. However, an important difference to the situation in Ocracoke is that older speakers in these communities did not show non-standard positive *were* but rather a levelled *was/wasn't* pattern that is more characteristic of vernacular U.S. varieties. Thus, in these communities, there was an even more dramatic reorganisation of the past BE paradigm from *was(n't)* generalization to regularisation to *weren't* in negative clauses. Interestingly, however, local teens and young adults behaved similarly to their peers in Ocracoke in that an increase in *weren't*-levelling at the expense of *wasn't* has gone hand in hand with a decreasing usage of non-standard levelled *was* in positive sentences.

13. Natalie Schilling has recently returned to Ocracoke for data collection (p.c.) and it remains to be seen whether she will now find 'ideal' restructuring into a neatly symmetrical paradigm split along positive/negative lines.

14. Jespersen (1954: 431 ff.) dates the emergence of positive and negative verb forms in spoken English around 1600. The reader is referred to his work for details of these verb forms as well as an account of the way in which the form *ain't* has developed from the verb *be* via the trajectory *aren't* > [ɑːnt] > [eɪnt].

15. Similarly, Amos et al. (2007) showed that in the Fenland town of Wisbech, the local equivalent of *ain't*, namely *in't* [ɪn?], accounted for 89% of all cases of negated BE and auxiliary HAVE. It can be robustly argued, given high levels of *weren't* levelling in the Fens, that *ain't-weren't* are a present-past duo as Schilling-Estes and Wolfram (1994) argued for Ocracoke.

16. Ihalainen (1987; cited in Ojanen n.d.: 4) has similarly observed that East Somerset speakers in the south-west of England tend to generalise the past tense form of *were* while west Somerset speakers tend to generalise *was*.

17. Vasko also reports other dialectologists' findings of *were* in Cambridgeshire, amongst other localities. One example is Anderwald's (2001: 5) study which lists the south Midlands (incorporating Cambridgeshire) as preferring *were* levelling (15.3%) over *was* levelling (5.2%).
18. See Moore (2011: 348) for a list of studies that confirm the use of *were* in the Bolton area.
19. Rates of *weren't it* were lowest in Inner London; Cheshire and Fox (2009: 33) point out that *weren't it* faces strong competition from invariant *innit* there. Pichler (2018) demonstrates that *innit* has meanwhile taken over.
20. Eisikovits (1991: 250) has reported that the English spoken by adolescents in Inner Sydney shows the opposite pattern with *wasn't*, viz.

    (32)   You're going, **wasn't** you?

21. Tagliamonte and Smith (2000) do not report the occurrence of the NSR with verbal –s in Guysborough Village but it is not clear if the data challenge Pietsch's (2005) claim that the NSR with past BE is a spin-off. Note also that neither Tagliamonte and Smith nor Wolfram and Sellers (1999) could test for the Proximity Effect of the NSR (only the Type-of-Subject Effect) due to very small numbers of non-adjacent contexts.
22. A statistical analysis using Goldvarb was conducted on the Fens data to inspect the differences in the use of *was* between subjects that would, in the standard, require *were*. The pronoun 'you' favoured *was* the most (0.648), then 'we' (0.600), then 'they' (0.426), with plural NP subjects most disfavouring (0.409). This difference was significant at $p < 0.001$ (Input 0.527, Log Likelihood -1835.089). When all pronouns are grouped together, we find pronouns unsurprisingly therefore also favouring *was* (0.519), and plural NPs again disfavouring (0.411). Again, the difference is significant ($p < 0.001$, Input 0.525, Log Likelihood -1849.154). When only 3rd pl. pronoun subjects (0.505) were compared with 3rd pl. NPs (0.488), again, the difference was significant at $p < 0.001$ (Input 0.447, Log Likelihood -1873.226). Whichever way we observe the differences between pronoun and NP subjects, we find that pronoun subjects in the Fens significantly favour *was*.

4 Past BE 225

23. On the basis of a separate Varbrul run in each case.
24. We would like to thank Sue Fox and Sue Baker for extracting the tokens of past BE from their datasets for us.
25. Note that while the emergence of 3rd sing. –s on regular present tense forms to the east of the Fens in vernacular East Anglian dialects (the gradual loss of zero marking) is a late twentieth century phenomenon, verbal zero has only traditionally been found in the eastern areas of the Fens, and is now obsolescent (Britain 2015).
26. We refer to Adger (2006) for an outline of the particulars of feature-checking, an operation that ensures that a syntactic structure converges (= well-formed). It is not central to the basic line of the argument.
27. We refer to his work for the theoretical reasoning behind this argument. Note, for example, that assuming that lexical items carry full bundles of agreement features (that is [singular: ±] [participant: ±] [author: ±]) misses the generalisation that all [singular: -] as well as all [author: -] forms are *are*.
28. Adger takes one of the principles of the procedure to be 'Reject Optionality'. This rules out the specification [*u*participant: -] because there will be <u>two</u> different forms associated with it: *was* in the context of a 3rd sing. pronoun and *were* in the context of a 3rd pl. pronoun.
29. Person/number marking on past BE has been in decline since the Old English period, where a distinction between 2nd sing. (*wǣre*) and pl. (*wǣron*) was made (for example Willis 2016: 213).
30. Others (most prominently, Lakoff 1973: 54) have famously argued that in some contexts the use of tag-questions signals lack of confidence.
31. In view of the lack of stigmatisation of levelling to *weren't* in Ocracoke (and the Fens; Britain 2002), Schilling-Estes and Wolfram (1994: 295) note: '[W]e realize that there is a delicate balance between the perceptual unobtrusiveness that allows for social acceptance and the perceptual obtrusiveness that renders *weren't* a salient marker of negativity'.
32. Richards (2010) reports that speakers in Morley, a suburb of the city of Leeds in the north of England, use two local, 'intermediate' independent forms in the polarity split: [wə] and [wɒ(nʔ)] (see Richards 2010: 70–72 for discussion of the nature of these forms). Interestingly, the intermediate form [wə] is the dominant form used across the verb paradigm in positive constructions, and [wɒnʔ] is dominant in negative constructions. Richards notes that if [wə] derives from *were* and

[wɒ(n?)] from *was(n't)*, this would make an extremely unusual case of a *were-wasn't* levelled dialect. However, because, so Richards found, speakers do not actually use the forms *were* and *wasn't* in the same way, she thinks that the intermediate variants are best seen as separate, leaving the nature of the past BE pattern in Morley somewhat ambiguous (2010: 78).

References

Adger, D. (2006). Combinatorial variability. *Journal of Linguistics, 42,* 503–530.

Adger, D., & Smith, J. (2005). Variation and the minimalist program. In L. Cornips & K. Corrigan (Eds.), *Syntax and variation: Reconciling the biological and the social* (pp. 149–178). Amsterdam: John Benjamins.

Adger, D., & Smith, J. (2010). Variation in agreement: A lexical feature-based approach. *Lingua, 120,* 1109–1134.

Ahava, S. (2010). *Intermediate past BE: A paradigm reshaped with data drawn from HARES* (MA dissertation). University of Helsinki, Helsinki.

Amos, J., Brana-Straw, M., Britain, D., Grainger, H., Piercy, C., & Rigby, A. (2007). *It's not up north but it's down south, ain't it? A regional examination of auxiliary versus negator contraction.* Paper presented at UK Language Variation and Change 6, University of Lancaster, UK.

Anderwald, L. (2001). *Was/were* variation in non-standard British English today. *English World-Wide, 22,* 1–22.

Anderwald, L. (2002). *Negation in non-standard British English: Gaps, regularizations, asymmetries.* London: Routledge.

Anderwald, L. (2004). The varieties of English spoken in the south-east of England: Morphology and syntax. In B. Kortmann & E. W. Schneider (with K. Burridge, R. Mesthrie, & C. Upton) (Eds.), *A handbook of varieties of English (Vol. 2): Morphology and syntax* (pp. 175–195). Berlin: Mouton de Gruyter.

Antieau, L. (2011). *Was/were* variation in the Middle Rocky Mountains. *Kansas Working Papers in Linguistics, 32,* 48–66.

Bauer, L. (1994). English in New Zealand. In R. Burchfield (Ed.), *The Cambridge history of the English language (Vol. 5): English in Britain and overseas: Origins and development* (pp. 382–429). Cambridge: Cambridge University Press.

Beal, J. (2004). English dialects in the North of England: Morphology and syntax. In B. Kortmann & E. W. Schneider (with K. Burridge, R. Mesthrie, & C. Upton) (Eds.), *A handbook of varieties of English (Vol. 2): Morphology and syntax* (pp. 114–195). Berlin: Mouton de Gruyter.

Beal, J., & Corrigan, K. (2000). Comparing the present with the past to predict the future for Tyneside English. *Newcastle and Durham Working Papers in Linguistics*, 6, 13–30.

Britain, D. (2002). Diffusion, levelling, simplification and reallocation in past tense BE in the English Fens. *Journal of Sociolinguistics,6*, 16–43.

Britain, D. (2008). The importance of 'elsewhere': Looking beyond London and Ireland in the creation of Australian English. *Essex Research Reports in Linguistics,57*, 79–114.

Britain, D. (2015). Between North and South: The Fenland. In R. Hickey (Ed.), *Researching Northern English* (pp. 417–435). Amsterdam: John Benjamins.

Britain, D., & Rupp, L. (2005). *Subject-verb agreement in English dialects: The East Anglian Subject Rule.* Paper presented at the International Conference on Language Variation in Europe 3, Amsterdam, The Netherlands.

Britain, D., & Sudbury, A. (2013). Falkland Island English. In B. Kortmann & K. Lunkenheimer (Eds.), *The Mouton world atlas of variation in English* (pp. 669–676). Berlin: Mouton de Gruyter.

Britain, D., & Trudgill, P. (2005). New dialect formation and contact-induced reallocation: Three case studies from the Fens. *International Journal of English Studies,5*, 183–209.

Brunner, K. (1963). *An outline of Middle English grammar.* Oxford: Blackwell.

Bybee, J., & Hopper, P. J. (2001). Introduction to frequency and linguistic structure. In J. Bybee & P. J. Hopper (Eds.), *Frequency and the emergence of linguistic structure* (pp. 1–27). Amsterdam: John Benjamins.

Carpenter, J. (2004). *The lost community of the Outer Banks: African American speech on Roanoke Island* (MA dissertation). North Carolina State University, Raleigh, NC.

Cheshire, J. (1981). Variation in the use of *ain't* in an urban British dialect. *Language in Society,10*, 365–388.

Cheshire, J. (1982). *Variation in an English dialect: A sociolinguistic study.* Cambridge: Cambridge University Press.

Cheshire, J., & Fox, S. (2009). *Was/were* variation: A perspective from London. *Language Variation and Change, 21*, 1–38.

Cheshire, J., Edwards, V., & Whittle, P. (1989). Urban British dialect grammar: The question of dialect levelling. *English World-Wide, 10,* 185–225.

Chomsky, N. (1995). *The minimalist program.* Cambridge, MA: MIT Press.

Christian, D., Wolfram, W., & Dube, N. (1988). *Variation and change in geographically isolated communities: Appalachian English and Ozark English.* Tuscaloosa, AL: American Dialect Society.

Clarke, S. (1997). English verbal *-s* revisited: The evidence from Newfoundland. *American Speech, 72,* 227–259.

Cole, M. (2008). What is the Northern Subject Rule? The resilience of a medieval constraint in Tyneside English. *Journal of the Spanish Society for Medieval Language and Literature, 15,* 91–114.

Cole, M. (2014). *Old Northumbrian verbal morphosyntax and the (Northern) Subject Rule.* Amsterdam: John Benjamins.

Corrigan, K. P. (1997). *The syntax of South Armagh English in its socio-historical perspective* (Doctoral dissertation). University College Dublin, Dublin.

Corrigan, K. P., Beal, J. C., & Moisl, H. L. (2001–2005). *The Newcastle electronic corpus of Tyneside English.* Newcastle University, UK.

Croft, W. (2000). *Explaining language change: An evolutionary approach.* Harlow: Pearson Education.

Dubois, S., & Horvath, B. (2003). Verbal morphology in Cajun Vernacular English: A comparison with other varieties of Southern English. *Journal of English Linguistics, 31,* 34–59.

Durham, M. (2013). Was/were alternation in Shetland English. *World Englishes, 32,* 108–128.

Eckert, P. (2008). Variation and the indexical field. *Journal of Sociolinguistics, 12,* 453–476.

Edwards, V., & Weltens, B. (1983). Research on non-standard dialects of British English: Progress and prospects. In W. Viereck (Ed.), *Focus on England and Wales* (pp. 97–135). Amsterdam: John Benjamins.

Eisikovits, E. (1991). Variation in subject-verb agreement in inner Sydney English. In J. Cheshire (Ed.), *English around the world: Sociolinguistic perspectives* (pp. 235–256). Cambridge: Cambridge University Press.

Ellis, A. (1889). *On Early English pronunciation (Part V).* London: Truebner.

Errington, J. J. (1985). *Language and social change in Java: Linguistic reflexes of modernization in a traditional royal polity.* Athens, OH: Ohio University Center for International Studies.

Feagin, C. (1979). *Variation and change in Alabama English: A sociolinguistic study of the white community.* Washington, DC: Georgetown University Press.

Forby, R. (1830). *The vocabulary of East-Anglia: An attempt to record the vulgar tongue of the twin sister counties Norfolk and Suffolk, as it existed in the last twenty years.* London: J. B. Nichols and Son.

Forsström, G. (1948). *The verb 'to be' in Middle English: A survey of forms.* Lund: C. W. K. Gleerup.

Fries, C. C. (1940). *American English grammar: The grammatical structure of present-day American English with especial reference to social differences or class dialects.* New York: Appleton-Century-Crofts.

Gardani, F. (2016). Allogenous exaptation. In M. Norde & F. Van de Velde (Eds.), *Exaptation and language change* (pp. 227–260). Amsterdam: John Benjamins.

Greene, R. (2010). *Language, ideology and identity in rural eastern Kentucky* (Doctoral dissertation). Stanford University, Palo Alto.

Halle, M., & Marantz, A. (1993). Distributed morphology and the pieces of inflection. In K. Hale & J. Keyser (Eds.), *The view from Building 20* (pp. 111–176). Cambridge, MA: MIT Press.

Hay, J., & Schreier, D. (2004). Reversing the trajectory of language change: Subject-verb agreement with *be* in New Zealand. *Language Variation and Change, 16,* 209–235.

Hazen, K. (2000). Subject-verb concord in a postinsular dialect: The gradual persistence of dialect patterning. *Journal of English Linguistics, 28,* 127–144.

Hendery, R. (2016). Untangling synchronic and diachronic variation: Verb agreement in Palmerston English. *Australian Journal of Linguistics, 36,* 429–450.

Henry, A. (1995). *Belfast English and Standard English: Dialect variation and parameter setting.* Oxford: Oxford University Press.

Hock, H. (1986). *Principles of historical linguistics.* Berlin: Mouton de Gruyter.

Hopper, P. J. (1991). On some principles of grammaticization. In E. C. Traugott & B. Heine (Eds.), *Approaches to grammaticalization (Vol. I): Theoretical and methodological issues* (pp. 17–36). Amsterdam: John Benjamins.

Ihalainen, O. (1987). Towards a grammar of the Somerset dialect: A case study of the language of J. M. In L. Kahlas-Tarka (Ed.), *Neophilologica Fennica* (Modern Language Society 100 years) (pp. 71–86). Helsinki: Société néophilologique.

Ito, R., & Tagliamonte, S. (2003). Well weird, right dodgy, very strange, really cool. *Language in Society, 32,* 257–279.

Jankowski, B. L., & Tagliamonte, S. A. (2017). A lost Canadian dialect: The Ottawa Valley 1975–2013. In T. Säily, A. Nurmi, M. Palander-Collin, & A. Auer (Eds.), *Historical linguistics: A Festschrift for Terttu Nevalainen on the occasion of her 65th birthday* (pp. 239–274). Amsterdam: John Benjamins.

Jespersen, O. (1954). *A modern English grammar on historical principles*. London: Allen and Unwin.

José, B. (2007). Appalachian English in Southern Indiana? The evidence from verbal -*s*. *Language Variation and Change, 19,* 249–280.

Joseph, B. D. (2016). Being exacting about exapting: An exaptation omnibus. In F. Van de Velde & M. Norde (Eds.), *Exaptation and language change* (pp. 27–55). Amsterdam: John Benjamins.

Khan, A. (2007). *A sociolinguistic study of Birmingham English: Language variation and change in a multi-ethnic British community* (Doctoral dissertation). University of Lancaster, Lancaster.

Kingston, M. (2000). *Dialects in danger: Rural dialect attrition in the East Anglian county of Suffolk* (MA dissertation). University of Essex, Colchester.

Klemola, J. (2006). Was/were *variation in traditional dialects of England*. Paper presented at the International Conference of English Historical Linguistics 14, University of Bergamo, Italy.

Kökeritz, H. (1932). *The phonology of the Suffolk dialect*. Uppsala: Aktibolag.

Kortmann, B., & Wagner, S. (2005). The Freiburg Dialect Project and Corpus. In B. Kortmann, T. Herrman, L. Pietsch, & S. Wagner (Eds.), *A comparative grammar of British English dialects: Agreement, gender, relative clauses* (pp. 1–20). Berlin: Mouton de Gruyter.

Kroch, A. (1989). Function and grammar in the history of English: Periphrastic 'do'. In R. Fasold (Ed.), *Language change and variation* (pp. 133–172). Amsterdam: John Benjamins.

Kuryłowicz, J. (1949). La nature des proces dits 'analogiques'. *Acta Linguistica, 5,* 121–138.

Labov, W. (1969). Contraction, deletion and inherent variability of the English copula. *Language, 48,* 773–818.

Lakoff, R. (1973). Language and woman's place. *Language in Society, 2,* 45–80.

Lass, R. (1990). How to do things with junk: Exaptation in language evolution. *Journal of Linguistics, 26,* 79–102.

Lass, R. (1997). *Historical linguistics and language change*. Cambridge: Cambridge University Press.

Levey, S. (2007). *The next generation: Aspects of grammatical variation in the speech of some London preadolescents* (Doctoral dissertation). Queen Mary University of London, London.

Malcolm, I. (1996). Observations on variability in the verb phrase in Aboriginal English. *Australian Journal of Linguistics, 16,* 145–165.

Mallinson, C., & Wolfram, W. (2002). Dialect accommodation in a bi-ethnic mountain enclave community: More evidence on the development of African American English. *Language in Society, 31,* 743–775.

Mańczak, W. (1958). Tendences générales des changements analogiques. *Lingua, 7,* 298-325 and 387-420.

Mańczak, W. (1980). Laws of analogy. In J. Fisiak (Ed.), *Historical morphology* (pp. 283–288). Berlin: Mouton de Gruyter.

McMahon, A. M. S. (1994). *Understanding language change.* Cambridge: Cambridge University Press.

Meechan, M., & Foley, M. (1994). On resolving disagreement: Linguistic theory and variation—*There's bridges. Language Variation and Change, 6,* 63–85.

Mittelstaedt, J., & Parrot, J. (2002). *A distributed morphology account of weren't levelling.* Paper presented at New Ways of Analyzing Variation 31, Stanford University, U.S.

Montgomery, M. (1994). The evolution of verb concord in Scots. In A. Fenton & D. McDonald (Eds.), *Studies in Scots and Gaelic: Proceedings of the Third International Conference on the Languages of Scotland* (pp. 81–95). Edinburgh: Canongate.

Montgomery, M. (1999). Sierra Leone Settler English: Another exported variety of African American English. *English World-Wide, 20,* 1–34.

Moore, E. (2003). *Learning style and identity: A sociolinguistic analysis of a Bolton high school* (Doctoral dissertation). University of Manchester, Manchester.

Moore, E. (2011). Interaction between social category and social practice: Explaining *was/were* variation. *Language Variation and Change, 22,* 347–371.

Moore, E., & Podesva, R. J. (2009). Style, indexicality and the social meaning of tag questions. *Language in Society, 38,* 447–485.

Mossé, F. (1952). *A handbook of Middle English.* Baltimore, MD: John Hopkins University Press.

Mufwene, S. S. (1996). The founder principle in creole genesis. *Diachronica, 13,* 83–134.

Murray, J. (1873). *The dialect of the Southern Counties of Scotland: Its pronunciation, grammar and historical relations.* London: Asher.

Narrog, H. (2007). Exaptation, grammaticalization, and reanalysis. *California Linguistic Notes, 23,* 1–27.

Nevalainen, T. (2006). Vernacular universals? The case of plural *was* in Early Modern English. In T. Nevalainen, J. Klemola, & M. Laitinen (Eds.), *Types of variation: Diachronic, dialectal and typological* (pp. 351–369). Amsterdam: John Benjamins.

Ojanen, A.-L. (n.d. a). *Past tense forms of the verb BE in the dialect of Cambridgeshire* (Unpublished manuscript).

Ojanen, A.-L. (n.d. b). *Past-tense negative forms of the verb BE in the dialect of Cambridgeshire* (Unpublished manuscript).

Orton, H., & Dieth, E. (1962–1971). *Survey of English Dialects*. Leeds: E. J. Arnold.

Orton, H., & Tilling, P. M. (1971). *Survey of English Dialects (B): The basic material (Vol. 3.1 and 3.3): The East Midland counties and East Anglia*. Leeds: E. J. Arnold.

Parrott, J. K. (2007). Distributed morphological mechanisms of Smith Island *weren't* leveling. *University of Pennsylvania Working Papers in Linguistics, 13*, 295–308.

Petyt, K. M. (1985). *Dialect and accent in industrial West Yorkshire*. Amsterdam: John Benjamins.

Pichler, H. (2018). *From complexity to uniformity, via (contact-induced) grammaticalization: Tracing the evolution of the London question tag 'system'*. Paper presented at the Discourse-Pragmatic Variation and Change Conference 4, University of Helsinki, Helsinki.

Pietsch, L. (2005). "*Some do and some doesn't*": Verbal concord variation in the north of the British Isles. In B. Kortmann, T. Herrman, L. Pietsch, & S. Wagner (Eds.), *A comparative grammar of British English dialects: Agreement, gender, relative clauses* (pp. 125–210). Berlin: Mouton de Gruyter.

Poplack, S., & Tagliamonte, S. (1989). There's no tense like the present: Verbal *-s* inflection in Early Black English. *Language Variation and Change, 1*, 47–84.

Poplack, S., & Tagliamonte, S. (1991). African American English in the diaspora: Evidence from old-line Nova Scotians. *Language Variation and Change, 3*, 301–339.

Pyles, T., & Algeo, J. (2005). *The origins and development of the English language* (5th ed.). Boston: Thomson Wadsworth.

Richards, H. (2010). Preterite *be*: A new perspective? *English World-Wide, 31*, 62–81.

Schilling-Estes, N. (2002). On the nature of isolated and post-isolated dialects: Innovation, variation and differentiation. *Journal of Sociolinguistics, 6*, 64–85.

Schilling-Estes, N. (2004). Constructing ethnicity in interaction. *Journal of Sociolinguistics, 8,* 163–195.

Schilling-Estes, N. ([2008] 2013). Investigating stylistic variation. In J. Chambers, P. Trudgill, & N. Schilling-Estes (Eds.), *Handbook of language variation and change* (2nd ed., pp. 327–349). Oxford: Blackwell.

Schilling-Estes, N., & Wolfram, W. (1994). Convergent explanation and alternative regularization patterns: *Were/weren't* levelling in a vernacular English variety. *Language Variation and Change, 6,* 273–302.

Schilling-Estes, N., & Zimmerman, L. (2000). *On the progress of morphological change:* Was/weren't *leveling in Smith Island English.* Paper presented at the Linguistic Society of America Annual Meeting, Chicago, IL.

Schreier, D. (2002a). *Terra incognita* in the Anglophone world: Tristan da Cunha, South Atlantic Ocean. *English Word-Wide, 23,* 1–29.

Schreier, D. (2002b). Past *be* in Tristan da Cunha: The rise and fall of categoricality in language change. *American Speech, 77,* 70–99.

Shorrocks, G. (1999). *A grammar of the dialect of the Bolton area (Part II): Morphology and syntax.* Frankfurt: Peter Lang.

Silverstein, M. (1979). Language structure and linguistic ideology. In P. R. Clyne, W. F. Hanks, & C. L. Hofbauer (Eds.), *The elements: A parasession on linguistic units and levels* (pp. 193–247). Chicago: Chicago Linguistic Society.

Singler, J. V. (1997). The configuration of Liberia's Englishes. *World Englishes, 16,* 205–231.

Smith, J. (2000). *Synchrony and diachrony in the evolution of English: Evidence from Scotland* (Doctoral dissertation). University of York, York.

Smith, J., & Tagliamonte, S. (1998). '*We* were *all thegither, I think we* was *all thegither':* Was regularization in Buckie English. *World Englishes, 17,* 105–126.

Strang, B. M. H. (1970). *A history of English.* London: Methuen.

Sudbury, A. (2001). Falkland Island English: A southern hemisphere variety? *English World-Wide, 22,* 55–80.

Tagliamonte, S. (1998). *Was/were* variation across the generations: View from the city of York. *Language Variation and Change, 10,* 153–192.

Tagliamonte, S. A. (2009). There *was* universals, then there *weren't*: A comparative sociolinguistic perspective on 'default singulars'. In M. Filppula, J. Klemola, & H. Paulasto (Eds.), *Vernacular universals and language contacts: Evidence from varieties of English and beyond* (pp. 103–129). London: Routledge.

Tagliamonte, S., & Smith, J. (1999). Analogical levelling in Samaná English: The case of *was* and *were*. *Journal of English Linguistics, 27*, 8–26.

Tagliamonte, S., & Smith, J. (2000). Old *was*, new ecology: Viewing English through the sociolinguistic filter. In S. Poplack (Ed.), *The English history of African American English* (pp. 141–171). Oxford: Blackwell.

Traugott, E. C. (2001). Zeroing in on multifunctionality and style. In P. Eckert & J. R. Rickford (Eds.), *Style and sociolinguistic variation* (pp. 127–136). Cambridge: Cambridge University Press.

Traugott, E. C. (2004). Exaptation and grammaticalization. In M. Akimoto (Ed.), *Linguistic studies based on corpora* (pp. 133–156). Tokyo: Hituzi Syobo Publishing.

Trüb, R. (2006). Nonstandard verbal paradigms in earlier white southern American English. *American Speech, 81*, 250–265.

Trudgill, P. (1986). *Dialects in contact*. Oxford: Blackwell.

Trudgill, P. (1989). Contact and isolation in linguistic change. In L. Breivik & E. Jahr (Eds.), *Language change: Contributions to the study of its causes* (pp. 227–238). Berlin: Mouton de Gruyter.

Trudgill, P. (1996). Language contact and inherent variability: The absence of hypercorrection in East Anglian present-tense verb forms. In J. Klemola, M. Kytö, & M. Risannen (Eds.), *Speech past and present: Studies in English dialectology in memory of Ossi Ihalainen* (pp. 412–425). Frankfurt: Peter Lang.

Trudgill, P. (2008). English dialect "defaults singulars", *was* versus *were*, Verner's law, and Germanic dialects. *Journal of English Linguistics, 36*, 341–353.

Vasko, A.-L. (2010). Past tense BE: Old and new variants. In B. Heselwood & C. Upton (Eds.), *Proceedings of methods XIII: Papers from the Thirteenth International Conference on Methods in Dialectology, 2008* (pp. 289–298). Frankfurt: Peter Lang.

Vermandere, D., & Meul, C. (2016). How functionless is junk and how useful is exaptation? Probing the -I/ESC- morpheme. In F. Van de Velde & M. Norde (Eds.), *Exaptation and language change* (pp. 261–285). Amsterdam: John Benjamins.

Visser, F. Th. (1970). *An historical syntax of the English language (Part one): Syntactical units with one verb* (2nd impression). Leiden: E. J. Brill.

Walker, J., & Van Herk, G. (2003). "We labors under a great deal of disadvantiges": Verbal -*s* in Early African American English. In S. Burelle & S. Somesfalean (Eds.), *Proceedings of the 2002 Annual Conference of the Canadian Linguistics Association* (pp. 365–377). Montreal: Canadian Linguistics Association.

Williams, K. (2007). *Ethnic identity and Past be configuration in the Lumbee Community of Baltimore, Maryland.* Paper presented at New Ways of Analyzing Variation 36, University of Pennsylvania, U.S.

Willis, D. (2016). Exaptation and degrammaticalization within an acquisition-based model of abductive reanalysis. In F. Van de Velde & M. Norde (Eds.), *Exaptation and language change* (pp. 197–225). Amsterdam: John Benjamins.

Wolfram, W. (2004). The grammar of urban African American Vernacular English. In B. Kortmann & E.W. Schneider (with K. Burridge, R. Mesthrie & C. Upton) (Eds.), *Handbook of varieties of English (Vol. 2): Morphology and syntax* (pp. 111–132). Berlin: Mouton de Gruyter.

Wolfram, W., & Christian, D. (1976). *Appalachian speech.* Arlington: Center for Applied Linguistics.

Wolfram, W., & Schilling-Estes, N. (2003a). Language change in "conservative" dialects: The case of past tense *be* in southern enclave communities. *American Speech, 78,* 208–227.

Wolfram, W., & Schilling-Estes, N. (2003b). Parallel development and alternative restructuring: The case of *weren't* intensification. In D. Britain & J. Cheshire (Eds.), *Social dialectology: In honour of Peter Trudgill* (pp. 131–154). Amsterdam: John Benjamins.

Wolfram, W., & Schilling-Estes, N. (2005). Remnant dialects in the coastal United States. In R. Hickey (Ed.), *Legacies of colonial English: Studies in transported dialects* (pp. 172–202). Cambridge: Cambridge University Press.

Wolfram, W., & Sellers, J. (1999). Ethnolinguistic marking of past *be* in Lumbee Vernacular English. *Journal of English Linguistics, 27,* 94–114.

Wolfram, W., & Thomas, E. (2002). *The development of African American English.* Oxford: Blackwell.

Woolard, K. (2008). Why *dat* now? Linguistic-anthropological solutions to the explanation of sociolinguistic icons and change. *Journal of Sociolinguistics, 12,* 432–452.

Zwicky, A., & Pullum, G. (1983). Clitization vs. inflection: English *n't. Language, 59,* 502–513.

5

Verbal –s in Existential *there* Sentences

5.1 Introduction

In this chapter we address verbal –s in existential *there* sentences. We define verbal –s in existentials as the use of –s in the context of a plural subject, which occurs following the verb. In the examples in (1), strings with verbal –s are in bold, and strings with subject-verb agreement according to Standard English are italicised.

(1) a. **Is there any nets** out there? (Eisikovits 1991: 245)
     b. *There are houses* where people have grown up and lived there for many years. (Meechan and Foley 1994: 72)
     c. **There was**, I think **more partridges** about there than what *there were pheasants*, yeah. (Peitsara 1988: 84)
     d. **There's two doors**. (Hay and Schreier 2004: 217)

Existential *there* sentences have been a focus of research in both generative syntax (see Felser and Rupp 2001 for an overview) and functional grammar, which postulates that the form that linguistic structures take is more

© The Author(s) 2019
L. Rupp and D. Britain, *Linguistic Perspectives on a Variable English Morpheme*,
https://doi.org/10.1057/978-1-349-72803-9_5

strongly determined by usage-based considerations (Hannay 1985), as well as in studies in language variation and change (LVC). We will show that the respective findings are clearly complementary and can inform each other. Existential *there* sentences, therefore, are among research areas in which collaboration between formal, functional and LVC-linguists would seem particularly fruitful. Functionally-oriented linguistics has inquired into the particular pragmatic function of existential *there* sentences, and the apparent relation between this function and the particular role and positioning of *there* and the denotational subject. Generative syntacticians have gone to great lengths to determine the conditions whereunder agreement between the subject and the verb can be established in a structure where the subject follows the verb. Variationist studies, however, have found that speakers actually very frequently use verbal –s in existential *there* sentences; that is, that existential *there* sentences quite readily show apparent 'non-agreement'. In fact, verbal –s in existentials is so pervasive that it has been demonstrated (i) to occur across varieties of English worldwide; (ii) to show higher rates of usage than in any other clause type; and (iii) to be even deployed by speakers in whose dialect verbal –s is otherwise (virtually) non-existent. Britain and Sudbury (2002: 214–216) provide an overview of quantitative studies that shows the percentage of verbal –s in present tense existentials to range between 87% and 98%, and in past tense existentials between 50% and 100%. In view of the pervasiveness of verbal –s in existential *there* sentences, variationists commonly treat this use separately from the use of verbal –s in other clause types. Here is a selection of quotes from variationist linguists who have commented on the situation accordingly:

- Cheshire et al. (1989: 199–200) in their survey of 89 schools across Britain found verbal –s in existential *there* sentences to be very widespread and conclude that 'they are best seen as a stylistic feature of English, characteristic of colloquial, informal speech, rather than as a non-standard feature';
- Trudgill (2008: 324) states: '[C]onstructions of the type *there's lots of people/there was lots of people* ... [are] often labeled "vernacular" or "nonstandard" despite the fact that [they] are used by most native speakers of English';

- In a comparative analysis of 13 English speaking locales across the world, Tagliamonte (2009: 115, 110) reports that existential constructions are 'perhaps the best example of a scale-independent constraint [on verbal –s]'; where 'scale' can be the community, the region, the nation, or the supranational level.[1]

The central question of this chapter therefore is:

Why is verbal –s currently so pervasive in existential there *sentences and how is the nature and function of verbal –s in existentials best explained?*

Other major questions are:

Can structural- and LVC-researchers work together in explaining the patterning of verbal –s in existential there *sentences?* Specifically,

How can insights from generative syntax into the structure of existential there *sentences help identify grammatical factors that favour verbal –s in this clause type,* and

What are the implications of the pervasiveness of verbal –s for generative assumptions about the mechanism of subject-verb agreement in existential there *sentences and perhaps in syntax more generally?*

The structure of this chapter is as follows. Section 5.2 provides a description of relevant properties of existential *there* sentences and outlines grammatical analysis of subject type, subject positioning, and subject-verb agreement in this construction. Section 5.3 presents variationist studies that have documented the robustness of verbal –s in existential *there* sentences. In Sect. 5.4 we examine the ways in which different linguistic traditions can work together in research on existentials; generating understanding of the grammatical factors that condition verbal –s in existentials on the one hand, and of the configuration for subject-verb agreement on the other. Finally, in Sect. 5.5, we will address the central question of this chapter. For this purpose, we will follow work by Breivik and Swan (2000) who have traced the history of *there* and argue that in the course of the history of English, existential *there* has grammaticalised from the locative adverb *there* in both form and meaning/function. For introductory illustration, note first that existential *there* has a 'weak form' compared to locative *there* (/ðεə(r)/) to the extent it can be pronounced with a reduced vowel

240   L. Rupp and D. Britain

(/ðə(r)/) and cannot bear emphatic stress. The illustrating examples in (2–3) have been adapted from Milsark (1974: 121):

(2)   Maybe I was here on March 2, but I was THERE on March 1.
        [locative adverb *there*]
(3) a. Bill didn't say that he caught a large snake, only that
        *THERE was one.
    b. Bill didn't say that he caught a large snake, only that there
        WAS one.
        [existential *there*]

Second, note that rather than conveying (concrete) locative reference, existential *there* has a more abstract, pragmatic function of alerting 'the addressee that she must be prepared to direct her attention towards an item of new information' (Breivik and Swan 2000: 28). We will argue that existential *there* is currently undergoing further, 'secondary', grammaticalisation of the type proposed by Traugott (2002). We assume that this grammaticalisation process was triggered in part by –s losing its function as an agreement morpheme in a context where the denotational subject was no longer in subject position. Following Hopper and Traugott's (2003) account of the grammaticalisation of the string *let us* → *let's* → *lets*, we specifically propose that in existentials, the morphemes *there* and –s have contracted into the form *there's*, and that this form may continue to grammaticalise into a single, merged morpheme '*theres*'. Entertaining a similar idea that *there(')s* represents an advanced stage in a grammaticalisation cline, Breivik and Martínez-Insua (2008) and Pfenninger (2009) have argued that *there(')s* has also developed concomitant functions. We will suggest that the development of the form *there(')s* has restored isomorphism and that *there(')s* is iconically motivated as a signpost that points out new information in the discourse. Here we will draw on Breivik and Swan (2000) who take existential *there(')s* to have the nature of a presentative signal. On this analysis, the usage of verbal –s in existentials is not strictly a 'separate' phenomenon, as it has been commonly characterised. Rather, it demonstrates one of a range of types of functional shift that verbal –s may undergo. In a similar way, use of the form *there(')s* in the function of a presentative signal is 'only' one manifestation of our 'Iconicity Hypothesis', according to which, so we hypothesised in Chapter 2, the particular functional shifts of verbal –s (re)introduce a diagrammatic iconic relation. Additionally, we will show (as Walker 2007 has previously advocated) that an examination of grammatical and social constraints on verbal –s can help establish the nature and function of the form *there(')s*.

5.2 Description and Formal Analysis of Existential *there* Sentences

It is well known that there are two kinds of *there* in English: existential *there*[2] and locative *there*. They are exemplified in the sentences (4) from Breivik and Swan (2000: 19) who term them *there*$_1$ and *there*$_2$:

(4) a. **There**$_1$ are linguists in the English Department who are worryingly ignorant of historical syntax.
 b. The linguist over **there**$_2$ behind the lamppost.

In Sect. 5.5 we will see that existential *there* diachronically derived from locative *there* in a grammaticalisation process. We will discuss differences in form and meaning/function between the two kinds of *there* in detail at that point. In the current section we provide an overview of the main grammatical characteristics of existential *there* sentences and focus particularly on aspects which are relevant to an analysis of verbal –s in this construction. In practice, this means that we will largely restrict ourselves to functionally oriented approaches to existentials and the properties of subjects there. We then turn to generative accounts of the syntax of subjects and subject-verb agreement in existential *there* sentences.

242   L. Rupp and D. Britain

The basic structure of existentials can be represented as *There* + *be* + *NP* + *XP*. Within this structure, existential *there* occurs in positions typically occupied by subject-NPs in English. It also behaves like a subject-NP in undergoing particular syntactic operations, such as inversion with the verb in (tag-)questions. For this reason, *there* is called the 'grammatical' subject of existentials. The subject-like behaviour of existential *there* is shown in (5a–d) from Felser and Rupp (2001: 290).

(5)   a.   Is there any hope?   [INTERROGATIVE]
        b.   There is no hope, is there?   [TAG-QUESTION]
        c.   There is believed [*t* to have been a   [PASSIVE]
               revolution].
        d.   There seems [*t* to have been something   [RAISING]
               brewing].

Existential *there* sentences also have a denotational subject, known as the 'associate-NP', which occurs in an unusual position following the verb (usually *be*). Hannay (1985) ascribes the positioning of the associate-NP to the pragmatic function of existential *there* sentences. He proposes to treat the existential as a presentative device that introduces new referents into the discourse (1985: 51).[3] Following cross-linguistic principles of functional grammar that govern the distribution of given and new information in a text (Halliday 1994), the associate-NP is placed in a position following the verb because this is the canonical position for items that have high information value (that is, items that carry the 'focus' function of presenting the relatively most important or salient information). Breivik (1981: 22) noted that while syntactically existential sentences take many forms across languages, '[t]here can be no doubt, however, that the various manifestations are strategies for accomplishing the same communicative goal: the introduction of new information. Indeed, in many languages, existential sentences are the only means of introducing indefinite non-generic NP's into the discourse.' Since the initial mention of an entity is typically introduced by an indefinite NP, the associate-NP is more frequently indefinite than a definite NP. This observation led to the postulation of the Definiteness Restriction (Milsark 1974). Compare the (a) to the (b) in examples (6–9) below (adapted from Felser and Rupp 2001: 291):

5 Verbal –s in Existential *there* Sentences   243

(6) a. There suddenly broke out **a fight**.
     b. *There suddenly broke out **the fight**.   [DEFINITE NP]
(7) a. There appeared to be **a ghost** in the attic.
     b. *There appeared to be **Elvis** in the attic.   [PROPER NAME]
(8) a. There seemed to be **someone** in the room.
     b. *There seemed to be **she/her** in the room.   [PRONOUN]
(9) a. There arrived **three new lecturers** today.
     b. *There arrived **every new lecturer** today.   [QUANTIFIER]

Definite descriptions, proper names and pronouns are usually excluded from existential *there* sentences because they convey given information, and this is also true of quantified noun phrases introduced by a universal quantifier such as *every* or *most*. Milsark (1977: 8) labelled NPs that are excluded from functioning as the associate-NP in an existential *there* sentence 'strong' NPs, and those that are permitted 'weak' NPs. However, Milsark (1974) already pointed out a notable exception to the definite restriction; namely, the 'list reading' of existentials exemplified in (10). (11–12) show some other situations in which a definite associate-NP can be perfectly normal:

Listing:
(10) a. Is there anything worth seeing around here? Well there's **the Necco factory**. (Milsark 1974: 208)
     b. If you have any trouble at least there's **John and Fred** to fall back on. (Hannay 1985: 18)

Reminders:
(11) a. Don't go yet. There's still **the football coupons** to be filled in. (Hannay 1985: 18)
     b. I'd like to go with you, but there's **all this work** to do! And there's **my mother-in-law** who's got to be taken to the airport. (Bolinger 1977: 119)

Typing (indicating a typical token of a particular type):

(12) a. There was **the most beautiful sunset** this evening. (Hannay 1985: 19)

  b. There's **the oddest-looking man** standing at the front door! (Bolinger 1977: 119)[4]

In an attempt to come to grips with such exceptions, Hannay points to the significance of the communicative setting of existentials (as presentative constructions they introduce the subject entity in a particular state of affairs into the world of the discourse) and contends that the issue at stake really is: 'in what sense must information be new in order to qualify for being introduced?' (1985: 3). According to Bolinger (1977: 117), the relevant factor is not grammatical definiteness but *semantic* definiteness (knownness), while Prince's (1992) taxonomy of given/new information crucially distinguishes between 'hearer old/new' and 'discourse old/new' information (see also Birner and Ward 1998: 13 ff.). In the case of 'reminders', a definite NP (like *the football coupons* in (11a)) may be known from the previous context, but it is recalled onto the scene. 'Reminders' can bring something back into awareness as well as make us aware of it for the first time in a new context. In a similar way, the NPs *John* and *Fred* in (10b) are definite, but they invoke new information in the sense that in the situation at hand, they provide the identity of people that the addressee can fall back on. This information may have been explicitly sought by a person asking the question 'Who do you think I could turn to?'. Hannay concludes that there exists no Definite Restriction as such. Indeed, Pfenninger (2009: 161) calls the constraint 'outdated', Bolinger (1977) maintains that none of the older comprehensive handbooks actually noted the constraint, while Martìnez-Insua (2013: 219) has shown that definite descriptions have been used in existential *there* sentences across the history of English. Various definite subjects are perfectly acceptable if they present salient information or are 'in focus' *in the given setting* (Hannay 1985: 101, 128) or, as Bolinger (1977: 94) has put it, if they '[bring] a piece of knowledge into consciousness'.[5] We will draw on the observed association of existentials with new information in our analysis of the form *there(')s* in Sect. 5.5.

A last property that has been associated with the associate-NP is that it can be structurally complex; a property that Hannay (1985) has termed 'extension', Martínez-Insua and Palacios Martínez (2003: 276) have related to the 'newness' of the referent, and one that seems to derive from a tendency for 'heavy' NPs to be placed in the right-periphery of the clause (Ross 1967). In fact, in corpus research on spoken and written data in the *British National Corpus* (BNC), Martínez-Insua and Palacios Martínez (2003) observed a markedly higher frequency of verbal –s in the context of 'heavy' NPs (containing PPs, relative clauses, etc.): 71.3% compared to 28.7% with 'minimal' associate-NPs (2003: 276–277). Some examples are shown in (13):

(13) a. Cos even in the shadow area you see there's still **nice textures shown on the front of the steps** …
     b. There was **lots of bare people on the beach.**

Martínez-Insua and Palacios Martínez envisage that 'the short-term memory of the speaker/writer may be affected by the length or possibly higher complexity of those constructions' (2003: 280) to the extent that s/he may lose sight of the connection between the subject and the verb. In Sect. 5.4.1, we will have a closer look at the internal structure of NPs and the effect on the occurrence of verbal –s.

Finally, one of the properties that has especially intrigued formal linguists is that in existentials the verb (in formal written Standard English, the most scrutinised variety in generative analyses) agrees with the associate-NP rather than with existential *there* in subject position.[6] This is shown in (14) which contains a plural associate-NP *seven blond girls*:

(14) There **were/*was three blond girls** in my group.

Generative syntacticians have been concerned with the question of how subject-verb agreement is ensured in existential *there* sentences throughout the development of the framework, as Felser and

Rupp (2001) have shown. Chomsky (1995) proposed that existential *there* is base-generated in (Spec,TP), the canonical subject position. Note that in the 1995 model, agreement does not constitute a separate phrase in the clause structure anymore; rather, agreement features are checked within TP. Under the VP-internal Subject Hypothesis (Koopman and Sportiche 1991), two subject positions are available: an external one in (Spec,TP) and an internal one in (Spec,VP). An existential *there* sentence such as *There were many people watching* can, accordingly, be assigned the representation in (15), where the associate-NP occupies (Spec,VP).

(15)

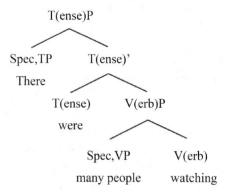

This raises the question of how the associate-NP 'checks' its plural agreement features against those of T. In the Minimalist Program (Chomsky 1995), features can only be checked in certain structurally 'local' relations, chiefly between specifier (Spec) and head, and hence constituents need to move to these positions. Note that in the configuration in (15), the associate-NP is not in the checking domain of *were* in T, and existential *there* already occupies (Spec,TP).

In response to the more general dilemma of not having the subject in the canonical subject position, Chomsky (1986) earlier suggested that the associate-NP raises to the subject position at the 'covert' syntactic level of Logical Form (LF), replacing existential *there* and enabling it to agree with the verb. This analysis is shown in (16), from Felser and Rupp (2001: 295):

(16) a. There was a fly in my soup.
     b. [a fly] was t in my soup

However, the proposal that existential *there* sentences and their non-existential counterparts are essentially structurally equivalent has proven somewhat difficult to maintain. We would expect (i) that (16a) and (16b) should be synonymous, and (ii) that for every existential *there* sentence, there is a non-existential counterpart. That this is not in fact the case is shown by a minimal pair like (17a–b) from Jenkins (1975: 49), cited in Felser and Rupp (2001: 296).

(17) a. There's a difference between X and Y.
     b. *A difference is between X and Y.

Bolinger (1977: 121, Footnote 1) has argued that such contrasts show that '*there* is neither empty nor redundant, but is a fully functional word that contrasts with its absence.' This view has received support from Pérez-Guerra (1999: 81) who suggests that '*there* is not a prototypical dummy element but rather a grammaticalized meaningful discourse marker with informative consequences on the utterance in which it occurs' (Martìnez-Insua 2013: 2014). Having discussed the pragmatics of existential sentences in this section, we will address the specific function of existential *there* in more detail in Sect. 5.5.

In Chomsky's (1995) framework, 'covert' raising of the associate-NP at LF is reanalysed as the adjunction of just the associate's agreement feature(s) to T. In this way, they can be 'checked' with the verb. The procedure is indicated in (18) below (based on Chomsky 1995: 370).

(18)

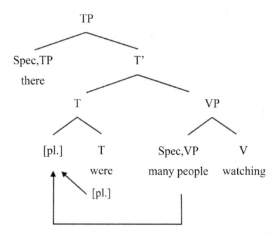

This analysis would not only account for subject-verb agreement in existential *there* sentences, but also for other characteristics of the construction, such as the absence of wide scope readings for associate-NPs. Felser and Rupp (2001: 291) note that an associate-QP (quantifier phase) like *many* in (19) has narrow scope only. That is, the associate-QP is necessarily in the scope of negation; it cannot take scope over it. This follows if unlike the agreement features of the associate-QP, its semantic features do not raise to T across negation, a suggestion made by Jang (1997).

(19)　There are **not many students** in this class.
　　　i = It is not the case that many students are in　　NOT > MANY
　　　this class.
　　　ii ≠ Many students are such that they are not in　　*MANY > NOT
　　　this class.

In Chomsky (1998), the concept of feature raising is nonetheless replaced by the possibility of 'abstract' long-distance agreement by the operation Agree. Under this scenario, indicated in the diagram in (20), the features of the associate-NP remain 'in place' and can be checked with the verb there.

(20)

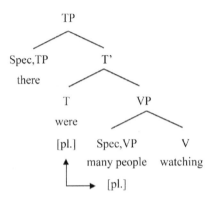

The idea that the associate-NP occurs in its base position in (Spec,VP) receives support from the favouring of indefinite subjects, as well as the obligatory stage-level properties of the predicate of existential *there* sentences, a fact orginally noted by Milsark (1974: 211). Following Carlson (1980: 152), who introduced the conceptual terminology, stage-level predicates are predicates that apply to transitional 'stages of individuals' (e.g. activities, events), whereas individual-level predicates express more permanent states. In existential *there* sentences, predicates that induce an individual-level reading such as *be blond* or *be intelligent* are normally not possible. Compare the (a) and (b) sentences of (21–22):

(21) a. There was a girl **in my group**.
 b. *There was a girl **blond**.
(22) a. There were many people **watching**.
 b. *There were many people **intelligent**.

Diesing (1992) has shown that the availability of the predicates can be explained by assuming that subject-NPs occupy different positions in the clause structure depending on their semantics. In this relation, note first that where the subject of an individual-level predicate is a bare plural, the bare plural subject can only have a 'strong' generic interpretation, as indicated in (23a). By contrast, bare plural subjects of stage-level predicates also admit a 'weak' existential reading (Diesing 1992: 17), as indicated in (23b).

(23) a.   Firemen are **intelligent.**   (individual-level predicate; generic reading only)
          = people working for the fire-brigade generally have a high IQ.
      b.   Firemen are **available.**   (stage-level predicate; existential reading also)
          = there currently are some firemen on call.

On the model of the semantic framework of Heim (1982), the details of which need not concern us here, Diesing postulates that the VP in the clause structure is subject to a process of 'existential closure' (1992: 10). Accordingly, subjects that occur in (Spec,VP) receive a 'weak' interpretation (i.e. indefinite NPs), while subjects that are interpreted in (Spec,TP) are assigned a 'strong' reading (i.e. definite NPs). Kratzer (1995: 141) has proposed that only stage-level predicates provide an internal (Spec,VP) position. Therefore, bare plural subjects of stage-level predicates can be construed with a 'weak' existential reading (cf. (23b)). However, bare plural subjects of individual-level predicates are always external subjects in (Spec,TP), and hence will automatically be interpreted as a 'strong' generic NP (cf. (23a)). Note that if the associate-NP of existentials is in (Spec,VP), it follows that the associate-NP is canonically associated with a 'weak' reading and cannot be the subject of an individual-level predicate. This account also captures the earlier-mentioned fact that existential *there* sentences and their non-existential counterparts are not necessarily equivalent. Recall the minimal pair in (17a–b), which we have reproduced in (24a–b) below, and to which we added (25a–b).

(24) a. There was [Spec,VP **a fly**] in my soup.
 b. [Spec,TP **A fly**] was in my soup.
(25) a. There were [Spec,VP **some girls**] at the party.
 b. [Spec,TP **Some girls**] were at the party.

The same interpretative difference can be observed. As the associate of an existential in (Spec,VP), indefinite NPs have a 'weak' reading, like a non-specific reading in (24a) or a so-called 'cardinal' reading in (25b) (where 'some girls' simply means 'more than one girl'). Compare (24b) and (25b) where the indefinite subject is in (Spec,TP) and can have a strong, specific or a so-called 'partitive' or 'presuppositional' meaning (in this case 'some girls' is understood as '*some of* the girls').

It seems to us that, in addition to the considerations outlined above, there is another reason for assuming that in existentials the associate-NP occupies its base (that is (Spec,VP)) position outside the checking domain of agreement proper. This is that agreement between the verb and the associate-NP has been shown to be frequently absent in varieties of English all over the world. The findings of variationist studies of verbal –s are discussed in the next section. In Sect. 5.5 we will demonstrate that the properties of existential *there* sentences described here (the 'presentative' pragmatic function of existentials and the particular semantic properties and low structural positioning of the associate-NP in (Spec,VP)) jointly help understand the central question of this chapter regarding the nature and function, as well as the pervasiveness, of verbal –s in this construction.

5.3 Socio-Historical Linguistic Work on Verbal –s in Existentials

Variationist studies have found a preponderance of verbal –s in existential *there* sentences.[7] They have shown that (1) diachronically, verbal –s has occurred in existential *there* sentences since the Old English period; and (2) speakers use verbal –s in existential *there* sentences in varieties where use of verbal –s in other contexts is declining, has been lost, or was never found. We will discuss the major results of these studies below.

5.3.1 The History of Verbal –s in Existentials

A number of researchers (Meechan and Foley 1994; Smith and Tagliamonte 1998; Walker 2007) have noted that verbal –s in existentials has a long history in English, dating back to the Old English period. In (26a–c) below are some historical examples from Visser (1970: 73–74).

(26) a. **þær wæs syx hund manna.** (*The Blickling Homilies* 203, 27 [971 A.D.])
'There was six hundred men.'
b. **There is more nobler portes** in England. (1542-47 Andrew Boorde, *Intro & Dyetary*, p. 120)
c. **There's two crowns** for thee, play. (1592 Marlow, *Jew Malta* IV, v)

Not only has variation in existentials—between agreement and non-agreement—persisted through to contemporary varieties of English, but the use of verbal –s in existentials today also appears to be increasingly common. We will take up this matter again in Sect. 5.5.

Pietsch (2005) has argued that the occurrence of verbal –s in existential clauses should be set aside and requires separate consideration from non-existentials, not only in view of its current scope but also because it has had a different diachronic trajectory. He maintains that the strong tendency for verbal –s in existentials derives from the fact that the post-verbal associate-NP has effectively lost its subject status. He claims that 'historically, this can be seen as part of a long-term trend of grammaticalization of the *there* construction, in which *there* has gradually changed its status from being originally a deictic adverb to being a subject' (2005: 156). We will discuss the grammaticalisation of the existential *there* construction at length in Sect. 5.5 in the context of our 'Iconicity Hypothesis'. Pietsch (2005), among others, also goes on to point out that the use of verbal –s in existentials has a different socio-linguistic status than other uses, to the extent that it occurs much more widely (even amongst speakers of Standard English; Trudgill 2008). In addition to this, the use of verbal –s is governed by a different set of linguistic constraints. The (socio-)linguistic conditioning of verbal –s in existentials is discussed in Sect. 5.4.

Some scholars have, however, pointed to similarities between existen-tials and other uses of verbal –s. In an experimental study with residents from southern Ontario, Canada, Smallwood (1997) tested for the use of verbal –s in locative inversion structures like (27) and found rates com-parable to existentials. She therefore assumes one of the relevant factors in verbal –s to be the occurrence of a postverbal subject. She proposes that postverbal positioning of the subject triggers default agreement marking (a 3rd sing. form).

(27) a.   On the centre of the page **is two houses.**
      b.   In the bottom **is three stars.**

Tagliamonte (1998: 69) observed tokens of non-standard *was* in locative inversion structures in York English (*And on that island **was the cooling towers**; And in my drawer **was all the road maps***) and similarly assumes a role for the particular structural configuration that locative inversion structures and existential *there* sentences share. The correlation between the two constructions suggests to us that verbal –s may be a function of a more general schema of locative inversion that initially included deic-tic *there*. We refer to Sect. 5.5 for in-depth discussion of the develop-ment of existential *there* from the locative (deictic) adverb *there*. Brinton and Stein (1995: 38 ff.) have demonstrated that, similar to *there* sen-tences, locative inversion structures underwent changes in both func-tion and frequency between the Old and Middle English periods. In Old English, locative inversion was triggered by a Verb-Second rule in the context of initial adverbs and served to introduce referents; in Middle English rates dramatically decrease, while from late Middle English locative inversion is on the rise again and used as a focusing strategy. Breivik (1981: 11) has argued that both preposed locative adverbials and *there* in the function of a 'compensatory subject-NP'

254 L. Rupp and D. Britain

provide a means of placing NPs in the focused position where elements conveying new information are expected to stand (as with: *Away ran the sheep*; *In the doorway stood my brother*). Brinton and Stein (1995) find that the use of locative inversion invokes a sense of surprise or unexpected developments (which is weakened when word order is changed towards the canonical order—compare: *Away the sheep ran as soon as they saw the dog*). They tie the emergence of this additional discourse meaning to the loss of systematic Verb-Second and the establishment of SVO order in Middle English; benchmarked against SVO, locative inversion will be perceived as 'marked'. Despite all similarities, present-day locative inversion structures would seem to have a different structure than existentials, though, since the preposed prepositional phrase cannot function as a subject and may be in a higher position than (Spec,TP) (for example (Spec,CP)).

5.3.2 Variationist Studies

A number of variationist studies have found that some varieties that used to display verbal –s in both non-existentials and existentials, have been moving to a situation in which speakers use verbal –s in existentials only. This is suggestive of verbal –s being abolished in non-existentials under the pressure of prestige norms and standardisation, while verbal –s in existentials has rather become the norm. It also suggests that verbal –s in non-existentials on the one hand and existentials on the other are—or may become—two separate phenomena. From a cross-comparison of a range of different varieties of English in the world, Tagliamonte has concluded that separation of the two contexts typically happens among current generations of speakers in urban mainstream communities. By contrast, the occurrence of verbal –s in both existential and non-existential constructions usually involves the persistence of a long-term feature of the traditional vernacular (2009: 124–125).

Hay and Schreier (2004) have demonstrated that New Zealand English (NZE) constitutes a prototype of a variety where the two contexts were separated. They studied verbal –s (in the form of past BE) in data from three different corpora that together contained 146 speakers born between 1853 and 1980, including recordings of first- and second-generation

5 Verbal –s in Existential *there* Sentences 255

New Zealanders, spanning the entire formation period of NZE in apparent time. The time-depth of their database gave them the opportunity to explore and trace the historical evolution of verbal –s in NZE over the past 150 years from the inception of English colonisation in New Zealand to the present day.

They found that verbal –s was used in non-existentials in early, nineteenth century New Zealand English. An example of this is (28) (2004: 223):

(28) **the volunteers was** there resting

They go on to show that verbal –s in non-existentials declined steadily throughout the second half of the nineteenth century and became marginal from 1900 to the extent that it all but disappeared in speakers born in the twentieth century (2004: 221–222). In contrast, existential *there* sentences show a different pattern. Usage of verbal –s in existentials similarly dropped during the late nineteenth century; however, this change was reversed, and the feature was re-established in modern New Zealand English (2004: 221–222). For illustration, Hay and Schreier cite two excerpts from an interview with a speaker of early NZE, Mr. R., who was born in New Zealand in 1898. Both excerpts show an occurrence of verbal –s. Hay and Schreier comment (2004: 209–210): 'an example such as that in [29] would be unusual in contemporary NZE whereas that in [30] would be unremarkable. Such examples indicate that patterns of subject-verb agreement with the verb *be* may have changed over the history of New Zealand – at least in non-existential environments such as [29].'

(29) Interviewer: What was the story about the bridge going away, Mr. R.?
        Mr. R.: Well they had the ice coming down and it was on piles you see. they weren't sunk in [unclear] **they was** getting loose
(30) Interviewer: Were you on your own?
        Mr. R.: Yes, I was on me own I ah, left Bannockburn in the morning it was. **there was three passengers** to go so it came on very rough

They conclude that while nineteenth century NZE had verbal –s in both existentials and in non-existentials, there were two subsequent developments: (1) standardisation in the nineteenth century led to the loss of verbal –s in around 1900 in existentials and non-existentials alike; and (2) a following increase of verbal –s in existential *there* sentences in the twentieth century led to a disassociation of the two paradigms and they were no longer conceived of as related. Hay and Schreier (2004) maintain that the view that the two uses of verbal –s (existential and non-existential) currently operate independently of one another is supported by the fact that they are subject to different social and grammatical constraints. For example, in the oldest age group born before 1870, men showed markedly higher rates of verbal –s in non-existentials compared to women (23% vs. 3%), but males and females in the youngest age group born after the 1950s did not show different rates of verbal –s in existentials (72% vs. 73%) (2004: 220, 223). One of the distinguishing grammatical constraints that they found was that contraction proved an important determinant of the rate of verbal –s in existentials (*there's*), whilst it had an inhibiting effect on the use of verbal –s in non-existentials. This constraint is discussed at more length in Sect. 5.4 and we will probe the nature of the contracted form *there's* in Sect. 5.5.

More studies have reported that verbal –s in existential *there* sentences has gone its own way in what were previously more general verbal –s areas: Feagin (1979) for Aniston, Alabama in the eastern U.S.; Petyt (1985) for three towns in West Yorkshire in northern England; Eisikovits (1991) for Inner Sydney in Australia; Tagliamonte (1998) for York in north-eastern England, and Antieau (2011) for Colorado, Utah and Wyoming in the Middle Rocky Mountains in the western U.S.

Eisikovits (1991) found highly differential frequencies of verbal –s between existentials and non-existentials in her study of 40 adolescents in an inner city area of Sydney. In existential *there* sentences, there was almost categorical use of non-standard *is* (97.7%) and *was* (88.9%), whereas in constructions other than existentials, the use of *is* and *was* fell drastically (3.9 and 12.9%, respectively). Some of her data are shown in (31–32) (1991: 242):

5 Verbal –s in Existential *there* Sentences   257

(31) a. **All the kids at school is** calling me 'sissy' and that.
      b. I thought **you was** talking about Rhonda.
(32) a. **Isn't** there **any girls** going?
      b. There **was five of us** there.

All 40 speakers deployed verbal –s in existentials, while 30 speakers used it categorically (1991: 243). To Eisikovits's (1991) mind, these numbers suggest that usage of verbal –s in existentials has become local 'standard' practice and does not carry any social meaning. Additionally, she noted that non-standard *present* BE is more frequent in existentials but non-standard *past* BE more frequent in non-existentials (Hay and Schreier 2004 and Pietsch 2005 have later made the same observation). In Sect. 5.4 and Sect. 5.5 we will take account of these findings also.

For the backdrop to Tagliamonte's (1998) study of the variety of English spoken in York, we refer readers back to Chapter 4. There we discussed the use of non-standard *were(n't)* in negative tags. It proved a separate development in York English where use of non-standard *were* in other standard *was* contexts is rare, demonstrating that levelling in the past BE paradigm can proceed in various directions. While York may be situated in a region of historical *were*-levelling, Tagliamonte inferred from data from the *Survey of English Dialects* (SED; Orton and Dieth 1962–1971) that the predominant pattern used to be generalised *was*. She shows that in York English, past BE is still variable across all persons. Here are some examples in which alternation between standard *were* and non-standard *was* can be observed (1998: 155):

(33) a. **You were** mentioning windscreen wipers …
      b. **You was** only away a bit.
(34) a. **The teachers were** all right.
      b. **All their belongings was** taken to the cattle market.

Evidence for the idea that non-standard *was* is a synchronic holdover derives from the specific way in which verbal –s is used in York. Current constraints mirror the historical northern pattern of conditioning (see Chapter 4 on Past BE): namely, highest rates of non-standard *was* with

2nd sing. *you* (12%), less *was* in the context of *we* (9%) and plural NPs (7%), and least with the 3rd person pronoun *they* (3%) (1998: 162).

Further, clause type exerted a strong effect. Tagliamonte (1998) found that 17% of all affirmative standard *were* contexts were realised as *was*; however, the vast majority of tokens of non-standard *was* were attested in existential *there* sentences (66% as opposed to 6% in all other contexts). Note also that non-standard *wasn't* only occurred in plural existential contexts (17%) and not elsewhere. Some examples of existentials in York English are shown in (35) (1998: 169):

(35) a. They were good. There **was a lot of them** were all right.
b. And there **was always kids** that were going missing.

Tagliamonte (1998) thinks that unlike –s in non-existentials, the verbal –s in existential constructions is presumably not a remnant that goes back to earlier stages in the history of English. First, she reminds us that the feature is very robust in English varieties worldwide, even in varieties that lack historical documentation of verbal –s. Second, young females in York showed particularly suggestive behaviour: overall they used non-standard *was* less than females of any other age group, except for existentials where they used non-standard *was* the most (1998: 182). Tagliamonte argues that younger females have not simply taken over a linguistic feature from their elders; rather, they have reorganised the system by specialising the use of non-standard *was* for deployment in existential *there* sentences. Tagliamonte concludes that non-standard *was* is not an innovative feature of York English grammar but one that has been undergoing contemporary change.

Antieau (2011) has reported a similar situation to obtain in three localities in the Middle Rocky Mountains, where he studied a sample consisting of 36 males and 34 females with different levels of education. As the following examples from his corpus show, *was* appeared in the context of all sorts of subject (2011: 53):

5 Verbal –s in Existential *there* Sentences   259

(36) a. Post office. Oh **you was** at the library …
      b. **They was. They was** going to burn it to the ground …
      c. … **the big rocks was** dropped …
      d. **We was** all healthy, every one of us …
      e. There **wasn't any great bands** of wild horses.

He found that 65 of his 70 informants used non-standard *was* in plural existential constructions (concluding that the use of *was* in plural existentials seems customary in the region) and that this number was nearly twice as high as the number of speakers who used non-standard *was* in other types of sentence. In addition to this it was noteworthy that education level had no effect on rates of non-standard *was* in existential contexts, replicating the finding of numerous other studies that this use is not socially stratified. Antieau (2011) observed a constraint ranking of *there* (61%), *you* (41%), *we* (23%), NP-plural (21%) and *they* (12%) (2011: 55). In comparison to other studies of past BE, frequencies of *they was* were relatively high, which Antieau has attributed to the fact that some speakers realised existential *there* as *they*. Here are some examples (2011: 61):

(37) a. I think **they** was two bedrooms upstairs.
      b. … they claim that **they** was four trains a day coming in here …[8]

Studies that have reported the favouring of verbal –s in existential *there* sentences without concomitant verbal –s in non-existentials (or evidence to this effect) include Peitsara (1988) for the dialect of Suffolk in eastern England that otherwise has verbal zero (see Chapter 3); Meechan and Foley (1994) for Nova Scotia and Ottawa in Canada; Tagliamonte and Smith (1999) for Nova Scotian Vernacular English in Guysborough Village, Canada (past tense only); Walker (2007) for Quebec English, Canada; Tagliamonte (2009) for Toronto, Canada (in the past tense); Moore (2011) for Bolton in north-west England; and Durham (2013) for Lerwick on the Scottish Shetland Islands. The latter two varieties traditionally show generalisation towards *were*. However, existentials disfavoured *were* and they were one of the only few contexts to show marked levels of non-standard *was*. Durham reports 42% levelled *were* in contexts of singular associate-NPs, as in (38a), and 56% levelled *was* in contexts of plural associate-NPs, as in (38b) (2013: 115–116).

(38) a. There **were** just **the one peerie stair** gan down.
   b. There **was lots of chairs**.

She demonstrates that the traditional form *There were* + singular associate-NP is used in the old and middle generations but has completely died out in the youngest generation of speakers. By contrast, the use of *There was* + plural associate-NP has increased incrementally across the generations and is now nearly categorical for the young speakers (2013: 118). Durham ascribes this pattern to the existence of a supralocal norm.

In sum, variationist studies have identified an abundance of verbal –s in existential *there* sentences, which extends to varieties in which verbal –s is otherwise in decline or does not occur. The finding that the use of verbal –s in existentials is on the increase amongst younger generations of speakers (Tagliamonte 1998; Durham 2013) suggests an ongoing diffusion of this form. In Sect. 5.5 we ascribe this development to ongoing (secondary) grammaticalisation of verbal –s in existentials, which, we suggest, has given rise to the diagrammatically iconic, presentative form *there(')s*.

5.4 Tying Together the Aims of Formal Linguistics and Variationist Studies

In this section we return to two major questions of this chapter: how can insights from generative syntax into the structure of existential *there* sentences help identify grammatical factors that favour verbal –s in this clause type, and what are the implications of the pervasiveness of verbal –s for generative assumptions about the mechanism of subject-verb agreement in existential *there* sentences and perhaps in syntax more generally? Inspired by a perspective afforded by Walker (2007), we will later, in the discussion in Sect. 5.6, argue that generative and variationist

5 Verbal –s in Existential *there* Sentences   261

linguists can also join forces in addressing the central question of this chapter. Specifically, we will show that exploring grammatical and social constraints on verbal –s in existentials sheds light on its pervasiveness and the nature and function of the form *there(')s*. In Sect. 5.4.1 below we will first demonstrate the usefulness of principles of generative syntax for determining grammatical conditioning of verbal –s in existentials, taking as a case study grammatical properties of the associate-NP. In Sect. 5.4.2 we will address other grammatical factors in the use of verbal –s, including the factors of distance between the verb and the associate-NP as well as contraction (*there's*). We then assess the significance of the findings for syntactic theorising on subject-verb agreement.

5.4.1 Conditioning of Verbal –s by Properties of the Associate-NP

Of the variationist studies that have inquired into conditioning of verbal –s by grammatical properties of the associate-NP, Meechan and Foley (1994) and Britain and Sudbury (2002) are among the most extensive. Meechan and Foley examined data from two corpora of varieties of English spoken by 31 speakers aged 55–95 in Nova Scotia and Ottawa in Canada, while Britain and Sudbury studied data of speakers between 20 and 70 years old in two corpora of New Zealand English and Falkland Island English. (We refer to their work for more details of the corpora and the data.) Britain and Sudbury explored the effect of the following properties of the associate-NP on the occurrence of verbal –s (2002: 218–219): determiner type, plural marking on the noun, and type of quantifier.

(39)   Determiner type:
   a.   <u>no</u>: there was **no** wool-beams then.[9]
   b.   <u>definite</u>: come down to the left of the tower, there's **those** pointy bits.
   c.   <u>numeric</u>: there was **four** suitcases one inside each other.
   d.   <u>bare</u>: if there's __medicals, they can always fit them on.
   e.   <u>quantifier</u>: there's **quite a few** dams built on dodgy sites down there.
   f.   <u>adjective</u>: there's **different Spice Girls** ones.

(40) Plural marking on the noun:
    a.   <u>Present</u>: there's half a dozen **garages**.
    b.   <u>Absent</u>: there's just a few more **sheep** around these days.
(41) Quantifier type:
    a.   <u>Quantifier containing an indefinite article</u>: there was **a lot of** single fellas around.
    b.   <u>Other quantifiers</u>: there were **heaps of** people at Juice.

Meechan and Foley also coded for strong and weak determiners on the associate-NP, following Milsark (1974: 73, 1977). Applying Diesing's (1992) 'mapping' hypothesis discussed in Sect. 5.2 to their investigation of existentials, Meechan and Foley (1994) predict a favouring of agreement in the context of associate-NPs that contain strong determiners. These will occur in (Spec,TP), a configuration in which subject-verb agreement is established. NPs with weak determiners remain in a VP-internal position.

(42) Weak:
    a.   There's not **too many** good places where you can swim around Ottawa.
    b.   There are definitely **two** views to the history.
    c.   There was **no** wild animals.
(43) Strong:
    a.   There's **my** two girls there.
    b.   There's **the** old remedies they had to have years ago.

For the factor of determiner type, Britain and Sudbury (2002: 224) attested the following hierarchy of effect (from most to least verbal –s): *no* > definite > numeral > bare > quantifier > adjective. In a separate analysis, they found that quantifiers that contained an indefinite (singular) article (such as *a lot of* in (41a)) were more likely to have verbal –s than other quantifiers. They point out that their results correspond to the results of other research that inquired into the role of the properties of the associate-NP. Meechan and Foley (1994: 76) found: *no* > numeral > weak/strong determiner. Tagliamonte (1998: 171), who studied only past tense existentials in York, observed the following ranking: *no* > partitives > definite > numbers > quantifiers > bare. Hay and Schreier's (2004: 218) findings for New Zealand English were similarly largely in line, as they reported: numeral > *no* > quantifiers containing *a* > definite > other quantifiers > bare > adjective. Later, Walker (2007) also coded for determiner type in his study of Quebec City English and obtained a result that matched that of Britain and Sudbury (2002): *a* quantifier > definite > no bare > numeral > other quantifier > adjective (2007: 159). Overall, determiners that occurred high in the ranking were: *no*, definite, *a* quantier; and determiners that occurred low in the ranking: numeral, bare and adjective.

In addition to this, results for the influence of plural marking on the noun also converged (Meechan and Foley 1994; Britain and Sudbury 2002; Walker 2007). If an associate-NP was marked for number by the plural morpheme –s, there was a slightly lower likelihood of verbal –s than if there was no marking, though the results were not statistically significant, except for Walker's. Meechan and Foley (1994)'s investigation of the influence of strong and weak determiners showed that neither of them impacted on the probability of verbal –s and so the hypothesis that the occurrence of verbal –s would correlate with different configurational positions of NPs was not confirmed. They concede that it is difficult to prove it because strong determiners are usually excluded from existentials by the Definiteness Restriction (as we saw in Sect. 5.2).[10] Tagliamonte (1998) also found that strong determiners did not behave differently in existentials in York English, and that tokens of strong determination made up a small proportion of the total at any rate: 16% of the plural associate-NPs (1998: 189, Footnote 4).

Britain and Sudbury (2002) conclude that there is a remarkable similarity in the grammatical constraints on verbal –s, not just between the two southern hemisphere varieties of New Zealand and the Falkland Islands—which, paradoxically, are themselves thousands of kilometres apart and in other respects diverge—but in comparison with other varieties, too. Walker (2013) has similarly reported that speakers in Quebec and Toronto in Canada show common conditioning of verbal –s in existentials, despite the fact that the communities have different sociolinguistic histories and ethnic compositions. Britain and Sudbury (2002) contemplate the notion of 'drift' as an explanation for the parallelism. The notion of drift goes back to work by Sapir (1933) and has subsequently been entertained in different forms by a number of linguists, including Trask (1996: 150) who has defined it as 'the curious tendency of a language to keep changing in the same direction'. Britain and Sudbury admit that variationist research has shed more light on external motivations for language change, such as language contact and prestige, than motivations for 'inherent' and 'intrinsic' changes (2002: 232).

However, since generative syntax postulates grammatical principles that are internal to our linguistic system, the framework should be able to make predictions as to when an associate-NP is more or less likely to favour verbal –s. Recall from Sect. 5.2 that the clause structure of existential *there* sentences is assumed to look like (44) (where PredP stands for any predicate: VP, AdjP, and so on). Agreement between the verb and the associate-NP can be achieved via a range of potential covert mechanisms: raising of the associate (- - -), feature-raising (...), or long distance-agreement (—).

(44)

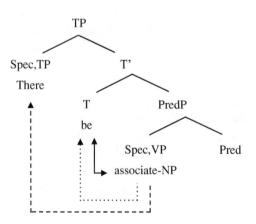

Here, we will remain agnostic as to which covert mechanism might apply. Rather, we zoom in on the internal structure of NPs in an attempt to find out when we might expect verbal –s to occur. Generative analyses traditionally characterised the nominal domain as an NP, a phrase in which determiners, such as definite articles, were generated in (Spec,NP). A proposal that is usually attributed to Abney (1987) considers the possibility that determiners project into a Determiner Phrase (DP) that dominates the NP. The NP-hypothesis and DP-hypothesis are illustrated for the phrase *the book* in (45a) and (45b), respectively:

(45) a.   b.

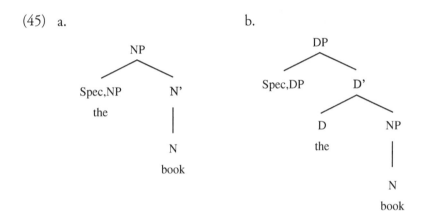

There have since been numerous proposals that in addition to this, other grammatical categories associated with nominal expressions each project phrases that are situated in between DP and NP; for example, an A(djective)P that hosts adjectives (Cinque 1994) and perhaps least controversially, a Num(ber)P reflecting number marking on the noun and hosting noun suffixes like plural –s (Lyons 1999). These proposals would give a structure like (46) for the DP *the really nice red books*.

(46)

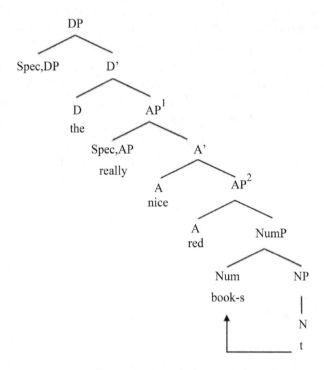

Bernstein (2001) provides a survey of theoretical and empirical arguments that have been put forward in favour of the DP-hypothesis. The primary theoretical motivation has been that the DP-hypothesis unifies the treatment of noun phrases and clauses, such that the nominal equivalent of the clause is DP. Ever since Chomsky (1986), it has been assumed that verbs project into the functional categories of Complementiser Phrase (CP) and Inflectional Phrase (IP). This gave clauses the structure CP–IP–VP in accordance with the X-bar schema. IP was later split up into further functional categories: T(ense)P and Agr(eement)P (Pollock 1989). Exploiting this idea, the DP-hypothesis extends this analysis to the effect that (following Grimshaw 1991) the DP similarly constitutes an 'extended' functional projection of the lexical head N that anchors the noun in the discourse (by the notion of

5 Verbal –s in Existential *there* Sentences   267

referentiality, similar to what Tense does for the verb). Advocates of the DP-hypothesis have argued that the existence of DP receives emprical support, too. One piece of evidence derives from the order between adjectives and nouns. Following Longobardi (1994: 623), in Italian, possessive adjectives obligatorily follow a proper name in the absence of a determiner, whereas in Germanic languages, the order is the reverse: adjectives precede nouns (viz. ***Gianni mio** ha finalmente telefonato* versus ***My John** has finally called*). Under the DP-hypothesis, the order noun-adjective derives from N-to-D raising across the A(djective)P. Further evidence is provided by the fixed ordering between different semantic types of adjectives (cf. *the nice, red book* but **the red, nice book*). In a more highly articulated DP structure, this no longer needs to be stipulated but derives from a particular 'stacking' of adjectives within the structure of the DP (Cinque 1994). Semantic classes of adverbs that are lowest in the hierarchy will occur closest to the noun in their distribution within the NP.

The DP-hypothesis has not been fully settled and it continues to be a subject of debate which nominal expressions constitute a functional category, whether they function as heads or specifiers in a phrase, or whether functional projections like DP are part of the clause structure when there is no N-related material; for example, in languages that lack articles—Alexiadou et al. (2007) provide extensive discussion. Following Bruening et al. (2015: 4), 'what is necessary in order to argue for the DP-Hypothesis is a demonstration that the relevant facts can only be accounted for by taking the head of the nominal projection to be D (or some other functional head) and not N'.

We note that one of the major differences between the DP-hypothesis and NP-hypothesis is that under the former, subject-verb agreement will involve the checking of agreement features between the verb and the head D of DP. In this context, we will explore one of five possible hypotheses put forward by Den Dikken et al. (2007) that may account for the observed favourings of verbal –s according to properties of the associate-NP. Among these is the 'Two position hypothesis': a hypothesis that we examined in Chapter 2 in relation to Henry's (1995) and Tortora and Den Dikken's (2010) account of verbal –s. Here we explore their 'D-head hypothesis', which Den Dikken et al. define as follows: 'The D-head Hypothesis (Hypothesis 5) ... is predicated on the premise that agreement between subject and finite verb is purely a function of the featural specifications of D: whenever D is explicitly plural, the noun phrase it heads will trigger plural agreement; but in cases in which there is no unambiguously plural D-head (because D is absent, null, or filled by an element, like *the*, that is number-neutral), a retreat to the singular default is available. This hypothesis is easily testable for varieties such as [Buckie English], in which D and its complement NP can differ in number (e.g. *that photos*; [Adger and Smith 2005: 169]); Hypothesis 5 would predict that such DPs could yield singular concord.' (2007: 1).

Along the lines of Den Dikken et al.'s (2007) hypothesis, we assume the following four structures for nominal expressions: (47a) a DP with a D specified for number (for example, *a*); (47b) a DP with a number-neutral D (for example, *no*, *the*); (47c) an NP from which D is absent (for example, in the case of bare nouns) and (47d) an extended structure of NP that is headed by a quantifier Q specified for number (for example, *a lot of, heaps*).

(47) a.   b.

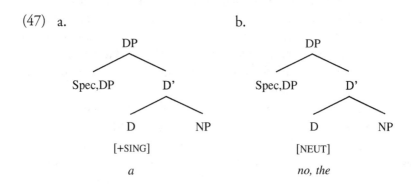

5 Verbal –s in Existential *there* Sentences

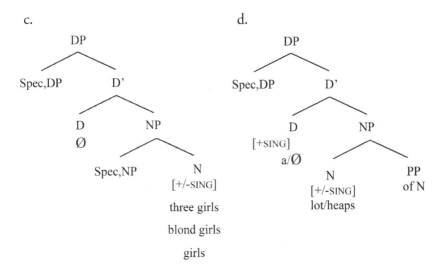

This analysis of the structure of nominal expressions predicts the basic constraint hierarchy that can be extrapolated from variationist studies: (from most to least verbal –s): quantifier *a* > *no* > definite > numeral > bare > other quantifier > adjective. Recall the basic claim of the DP-hypothesis that the head of the nominal projection is not N but D. Both (47a) and (47d) trigger agreement of the verb with the singular D *a* (for example, *a lot of*), thus favouring –s. In (47b), D is unspecified for number, or number neutral and therefore verbal –s is admitted in the context of the negative determiner *no* and definite descriptions with *the*. In (47c), subject-verb agreement will arguably be with features of N (possibly via a head Num of NumP shown in (46)) because D is covert or perhaps absent; this configuration should trigger plural agreement if the NP is plural, thus disfavouring –s. The same applies to the quantifier *heaps of* in (47d). Note that from the perspective of existentials, it seems that adjectives cannot be heads of an AdjP (an idea discussed in Alexiadou et al. 2007) as they would block agreement from N by the

270 L. Rupp and D. Britain

Head Movement Constraint (Travis 1984) or Relativized Minimality (Rizzi 1990) in for example *There BE three blond girls in my group* (cf. (47c)). (Hankamer and Mikkelsen 2002 express the same view on the basis of argumentation having to do with the semantics of adjectives.) Finally, with a view to the forthcoming discussion of the nature of the form *there(')s* in Sect. 5.5, it is important to highlight here that for the constraint hierarchy to hold, verbal –s must constitute a singular verb form.

5.4.2 Implications of the Effects of 'Distance', 'Tense' and 'Contraction'

Three other factors that have been identified as impacting on verbal –s by nearly all variationist studies are the factors of 'distance' between the verb and the associate-NP, 'tense' and 'contraction' (*there's*). They are illustrated by data from Britain and Sudbury (2002: 218–219) below. (48c) and (49a) include a token of contraction of *there* and *'s* into *there's*.

(48) *Distance between Verb and NP*
   a. <u>none</u>: I knew there **were hymns** in Welsh.
   b. <u>small</u>: there **aren't** really **any muscles** there at all.
   c. <u>large</u>: I mean **there's** probably often **times** people collecting.
(49) *Tense of the verb*
   a. <u>Present</u>: **there's** some pork pieces left up here too.
   b. <u>Past</u>: there **was** icebreakers iced in with her.

In this section we will address these effects and any potential implications they might have for generative assumptions about the mechanism of subject-verb agreement in existential *there* sentences and perhaps in syntax more generally.

We begin with the effect of 'distance'—the amount of lexical material between the verb and the associate-NP. Sobin (1997) has argued that adjacency is a strong factor in agreement between the verb and the associate-NP; a phenomenon that he terms 'flat agreement' (p. 325). A number of variationist studies have accordingly examined if a rise

5 Verbal –s in Existential *there* Sentences   271

in the proportion of verbal –s can be observed the greater the distance between the verb and the associate-NP; the idea being that any material that intervenes between the verb and the associate-NP can potentially hamper agreement. Tagliamonte (1998) coded for up to more than four words in her research on York English; one example is *There was [about seven] lads got into a Bedford Van* (1998: 173). She found that non-adjacent postverbal subjects were more likely to occur with non-standard *was* (68%) than adjacent subjects (45%) (1998: 174). Britain and Sudbury (2002: 229) report the same trend in the English spoken in New Zealand and on the Falkland Islands. In their New Zealand data, for example, scores ranged from 61% verbal –s where the verb and the NP were adjacent, to categorical verbal –s where there were three or more lexical expressions occurring between the verb and the associate-NP. In Meechan and Foley's study of Canadian English, 'distance' yielded a significant result although no effect was found for different types and length of intervening material (1994: 83, Footnote 14). For New Zealand English again, Hay and Schreier (2004: 221) also observed an (albeit non-significant) effect whereby the frequencies of verbal –s increased according to the number of words breaking up the adjacency. Walker (2007: 158) has added that the use of singular agreement in Quebec City English, too, is similarly influenced by the presence of intervening material.[11]

Note that the observed favouring effect of 'distance' on verbal –s in existential *there* sentences seems at odds with the generative assumption that agreement between the verb and the associate-NP can take place via a covert operation, be it covert raising of the associate-NP, or feature-raising from the associate-NP into TP, or long distance-agreement between T and the associate-NP. (Sobin 1997 has expressed the same view on somewhat different grounds.) The intervening material between the verb and associate-NPs that variationist studies have reported on frequently concerns adjuncts like adverbs. Rather than constituting independent heads or specifiers, adjuncts adjoin to layers in X-bar structure because they do not 'check with' features of other constituents. Being adjuncts, they are in fact not expected to interfere with covert subject-verb agreement under the Head Movement Constraint of Travis (1984) or Rizzi's (1990) Relativized Minimality.[12] This apparently challenges one of the reasons (i.e. the syntax of existentials) for assuming that covert agreement operations exist.

A number of alternative solutions have been proposed to account for the propensity of verbal –s in the presence of a postverbal subject. Some researchers assume a processing account and attribute the pattern to the fact that the speaker is not yet aware of the exact nature of the subject in postverbal position (Meechan and Foley 1994; Chambers 2004; Walker 2007). In constructions where 'regular' agreement with the denotational subject is not possible because it is separated from the verb, a different mechanism is needed to generate an outcome. The insertion of a default form, which in English happens to be 3rd sing. –s, has been alluded to (Tortora 1997; Schütze 1999; Walker 2007). Such accounts assume that *there* cannot participate in subject-verb agreement. Yet others postulate that existential *there* itself exerts pressure towards singular agreement with the verb (Eisikovits 1991; Sobin 1997).

We move on to the second indicator of verbal –s to be discussed in this section, that of 'tense'. Britain and Sudbury (2002) found that verbal –s was significantly more frequent in the present than in the past tense in their southern hemisphere data. This has proven to be one of the most distinguishing features of verbal –s in existentials and it suggest that present and past tense existentials are of a different nature (Pietsch 2005). Hay and Schreier (2004) have argued that in non-existential clauses with *be*, by contrast, verbal –s occurs more frequently in the past tense than in the present (past BE). However, it is important to point out here that all of the studies that have been referred to in this chapter report that contraction significantly enhances the occurrence of verbal –s (*there's*). For example, in their data from Nova Scotia and Ottawa, Meechan and Foley (1994: 75, 77) found that in the context of contraction, the rate of verbal –s increased to 92% from 72% overall, while *there's* occupied almost half of Walker's (2007: 157) data set of existentials in his study of Quebec City English. In this light, Meechan and Foley (1994) have argued that the purported effect of tense is actually an effect of contraction where contraction is only possible in the present tense (*there's*). That is, in varieties that have no contracted past, the factors of tense and contraction are not independent. They conclude that any effect of past and present tense is therefore better explained as due to contraction and not tense.[13] Many scholars have commented on the status of *there's* in this relation and have alternatively labelled it a 'discourse device' (Hannay 1985: 3), 'a frozen form' (Schilling-Estes and Wolfram 1994: 286), 'a prefabricated phrase' (Cheshire 1999: 138), 'an unanalyzed "chunk" of language' (Crawford 2005: 49), as having 'lexicalized status' (Walker 2007: 162), and an 'invariant prefabricated expression used to introduce new topics in the discourse' (Cheshire and Fox 2009: 8).

In the following Sect. 5.5 we will propose that the contracted form *there's* embodies a stage in an ongoing process of the grammaticalisation of existential *there*. In that section we will address the central question of this chapter: Why is verbal –s currently so pervasive in existential *there* sentences and how is the nature and function of verbal –s in existentials best explained? We will argue that *there(')s* is a grammaticalised form that has come to iconically serve as a presentative signal or sign.

5.5 The Grammaticalisation of Existential *there* into a Presentative Sign

In this section we address the central question of this chapter: Why is verbal –s currently so pervasive in existential *there* sentences and how is the nature and function of verbal –s in existentials best explained? We will show that the properties of existential *there* sentences discussed in Sect. 5.2 (the pragmatic 'presentative' function of existentials and the particular 'weak' semantic properties and low structural positioning of the associate-NP in (Spec,VP)) all contribute to an understanding of this question. In our analysis, we will draw on work by Breivik and Swan (2000) who offer a diachronic perspective and have argued that existential *there* grammaticalised from the locative adverb *there*. The view that existential *there* derived from the adverbial of place dates back to Lyons (1975). In light of Hopper and Traugott's (2003) account of the grammaticalisation of the string *let us → let's → lets*, we envisage that as a function of the postverbal positioning of the subject, –s has been losing its function as an agreement morpheme in existentials and that, at present, further, secondary grammaticalisation of the morpheme *there* and verbal –s is taking place (in the sense of Traugott 2002) from *there is* → *there's* → *theres*. Further, we will argue that in accordance with our 'Iconicity Hypothesis', secondary grammaticalisation has implemented an isomorphic relation between form (*there(')s*) and function (alerting the addressee to new information in the discourse). In addition to this, we will build on Breivik and Swan's (2000) characterisation of *there(')s* as a presentative signal and suggest that the form *there(')s* is iconically motivated as a signpost of new information. Inspired by Walker (2007), we will in the discussion in Sect. 5.6 suggest that views from formal and LVC-linguists on the grammatical and social conditioning of verbal –s can also complement one another in establishing more robustly the nature of the form *there(')s*.

Breivik and Swan (2000) document the diachronic development of existential *there* from Old English to present-day English and offer a principled account which makes particular reference to the concepts of 'grammaticalisation' and 'subjectification'. They cite Jespersen (1969: 129) as one of the first to have claimed that 'it is evident that existential *there* originated as the ordinary *there*, a "pronominal adverb" meaning "at that particular place", but in the course of time it has diverged very considerably from its origin, not only in pronunciation [...] but in other respects as well'. Breivik and Swan (2000) look for evidence in data from Old English. While, as they note, the exact timing of the separation between the two tokens of *there* has been subject to some debate, they assume that existential *there* split off from the locative adverb *there* and began to function as an expression without (concrete) locative reference as early as the Old English period. Most probably, then, there was some transitional stage: Breivik and Swan (2000) give (50a) as an example illustrating the use of the locative adverb *there*, (50b) as an example that is ambiguous between locative and existential *there*, and (50c) as an unambiguous example of existential use (2000: 20–21).

5 Verbal –s in Existential *there* Sentences   275

(50) a. On he siþþan hwearf hamweard to Babylonia. **þær** wœron
œrendracan on anbide eallre worolde …
'He afterwards went home to Babylon. There ambassadors
from all over the world were waiting' (Orosius 136: 3–4)
b. Gif **ðær** beoð fiftig wera wunigende on þam earde …
'If there are fifty men living in the place' (Ælfric 1 XIII: 196)
c. **þær** wœs sang ond sweg samod œtgœdere fore Healfdenes
hildewisan …
'There was singing and music joined together in the presence of Healfdene's warlike chieftain' (Beowulf 1063–1064)

Breivik and Swan (2000) argue that the locative adverb would regularly
have been preposed to the beginning of the sentence as a corollary of
the application of Verb-Second (cf. (50a)). Both Breivik (1981) and
Pfenninger (2009: 44) have argued that Old English 'þær' and other
adverbs of place may have acted as 'linking' words; namely, 'as a transitional adverb that refers to a locative element or word group in the
preceding sentence', as in (51) below:

(51) hlūdne in healle; **þǣr** wæs hearpan sweg
(*Beowulf* ed. Jack 33, 86–90)
'loud in the hall, there was the sound of harps'

Breivik and Swan (2000) suggest that subsequently, *there* came to be
deployed as an empty topic with no concrete referential meaning at all.
It was placed in a fixed, sentence-initial position to trigger movement
of the verb to second position. Then, 'the Old English empty topic
[*there*] was syntactically reanalyzed as an empty subject when in [the
course of Middle English], English changed typologically from verb-second (TVX) to verb-medial (SVX)' (2000: 22). The reordering generated strings in which the verb occurs following the subject. In relation
to the emergence of the form *there(')s*, it is important to note here that
as a result of this typological change, the notational subject (the associate-NP) no longer occurred in the canonical subject position to enter
into agreement with the verb, since this position was now occupied by

there. The function of the emergent category of existential *there* has variably been described along the lines of an 'empty subject-marker rather than a true adverb' (Traugott 1992: 218), an 'expletive [that] is inserted as a "dummy" filler of the structural subject position' (references in Felser and Rupp 2001: 295), and as an element 'with a more or less empty semantic content that [is] inserted to fill a semantically empty slot for syntactic and pragmatic reasons' (Pfenninger 2009: 9). Breivik (1981: 16) has argued that the use of existential *there* as an empty topic/subject remained optional until Early Modern English, citing a comparison of the (a) and (b) sentences with and without *there* in (52).[14] The Old English *there*-less example in (53) is from Breivik and Martínez-Insua (2008: 353).

(52) a.   There was a knight / that hadde two doughters … (Offord, 17)
      b.   And in alle the world is no gretter treason / than for to
           deceyue gentyll wymmen … (Offord, 12)
(53) On ðære byrig wæs sum þegn bonifacius gehaten …
      'In that city there was a certain noble named Bonifacius'
      (Ælfric's *Lives of Saints*)

In a large corpus study covering a period from the ninth to the eighteenth century, Jenset (2010) has confirmed the analysis of the evolution of existential *there* sketched thus far: it was a gradual progress which had already begun in Old English, gained momentum in late Middle English and was not complete until the beginning of the Early Modern English period.

Breivik and Swan (2000) analyse the diachronic development of existential *there* from locative *there* as an occurrence of grammaticalisation. The term 'grammaticalisation' originates in work by Meillet, the pioneer of grammaticalisation studies. He defined it as 'le passage d'un mot autonome au rôle d'élément grammatical' (1912: 285); that is, the process whereby an independent word assumes a grammatical function. Hopper and Traugott (2003: 10–11) identify a number of properties that are typically associated with grammaticalisation. These include:

5 Verbal –s in Existential *there* Sentences   277

(1) reanalysis of a grammatical category in local contexts;
(2) phonological reduction[15];
(3) loss of concrete meaning;
(4) addition of new, more abstract and speaker-based meanings;
(5) generalisation to other contexts of use.

We refer readers to Hopper and Traugott (2003: 2–3) for an illustration of these and other characteristics in a case study of the future *be going to/be gonna* construction. Regarding (3–4), Hopper and Traugott (2003) have argued that while one may expect grammaticalisation to result in the weakening of concrete meaning, in the early stages of the grammaticalisation process it is actually not adequate to speak of an expression showing semantic 'bleaching'. 'Rather, there is a balance between loss of older, typically more concrete, meanings, and development of newer, more abstract ones that at a minimum cancel out the loss. Many are the result of pragmatic strengthening ...' (2003: 101). Equally, as a result of reanalysis, an expression is likely to lose its membership of a major lexical category such as verb or adverb. However, Hopper and Traugott suggest that this process is better thought of as 'a functional shift from one kind of role to another in the organization of discourse' than the 'decay or deterioration' of a form (2003: 108).

Breivik and Swan (2000: 27) point out that the emergence of existential *there* shows many of the characteristics usually involved in grammaticalisation. They are listed in (i–iv):

(i) The change occurred in a very local context (namely, in sentence-initial position);
In this context, the grammatical category of locative adverb was reanalyzed and existential *there* acquired the syntactic status of an expletive that functioned as a topic/subject-position holder[16];
(ii) The form of existential *there* was phonologically reduced to /ðə(r)/ from the /ðɛə(r)/ of the locative adverb *there*;
(iii) The original meaning was lost and existential *there* can no longer refer to concrete location;

278 L. Rupp and D. Britain

(iv) The grammatical development has been accompanied by an increase in 'subjectification' to the effect that existential *there* now is an item that is used by the speaker to signal new information;

(v) Existential *there* has come to be used in the contexts of discourse-new subjects.

Regarding (ii–iv), Breivik and Swan (2000) maintain that the reduction of form and the semantic weakening in existential *there* sentences have been accompanied by a concurrent pragmatic shift. Whereas in the earliest stages of English, *there* had a purely syntactic function, namely, that of topic-/subject holder, increasingly *there* came to serve pragmatic and speaker-based functions (Breivik and Martínez-Insua 2008: 356). Breivik and Swan (2000) believe that existentials crucially demonstrate the phenomenon of 'subjectification'. Elizabeth Traugott has been the main proponent of the concept of subjectification in diachronic change. Traugott has argued that it is specifically the subjective stance of the speaker that is strengthened in early stages of grammaticalisation (1995: 49). She has characterised 'subjectification' as an 'historical pragmatic-semantic process whereby meanings become increasingly based in the SP[eaker]/ W[riter]'s subjective belief state or attitude toward what is being said and how it is being said' (2003: 125). Accordingly, Breivik and Swan describe the current function of existential *there* as follows: 'Today the speaker uses it as a signal to tell the addressee that she must be prepared to direct her attention towards an item of new information.' (2000: 28). That is, '[t]he pragmatic function of [existential] sentences is to introduce new information into the discourse' (Breivik and Martínez-Insua 2008: 353).

Breivik and Swan (2000) link this specific application of subjectification to the fact that existential *there* was found in a particular syntactic context where it preceded a subject noun phrase conveying new information. Breivik (1981: 11) had earlier suggested that as a 'compensatory subject-NP', *there* provided a means of placing NPs in the focused position where elements conveying new information are expected to stand (the so-called end-weight principle). Smirnova (2015: 219) has aptly defined such reanalysis in a constructionist framework as 'constructualization': 'the formation of a new construction by way of ... contextual restrictions with resulting semantic and structural reorganization of language.

5 Verbal –s in Existential *there* Sentences 279

It is constituted by two relevant processes: semanticization and pragmatic implicatures (or "invited inferences", Traugott and Dasher 2002) on the one hand and structural reanalysis on the other.' Note that the current function of existential *there* was arguably dormant to the effect that there is an inference of 'existential predication' from the concrete location that a locative expression designates. The way that Breivik and Swan have put it is that existential *there* 'has not undergone complete desemanticization; it retains a vestige of spatiality' (2000: 29). The notion of location conveyed, however, is a more 'abstract' location; Breivik and Swan (2000) propose that existential *there* serves to bring into the addressee's awareness conceptual entities that are located in *a mental space*. Following Hopper and Traugott (2003: 3), the new meaning of a grammaticalising expression (in our case: a mental space) can become salient where the original meaning (a concrete location) is not obvious. Consider (54):

(54) There is an answer to the question (?there/?in the book/?near the café).

The described effect of 'inference' (Hopper and Traugott 2003: 3) is also observed in Hopper's (1991: 22) grammaticalisation principle of 'Persistence': 'When a form undergoes grammaticalization from a lexical to a grammatical function, so long as it is grammatically viable some traces of its original lexical meanings tend to adhere to it'.[17] Accordingly, Pfenninger (2009: 247–248) has stated that the original semantics of locative *there* determines and remains visible in existential *there*: the slight locative colouring of existential *there* can be understood as a continuation of its original lexical meaning. We note that Felser and Rupp (2001) have independently, in their generative account of existentials, proposed that existential *there* is the overt realisation of a spatio-temporal argument on the model of Kratzer (1995) and Ramchand (1996). Specifically, they argue that a spatio-temporal argument compares to a quasi-argument in that it is 'thematic without referring to an actual participant in the action or event depicted'—Felser and Rupp take it to be associated with an abstract location (2001: 312). Bolinger (1977) earlier argued that existential *there* is an extension of locative *there*, with a meaning that refers to a generalised 'location'. While locative *there* 'presents something on the

280   L. Rupp and D. Britain

immediate stage (brings something literary or figurative before our presence), [existential *there*] presents something to our minds (brings a piece of knowledge into consciousness)' (1977: 93–94). Bolinger argues that both existential *there* (raising awareness) and *to be* (as a verb 'of emergence' or bringing into existence) have meaning, and that existential meaning is conveyed by the combination of *there +be*.

Hopper and Traugott (2003) note that although a grammatical development may originate in the earliest stages of English, the products of various stages of grammaticalisation may continue to coexist, sometimes for many centuries, up to the present time. This the phenomenon of 'layering' (Hopper 1991) that we discussed in previous chapters in relation to overlapping uses of verbal –s and past BE. In this context, Breivik and Swan (2000) have pointed out that while the grammaticalisation of existentials started very early (in their opinion, in Old English), traces of the process are present in Modern English in that the locative adverb *there* and existential *there* are still identical in their written form and have remained side by side.

At this point, we would like to appeal to Hopper and Traugott's (2003) inventory of properties of grammaticalisation to argue that there has been a further development in the grammaticalisation of existential *there*, the result of which is the form *there(')s*. We have repeated their inventory below for convenience.

(1) reanalysis of grammatical category in local contexts;
(2) phonological reduction;
(3) loss of concrete meaning;
(4) new, more abstract and speaker-based meanings are added;
(5) generalisation to other contexts of use.

Our analysis is framed in Hopper and Traugott's (2003: 10–12) case-study of *let*-constructions; a construction, which, they say, 'illustrates vividly that grammaticalization is an everyday fact of language'. They begin by noting that in contemporary English there is a construction that involves a 2nd person imperative with the verb *let*:

5 Verbal –s in Existential *there* Sentences   281

(55) (You) Let us/Bill go.   (that is, release us)

Alongside this ordinary imperative construction with *let* in (55), there is a construction that Hopper and Traugott (2003: 10) report is sometimes termed 'adhortative' (=urging, encouraging). This construction can be paraphrased as 'I suggest that you and I ...'. An important characteristic of this construction is that the constituents *let* and *us* (the subject of the main verb *go* in (55)) are contracted into the form 'let's', as shown in (56):

(56) Let's go to the circus tonight.

Hopper and Traugott credit Quirk et al. (1985: 829) for observing that the use of this construction has been extended beyond 1st pl. subjects. What is more, these subjects can be overtly expressed, as in (57b):

(57) a. Let's give you a hand.
          (that is, let me give you a hand; first person singular)
      b. Let's you go first, then if we have any money left I'll go.
          (second person singular) (2003: 10–11)

While Quirk et al. (1985: 230) describe *let's* as 'no more than an introductory particle', Hopper and Traugott argue that the sense of *let's* has undergone subjectification to the extent that it 'has become more centred in the speaker's attitude to the situation' (2003: 11) in conveying the speaker's encouragement. (Traugott 1995: 37 describes it as the speaker's 'condescending support-style'.) They argue that this change in meaning (from the full verb *let* 'allow, permit') has gone hand-in-hand with reanalysis and a change in form. First, the 1st pl. pronoun *us* became cliticised (*let's*) (cf. (58a) versus (58b)). However, when usage of *let's* spread to subjects other than first person plural (cf. (58b) and (58c)), it was no longer valid to analyse it as a cliticised form. They (2003: 12) propose that '(t)he final *s* of *lets*, then, is losing its status as a separate morpheme, and is in the process of becoming a simple phonemic constituent of a (monomorphemic) word'. They take the historical trajectory of the *let's* construction to be as in (58) and to reflect a more general cline in grammaticalisation of *word* > *affix* > *phoneme*.

(58) (let) us > (let)'s > (let)s
a. Please, let us go.   [let [us V]]
b. Let's (you and I) go to the circus tonight. [let's [you and I V]]
c. Lets me give you a hand.   [lets [me V]]

We would now like to return to some of the major findings of variationist studies on existentials as reported in Sects. 5.3 and 5.4. Recall that they have demonstrated that the use of verbal –s is very common in existential *there* sentences, and that contraction into *there's* enhances the rate of usage of verbal –s in the context of plural associate-NPs. Along the lines of Hopper and Traugott (2003), we think that existential *there*, once it had grammaticalised from the locative adverb *there*, continued to develop a new grammatical form and function in the manner sketched in (59).

(59) a.

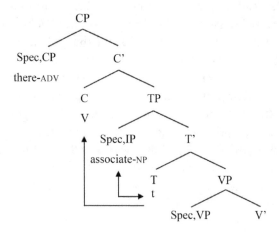

5 Verbal –s in Existential *there* Sentences

b.
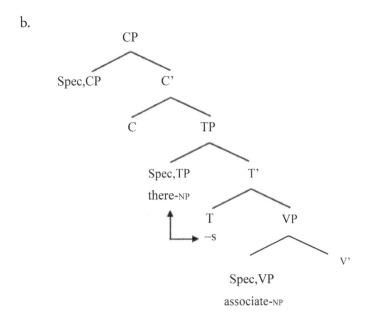

Preposed locative *there* triggered movement of the verb from T to C (Verb Second). On its way from T to C, the verb could enter in a subject-verb agreement relation with the subject in (Spec,TP) (as in (59a)). When locative *there* was reanalysed as (what now is) existential *there*, it acquired the categorical status of an NP and came to occupy (Spec,TP). As a result, agreement between the verb and the associate-NP no longer obtained and the agreement morpheme on the verb would have lost its function (cf. Pietsch 2005: 156). Given that it is in particular the singular agreement marker –s that has specialised, we consider it likely that agreement was at first re-established as a relation between the verb and *there* (as Sobin 1997 assumes). Alternatively, singular –s might have spread via the contexts that admitted or promoted singular –s in existentials; for example, in the context of number-neutral determiners like *no* and *the*, or adverbs that intervene between the verb and the associate-NP (e.g. *And, there's [at least eight] discs available at*

the present time ... from Martínez-Insua and Palacios Martínez (2003: 279)). Recall from Chapter 2 that the latter factor of 'distance' favours verbal –s in non-existentials also by the 'Proximity Effect' of the NSR. Such developments can have given rise to the situation of variation that exists today, in which speakers variably use (standard) plural subject-verb agreement (*there are/were* + plural associate-NP) and singular –s in the context of a plural associate-NP (*there is/was* + plural associate-NP). At this stage, singular –s also occurs as a contracted form (*there's* + plural associate-NP).[18]

In the end, however, –s must have lost its function as an agreement morpheme altogether and this, we assume, triggered reanalysis of *there* and (what had become) verbal –s. On the model of Hopper and Traugott's (2003) account of *let('s)* constructions, we would like to argue that the reanalysis involved a change in constituency as indicated in (60).

(there) is/are > (there)'s > (there)s

(60) a. There are hundreds of shells on the beach.   [there [are NP-plural V]]

b. There is hundreds of shells on the beach.   [there is [NP-plural V]]

c. There's hundreds of shells on the beach.   [there's [NP-plural V]]

d. Theres hundreds of shells on the beach.   [theres [NP-plural V]]

Specifically, we envisage that the morpheme *there* was reassigned from the category of 'existential' *there* to acquire the status of a particle *there(')s*, a trajectory in which the contracted form *there's* constituted an intermediate stage.[19] This may in effect mean that –s in *there(')s* is no longer of a verbal nature. The application of reanalysis is evident from the fact that the syntactic contexts in which *there* can occur have been generalised to contexts that were unavailable before; namely, contexts with (all sorts of) plural NP-associates.[20]

Overall, on the basis of this analysis, it seems opportune to hypothesise that we are dealing with a process of further, 'secondary' grammaticalisation. In the literature, two main models of secondary grammaticalisation

5 Verbal –s in Existential *there* Sentences   285

have been proposed; one by Givón (1991), who coined the term, and one by Traugott (2002), who was the first to use the term in contrast to 'primary' grammaticalisation. Underlying both models is the assumption that two types of grammaticalisation can be distinguished: primary grammaticalisation, which involves an initial change from lexical to grammatical status, while secondary grammaticalisation involves a subsequent change from a grammatical(ised) function to a further grammatical function (Traugott 2010: 41). The terms primary versus secondary indicate the temporal order of changes, such that 'changes of type B are later than, or at least start at the same time as changes of type A, and crucially not before them' (Traugott 2002: 28). The output of a previous stage in a grammatical development, primary grammaticalisation, serves as input for the next stage, secondary grammaticalisation. We will first outline the two models before we interpret the envisaged grammaticalisation of *there('s)* within the framework of these models.

In Givón's (1991) model, grammaticalisation can be conceived of as a chain (Breban 2015) or tree (Smirnova 2015) in which distinct, fully-fledged, and independent processes of grammaticalisation occur in succession. He observed that in Biblical Hebrew, the (already) grammaticalised subordinator of relative clauses, *asher*, came to serve two other constructions: adverbial clauses and verbal complements. Following Breban (2010: 69), the secondary grammaticalisation of Givón concerns 'the development of *new* (more) grammatical meanings on the basis of existing grammatical meanings of a linguistic element' [our italics LR&DB]. (Note that Hopper and Traugott (2003: xv) appear to have defined 'grammaticalisation' in a similar way as 'a change whereby lexical items and constructions come in certain linguistic contexts to serve grammatical functions and, once, grammaticalized, continue to develop grammatical functions'.) Breban (2015) points out that the major way in which the model of Givón (1991) differs from that of Traugott (2002) lies in the availability of semantic/pragmatic change. Only secondary grammaticalisation in the sense of Givón (1991) can be semantically/pragmatically driven.

In a volume of research, Traugott has developed a typology of types of semantic and pragmatic change that can occur during the process of grammaticalisation. In the first version of this typology, Traugott

(1982) adapted the three-layered model of language from Halliday and Hasan (1976). She postulated that semantic change is most likely to evolve from 'less personal to personal'; namely, it typically proceeds from an objective (truth-conditional) propositional meaning, to a textual meaning, and then an expressive, speaker-centred meaning, denoting attitudes to discourse situations or a speaker's feelings or relationships with his interlocutors. Textual meaning is conveyed by 'resources ... creating a cohesive discourse' (1982: 248). At the heart of Traugott's typology is the idea that grammaticalisation derives from a series of smaller transitions that over time unfold in the same direction across languages (namely, the hypothesis of the unidirectionality of change, as addressed in Chapter 4). This has been conceptualised in the metaphor of a 'cline'; a natural 'pathway' along which expressions evolve (Hopper and Traugott 2003: 6), both structurally (cf. the earlier discussion of the derivation of the form *lets*) and semantically/pragmatically. A shift from textual to expressive is found, for example, in the case of the grammaticalisation of the definite article *the*, which developed from the Old English demonstrative paradigm. In one of its earliest uses, the article has the textual function of an anaphora since *the book* can be used to refer back to some entity previously mentioned, but in an historically later use it can also establish common ground between the speaker and the hearer, as in *The book that I told you about* (Lyons 1999: 332). Narrog (2015) has forcefully argued that the restrictions on the direction of grammaticalisation have not yet been definitively established. He has particularly taken issue with the idea that textual information is a fixed transitional stage between the shift from the propositional to the expressive. The evolution of the meaning of the expression *actually* seems one such counterexample. Following Traugott and Dasher (2002: 169–70), the history of *actually* illustrates a shift in meaning from propositional 'in action, in practice' (expressing commitment to the truth of the proposition) > subjective 'epistemic adversative' (embodying surprise, incredulity) > textual 'additive discourse marker' (signalling additivity). Narrog has highlighted that advanced stages of grammaticalisation can in fact show development towards textual/discourse-oriented functions and in (2012) postulated an alternative model of increased 'speech-act orientation'.

5 Verbal –s in Existential *there* Sentences 287

In view of such unclarity about the ordering of textual and the expressive changes, Traugott (1995: 47) subsumes change in textual meaning under expressive meaning. Textual functions like turn-taking and the formation of a coherent discourse were now seen as embedded in expressive functions. Narrog (2015: 154) has recently questioned the idea that the textual domain is part of the expressive domain proper. In later work (Traugott and Dasher 2002: 34 ff.), Traugott's original typology of semantic/pragmatic change has given way to a mechanism of nonsubjective > subjective (speaker-orientation) > intersubjective (hearer-orientation). The stages in this model involve increased subjectivity and ultimately intersubjectivity. Subsequently, expressions gradually develop semantic or pragmatic meanings that primarily convey the speaker's attitude or viewpoint (subjectivity), while subsequent to this they are deployed to encode meanings more centred on the addressee (intersubjectivity) (for example, turn relinquishing or elicitation of response, or meanings oriented towards the addressee's stance and participation in the communicative situation). The adverb *well* may be an example of an expression that has been proceeding according to this trajectory. Following Jucker (1997), the earliest, propositional meaning associated with the adverb *well* is 'in accordance with a good or high standard of conduct or morality; in a way which is morally good' (1997: 95). Later on, Jucker argues (1997: 94–95), *well* came to be associated with a range of other uses, and developed from a predominantly textual (that is, framing) marker (for example, indicating a topic change) into a predominantly interpersonal marker. In one of its intrapersonal uses, *well* can be recruited as a 'face-threat mitigator', indicating problems occurring at the intrapersonal level. This can involve situations where either the face of the speaker or that of the hearer is threatened; for instance when the speaker thinks that the upcoming text or discourse may be socially sensitive in some way.[21]

Already in relation to Traugott's (1982) first typology, McMahon (1994: 170) cautioned that while the tendencies that have been empirically observed towards types of semantic/pragmatic change are clearly relevant to grammaticalisation, the boundaries between them are rather vague. Herring (1991: 253–254) has more strongly expressed concern that it is not clear why we might expect the characterisation of direction

288   L. Rupp and D. Britain

of effect to obtain. Note, for example, that Breban (2010: 112–117) has argued that the textual domain can be interpersonal to the effect that it frequently involves interaction between the speaker and the hearer: the speaker may organise the discourse in order to facilitate the processing and correct interpretation of information by the hearer. In this light, she assumes the occurrence of 'textual (inter)subjectification'. McMahon has stated that more data and more rigorous testing is required in the programme of grammaticalisation research (1994: 170).

Having outlined the types of semantic/pragmatic change that Givón's (1991) model of secondary grammaticalisation allows for, we now turn to Traugott's (2002) model. In Traugott's model, secondary grammaticalisation can be conceived of as a cline. Accordingly, primary grammaticalisation leads to a change in function from the lexical to the grammatical, and secondary grammaticalisation leads to a change in form from a less grammatical status to a more grammatical status. She comments: 'With respect to such changes, it does make sense to talk about shifts towards more grammatical status, although it would be more accurate to say that "expressions of functional categories become more bonded over time"' (2002: 27). Typical effects of an increase in bondedness include: morphological binding/fusion, phonetic erosion, bleaching and the like. For illustration, Traugott cites the reduction of auxiliaries after they developed from lexical verbs: *will* → *'ll*. Crediting Bybee (1995), Hopper and Traugott (2003: 127) have argued that especially words that often occur adjacent to another may become fused and automated to the effect that they are stored and uttered 'as a block'; an example of this is *going to* > *gonna*. (Joseph (2004: 154) rejects the necessity of alluding to frequency and assumes an effect of the 'low salience in phrasal prosody and stresslessness of function words' instead.) On this perspective, Traugott's (2002) secondary grammaticalisation is not a grammaticalisation process in its own right but an 'extended' development; that is, a (later) stage in a single process of grammaticalisation.[22] It is more a continuous development than the diversification in the grammaticalisation chain of Givón (1991), in which new functions develop alongside the old functions that continue to exist. Traugott (2010) has argued that subjectification is less likely to occur in secondary grammaticalisation than in primary grammaticalisation. 'This

5 Verbal –s in Existential *there* Sentences   289

is because primary grammaticalization often requires prior strengthening of pragmatic inferences that arise in very specific linguistic contexts prior to their semanticization and reanalysis as grammatical elements. Further grammaticalization, however, often involves development into automatized structures (especially in the case of inflections)' (2010: 40–41). Breban (2015) has argued that to the extent that semantic change happens in Traugott's (2002) model at all, it will be a tendency towards intersubjectivity. In an examination of a set of cross-linguistic data, Narrog (2015) concurs that secondary grammaticalisation often involves the loss of subjective meaning.

Traugott (2002) has linked her sense of 'secondary grammaticalisation' to the definition of grammaticalisation put forward by Kuryłowicz ([1965] 1976: 52): 'the increase of the range of a morpheme advancing from a lexical to a grammatical or from a less grammatical to a more grammatical status'. This way of putting it has been met by fierce criticism of Von Mengden (2016), who has argued that it is not clear how to conceive of a 'more or less' grammatical expression, or how to measure any such hierarchy for that matter. Askedal (2008: 47) has earlier (rightly) pointed out that an increase in bondedness (as in the case of *will* → *'ll*) does not imply an increase in grammaticality.[23] However, taking account of research on *there('s)* to date, we think that the extended grammaticalisation of *there(')s* that we have in mind fits Traugott's (2002) sense of secondary grammaticalisation best. Smirnova (2015: 218) points out that while secondary grammaticalisation on the model of Givón (1991) may be visualised as a split, on the model of Traugott, it is best thought of as a linear representation that starts with a lexical source and runs all the way down. Along the lines of the latter model, we conceive of secondary grammaticalisation of *there('s)* as a follow-up process. First, *there(')s* has undergone additional phonetic reduction. Second, *there(')s* does not seem to have acquired any new functions towards greater subjectivity; if anything, textual/discourse orientation and intersubjectivity appear to have emerged. Below we will present a number of pragmatic deployments of *there(')s* that have been identified in the literature and differ from the subjective 'existential' use of *there* of Breivik and Swan (2000).

290   L. Rupp and D. Britain

To begin with, Crawford (2005) has argued that *there's* is recruited with a textual meaning. He speaks of *there's* as 'an unanalyzed "chunk" of language that allows speakers to use a well-established principle of discourse organization': 'the principle of end weight … that heavier NPs tend to be found at the end of clauses' (2005: 42, 49). He and other researchers have pointed out that in addition to this, existential *there* sentences play a role in conversational management and 'organizing talk' (Schiffrin 1994: 239–240), such as turn-taking and topic organisation. We refer to Schiffrin (1994: 239–279) and Crawford (2005: 49–58) for detailed discussion of such other discourse functions. Here we illustrate with one example of the function of 'topic manager' from Crawford (2005: 50):

(61)   a.   … what do we have to do?
       b.   Well, I think **there's two things**. I think Joe and I should talk about it okay and I wanted to know what you feel.

Following Crawford, in (61) *there's* serves to introduce 'two things' so that the speaker can go on to explain each 'thing' in depth. In his multiregister corpus study, he observed that particular discourse functions of *there(')s* correlated with 'situational factors'. For example, he attested (perhaps somewhat unexpectedly) that *there's* functioned as 'topic manager' more frequently in formal academic lectures than in conversation. Crawford explains that academic lectures involve longer stretches of speech. Because of the cognitive burden that this imposes, there is a greater need to package information for the audience in such a manner that relationships are shown between topics.

In a corpus study of components of the *British National Corpus* (including the *Bergen Corpus of London Teenage Language*), Breivik and Martínez-Insua (2008: 359) earlier entertained the idea that 'it would appear that not only [existential *there*], but also [*there*]+singular *be* (particularly the contracted form [*there's*]), has undergone grammaticalization'. They subscribe to the observation that *there's* has come to serve a number of other functions than its original existential use, but do analyse these as speaker-based and the result of an ongoing process of subjectification. Citing earlier work by Martínez-Insua (2004), they say that

5 Verbal –s in Existential *there* Sentences 291

existential *there* sentences can be used to perform a variety of speech acts that express relatively high degrees of involvement and personal commitment on the part of the speaker. 'Generally speaking, the grammaticalization of existential [*there* + *be*] seems to endow this sequence with the capacity to convey what may be referred to as prospective and retrospective communicative functions.' (2008: 359). According to Breivik and Martínez-Insua, retrospective [*there* + *be*] points back to the previous discourse, allowing the speaker/writer to comment on, complete or summarise what has been stated before (for example, *Perhaps* **there** *ought to* **be** *a law like that, but* **there isn't** *at the moment*; 2008: 360). Prospective [*there* + *be*], on the other hand, allows the speaker/writer to introduce new information that is largely independent of the previous context and may be elaborated upon in subsequent discourse (for example, ***There*** *were those amongst his small circle of intimates who said it would be his undoing, but they or their predecessors had been prophesying the same for three decades, and Klein had out-prospered every one of them*; (2008: 360)). In a consideration of new functions of *there('s)*, it is somewhat unfortunate that only one of the tokens that Breivik and Martínez-Insua present contains the form *there's*. Further, the additional speaker-based functions that they describe might perhaps just as well be seen as having a textual orientation, rather than expressing a novel subjective meaning.[24]

Finally, Pfenninger (2009) finds that existential *there* sentences epitomise the phenomenon of intersubjectification. Drawing on Grzegorek (1984), for her there is a clear distinction between (1) existential *there* 'that assert[s] the existence of the referent of the displaced NP', and (2) a later, non-existential form *there's* 'that raise[s] the referent of the subject to the addressee's consciousness' (2009: 238). She argues that whereas existential *there* carries traces of its original locative meaning as a result of persistence (Hopper 1991), non-existential *there's* has lost a locative sense altogether. While Pfenninger does not exclusively associate the form *there's* with non-existential use, she claims that it is most commonly associated with a list reading (see (61a–b) again) and categorises constructions with the form *there's* as 'enumerative' *there* constructions (2009: 249). She cites the following example as a good illustration of this: *Vheissu is hardly a restful place.* ***There's barbarity, insurrection, internecine feud*** (2009: 265).

However, the association between the form *there's* and any particular semantic/pragmatic uses, such as the list reading, is still to be established more robustly in future research.

Summarising, this is the 'secondary' development of the expression *there(')s* that we have in mind:

(1) reanalysis of grammatical category in local contexts: *there* + –s has been reanalysed as one morpheme: *there(')s*[25];
(2) phonological reduction and routinisation: the verb *be* has merged with *there* into a single morpheme[26];
(3) an altogether loss of locative sense;
(4) new, intersubjective meanings are added;
(5) generalisation to other contexts of use: new distributional possibilities have opened up for the form *there(')s*, namely, contexts with plural associate-NPs.

The scenario we have in mind extends Hopper's (1991: 22) 'layering' principle of grammaticalisation from locative *there* to existential *there* to *there(')s*. Hopper and Traugott (2003: 125) say: 'In any single language there is always considerable synchronic diversity within one domain. Some of the most obvious cases are those where a full and a reduced form coexist, with related forms and only minimally different functions.' The different layers of 'older' and 'newer' *there(')s* constructions would seem to provide an excellent example of the synchronic result of successive grammaticalisation of forms.

Lastly, it seems to us that similar to the particular functional shifts that other tokens of verbal –s have undergone, secondary grammaticalisation of *there(')s* has imposed diagrammatic iconicity along the lines of the 'Iconicity Hypothesis' that we outlined in Chapter 2. Note that in an analysis of the grammaticalisation of a Latin analytic modal construction into future tense markers in Romance, Ramat (1995: 123) has previously argued that changes that are part of the grammaticalisation process themselves may preserve iconicity at the morphological level where iconicity has declined due to the weakening of semantic content and phonetic substance. We envisage that as a result of the (primary) grammaticalisation (or: reanalysis) of the locative adverb *there* as an

NP in (Spec,TP), neither –s nor any forms of the verb *be* (*is*, *are*) were used for agreement with the notational subject any longer, which had been placed postverbally in (Spec,VP). The use of verbal –s was subsequently extended across singular and plural subjects. In further (secondary) grammaticalisation, verbal –s was incorporated into *there* and *there('s)* acquired other (intersubjective) meanings. Recall from Chapter 2 that diagrammatic iconicity divides into two types: 'isomorphism' and 'motivation' (Haiman 1980). The way in which existentials developed has resulted in (or further enforced, see Note 16) an isomorphic one-to-one relationship between form (*there(')s*) and function (alerting the addressee to new information and so on). In addition to this, we would like to put forward the possibility that the form *there(')s* is also iconically *motivated*. Citing data from the spoken material of the *Survey of English Usage*, Breivik (1981: 15) anticipated this analysis, first noting that 'sometimes it would appear that [existential *there*] and the verb *be* have become fused into a single presentative formula [there's]', as in[27]:

(62) a. and they've sold the back of their garden and **there's two houses.**

b. … just in case—**there's no toys** on Christmas morning.

Breivik goes on to propose that '[s]ince [existential *there*] has come to be associated with the introduction of new information, it has itself acquired the status of a presentative signal' (1981: 16). Note that on this perspective, existential *there(')s* is naturally expected to occur with definite associate-NPs as long as (as we saw in Sect. 5.2) its function is to (re)call the referent of the definite NP into the focus of attention, as in the list reading in (63):

(63) Who's attending the meeting?
Well, **there's Noel, Michael, and Sue.**

Breivik (1981: 16) points out that his hypothesis about the status of *there(')s* as a presentative unit receives support from the fact that sentences like (63) are ill-formed when the verb *to be* is made to agree with the associate NP: **Well, there **are** Noel, Michael and Sue.*

We would like to suggest that the form *there(')s* is a presentative device that resembles a signpost in signalling (new) information. Factors that have contributed to its iconic nature are (1) it has grammaticalised into one morpheme, and (2) it has no concrete meaning. Following important observations in Schiffrin (1994: 276–277), in order to qualify for presenting new information, the presentative signal should be material that imposes few processing demands upon the hearer. The form *there(')s* is a highly appropriate device to introduce a referent in the discourse because it predicates very little (if anything) of an entity and because the verb *be* is a weak predicate (see Cheshire 1999 and Crawford 2005 for discussion of the role of processing demands in this; also see Detges and Waltereit (2002: 178, 181) for the effect of routinisation on perceptual saliency in a broader context). In a similar vein, Pfenninger (2009: 260) has said: 'since *be* carries a more or less neutral meaning from the semantic point of view ... it facilitates emphasis on the NP by not attracting attention to itself'.

5.6 Discussion

Chomsky (1995) and Walker (2007), too, have argued that the morpheme *there's* has special status. Chomsky (1995: 384) writes:

> As is well known, agreement with the associate is sometimes overridden, as for example in *there's three books on the table, there's a dog and a cat in the room* (vs *a dog and a cat is in the room*). The phenomenon, however, seems superficial: thus it does not carry over to **is there three books ... *there isn't any books ...* and so on. The form *there's* simply seems to be a frozen option, not relevant [to the account of agreement LR&DB].

However, Smallwood (1997) has previously responded that non-contracted forms of verbal –s did occur in her data, as in (64a), and many others have found the same. (64b–c) are from Eisikovits (1991: 245) and (64d) from Britain and Sudbury's (2002) data from the Falkland Islands.

5 Verbal –s in Existential *there* Sentences   295

(64)   a.   On the top, just about centre, **there is** stick people.
        b.   **Is there** any nets out there?
        c.   **There isn't** any girls going, is there?
        d.   Yes, **there is** quite a few women golfers in Stanley.

We have proposed an analysis of existential *there* sentences in which the form *there(')s* has a place at the end of a grammaticalisation trajectory. In the envisaged trajectory, the separation between locative and existential *there* represents the first stage. Via a number of intermediate stages involving non-contracted verbal –s (*there is/was*) and contracted *there's*, the occurrence of the presentative signal *there(')s* represents the final stage. We would agree (with Chomsky 1995) that the morpheme *there(')s* no longer has a role in subject-verb agreement. In the completely different context of past BE, Trudgill (2008: 324) has said that 'what is involved here is not a question of singular versus plural', and this is exactly what we think applies to *there(')s*. We think that no term such as 'singular concord/agreement/*be*' or 'non-standard concord/agreement' is fully appropriate, and ascribe to Schütze's position that 'non-agreement is really *absence* of agreement' (1999: 480). Tortora (1997: 294, Footnote 25) says that 'this raises the question of what in fact -'s is ... I do not offer an analysis here (although I do think it is possible to pursue the idea that -'s may not even be the contracted form of *is* at all; only future research can tell whether it may be, in fact, a functional morpheme of a different nature)'. We have proposed that *there(')s* has been reanalysed as a presentational device that has acquired the intersubjective function of guiding the addressee to new information.

However, the hypothesis that *there(')s* is a single morpheme awaits analytical testing in future research, examining to what extent *there(')s* in fact shows idiosyncratic behaviour. This is another aspect of existentials in respect of which variationist research and grammatical theory can join forces, and provide important evidence for accounts of grammaticalisation. Krejci and Hilton (2015) have previously advocated the position that there are two realisations of 'non-agreement' in existentials and that sociolinguistic and syntactic analysis can be deployed to find out whether *there's* is turning into an unanalysable lexical unit. Walker (2007) has been among the first to look for independent evidence demonstrating that *there's* is of a different (lexicalised) nature than *there is/was*.[28] In Walker (2014) he has made a case for using constraint hierarchies as a diagnostic tool for assessment. He notes that in studies from the field of comparative sociolinguistics (like Poplack and Tagliamonte 2001) 'it is a commonplace that if the hierarchy of linguistic conditioning of variant *x* is the same in Community A and Community B, the two communities can be inferred to share the same linguistic system (and furthermore the same source variety)' (2014: 9). Walker thus extends the utility of the constraint hierarchy to compare the variants *there is* and *there's*: does or doesn't the putatively lexicalised form *there's* demonstrate its own distinct conditioning? If *there is* and *there's* share the same linguistic conditioning, we can infer that they are related forms; but if their linguistic conditioning differs, they must be of a different nature. Walker (2007) inquired into *there* sentences in Quebec English, whilst Walker (2014) extended the analysis with data from Toronto and the island of Bequia in the Caribbean. One of the results was that uncontracted *there is/was*, on the one hand, and contracted *there's*, on the other, showed different conditioning by determiner type. The direction of effect exerted for *there's* was significant and almost diametrically opposed to the results of other studies which did not separate *there is/was* and *there's* in their analysis: *a* quantifier > adjective > bare > negative > definite > number > other quantifier (see Sect. 5.4.1 again). In contrast, the direction of effect observed for *there is/was*, albeit not significant, rather patterned with the results reported by other studies which combined *there is/was* and *there's*: *a* quantifier > definite > negative > bare > number > other quantifier > adjective (2007: 160–161). We fully subscribe to Walker's (2007, 2014) insightful approach, though more research needs to be carried out to explore the universality of his finding across other varieties of English. His findings are challenged by, for example, the results from Crawford's (2005) corpus analysis of existential *there* sentences in five different registers of present-day American English. Crawford found that *there's* behaved like *there is* with respect to determiner type (2005: 55). Further, it is a somewhat unexpected outcome on Walker's own account that his results for uncontracted strings *there is/was* corresponded to the results of studies which combined contracted and uncontracted forms, such as Britain and Sudbury (2002). This said, it seems telling that while many studies

5 Verbal –s in Existential *there* Sentences   297

may not have treated *there's* separately from *there is/was*, they reported a strong favouring of the form *there's* in their data (for example Meechan and Foley 1994).

Fortunately, we were able to go back to the New Zealand English data explored in Britain and Sudbury (2002) to see both if *there's* patterned differently from *there is/was* with respect to determiner type, and to see if each form patterned similarly to its equivalent in Walker's Canadian data. In Britain and Sudbury (2002), when *there's* and *there is* and *there was* were combined in the analysis (vs. *there are/there were*), the data patterned for determiner type as follows:

a-quantifiers > *no* > Definite > Number > Bare > Other quantifiers > Adjective

Following Walker (2007: 158), we first reanalysed the data, excluding *there's*, and considering only full singular forms versus full plural forms. As in Walker's case, determiner type was not significant, but only marginally so ($p = 0.055$). The data compared as follows, with the underlined factors favouring the use of the full singular form, and the rest not:

<u>no</u> > <u>Definite</u> > <u>*a*-quantifiers</u> > Number > Adjective > Bare > Other quantifiers

(cf. Walker 2007: 158: <u>*a*-quantifiers > Definite > *no*</u> > Bare > Number > Other quantifiers > Adjective).

We then reanalysed the New Zealand data, again following Walker (2007: 160); this time contrasting *there's* with all other forms. As he suggests, 'If the choice of *there's* reflects the more general process of singular agreement, we expect to see similar linguistic conditioning of its occurrence. If it reflects a process of lexicalization, we expect to find different conditioning' (2007: 160). This time the effect of determiner type was as follows, and statistically significant ($p = 0.006$):

<u>*a*-quantifiers > Bare > Number</u> > *no* > Other quantifiers > Definite > Adjective

(cf. Walker 2007: 160): <u>*a*-quantifiers > Adjective > Bare</u> > *no* > Definite > Number > Other quantifiers.

Clearly the effect of determiner type operates differently on full singular forms than it does on *there's* in the New Zealand data. Leaving aside *a*-quantifiers, the effect of *no* and definites on the one hand, and bare nouns and adjectives on the other, differs quite considerably from one analysis to the other. What seems to be going on is that *there(')s* more readily allows for subjects that can be plural in the absence of an overt D (recall the discussion in Sect. 5.4.1), consistent with the secondary grammaticalisation process that we have proposed. These results, then, support Walker's (2007: 162) lexicalisation argument[29] as well as his appeal for more researchers to differentiate *there's* forms from full singular forms. Although not alone conclusive, further support for the *there's ≠ there is* hypothesis possibly comes from a perception experiment conducted by Hilton (2016). Over 900 American English speakers evaluated stimuli by eight native speakers recorded reading four existential sentences with plural associate-NPs, one each with *there's, there is, there are* and *there were*.[30] They were asked to assess whether the speaker in each case was intelligent, articulate, educated and came from a wealthy or middle class family. She finds that 'listener evaluations of *there's* were nearly indistinguishable from evaluations of the standard agreement guises with *there are*' (2016: 64). Guises who used *there is*, however, were rated as significantly less educated, intelligent, articulate, and less likely to be from wealthy or middle class backgrounds than the guises who used *there are* or *there's*. She concludes that her study 'casts serious doubt' on the idea that *there's* and *there is* are sociolinguistically and syntactically equivalent (2016: 69).

What can social factors tell us about the nature of *there's*? Given its function as a useful presentative device, we would not necessarily expect the use of *there('s)* to convey a strong social meaning. Consistent with this expectation, Tagliamonte and Smith (1999: 157) claim that the patterning of verbal –s in existentials is robust and reported 'regardless of geographical location, rural or urban status, or social characteristics of the speakers', while Smith and Tagliamonte (1998: 112) maintain that 'in existentials there is little extra-linguistic conditioning'. Nonetheless, reports of social conditioning are not entirely absent. Among the significant social factors reported in the literature are: age (higher rates of verbal –s among younger speakers; Britain and Sudbury 2002); level of education (lower frequencies of verbal –s amongst speakers who obtained higher levels of education; for example Meechan and Foley

1994); similarly, employment (for example Hay and Schreier 2004); style (more verbal –s in informal registers; for example Smallwood 1997); style as a function of spoken language (verbal –s is more frequent in speech than in writing; for example Cheshire 1999; Crawford 2005) and gender (boys increasingly use verbal –s the older they get, whereas the older girls are, the less verbal –s they use; Eisikovits 1991, who suggests that this gender difference might reflect orientation towards covert prestige forms versus overt prestige norms, respectively) (but see Tagliamonte 1998 for a different gender pattern in York, discussed in Sect. 5.3.2). We take the favouring of *there's* by younger generations of speakers to be indicative of the ongoing grammaticalisation of *there(')s*, and the education factor to demonstrate pressure of prescriptive norms of correctness in favour of Standard English.[31] In a study of California's Central Valley, Krejci and Hilton (2015) inquired into social factors as a means of distinguishing *there's* from *there is*. They found a greater use of the string *there is* by male speakers and speakers with less education, whereas younger speakers showed significantly higher rates of *there's*. They similarly considered this suggestive of a change in progress leading to the lexicalisation of *there(')s*.[32] We also examined the New Zealand data for possible social constraints, distinguishing *there is* from *there's*. *There is* was used more by male, older speakers in blue collar occupations with few educational qualifications—NORMs, in a sense—whereas *there's* was favoured by young speakers with mid-ranking occupations and educational achievement—a profile typical of the leaders of change (Milroy and Milroy 1985).

In future work it will also be interesting to explore more closely whether use of *there is* versus *there(')s* correlates with particular discourse-pragmatic functions (recall the discussion of subjective, intersubjective and textual meanings in Sect. 5.5). In the context of *there* sentences, we may more generally ask to what extent discourse-pragmatic factors influence results that have thus far been ascribed to structural factors.[33] Cheshire (1999: 137) and later Crawford (2005) have warned formal linguists against conducting too narrow an investigation of existential *there* sentences in isolation from their discourse context. The importance of the discourse context warrants more qualitative analysis than has been undertaken thus far, and this applies to variationist studies, too. We would conclude that over time the functions of verbal

–s in *there* sentences have been determined by an interaction of structural–, social–, and discourse-pragmatic factors to an extent that is still to be fully decided, and that LVC-researchers and formal and functional linguists can jointly unravel the full story.[34]

Notes

1. The generative linguist Sobin (1997: 319) has even defined subject-verb agreement in existentials as constituting a 'grammatical virus'. He argues that 'grammatical viruses' are imposed by prescriptivist considerations of prestige and correctness and embody rules that are contrary and external to natural grammar.

2. Existential *there* sentences have been loosely described as asserting the existence of something (Jespersen 1924 was among the first to identify them as such). We will qualify this description in Sect. 5.5 on the grammaticalisation of existential *there*. Hannay (1985: 12) has argued that it may in fact not be appropriate to label the *there* in existentials as 'existential *there*' as it is not obvious that it has inherent 'existential' features. From this perspective, it might be better labelled 'introductory *there*', as Hannay (1985) does, according to its pragmatic function, or 'expletive *there*' in view of its syntactic status (Felser and Rupp 2001). For the sake of transparency, however, we will continue to refer to it as 'existential *there*', reflecting the nature of the construction in which it occurs.

3. As is well known, there is another type of 'presentative' construction which involves *there* and a verb other than *be*. The examples in (65) are from Hannay (1985: 9). However, he and others (see the references in his work) have argued that these should be distinguished from the existential *there* construction. The precise argument for treating them separately need not concern us here.

> (65) a. In a dark towering castle **there** once lived a beautiful princess.
> b. **There** exists some doubt about the future of the Labour party.
> c. **There** emerged the frightening possibility that she would leave him.

5 Verbal –s in Existential *there* Sentences 301

Following Schütze (1999), presentative constructions are not used with verbal –s. Pfenninger (2009: 240) has argued that the rise of existential *there* sentences has caused the use of presentational constructions to decline.
4. Huddleston and Pullum (2002: 1400–1401) provide two further examples that defy the definiteness restriction: first, definite descriptions that are hearer-new but nonetheless identifiable from a descriptor like a relative clause, as in (66a), and second, what they term 'false definite *this*', as in (66b), where *this* can be replaced by the indefinite singular determiner *a* but not by *the*.

(66) a. In Johnson's latest article, there is **the claim that earthquakes are affected by the tides**.
      b. %Last week, there was **this strange dog** wandering around the neighbourhood.

5. An apparently different kind of exception to the definiteness restriction derives from non-initial existential sentences in Indian English, which may convey old information (for example Lange 2012: 107):

(67) C: Something and some places like *Majestic* and all that …
      Yeah *Majestic* is there.

6. This is one of the ways in which existential *there* sentences differ from 'dummy' *it* or 'weather-*it*'; cf. *It was raining*.
7. Some varieties rather show the reverse pattern; thus, r-generalisation in the context of a singular associate-NP. These are mostly varieties that have been moving from traditional *were*-levelling to a mixed *was/weren't* system, as discussed in Chapter 4. Among them are the Fens of eastern England (Britain 2002). Here, speakers, while continuing to show low rates of *were*-levelling (9%) in positive existentials (*There were a farm*) as compared to 81% *was*-levelling (*There was farms*) (2002: 27), showed 83% *weren't*-levelling (*There weren't a farm*) and 0% *wasn't*-levelling (*There wasn't farms*) in negative existentials (2002: 29). The corresponding figures reported for Ocracoke by Schilling-Estes and Wolfram (1994: 283) amounted to 8.1% levelled *were*, 67.9% levelled *was*, 61.1% levelled *weren't* and 28.6% levelled *wasn't*. In data from the *Northern Ireland Transcribed Corpus of Speech* (NITCS) and the *Freiburg Corpus of English Dialects* (FRED), Pietsch (2005) found r-generalisation in both the present and the past tense of *be* in parts of

Northern Ireland and Scotland. In the NITCS data, this was especially apparent in negative existentials with singular denotational subjects, where the use of –r was three times more frequent than in non-negated constructions (27% as opposed to 9%; 2005: 160). He has argued that this negation effect reflects the more general finding that some dialects prefer generalised *weren't* over *wasn't* (see the discussion in Chapter 4). Cheshire and Fox (2009: 28) think the same regarding the use of *weren't* in existentials by their outer London adolescent group.

8. While Antieau (2011) says that this phenomenon has received relatively little attention in the literature on past BE, Peitsara (1988) has reported on the occurrence of existential *they* in the dialect of Suffolk in eastern England and Tortora in the English of Appalachia (2006: 278; and references therein). One Appalachian example is *They's about six or seven guitar players here* (cited from Montgomery and Hall 2004: xlix). We refer to their work for speculations about the historical emergence of existential *they* (which both of them assume derives from existential *there*) and for a description of linguistic factors that promote existential *they*, which Peitsara (1988) discusses at some length. One such a favouring factor is that in the dialect of Suffolk, existential *they* was mostly used in the past tense, combining with non-standard *was* in affirmative sentences and the vernacular form *wa'n't* in negative sentences. Peitsara (1988: 86) comments: 'The status of *wa'n't* as a dialectal form seems to equal that of existential *they*, for whenever the variant *they* precedes, the verbal in negative sentences is *wa'n't*.' [Since in traditional East Anglian varieties, the /ɜː/ vowel in checked position was realised as [ɐ], we believe that *wa'n't* may in fact be the eye-dialect spelling of [wɐnt] or [wɐn?] LR&DB]. Richards (2010: 73) similarly finds that speakers in Morley in northern England use a non-standard mixed *were/wasn't* system exclusively with vernacular forms ([wə/wɒn?]), while they reserve the Standard English forms for subject-verb agreement.

9. Britain and Sudbury (2002) also tested for the effect of polarity. They found that negative contexts favoured standard plural forms, both in the present and (especially) in the past tense. Whilst their finding for the present arguably derives in part from the unavailability of cliticised forms like *there'sn't*, this explanation cannot be extended to the past tense (*wasn't*). However, we note that different studies appear to have categorised 'negative context' in different ways. For example, Martínez-Insua and Palacios Martínez (2003) include 'no', which Britain and

Sudbury (2002) treat separately as a negative determiner. The results for the factor of polarity may therefore not be directly comparable and somewhat skewed.

10. Meechan and Foley (1994) frame their solution to exceptional usage of definite associate-NPs in existentials in terms of partitive case assignment, drawing on Belletti (1988). We think that it may also fall out from a DP-hypothesis in which the feature of definiteness [+Def] is associated with a D-head in the clause structure, rather than with the nominal expression itself. This analysis follows Lyons (1999), who postulates that only definite determiners are associated with a DP (Definiteness Phrase), while other determiners are associated with some lower functional head. Definiteness is thus seen as being determined structurally, not lexically, as a feature of the DP, and it is induced by filling that position (1999: 290). On this account, we may argue that 'strong' DPs can escape the Definiteness Restriction (cf. Hannay 1985 in Sect. 5.2) and receive a 'weak' reading (of providing 'new' information in the discourse) when they do not raise as high as this Definiteness Phrase but remain low in the clause structure, a possibility that we established for the associate-NP of existentials on independent grounds. The DP-hypothesis is addressed at more length later in Sect. 5.2.1.

11. Some variationist studies have also tested for the effect of subject-auxiliary inversion in interrogative structures, which arguably similarly creates a distance between the verb and the associate-NP and leaves them non-adjacent. In Chapter 2 on verbal –s, we noted that a number of studies (except Henry 1995) have identified the structural configuration of interrogatives as one of the few prototypical verbal –s environments left (Pietsch 2005) for non-existentials. There, we ascribed this use of verbal –s as a means of signalling subjects with low accessibility. For the specific case of existentials, the results are not fully transparent. In their data sets of New Zealand and the Falkland Islands, Britain and Sudbury (2002: 228) found a clear preference for plural forms in inverted clauses as in (68a): 35% and 16%, respectively, where the result for the Falklands was significant. Eisikovits (1991: 242) presents several tokens of verbal –s in interrogative existentials (as in (68b)) in her Inner Sydney data, but does not comment on them.

304   L. Rupp and D. Britain

(68) a. **Are** there **any more sultanas** in the crumble?
      b. **Isn't** there **any girls** going?

12. On the assumption of a covert operation from VP into TP for subject-verb agreement, we arguably do expect a blocking effect of sentence negation. This is because ever since Pollock (1989), sentential *not* is commonly taken to be the Neg head of a NegP that is situated between V and T. Recall from Sect. 5.2 that in existentials like (69), *not* can take scope over the quantifier *many*, but not vice versa. This suggests that the *not* that is available in existentials is constituent negation, which is adjoined to VP. Sentence negation is possible when negation is attached to the verb, as with *aren't* in (70). Following work by Zwicky and Pullum (1983), such forms are best analysed as constituting lexical items (instead of derived forms; an idea that was discussed in relation to *weren't* in Chapter 4). Rupp (2003) proposes that are directly inserted into T. Therefore, they do not induce a blocking effect.

(69) There are not many students waiting outside.
      [TP There [T are][VP not [VP many students [V waiting outside]]]]
      i. = It is not the case that many students are   NOT > MANY
      waiting outside.
      ii ≠ Many students are such that they are not   *MANY > NOT
      waiting outside.
(70) There aren't many students waiting outside.
      [TP There [T aren't][VP many students [V waiting outside]]]

13. Some claim to have found contracted past BE. In the following example from Suffolk, Peitsara (1988: 83) says that context should help resolve the ambiguity.

(71) … an' he used to get an old pheasant sometimes. **There's** some ferrets, too.

We note that in East Anglia in England, in relaxed informal speech, *there was* can be reduced to [ðɛʌz]. That is to say, we wonder whether the source of the form in (71) is phonological, rather than morphological contraction.

5 Verbal –s in Existential *there* Sentences   305

Walker (2014: 12), in a study of speakers from Toronto, Quebec and the island of Bequia in the Caribbean, coded for past (72a) and non-past (72b) temporal reference of the verb, rather than present and past tense morphology, based on clues provided in the surrounding discourse.

(72) a. Of course, **there's** things that he wanted to ask. [PAST]

      b. **There's** only three of us here. [PRESENT]

He found an overwhelming preference for *there's* in present tense temporal contexts, whereas non-contracted forms were favoured in past tense temporal contexts (2014: 17).

14. On an alternative account, sentences with a preposed prepositional phrase like *in all the world* in (52b) are deployed to convey a different meaning than existential *there* sentences; recall the discussion of contemporary non-synonymous (non-)existential pairs in (17a–b).

15. See Harris and Campbell (1995: 61–93) for a detailed discussion of 'reanalysis'. Reanalysis need not go together with phonetic reduction: compare the use of *while* as a noun in the sense of 'a portion of time' to *while* as a temporal conjunct. Von Mengden (2016: 138) has argued that, therefore, 'erosive change' should not be taken as a defining feature of 'grammaticalization' or assumed to be part of it. Joseph (2004: 53) points out that phonetic reduction is an independent sound change that occurs outside of grammaticalisation, and so should be considered as due to phonetic factors and not as somehow 'occasioned' by grammatical status. He notes that phonetic reduction in grammaticalisation may rather reflect the low prosodic prominence that function words often show. In the same spirit, Smirnova (2015: 219–220) envisages that what she terms 'constructional changes' follow the formation of a new construction ('constructionalization'). In a series of papers, Joseph has more generally contended that 'grammaticalization' is not a process in itself, but a label given to a particular outcome of a series of traditionally recognised changes, such as reanalysis, phonetic reduction, and analogy. (Harris and Campbell (1995: 92) express a similar stance; Fischer (1999: especially 352–353) even sees an iconic basis for the various processes that have been distinguished in grammaticalisation.) As Fischer (2010: 295) has put it: 'An increasing number of formal and/or

historical linguists believe that grammaticalization should be considered an *epiphenomenon* rather than a mechanism of change in and by itself.' Hopper and Traugott (2003: xv) have acknowledged such concerns. On a positive note, Joseph (2004: 61) much appreciates the central role that grammaticalisation studies have assigned to actual language use(rs) in changes like reanalysis (see, for example, Detges and Waltereit 2002).

16. Jenset reports as one of the main results of his Ph.D. research the finding that there was no general increase of initial adverbs during the Old English period, and that *there* tended to occur with the verb *be* already from the Old English period (2010: 291).

17. Pfenninger (2009: 15), in comparative corpus study of the diachrony of existentials in English and German, demonstrates that other of Hopper's (1991) principles of grammaticalisation also apply; that of 'Divergence', whereby a lexical split separates the evolving grammatical element from its lexical mother (cf. the split between locative and existential *there*), and that of 'Specialization', whereby 'a variety of formal choices narrows and the smaller number of forms selected assume more general grammatical meanings' (1991: 22). In relation to 'Specialization', Pfenninger (2009) shows that German is less advanced in the grammaticalisation of existential sentences to the extent that German (still) uses a variety of different constructions, whereas in English, existential sentences have come to be restricted to constructions with *there* over time. (We refer to her work for more detailed discussion.) Note that this development seems to have constituted an emergent step towards isomorphism and diagrammatic iconisation of existential *there* sentences; the ensuing steps are discussed later in this section.

18. We are aware that this analysis is not directly compatible with Trudgill's (2009: 306–307) view that non-standard past tense existentials are subsidiary to the non-standard usage of present tense *there is* and *there's*. He believes that the spread of verbal –s in existentials was first triggered when *there's* grammaticalised into a single item parallel to French *il y a*. In this relation, we take note of Rosen's (2014: 135) finding that bilingual French-English speakers showed much higher rates of verbal –s in existentials than monolingual English speakers on the Channel Island of Jersey off the Normandy French coast.

    Our assumption does receive some support from Collins (2012). He used subcorpora of the *International Corpus of English* (ICE) to

5 Verbal –s in Existential *there* Sentences   307

study existential sentences in seven postcolonial varieties at different stages along the trajectory of new dialect development proposed in Schneider's (2003) Dynamic Model. He found that the more advanced the varieties were in the trajectory, the more verbal –s they showed, not only by means of *there's* but also in the past tense.

19. It seems natural that there should be a similar development in existentials with a singular associate-NP. The few studies that inquired into this matter have reported apparently contrastive findings. Martínez-Insua and Palacios-Martínez (2003: 273) found that the form *there's* occurred twice as much in existentials with a plural associate-NP than with a singular associate-NP in the *British National Corpus* (BNC). Krejci and Hilton (2015) claim to have found an increase amongst younger speakers in the use of *there's* (vis à vis *there is*) with a singular associate-NP. However, they have not (yet) presented any statistical analysis of their data from 144 sociolinguistic interviews with speakers aged 18–93 in three cities in California's Central Valley, collected between 2010 and 2012.

20. Melchers and Sundkvist (2010) report that, apparently parallel to *there's*, speakers on the Shetland and Orkney Isles off the coast of northern Scotland use one morpheme corresponding to *there is* and *there are*: *der* and *thir*, respectively. Here are some examples from Melchers (2004: 39):

(73) a. **Der** a boat hoose yonder.
      b. **Der** twa Women's Guilds been pitten aff da night.
      c. **Thir** a lock o fock here.

Interestingly, such unified forms also exist for the past tense: 'they wir' in Orkney (e.g. *They wir a coo lowse in the byre*) and 'dey wir' in Shetland (e.g. *Dey wir no money dan*) (Melchers 2004: 39). Melchers and Sundkvist do not comment on the precise nature of these forms, however.

21. Kranich (2008: 242, 2010: 103) speaks of 'objectification' (or: desubjectification) as the reverse of subjectification, and defines it as 'a process by which items become less available for the expression of the speaker's belief state/attitude toward the proposition'; that is, loss/absence of subjective, expressive meaning. We will stick to the term 'intersubjectivity/ intersubjectification', however.

22. The concept of 'secondary grammaticalisation' is still quite controversial. Does invoking 'secondary grammaticalisation' add to our understanding of the grammaticalisation process at large? Or is it captured in the existing framework? For in-depth discussion of this matter, we refer the reader to the special issue 47 of *Language Sciences* (2015) on secondary grammaticalisation. We take no position in this debate as it does not influence the line of argument here.

23. Andersen (2006: 233) put forward the alternative term of 'regrammation': 'a change by which a grammatical expression through reanalysis is ascribed different grammatical content (change with and among grammatical paradigms)'. This description seems reminiscent of Givón's (1991) notion of secondary grammaticalisation. Andersen has made a more general case for separating the various aspects of grammaticalisation, such as bondedness, in view of the fact that they can occur separately and for this reason are best interpreted in the concrete historical contexts in which they have occurred.

24. One complication is that there is some counter-evidence to the idea that the textual function of *there(')s* is an innovative use and one that is exclusively associated with contemporary uses of *there(')s*. In an analysis of data from three electronic corpora of consecutive periods in the English language, Martínez-Insua (2013) has demonstrated that existential constructions have been used as a textual strategy from as early as Old English; specifically, to locate a clause within its context and for scenario setting.

25. The scenario that we envisage here reminds us of Smirnova's (2015) constructionist model of grammaticalisation, which focuses on contextual factors during the grammaticalisation process. In her model, grammaticalisation involves a process of 'constructionalisation'. She defines 'constructionalisation' as the initial formation of a new construction in a language (here: the construction with *there('s)*) whereby contextual constraints (here: the occurrence of existential *there* in contexts of –s) are conventionalized and analysed as inherent parts of the new construction.

26. See Pfenninger (2009: 58) for extensive discussion that *be* in *there* sentences has undergone a cline from full verb > auxiliary > verbal clitic > verbal affix. Detges and Waltereit (2002: 178) say that '[t]he first consequence of a given construction's routinization is that it becomes part of the language's inventory of idiomatic expressions. This means that it is

5 Verbal –s in Existential *there* Sentences   309

increasingly used in a certain form, while other possible forms are progressively excluded.'

27. Peitsara, who claims to have found examples of *there's* in the past tense in a study of the dialect of Suffolk, commented that this 'would indicate a tendency towards extreme uniformity of system, where the single form *there's* introduces existential sentences as a kind of single morpheme, not analyzable into any constituents that would mark it for number or tense. The reduction of the verb in existential sentences has been described only as a meaningless "place-holder" in the same way as the anticipatory *there*. The reduction of the verb to a mere enclitic affix to *there* indicates that it is even less than that, because it does not seem to even need a place of its own, viz. a syllable or stress, even a weak one, in the intonation group to which it belongs' (1988: 83).

28. Arguably, the situation is even more complicated in that the form *there's is* potentially ambiguous. It may have derived from contraction of *there is* in the grammar, or now constitute an independent presentative signal in which –s is no longer of a verbal nature, a possibility that we have attempted to capture in the notation *there(')s → theres*.

29. The ranking of constraints in Walker's data and that in the New Zealand data differs in a number of respects, however, also. This could reflect regional differences, but, more likely, as both Walker (2007) and Hay and Schreier (2004) propose, differences in the distribution of different constructions in the data set. We note, for example, that while *a* quantifiers, bare nouns and other quantifiers make up 15%, 17% and 33% of the total number of tokens in the New Zealand data, these categories made up 27%, 27% and 17% of the total respectively in Walker's Canadian data (2007: 160).

30. Interestingly, though, *there was* was not used as a fifth alternative in the experiment.

31. Apparently contradictory to this is that among the different ethnic groups that they studied in Inner London, Cheshire and Fox (2009: 32–33) found that Bangladeshi speakers favoured non-standard *was* in existentials, even though this group acquires their English mainly from school and have been exposed to prescriptive norms by the influence of formal education.

32. Janda (2001: 289) has argued that the 'path(way)' metaphor in grammaticalisation studies in itself contributes little to our understanding

of how and why language changes, and is best understood as deriving from language change across successive generations of speakers.

33. For example, the factor of 'distance' between the verb and the associate-NP is commonly addressed from the perspective of phrase structure, but Martínez-Insua and Palacios-Martínez (2003: 278) speak in terms of distance agentively being *created* to allow the main focus to fall on the associate-NP.

34. On a final note, we note that similar principles seem to hold of 'here's' vs. 'here are' (*Here's two new pens*) (or 'where's', for that matter; cf. *Where's/*is my keys* (De Vos 2013: 60)). Pfenninger (2009: 52) has noted: 'most scholars fail to explain why *there* is inserted to play the orientation role in the spatio-temporal discourse, and not, say, *here*'. '(W)here's' is a topic for another research paper.

References

Abney, S. P. (1987). *The English noun phrase in its sentential aspect* (Doctoral dissertation). Massachusetts Institute of Technology, Cambridge, MA.

Adger, D., & Smith, J. (2005). Variation and the minimalist program. In L. Cornips & K. Corrigan (Eds.), *Syntax and variation: Reconciling the biological and the social* (pp. 149–178). Amsterdam: John Benjamins.

Alexiadou, A., Haegeman, L., & Stavrou, M. (2007). *Noun phrase in the generative perspective*. Berlin: Mouton de Gruyter.

Andersen, H. (2006). Grammation, regrammation and degrammation: Tense loss in Russian. *Diachronica, 23,* 231–258.

Antieau, L. (2011). *Was/were* variation in the Middle Rocky Mountains. *Kansas Working Papers in Linguistics, 32,* 48–66.

Askedal, J. O. (2008). 'Degrammaticalization' versus typology: Reflections on a strained relationship. In T. Eythórsson (Ed.), *Grammatical change and linguistic theory: The Rosendal papers* (pp. 45–77). Amsterdam: John Benjamins.

Belletti, A. (1988). The case of unaccusatives. *Linguistic Inquiry, 19,* 1–34.

Bernstein, J. (2001). The DP hypothesis: Identifying clausal properties in the nominal domain. In C. Collins & M. Baltin (Eds.), *Handbook of contemporary syntactic theory* (pp. 536–561). Oxford: Blackwell.

Birner, B. J., & Ward, G. (1998). *Information status and noncanonical word order in English*. Amsterdam: John Benjamins.

Bolinger, D. (1977). *Meaning and form*. London: Longman.

Breban, T. (2010). *English adjectives of comparison: Lexical and grammaticalized uses*. Berlin: Mouton de Gruyter.

Breban, T. (2015). Refining secondary grammaticalization by looking at sub-processes of change. *Language Sciences, 47*, 161–171.

Breivik, L. E. (1981). On the interpretation of existential *there*. *Language, 57*, 1–25.

Breivik, L. E., & Martínez-Insua, A. E. (2008). Grammaticalization, subjectification and non-concord in English existential sentences. *English Studies, 89*, 351–362.

Breivik, L. E., & Swan, T. (2000). The desemanticisation of existential *there* in a synchronic-diachronic perspective. In C. Dalton-Puffer & N. Ritt (Eds.), *Words: Structure, meaning, function: A Festschrift for Dieter Kastovsky* (pp. 19–34). Berlin: Mouton de Gruyter.

Brinton, L., & Stein, D. (1995). Functional renewal. In H. Andersen (Ed.), *Historical linguistics 1993: Selected Papers from the 11th International Conference on Historical Linguistics, Los Angeles, 16–20 August 1993* (pp. 33–47). Amsterdam: John Benjamins.

Britain, D. (2002). Diffusion, levelling, simplification and reallocation in past tense BE in the English Fens. *Journal of Sociolinguistics, 6*, 16–43.

Britain, D., & Sudbury, A. (2002). There's sheep and there's penguins: 'Drift', 'slant' and singular verb forms following existentials in New Zealand and Falkland Island English. In M. Jones & E. Esch (Eds.), *Language change: The interplay of internal, external and extra-linguistic factors* (pp. 209–242). Berlin: Mouton de Gruyter.

Bruening, B., Dinh, X., & Kim, L. (2015). Selection, idioms, and the structure of nominal phrases with and without classifiers. *Glossa: A Journal of General Linguistics, 3*, 42.

Bybee, J. (1995). Regular morphology and the lexicon. *Language and Cognitive Processes, 10*, 425–455.

Carlson, G. N. (1980). *Reference to kinds in English*. New York: Garland Publishing.

Chambers, J. (2004). Dynamic typology and vernacular universals. In B. Kortmann (Ed.), *Dialectology meets typology: Dialect grammar from a cross-linguistic perspective* (pp. 128–145). Berlin: Mouton de Gruyter.

Cheshire, J. (1999). Spoken Standard English. In T. Bex & R. Watts (Eds.), *Standard English: The widening debate* (pp. 149–166). London: Routledge.

Cheshire, J., & Fox, S. (2009). *Was/were* variation: A perspective from London. *Language Variation and Change, 21,* 1–38.

Cheshire, J., Edwards, V., & Whittle, P. (1989). Urban British dialect grammar: The question of dialect levelling. *English World-Wide, 10,* 185–225.

Chomsky, N. (1986). *Barriers.* Cambridge, MA: MIT Press.

Chomsky, N. (1995). *The minimalist program.* Cambridge, MA: MIT Press.

Chomsky, N. (1998). *Minimalist inquiries: The framework.* Cambridge, MA: MIT Occasional Papers in Linguistics, 15.

Cinque, G. (1994). On the evidence for partial N-movement in the Romance DP. In G. Cinque, J. Koster, J.-Y. Pollock, L. Rizzi, & R. Zanuttini (Eds.), *Paths towards universal grammar: Studies in honor of Richard S. Kayne* (pp. 85–110). Washington, DC: Georgetown University Press.

Collins, P. (2012). Singular agreement in *there*-existentials: An intervarietal corpus-based study. *English World-Wide, 33,* 53–68.

Crawford, W. J. (2005). Verb agreement and disagreement: A corpus investigation of concord variation in existential *There + Be* constructions. *Journal of English Linguistics, 33,* 35–61.

De Vos, M. (2013). Homogeneity in subject-verb concord in South African English. *Language Matters: Studies in the Languages of Africa, 44,* 58–77.

Den Dikken, M., Bernstein, J., Tortora, C., & Zanuttini, R. (2007). Data and grammar: Means and individuals. *Theoretical Linguistics, 33,* 335–352.

Detges, U., & Waltereit, R. (2002). Grammaticalization vs. reanalysis: A semantic-pragmatic account of functional change in grammar. *Zeitschrift für Sprachwissenschaft, 21,* 151–195.

Diesing, M. (1992). *Indefinites.* Cambridge, MA: MIT Press.

Durham, M. (2013). Was/were alternation in Shetland English. *World Englishes, 32,* 108–128.

Eisikovits, E. (1991). Variation in subject-verb agreement in inner Sydney English. In J. Cheshire (Ed.), *English around the world: Sociolinguistic perspectives* (pp. 235–256). Cambridge: Cambridge University Press.

Feagin, C. (1979). *Variation and change in Alabama English: A sociolinguistic study of the white community.* Washington, DC: Georgetown University Press.

Felser, C., & Rupp, L. (2001). Expletives as arguments: Germanic existential sentences revisited. *Linguistische Berichte, 187,* 289–324.

Fischer, O. (1999). On the role played by iconicity in grammaticalization processes. In O. Fischer & M. Nänny (Eds.), *Form miming meaning: Iconicity in language and literature* (pp. 345–374). Amsterdam: John Benjamins.

Fischer, O. (2010). An iconic, analogical approach to grammaticalization. In C. Jac Conradie, R. Johl, M. Beukes, O. Fischer, & C. Ljungberg (Eds.), *Signergy* (pp. 279–299). Amsterdam: John Benjamins.

Givón, T. (1991). The evolution of dependent clause morpho-syntax in Biblical Hebrew. In E. C. Traugott & B. Heine (Eds.), *Approaches to grammaticalization (Vol. 2): Focus on types of grammatical markers* (pp. 257–310). Amsterdam: John Benjamins.

Grimshaw, J. (1991). *Extended projection* (Unpublished manuscript). Brandeis University, Waltham, MA.

Grzegorek, M. (1984). *Thematization in English and Polish: A study in word order*. Poznan: UAM.

Haiman, J. (1980). The iconicity of grammar: Isomorphism and motivation. *Language, 56,* 515–540.

Halliday, M. (1994). *An introduction to functional grammar*. London: E. J. Arnold.

Halliday, M. A. K., & Hasan, R. (1976). *Cohesion in English*. London: Longman.

Hankamer, J., & Mikkelsen, L. (2002). A morphological analysis of definite nouns in Danish. *Journal of Germanic Linguistics, 14,* 137–175.

Hannay, M. (1985). *English existentials in functional grammar*. Dordrecht: Foris.

Harris, A. C., & Campbell, L. (1995). *Historical syntax in cross-linguistic perspective*. Cambridge: Cambridge University Press.

Hay, J., & Schreier, D. (2004). Reversing the trajectory of language change: Subject-verb agreement with *be* in New Zealand. *Language Variation and Change, 16,* 209–235.

Heim, I. (1982). *The semantics of definite and indefinite noun phrases* (Doctoral dissertation). University of Massachusetts, Amherst, MA.

Henry, A. (1995). *Belfast English and Standard English: Dialect variation and parameter setting*. Oxford: Oxford University Press.

Herring, S. C. (1991). The grammaticalization of rhetorical questions in Tamil. In E. Traugott & B. Heine (Eds.), *Approaches to grammaticalization (Vol. 1) Theoretical and methodological issues* (pp. 253–284). Amsterdam: John Benjamins.

Hilton, K. (2016). Nonstandard agreement in Standard English: The social perception of agreement variation under existential there. *University of Pennsylvania Working Papers in Linguistics, 22,* 61–70.

Hopper, P. J. (1991). On some principles of grammaticization. In E. C. Traugott & B. Heine (Eds.), *Approaches to grammaticalization (Vol. I): Theoretical and methodological issues* (pp. 17–36). Amsterdam: John Benjamins.

Hopper, P. J., & Traugott, E. C. (2003). *Grammaticalization* (2nd ed.). Cambridge: Cambridge University Press.

Huddleston, R., & Pullum, G. K. (2002). *The Cambridge grammar of the English language.* Cambridge: Cambridge University Press.

Janda, R. D. (2001). Beyond "pathways" and "unidirectionality": On the discontinuity of transmission and the counterability of grammaticalization. *Language Sciences, 23,* 265–340.

Jang, Y. (1997). Minimal feature-movement. *Journal of Linguistics, 33,* 311–325.

Jenkins, L. (1975). *The English existential.* Tübingen: Max Niemeyer.

Jenset, G. B. (2010). *A corpus based study on the evolution of* there: *Statistical analysis and cognitive interpretation* (Doctoral dissertation). University of Bergen, Bergen.

Jespersen, O. (1924). *The philosophy of grammar.* Chicago: University of Chicago Press.

Jespersen, O. (1969). *Analytic syntax.* New York: Holt, Rinehart and Winston.

Joseph, B. D. (2004). Rescuing traditional (historical) linguistics from grammaticalization 'theory'. In O. Fischer, M. Norde, & H. Peridon (Eds.), *Up and down the cline* (pp. 44–71). Amsterdam: John Benjamins.

Jucker, A. H. (1997). The discourse marker *well* in the history of English. *English Language and Linguistics, 1,* 91–110.

Koopman, H., & Sportiche, D. (1991). The position of subjects. *Lingua, 85,* 211–258.

Kranich, S. (2008). Subjective progressives in seventeenth and eighteenth century English: Secondary grammaticalization as a process of objectification. In M. Gotti, M. Dossena, & R. Dury (Eds.), *English historical linguistics 2006 (Vol. I): Syntax and morphology* (pp. 241–256). Amsterdam: John Benjamins.

Kranich, S. (2010). Grammaticalization, subjectification and objectification. In K. Stathi, E. Gehweiler, & E. König (Eds.), *Grammaticalization: Current views and issues* (pp. 101–122). Amsterdam: John Benjamins.

Kratzer, A. (1995). Stage-level and individual-level predicates. In G. N. Carlson & F. J. Pelletier (Eds.), *The generic book* (pp. 125–175). Chicago: University of Chicago Press.

Krejci, B., & Hilton, K. (2015). *Agreement variation under existential* there. Paper presented at the Annual Corpus Lunch, Stanford University, Stanford.

Kuryłowicz, J. (1976). *Esquisses linguistiques* (Vol. 2, pp. 38–54). Munich: Fink [Original work published in Kuryłowicz, J. (1965). The Evolution of Grammatical Categories. *Diogenes, 13*, 55–71.]

Lange, C. (2012). *The syntax of Indian English*. Amsterdam: John Benjamins.

Longobardi, G. (1994). Reference and proper names. *Linguistic Inquiry, 25*, 609–665.

Lyons, J. (1975). Deixis as the source of reference. In E. L. Keenan (Ed.), *Formal semantics of natural language* (pp. 61–83). Cambridge: Cambridge University Press.

Lyons, C. (1999). *Definiteness*. Cambridge: Cambridge University Press.

Martínez-Insua, A. E. (2004). *Existential there-constructions in contemporary British English: A corpus driven analysis of their use in speech and writing*. Munich: Lincom Europa.

Martínez-Insua, A. E. (2013). There-constructions as a choice for coherence in the recent history of English. In L. Fontaine, T. Bartlett, & G. O'Grady (Eds.), *Systemic functional linguistics: Exploring choice* (pp. 207–225). Cambridge: Cambridge University Press.

Martínez-Insua, A. E., & Palacios Martínez, I. (2003). A corpus-based approach to non-concord in present-day English existential *there*-constructions. *English Studies, 84*, 262–283.

McMahon, A. M. S. (1994). *Understanding language change*. Cambridge and New York: Cambridge University Press.

Meechan, M., & Foley, M. (1994). On resolving disagreement: Linguistic theory and variation—*There's* bridges. *Language Variation and Change, 6*, 63–85.

Meillet, A. (1912). L'évolution des formes grammaticales. Scientia (Rivista di Scienza) 12, No. 26, 6. In *Linguistique historique et linguistique générale* (pp. 130–148). Paris: Librairie Ancienne Honoré Champion.

Melchers, G. (2004). English spoken in Orkney and Shetland: Morphology, syntax and lexicon. In B. Kortmann & E. W. Schneider (with K. Burridge, R. Mesthrie & C. Upton) (Eds.), *A handbook of varieties of English (Vol. 2): Morphology and syntax* (pp. 34–47). Berlin: Mouton de Gruyter.

Melchers, G., & Sundkvist, P. (2010). Shetland and Orkney. In D. Schreier, P. Trudgill, E. W. Schneider, & J. P. Williams (Eds.), *The lesser-known varieties of English* (pp. 17–34). Cambridge: Cambridge University Press.

Milroy, J., & Milroy, L. (1985). Linguistic change social network and speaker innovation. *Journal of Linguistics, 21,* 339–384.

Milsark, G. (1974). *Existential sentences in English* (Doctoral dissertation). Massachusetts Institute of Technology, Cambridge, MA.

Milsark, G. (1977). Toward an explanation of certain peculiarities of the existential construction in English. *Linguistic Analysis, 3,* 1–29.

Montgomery, M., & Hall, J. (2004). *Dictionary of Smoky Mountain English.* Knoxville: University of Tennessee Press.

Moore, E. (2011). Interaction between social category and social practice: Explaining *was/were* variation. *Language Variation and Change, 22,* 347–371.

Narrog, H. (2012). Textual uses of modality and mood in subordinate clauses as part of *speech-act orientation.* In L. Brems, L. Ghesquière, & F. Van de Velde (Eds.), *Intersections of intersubjectivity* (pp. 29–52). Amsterdam: John Benjamins.

Narrog, H. (2015). (Inter)subjectification and its limits in secondary grammaticalization. *Language Sciences, 47,* 148–160.

Orton, H., & Dieth, E. (1962–1971). *Survey of English Dialects.* Leeds: E. J. Arnold.

Peitsara, K. (1988). On existential sentences in the dialect of Suffolk. *Neuphilologische Mitteilungen, 1,* 72–99.

Pérez-Guerra, J. (1999). *Historical English syntax: A statistical corpus-based study on the organisation of Early Modern English sentences.* München: Lincom.

Petyt, K. M. (1985). *Dialect and accent in industrial West Yorkshire.* Amsterdam: John Benjamins.

Pfenninger, S. E. (2009). *Grammaticalization paths of English and high German existential constructions.* Bern: Peter Lang.

Pietsch, L. (2005). *"Some do and some doesn't":* Verbal concord variation in the north of the British Isles. In B. Kortmann, T. Herrman, L. Pietsch, & S. Wagner (Eds.), *A comparative grammar of British English dialects: Agreement, gender, relative clauses* (pp. 125–210). Berlin: Mouton de Gruyter.

Pollock, J.-Y. (1989). Verb movement, universal grammar, and the structure of IP. *Linguistic Inquiry, 20,* 365–424.

Poplack, S., & Tagliamonte, S. (2001). *African American English in the diaspora: Tense and aspect.* Malden, MA: Blackwell.

Prince, E. F. (1992). The ZPG letter: Subjects, definiteness and information-status. In W. C. Mann & S. A. Thompson (Eds.), *Discourse description: Diverse linguistic analyses of a fund-raising text* (pp. 295–326). Amsterdam: John Benjamins.

Quirk, R., Greenbaum, S., Leech, G., & Svartvik, J. (1985). *A comprehensive grammar of the English language*. London: Longman.

Ramat, A. G. (1995). Iconicity in grammaticalization processes. In R. Simone (Ed.), *Iconicity in language* (pp. 119–139). Amsterdam: John Benjamins.

Ramchand, G. (1996). Two subject positions in Scottish Gaelic: The syntax-semantics interface. *Natural Language Semantics, 4*, 165–191.

Richards, H. (2010). Preterite *be*: A new perspective? *English World-Wide, 31*, 62–81.

Rizzi, L. (1990). *Relativized minimality*. Cambridge, MA: MIT Press.

Rosen, A. (2014). *Grammatical variation and change in Jersey English*. Amsterdam: John Benjamins.

Ross, J. R. (1967). *Constraints on variables in syntax* (Doctoral dissertation). Massachusetts Institute of Technology, Cambridge, MA.

Rupp, L. (2003). *The syntax of imperatives in English and Germanic: Word order variation in the minimalist framework*. Basingstoke: Palgrave Macmillan.

Sapir, E. (1933). La réalité psychologique des phonèmes. *Journal de Psychologie Normaleet Pathologique, 30*, 247–265. [English version published in 1949 as The psychological reality of phonemes. In D. G. Mandelbaum (Ed.), *Selected writings of Edward Sapir in language, culture and personality* (pp. 46–60). Oakland, CA: University of California Press.]

Schiffrin, D. (1994). *Approaches to discourse*. Oxford: Blackwell.

Schilling-Estes, N., & Wolfram, W. (1994). Convergent explanation and alternative regularization patterns: *Were/weren't* levelling in a vernacular English variety. *Language Variation and Change, 6*, 273–302.

Schneider, E. W. (2003). The dynamics of New Englishes: From identity construction to dialect birth. *Language, 79*, 233–281.

Schütze, C. (1999). English expletive constructions are not infected. *Linguistic Inquiry, 30*, 467–484.

Smallwood, C. (1997). Dis-agreement in Canadian English existentials. In *Proceedings from the 1997 annual conference of the Canadian Linguistic Association* (pp. 227–238). Calgary: University of Calgary.

Smirnova, E. (2015). When secondary grammaticalization starts: A look from the constructional perspective. *Language Sciences, 47*, 215–228.

Smith, J., & Tagliamonte, S. A. (1998). '*We were all thegither, I think we was all thegither*': *Was* regularization in Buckie English. *World Englishes, 17*, 105–126.

Sobin, N. (1997). Agreement, default rules and grammatical viruses. *Linguistic Inquiry, 28*, 318–343.

Tagliamonte, S. A. (1998). *Was/were* variation across the generations: View from the city of York. *Language Variation and Change, 10*, 153–192.

Tagliamonte, S. A. (2009). There *was* universals, then there *weren't*: A comparative sociolinguistic perspective on 'default singulars'. In M. Filppula, J. Klemola, & H. Paulasto (Eds.), *Vernacular universals and language contacts: Evidence from varieties of English and beyond* (pp. 103–129). New York and Oxford: Routledge.

Tagliamonte, S., & Smith, J. (1999). Analogical levelling in Samaná English: The case of *was* and *were*. *Journal of English Linguistics, 27*, 8–26.

Tortora, C. (1997). *The syntax and semantics of the weak locative* (Doctoral dissertation). University of Delaware, Newark, DE.

Tortora, C. (2006). The case of Appalachian expletive *they*. *American Speech, 81*, 266–296.

Tortora, C., & Den Dikken, M. (2010). Subject agreement variation: Support for the configurational approach. *Lingua, 120*, 1089–1108.

Trask, R. L. (1996). *Historical linguistics*. London: E. J. Arnold.

Traugott, E. C. (1982). From propositional to textual and expressive meanings: Some semantic-pragmatic aspects of grammaticalization. In W. P. Lehmann & Y. Malkiel (Eds.), *Perspectives on historical linguistics* (pp. 245–271). Amsterdam: John Benjamins.

Traugott, E. C. (1992). Syntax. In R. Hogg (Ed.), *The Cambridge history of the English language (Vol. 1): The beginnings to 1066* (pp. 168–289). Cambridge: Cambridge University Press.

Traugott, E. C. (1995). Subjectification in grammaticalization. In D. Stein & S. Wright (Eds.), *Subjectivity and subjectivisation in language* (pp. 31–54). Cambridge: Cambridge University Press.

Traugott, E. C. (2002). From etymology to historical pragmatics. In D. Minkova & R. Stockwell (Eds.), *Studies in the history of the English language* (pp. 19–49). Berlin: Mouton de Gruyter.

Traugott, E. C. (2003). From subjectification to intersubjectification. In R. Hickey (Ed.), *Motives for language change* (pp. 124–139). Cambridge: Cambridge University Press.

Traugott, E. C. (2010). (Inter)subjectivity and (inter)subjectification: A reassessment. In H. Cuyckens, K. Davidse, & L. Vandelanotte (Eds.), *Subjectification, intersubjectification and grammaticalization* (pp. 29–70). Berlin: Mouton de Gruyter.

Traugott, E. C., & Dasher, R. B. (2002). *Regularity in semantic change*. Cambridge: Cambridge University Press.

Travis, L. M. (1984). *Parameters and effects of word order variation* (Doctoral dissertation). Massachusetts Institute of Technology, Cambridge, MA.

Trudgill, P. (2008). English dialect "defaults singulars", was versus were, Verner's law, and Germanic dialects. *Journal of English Linguistics, 36,* 341–353.

Trudgill, P. (2009). Vernacular universals and the sociolinguistic typology of English dialects. In M. Filppula, J. Klemola, & H. Paulasto (Eds.), *Vernacular universals and language contacts: Evidence from varieties of English and beyond* (pp. 304–322). London: Routledge.

Visser, F. Th. (1970). *An historical syntax of the English language (Part one): Syntactical units with one verb* (2nd impression). Leiden: E. J. Brill.

Von Mengden, F. (2016). Functional changes and (meta-)linguistic evolution. In M. Norde & F. Van de Velde (Eds.), *Exaptation and language change* (pp. 121–162). Amsterdam: John Benjamins.

Walker, J. (2007). "There's bears back there": Plural existentials and vernacular universals in (Quebec) English. *English World-Wide, 28,* 147–166.

Walker, J. (2013). *Subject-verb agreement in English existentials: A cross-community comparison.* Invited paper presented at the University of Bern, Switzerland.

Walker, J. (2014). Contrasting patterns of agreement in three communities. In N. Dion, A. Lapierre, & R. Torres Cacoullos (Eds.), *Linguistic variation: Confronting fact and theory* (pp. 7–21). London: Routledge.

Zwicky, A., & Pullum, G. (1983). Clitization vs. inflection: English *n't. Language, 59,* 502–513.

6

Conclusion

Throughout this volume we have attempted to pull together formal, functional, variationist and historical linguistic perspectives on a number of distinct but related manifestations of verbal –s. One aim has been to see what we can gain by working on such topics in an interdisciplinary way. Another has been to attempt a single more holistic and all-embracing account of how verbal –s emerged, developed and works in the many forms and functions that it has today. In this concluding chapter, we recap our argument from each of the earlier chapters, highlight some of the areas on to which we have been able to shed new light in investigating verbal –s, as well as returning to our original research questions, and considering what more general advances we can claim from this work.

6.1   Verbal –s

In Chapter 2 we discussed the historical origins, sociolinguistic patterning and grammatical behaviour of verbal –s. We tracked its chronological trajectory from its origins as a regional form of the north of England

© The Author(s) 2019
L. Rupp and D. Britain, *Linguistic Perspectives on a Variable English Morpheme*,
https://doi.org/10.1057/978-1-349-72803-9_6

and Scotland, through to its present-day distribution and functions. It began its life as a 2nd sing. agreement morpheme, and, over time, generalising across person and number, came to lose its agreement function and grammaticalised. As a result of exaptation and regrammaticalisation, different communities came to adopt one amongst a wide range of linguistic, stylistic and social functions for –s. These include the emergence of linguistic constraints on verbal –s such as the Northern Subject Rule, the Following Complement Constraint and the marking of habituality, as well as more socio-stylistic factors such as its use in vernacular narrative, its heightened use, for example in Reading, in so-called 'vernacular verbs', and its strategic deployment as an identity marker, for example in the case of the Newfoundland drag queens. In the course of time, first uses of –s may be replaced by more innovative ones, giving rise to a transitional layering of different uses (Hopper 1991), as with the 'Old –s' and 'New –s' that Childs and Van Herk (2014) have observed in Newfoundland.

Despite the apparent diversity of functions, we argued that they all seem to share one common motivation—their direction of functional shift over time has been moving towards ever-greater diagrammatic iconicity.

6.2 Verbal Zero

In Chapter 3 we discussed a widely recognised but much less well-investigated manifestation of non-standard use of verbal marking, namely verbal zero, most commonly reported for AAVE in North America and East Anglia in England. We argued that, almost without exception, verbal zero has arisen in contexts of intensive language and dialect contact, whether it be the verbal zero that became adopted by African Americans in the last century, or that which emerged in, for example, multilingual Norwich in the seventeenth century as a result of the arrival of asylum seekers from the Low Countries, or that which has emerged as a result of colonial dialect mixture (for example Tristan da Cunha) or colonial language contact (for example the 'New' L2 Englishes), or, indeed, that which has become semi-stable in contemporary English as a Lingua Franca. In many of these varieties, 3rd sing. –s is making inroads into the system. We claim that this is the result of standardisation, whether by contact with –s-using speakers or through more formal means. In investigating verbal zero in East Anglia, we have uncovered what appears to be a previously unidentified but nevertheless, given recent empirical research, robust linguistic constraint on variability in 3rd sing. contexts—namely the East Anglian Subject Rule, a preference for –s after pronouns rather than after NPs, contrary to the Northern Subject Rule.

6.3   Past BE

Chapter 4 investigated verbal –s in the context of past BE. Here we noted that variant forms of past BE are not, in non-standard varieties, being used to mark agreement, similar to our claim for verbal –s in lexical verbs. We identified from the literature a range of variable uses of this kind. These include: varieties which are levelling away *were* forms in favour of *was* (leading them to be simply marking tense); varieties which deploy the variant forms to maximally mark polarity, with *was* used across affirmative contexts and *weren't* across the negative; varieties in which past BE forms are constrained by either the Northern or East Anglian Subject Rules, as well as a number of more specialised functions such as the use of *weren't* in question tags. We noted that a number of varieties across southern England (and diaspora varieties that historically had a significant input from southern England, such as Australian English) behave according to the East Anglian Subject Rule with respect to past BE variation, suggesting that the geographical scope of the rule may not be merely restricted to East Anglia. As in Chapter 2, we envisage here that it is a drive towards greater diagrammatic iconicity that may motivate these functional shifts.

6.4   Existentials

Chapter 5, finally, investigated verbal –s in the context of existential constructions. The variable use of *there's* in the context of plural NPs in existentials is ubiquitous across English varieties, even the Standard. It has been a stable feature of English for a very long time, but, we argue, appears to be undergoing continued grammaticalisation to the extent that –s should no longer be considered as a separate morpheme, but an element fused into a single unit which functions as a presentative marker for New information. Evidence for this fusion comes from empirical evidence demonstrating that distinct linguistic constraint hierarchies govern *there(')s* in contrast to *there is*. This case presents a classical dual example of the grammaticalisation cline, with the finite form of BE shifting from verb to contracted element to a fused form, and 'there' shifting from locative adverb to existential marker, to presentative device, once fused with –s.

Our probing of verbal –s, verbal zero, past BE and existential *there(')s* has led to a number of important new observations that help us understand the linguistic, socio-stylistic and functional parameters that condition this feature. We note here what, for us, are the most prominent:

1. The nature of the Northern Subject Rule. To recap, the NSR stipulates that –s forms are more likely to occur after NPs and non-adjacent pronouns than after adjacent pronouns. Earlier attempts to explain this phenomenon were never entirely satisfactory, because they were unable to capture both sub-constraints (NP>Pro; non-adjacent>adjacent) nor provide a motivation for why NPs should behave differently from pronouns in this context. Drawing upon a discourse-pragmatic approach, one of the well-established differences between pronouns and NPs is that the former have high accessibility, while the latter tend to have low accessibility (for example Epstein 2002). It has earlier been noted that more inaccessible items are more likely to be marked than accessible ones (for example Ariel 1999). Non-adjacent pronoun forms that are separated from the verb can, similarly, be seen as more inaccessible than when the pronoun is adjacent to the verb. We would expect therefore that NPs and non-adjacent pronouns, given their relative inaccessibility, would require more marking than adjacent pronouns, and this is indeed what we find with verbal –s within the Northern Subject Rule. While many varieties of English no longer demonstrate a fully operative Northern Subject Rule, some deploy verbal –s following certain specific types of subject—such as subjects of relative clauses

and structurally heavy subjects—which are especially inaccessible in this sense. This view on the Northern Subject Rule is of the same type as that which we saw in Chapter 5 with the newly grammatical-ised function of *there(')s* as a presentative marker—both forms appear motivated by discourse-pragmatic considerations.

2. Back in 2005, we (Britain and Rupp 2005) speculated on the basis of emerging empirical evidence from East Anglian dialects of British English that a different constraint was operative there for both 3rd sing. and past BE. In these varieties, –s forms were used more after pronouns than after NPs, reversing the NSR. This manifested itself through a greater use of 3rd sing. –s and 3rd pl. *was* after pronouns than after NPs. There is now more substantial empirical meat behind this speculation, with recent work (for example Potter 2018, based on a large, multilocality corpus), demonstrating a statistically signif-icant operative East Anglian Subject Rule. This pattern is, we argue, to be expected. A number of studies have shown that there is a correlation between agreement marking and the use of pronouns (for example Corbett 2003). We have provided a formal syntactic account which motivates this correlation in terms of pronoun dou-bling and the positioning of pronouns and NPs in the clause struc-ture. We continue our empirical and theoretical investigations of this phenomenon.

We can now return to the three research questions that we introduced at the beginning of the book. They were:

1. If verbal –s is not used as an agreement morpheme, what is it?
2. How has verbal –s come to be used for purposes other than for agree-ment marking?
3. Why is verbal –s used for these other purposes?

For verbal –s, past BE and existential *there(')s*, we addressed these ques-tions in the previous chapters. In doing so, it became evident that the answers were similar in each case and that we are in fact dealing with just one overarching phenomenon.

We propose that the underlying motivation behind the diachronic development of these in many ways highly diverse forms and functions of verbal –s is diagrammatic iconicity and therefore we earlier proposed a unified account of this phenomenon. This account argues that all of the uses of verbal –s are, in effect, restoring an isomorphic relationship between the form and the function of –s, a relationship that was lost when –s spread from 2nd sing. across the rest of the paradigm. We can therefore witness this isomorphic relationship, for example, between –s and polarity, –s and inaccessible subjects, –s and tags, –s and local identity, –s and the presentation of new information (together with *there*), and –s and narrative turns. In addition to this, we pointed out the apparent iconic motivation of these relationships; for example, with maximally different morphemes of past BE (*was/weren't*) indicating contrastive situations, discourse-heavy subjects being marked by extra material, and local identity being expressed by a vernacular form. In line with current thinking in research on iconicity (e.g. De Cuypere 2008), verbal –s appears to be used strategically and creatively to convey additional meaning.

In thinking about how we constructed our unified account of the development of verbal –s, we were struck by how many of the different manifestations of verbal –s are motivated by discourse-pragmatic factors—the Northern Subject Rule, vernacular narrative uses, the Following Complement Constraint, *weren't* tags, and existential *there(')s*. In a number of papers, Cheshire has argued for a much greater sensitivity towards discourse-pragmatic context in the analysis of syntactic variation. She suggests, for example, that 'speakers use syntactic forms to construct discourse, and through discourse they perform many different kinds of social activities and construct many different kinds of social meanings' (Cheshire 2005: 503). Our analysis suggests that discourse-pragmatic motivations are often evident in patterns of syntactic variation and we agree with Cheshire that they should be routinely explored in analyses of grammatical variability in order to fully understand the function of individual variants. Cheshire's account also foregrounds how, through the discourse constructed by syntactic variation, social activities can be performed—for example the telling of narratives—and social meanings constructed—such as the identity-building deployment of –s by the Newfoundland drag queens. The link, then, between the syntactic and the social appears in these cases to be indirect, filtered through discourse pragmatic context.

Finally, we believe we have once again (see also Cornips and Corrigan 2005, and the papers therein) highlighted how, for example, formal syntacticians, variationists, sociolinguists, historical linguists and functional grammarians can advance our theoretical understanding of grammatical variation by working together and drawing from each others' insights. We have, for example, demonstrated how grammatical analysis can help us understand the motivation behind the East Anglian Subject Rule, along with a discourse-pragmatic motivation behind the Northern Subject Rule. Variationists have, on the other hand, unearthed both a wide range of different systems of verbal –s deployment in different varieties of English, as well as the internal constraints governing variability in these systems. And sociolinguists have demonstrated how verbal –s performs a wide range of meaningful stylistic, discursive and social functions. In this volume we have attempted to argue that together they are telling one story about the occurrence of verbal –s.

References

Ariel, M. (1999). The development of person agreement markers: From pronouns to higher accessibility markers. In M. Barlow & S. Kemmer (Eds.), *Usage-based models of language* (pp. 197–260). Stanford: CSLI Publications.

Barlow, M. (1992). *A situated theory of agreement.* New York: Garland.

Barlow, M. (1999). Agreement as a discourse phenomenon. *Folia Linguistica, 33,* 187–201.

Britain, D., & Rupp, L. (2005). *Subject-verb agreement in English dialects: The East Anglian Subject Rule.* Paper presented at The International Conference on Language Variation in Europe 3, Amsterdam, The Netherlands.

Cheshire, J. (2005). Syntactic variation and beyond: Gender and social class variation in the use of discourse-new markers. *Journal of Sociolinguistics, 9,* 479–508.

Childs, B., & Van Herk, G. (2014). Work that -s! Drag queens, gender, identity, and traditional Newfoundland English. *Journal of Sociolinguistics, 18,* 634–657.

Corbett, G. (2003). Agreement: The range of the phenomenon and the principles of the Surrey database of agreement. *Transactions of the Philological Society, 101,* 155–202.

Cornips, L., & Corrigan, K. P. (Eds.). (2005). *Syntax and variation: Reconciling the biological and the social.* Amsterdam: John Benjamins.

De Cuypere, L. (2008). *Limiting the iconic: From the metatheoretical foundations to the creative possibilities of iconicity in language.* Amsterdam: John Benjamins.

Epstein, R. (2002). The definite article, accessibility, and the construction of discourse referents. *Cognitive Linguistics, 12,* 333–378.

Hopper, P. J. (1991). On some principles of grammaticization. In E. C. Traugott & B. Heine (Eds.), *Approaches to grammaticalization (Vol. I): Theoretical and methodological issues* (pp. 17–36). Amsterdam: John Benjamins.

Potter, R. (2018). *A variationist multilocality study of unstressed vowels and verbal -s marking in the peripheral dialect of East Suffolk* (Doctoral dissertation). University of Essex, Colchester.

References

Abney, S. P. (1987). *The English noun phrase in its sentential aspect* (Doctoral dissertation). Massachusetts Institute of Technology, Cambridge, MA.

Adger, D. (2006). Combinatorial variability. *Journal of Linguistics, 42,* 503–530.

Adger, D., & Smith, J. (2005). Variation and the minimalist program. In L. Cornips & K. Corrigan (Eds.), *Syntax and variation: Reconciling the biological and the social* (pp. 149–178). Amsterdam: John Benjamins.

Adger, D., & Smith, J. (2010). Variation in agreement: A lexical feature-based approach. *Lingua, 120,* 1109–1134.

Ahava, S. (2010). *Intermediate past BE: A paradigm reshaped with data drawn from HARES* (MA Dissertation). University of Helsinki, Helsinki.

Alexiadou, A., Haegeman, L., & Stavrou, M. (2007). *Noun phrase in the generative perspective.* Berlin: Mouton de Gruyter.

Amos, J., Brana-Straw, M., Britain, D., Grainger, H., Piercy, C., & Rigby, A. (2007). *It's not up north but it's down south, ain't it? A regional examination of auxiliary versus negator contraction.* Paper presented at UK Language Variation and Change 6, University of Lancaster, UK.

Andersen, H. (2006). Grammation, regrammation and degrammation: Tense loss in Russian. *Diachronica, 23,* 231–258.

Anderwald, L. (2001). *Was/were* variation in non-standard British English today. *English World-Wide, 22,* 1–22.

© The Editor(s) (if applicable) and The Author(s),
under exclusive licence to Springer Nature Limited 2019
L. Rupp and D. Britain, *Linguistic Perspectives on a Variable English Morpheme,*
https://doi.org/10.1057/978-1-349-72803-9

330 References

Anderwald, L. (2002). *Negation in non-standard British English: Gaps, regularizations, asymmetries*. London: Routledge.

Anderwald, L. (2004). The varieties of English spoken in the south-east of England: Morphology and syntax. In B. Kortmann & E. W. Schneider (with K. Burridge, R. Mesthrie, & C. Upton) (Eds.), *A handbook of varieties of English (Vol. 2): Morphology and syntax* (pp. 175–195). Berlin: Mouton de Gruyter.

Antieau, L. (2011). *Was/were* variation in the Middle Rocky Mountains. *Kansas Working Papers in Linguistics, 32*, 48–66.

Ariel, M. (1999). The development of person agreement markers: From pronouns to higher accessibility markers. In M. Barlow & S. Kemmer (Eds.), *Usage-based models of language* (pp. 197–260). Stanford: CSLI Publications.

Ariel, M. (2001). Accessibility theory: An overview. In T. J. M. Sanders, J. Schilperoord, & W. Spooren (Eds.), *Text representation: Linguistic and psycholinguistic aspects* (pp. 29–87). Amsterdam: John Benjamins.

Asante, M. (2012). Variation in subject-verb concord in Ghanaian English. *World Englishes, 31*, 208–225.

Askedal, J. O. (2008). 'Degrammaticalization' versus typology: Reflections on a strained relationship. In T. Eythórsson (Ed.), *Grammatical change and linguistic theory: The Rosendal papers* (pp. 45–77). Amsterdam: John Benjamins.

Asprey, E. (2007). *Black Country English and Black Country identity* (Doctoral dissertation). University of Leeds, Leeds.

Bailey, G., & Maynor, N. (1987). Decreolization. *Language in Society, 16*, 449–474.

Bailey, G., & Maynor, N. (1989). The divergence controversy. *American Speech, 64*, 12–39.

Bailey, G., & Ross, G. (1988). The shape of the superstrate: Morphosyntactic features of ship English. *English World-Wide, 9*, 193–212.

Bailey, G., Maynor, N., & Cukor-Avila, P. (1989). Variation in subject-verb concord in Early Modern English. *Language Variation and Change, 1*, 285–300.

Barlow, M. (1992). *A situated theory of agreement*. New York: Garland.

Barlow, M. (1999). Agreement as a discourse phenomenon. *Folia Linguistica, 33*, 187–201.

Bauer, L. (1994). English in New Zealand. In R. Burchfield (Ed.), *The Cambridge history of the English language (Vol. 5): English in Britain and overseas: Origins and development* (pp. 382–429). Cambridge: Cambridge University Press.

Beal, J. (1993). The grammar of Tyneside and Northumbrian English. In J. Milroy & L. Milroy (Eds.), *Real English: The grammar of English dialects in the British Isles* (pp. 187–213). London: Longman.

References   331

Beal, J. (2004). English dialects in the North of England: Morphology and syntax. In B. Kortmann & E. W. Schneider (with K. Burridge, R. Mesthrie, & C. Upton) (Eds.), *A handbook of varieties of English (Vol. 2): Morphology and syntax* (pp. 114–195). Berlin: Mouton de Gruyter.

Beal, J., & Corrigan, K. (2000). Comparing the present with the past to predict the future for Tyneside English. *Newcastle and Durham Working Papers in Linguistics, 6,* 13–30.

Belletti, A. (1988). The case of unaccusatives. *Linguistic Inquiry, 19,* 1–34.

Benskin, M. (2011). Present indicative plural concord in Brittonic and Early English. *Transactions of the Philological Society, 109,* 158–185.

Bernstein, J. (2001). The DP hypothesis: Identifying clausal properties in the nominal domain. In C. Collins & M. Baltin (Eds.), *Handbook of contemporary syntactic theory* (pp. 536–561). Oxford: Blackwell.

Bernstein, J. (2008). The expression of third person in older and contemporary varieties of English. *English Studies, 89,* 571–586.

Berretta, M. (1995). Morphological markedness in L2 acquisition. In R. Simone (Ed.), *Iconicity in language* (pp. 197–233). Amsterdam: John Benjamins.

Birner, B. J., & Ward, G. (1998). *Information status and noncanonical word order in English.* Amsterdam: John Benjamins.

Bolinger, D. (1977). *Meaning and form.* London: Longman.

Bonness, D. J. (2017). The Northern Subject Rule in the Irish diaspora: Subject-verb agreement among first- and second generation emigrants to New Zealand. *English World-Wide, 38,* 125–152.

Booij, G. (2010). *Construction morphology.* Oxford: Oxford University Press.

Börjars, K., & Chapman, C. (1998). Agreement and pro-drop in some dialects of English. *Linguistics, 36,* 71–98.

Bowerman, S. (2004). White South African English. In R. Mesthrie (Ed.), *Varieties of English (Vol. 4): Africa, South and South-East Asia* (pp. 472–487). Berlin: Mouton de Gruyter.

Breban, T. (2010). *English adjectives of comparison: Lexical and grammaticalized uses.* Berlin: Mouton de Gruyter.

Breban, T. (2015). Refining secondary grammaticalization by looking at subprocesses of change. *Language Sciences, 47,* 161–171.

Breivik, L. E. (1981). On the interpretation of existential *there. Language, 57,* 1–25.

Breivik, L. E., & Martínez-Insua, A. E. (2008). Grammaticalization, subjectification and non-concord in English existential sentences. *English Studies, 89,* 351–362.

332 References

Breivik, L. E., & Swan, T. (2000). The desemanticisation of existential *there* in a synchronic-diachronic perspective. In C. Dalton-Puffer & N. Ritt (Eds.), *Words: Structure, meaning, function: A Festschrift for Dieter Kastovsky* (pp. 19–34). Berlin: Mouton de Gruyter.

Bresnan, J., & Mchombo, S. A. (1986). Grammatical and anaphoric agreement. In A. Farley, P. Farley, & K. McCullough (Eds.), *Proceedings of the Chicago Linguistic Society 22: Papers from the Parasession on Pragmatics and Grammatical Theory* (pp. 741–782). Chicago: Chicago Linguistics Society.

Bresnan, J., & Mchombo, S. A. (1987). Topic, pronoun, and agreement in Chicheŵa. *Language, 63,* 741–782.

Bresnan, J., & Moshi, L. (1990). Object asymmetries in comparative Bantu syntax. *Linguistic Inquiry, 2,* 147–185.

Brinton, L., & Stein, D. (1995). Functional renewal. In H. Andersen (Ed.), *Historical linguistics 1993: Selected Papers from the 11th International Conference on Historical Linguistics, Los Angeles, 16–20 August 1993* (pp. 33–47). Amsterdam: John Benjamins.

Britain, D. (1997a). Dialect contact and phonological reallocation: 'Canadian Raising' in the English Fens. *Language in Society, 26,* 15–46.

Britain, D. (1997b). Dialect contact, focusing and phonological rule complexity: The koineisation of Fenland English. *Special Issue of University of Pennsylvania Working Papers in Linguistics, 4,* 141–170.

Britain, D. (2001). Welcome to East Anglia! Two major dialect 'boundaries' in the Fens. In P. Trudgill & J. Fisiak (Eds.), *East Anglian English* (pp. 217–242). Woodbridge: Boydell and Brewer.

Britain, D. (2002). Diffusion, levelling, simplification and reallocation in past tense BE in the English Fens. *Journal of Sociolinguistics, 6,* 16–43.

Britain, D. (2008). The importance of 'elsewhere': Looking beyond London and Ireland in the creation of Australian English. *Essex Research Reports in Linguistics, 57,* 79–114.

Britain, D. (2014). *Linguistic diffusion and the social heterogeneity of space and mobility.* Paper presented at the 3rd International Society for the Linguistics of English conference, Universität Zürich, Switzerland.

Britain, D. (2015). Between North and South: The Fenland. In R. Hickey (Ed.), *Researching Northern English* (pp. 417–435). Amsterdam: John Benjamins.

Britain, D. (2016). *Up, app and away? Social dialectology and the use of smartphone technology as a data collection strategy.* Paper presented at Sociolinguistics Symposium 21, Universidad de Murcia, Spain.

References 333

Britain, D., & Matsumoto, K. (2015). Palauan English. In J. Williams, E. W. Schneider, P. Trudgill, & D. Schreier (Eds.), *Further studies in the lesser known varieties of English* (pp. 305–343). Cambridge: Cambridge University Press.

Britain, D., & Rupp, L. (2005). *Subject-verb agreement in English dialects: The East Anglian Subject Rule.* Paper presented at The International Conference on Language Variation in Europe 3, Amsterdam, The Netherlands.

Britain, D., & Sudbury, A. (2002). There's sheep and there's penguins: 'Drift', 'slant' and singular verb forms following existentials in New Zealand and Falkland Island English. In M. Jones & E. Esch (Eds.), *Language change: The interplay of internal, external and extra-linguistic factors* (pp. 209–242). Berlin: Mouton de Gruyter.

Britain, D., & Sudbury, A. (2013). Falkland Island English. In B. Kortmann & K. Lunkenheimer (Eds.), *The Mouton world atlas of variation in English* (pp. 669–676). Berlin: Mouton de Gruyter.

Britain, D., & Trudgill, P. (2005). New dialect formation and contact-induced reallocation: Three case studies from the Fens. *International Journal of English Studies, 5*, 183–209.

Bruening, B., Dinh, X., & Kim, L. (2015). Selection, idioms, and the structure of nominal phrases with and without classifiers. *Glossa: A Journal of General Linguistics, 3*, 42.

Brunner, K. (1963). *An outline of Middle English grammar.* Oxford: Blackwell.

Bucholtz, M. (1999). You da man: Narrating the racial other in the production of white masculinity. *Journal of Sociolinguistics, 3*, 443–460.

Bucholtz, M., & Lopez, Q. (2011). Performing blackness, forming whiteness: Linguistic minstrelsy in Hollywood film. *Journal of Sociolinguistics, 15*, 680–706.

Buchstaller, I., Corrigan, K. P., Holmberg, A., Honeybone, P., & Maguire, W. (2013). T-to-R and the Northern Subject Rule: Questionnaire-based, spatial, social and structural linguistics. *English Language and Linguistics, 17*, 85–128.

Bybee, J. (1995). Regular morphology and the lexicon. *Language and Cognitive Processes, 10*, 425–455.

Bybee, J., & Hopper, P. J. (2001). Introduction to frequency and linguistic structure. In J. Bybee & P. J. Hopper (Eds.), *Frequency and the emergence of linguistic structure* (pp. 1–27). Amsterdam: John Benjamins.

Calle-Martín, J., & Romero-Barranco, J. (2017). Third person present tense markers in some varieties of English. *English World-Wide, 38*, 77–103.

334 References

Campbell, A. (1959). *Old English grammar*. Oxford: Clarendon Press.

Carlson, G. N. (1980). *Reference to kinds in English*. New York: Garland Publishing.

Carpenter, J. (2004). *The lost community of the Outer Banks: African American speech on Roanoke Island* (MA dissertation). North Carolina State University, Raleigh, NC.

Chambers, J. (2004). Dynamic typology and vernacular universals. In B. Kortmann (Ed.), *Dialectology meets typology: Dialect grammar from a cross-linguistic perspective* (pp. 128–145). Berlin: Mouton de Gruyter.

Chapman, C. (1998). A subject-verb agreement hierarchy: Evidence from analogical change in modern English dialects. In R. M. Hogg & L. van Bergen (Eds.), *Historical linguistics (Vol. 2): Germanic linguistics: Selected papers from the 12th International Conference on Historical Linguistics, Manchester, August 1995* (pp. 35–44). Amsterdam: John Benjamins.

Cheshire, J. (1981). Variation in the use of *ain't* in an urban British dialect. *Language in Society, 10*, 365–388.

Cheshire, J. (1982). *Variation in an English dialect: A sociolinguistic study*. Cambridge: Cambridge University Press.

Cheshire, J. (1999). Spoken Standard English. In T. Bex & R. Watts (Eds.), *Standard English: The widening debate* (pp. 149–166). London: Routledge.

Cheshire, J. (2005a). Syntactic variation and beyond: Gender and social class variation in the use of discourse-new markers. *Journal of Sociolinguistics, 9*, 479–508.

Cheshire, J. (2005b). Syntactic variation and spoken language. In L. Cornips & K. Corrigan (Eds.), *Syntax and variation: Reconciling the biological and social* (pp. 81–106). Amsterdam: John Benjamins.

Cheshire, J., & Fox, S. (2009). *Was/were* variation: A perspective from London. *Language Variation and Change, 21*, 1–38.

Cheshire, J., & Ouhalla, J. (1997). *Grammatical constraints on variation*. Paper presented at UK Language Variation and Change 1, University of Reading, UK.

Cheshire, J., Edwards, V., & Whittle, P. (1989). Urban British dialect grammar: The question of dialect levelling. *English World-Wide, 10*, 185–225.

Childs, C. (2011). *The Northern Subject Rule and coordination: Examining perceptions of verbal -s occurrence in Tyneside English* (BA dissertation). University of Newcastle, Newcastle.

Childs, C. (2012). Verbal *-s* and the Northern Subject Rule: Spatial variation in linguistic and sociolinguistic constraints. In Á. Pérez, X. Afonso, E. Carrilho, & C. Magro (Eds.), *Proceedings of the International Symposium* *on Limits and Areas in Dialectology, Lisbon, 2011* (pp. 319–344). Lisboa: Centro de Linguística da Universidade de Lisboa.

Childs, B., & Van Herk, G. (2010). Breaking old habits: Syntactic constraints underlying habitual effects in Newfoundland English. In J. Walker (Ed.), *Aspect in grammatical variation* (pp. 81–93). Amsterdam: John Benjamins.

Childs, B., & Van Herk, G. (2013). Superstars and bit players: Salience and the fate of local dialect features. In A. Barysevich, A. D'Arcy, & D. Heap (Eds.), *Proceedings of Methods XIV: Papers from the Fourteenth International Conference on Methods in Dialectology, 2011* (pp. 139–148). Frankfurt: Peter Lang.

Childs, B., & Van Herk, G. (2014). Work that -s! Drag queens, gender, identity, and traditional Newfoundland English. *Journal of Sociolinguistics, 18*, 634–657.

Chomsky, N. (1986). *Barriers.* Cambridge, MA: MIT Press.

Chomsky, N. (1995). *The minimalist program.* Cambridge, MA: MIT Press.

Chomsky, N. (1998). *Minimalist inquiries: The framework.* Cambridge, MA: MIT Occasional Papers in Linguistics, 15.

Christian, D., Wolfram, W., & Dube, N. (1988). *Variation and change in geographically isolated communities: Appalachian English and Ozark English.* Tuscaloosa, AL: American Dialect Society.

Cinque, G. (1994). On the evidence for partial N-movement in the Romance DP. In G. Cinque, J. Koster, J.-Y. Pollock, L. Rizzi, & R. Zanuttini (Eds.), *Paths towards universal grammar: Studies in honor of Richard S. Kayne* (pp. 85–110). Washington, DC: Georgetown University Press.

Clark, E. V., & Clark, H. H. (1979). When nouns surface as verbs. *Language, 55,* 767–811.

Clarke, S. (1997). English verbal -s revisited: The evidence from Newfoundland. *American Speech, 72,* 227–259.

Clarke, S. (1999). Search for origins: Habitual aspect and Newfoundland Vernacular English. *Journal of English Linguistics, 27,* 328–340.

Clarke, S. (2004). Verbal -s reconsidered: The subject type constraint as a diagnostic of historical transatlantic relationship. In C. Kay, S. Horobin, & J. Smith (Eds.), *New perspectives on English historical linguistics: Selected papers from 12 ICEHL. Glasgow, 21–26 August 2002 (Vol. I): Syntax and morphology* (pp. 1–14). Amsterdam: John Benjamins.

Clarke, S. (2010). *Newfoundland and Labrador English.* Edinburgh: Edinburgh University Press.

Clarke, S. (2014). The continuing story of verbal -s: Revisiting the Northern Subject Rule as a diagnostic of historical relationship. In R. T. Cacoullos,

N. Dion, & A. Lapierre (Eds.), *Linguistic variation: Confronting fact and theory* (pp. 75–95). London: Routledge.

Clarke, S., & Hiscock, P. (2009). Hip-hop in a post-insular community: Hybridity, local language, and authenticity in an online Newfoundland rap group. *Journal of English Linguistics, 37,* 241–261.

Cole, M. (2008). What is the Northern Subject Rule? The resilience of a medieval constraint in Tyneside English. *Journal of the Spanish Society for Medieval Language and Literature, 15,* 91–114.

Cole, M. (2014). *Old Northumbrian verbal morphosyntax and the (Northern) Subject Rule.* Amsterdam: John Benjamins.

Collins, P. (2012). Singular agreement in *there*-existentials: An intervarietal corpus-based study. *English World-Wide, 33,* 53–68.

Comeau, P. (2011). Verbal *-s* in Vernacular Newfoundland English: A combined variationist and formal account of grammatical change. *University of Pennsylvania Working Papers in Linguistics, 17,* 31–40.

Comrie, B. S. (1979). The animacy hierarchy in Chuckchee. In P. C. Clyne, W. F. Hanks, & C. L. Hofbauer (Eds.), *The elements: A parasession on linguistic units and levels, April 20–21, 1979* (pp. 322–329). Chicago: University of Chicago.

Corbett, G. (1979). The agreement hierarchy. *Journal of Linguistics, 15,* 203–224.

Corbett, G. (2003). Agreement: The range of the phenomenon and the principles of the Surrey database of agreement. *Transactions of the Philological Society, 101,* 155–202.

Corbett, G. (2006). *Agreement.* Cambridge: Cambridge University Press.

Cornips, L., & Corrigan, K. P. (Eds.). (2005). *Syntax and variation: Reconciling the biological and the social.* Amsterdam: John Benjamins.

Corrigan, K. P. (1997). *The syntax of South Armagh English in its socio-historical perspective* (Doctoral dissertation). University College Dublin, Dublin.

Corrigan, K. P., Beal, J. C., & Moisl, H. L. (2001–2005). *The Newcastle electronic corpus of Tyneside English.* Newcastle University, UK.

Coseriu, E. (1994). *Textlinguistik: Eine Einführung* (3rd ed., J. Albrecht, Ed.). Tübingen: Francke.

Crawford, W. J. (2005). Verb agreement and disagreement: A corpus investigation of concord variation in existential *There + Be* constructions. *Journal of English Linguistics, 33,* 35–61.

Croft, W. (2000). *Explaining language change: An evolutionary approach.* Harlow: Pearson Education.

References   337

Cukor-Avila, P. (2003). The complex grammatical history of African-American and white vernaculars in the South. In S. Nagle & S. Sanders (Eds.), *English in the Southern United States* (pp. 82–105). Cambridge: Cambridge University Press.

Cutler, C. (1999). Yorkville crossing: White teens, hip hop and African American English. *Journal of Sociolinguistics, 4,* 428–442.

D'Arcy, A. (2017). *Discourse-pragmatic variation and change: Eight hundred years of LIKE.* Amsterdam: John Benjamins.

De Both, F. (2019). Nonstandard periphrastic DO and verbal -s in the south west of England. *Journal of Historical Sociolinguistics, 5,* 1–35. https://doi.org/10.1515/jhsl-2018-0006.

De Cuypere, L. (2005). Exploring exaptation in language change. *Folia Linguistica Historica, 26,* 13–26.

De Cuypere, L. (2006). Iconiciteit in taal: Evolutionarisme en creativiteit. *Studies van de BLK, 1,* 1–12. Retrieved May 2019 from https://sites.uclouvain.be/bkl-cbl/wp-content/uploads/2014/08/cuy2006.pdf.

De Cuypere, L. (2008). *Limiting the iconic: From the metatheoretical foundations to the creative possibilities of iconicity in language.* Amsterdam: John Benjamins.

De Haas, N. K. (2011). *Morphosyntactic variation in Northern English: The Northern Subject Rule, its origins and early history* (Doctoral dissertation). Radboud University, Nijmegen.

De Klerk, V. (1996). *Focus on South Africa.* Amsterdam: John Benjamins.

De Saussure, F. (1915). *Course in general linguistics.* C. Bally & A. Sechehaye (Eds.) in collaboration with A. Riedlinger (W. Baskin, Trans.). New York: McGraw-Hill Book Company.

De Vos, M. (2013). Homogeneity in subject-verb concord in South African English. *Language Matters: Studies in the Languages of Africa, 44,* 58–77.

Den Dikken, M. (2001). "Pluringals", pronouns and quirky agreement. *The Linguistic Review, 18,* 19–41.

Den Dikken, M., Bernstein, J., Tortora, C., & Zanuttini, R. (2007). Data and grammar: Means and individuals. *Theoretical Linguistics, 33,* 335–352.

Deterding, D. (2007). *Singapore English.* Edinburgh: Edinburgh University Press.

Detges, U., & Waltereit, R. (2002). Grammaticalization vs. reanalysis: A semantic-pragmatic account of functional change in grammar. *Zeitschrift für Sprachwissenschaft, 21,* 151–195.

Dewey, M. (2006). *English as a Lingua Franca: An empirical study of innovation in lexis and grammar* (Doctoral dissertation). King's College London, London.

Diesing, M. (1992). *Indefinites.* Cambridge, MA: MIT Press.

338 References

Dubois, S., & Horvath, B. (2003). Verbal morphology in Cajun Vernacular English: A comparison with other varieties of Southern English. *Journal of English Linguistics, 31*, 34–59.

Durham, M. (2013). Was/were alternation in Shetland English. *World Englishes, 32*, 108–128.

Eckert, P. (2008). Variation and the indexical field. *Journal of Sociolinguistics, 12*, 453–476.

Eckert, P. (2011). Where does the social stop? In F. Gregersen, J. K. Parrott, & P. Quist (Eds.), *Language variation—European perspectives III: Selected papers from the 5th International Conference on Language Variation in Europe, Copenhagen, June 5, 2009* (pp. 13–30). Amsterdam: John Benjamins.

Eckert, P. (2012). Three waves of variation study: The emergence of meaning in the study of sociolinguistic variation. *Annual Review of Anthropology, 41*, 87–100.

Eckert, P. (2017). The most perfect of signs: Iconicity in variation. *Linguistics, 55*, 1197–1207.

Edwards, V., & Weltens, B. (1983). Research on non-standard dialects of British English: Progress and prospects. In W. Viereck (Ed.), *Focus on England and Wales* (pp. 97–135). Amsterdam: John Benjamins.

Eisikovits, E. (1991). Variation in subject-verb agreement in inner Sydney English. In J. Cheshire (Ed.), *English around the world: Sociolinguistic perspectives* (pp. 235–256). Cambridge: Cambridge University Press.

Ellis, A. (1889). *On Early English pronunciation (Part V)*. London: Truebner.

Ellis, M. (1994). Literary dialect as linguistic evidence: Subject-verb concord in nineteenth-century literature. *American Speech, 69*, 128–144.

Elworthy, F. T. (1877). *An outline of the grammar of the dialect of West Somerset*. London: Trübner.

Elworthy, F. T. (1886). *The West Somerset word book: A glossary of dialectal and archaic words and phrases used in the West of Somerset and East Devon*. London: Trübner.

Epstein, R. (1995). The later stages in the development of the definite article: Evidence from French. In H. Andersen (Ed.), *Historical linguistics 1993: Selected papers from the 11th International Conference on Historical Linguistics, Los Angeles, 16–20 August 1993* (pp. 159–175). Amsterdam: John Benjamins.

Epstein, R. (2002). The definite article, accessibility, and the construction of discourse referents. *Cognitive Linguistics, 12*, 333–378.

Epstein, R. (2010). The distal demonstrative as discourse marker in Beowulf. *English Language and Linguistics, 15*, 113–135.

References   **339**

Errington, J. J. (1985). *Language and social change in Java: Linguistic reflexes of modernization in a traditional royal polity.* Athens, OH: Ohio University Center for International Studies.

Fasold, R. (1972). *Tense marking in Black English.* Arlington: Center for Applied Linguistics.

Feagin, C. (1979). *Variation and change in Alabama English: A sociolinguistic study of the white community.* Washington, DC: Georgetown University Press.

Felser, C., & Rupp, L. (2001). Expletives as arguments: Germanic existential sentences revisited. *Linguistische Berichte, 187,* 289–324.

Fernández Cuesta, J. (2011). The Northern Subject Rule in first-person-singular contexts in Early Modern English. *Folia Linguistica Historica, 32,* 89–114.

Fernández Cuesta, J. (2015). The history of present indicative morphosyntax from a Northern perspective. In R. Hickey (Ed.), *Researching Northern English* (pp. 90–130). Amsterdam: John Benjamins.

Fernández Cuesta, J., & Rodríguez Ledesma, M. N. (2007). From Old Northumbrian to Northern Middle English: Bridging the divide. In G. Mazzon (Ed.), *Studies in Middle English forms and meanings* (pp. 117–133). Frankfurt: Peter Lang.

Filppula, M. (1999). *The grammar of Irish English: Language in Hibernian style.* London: Routledge.

Fischer, O. (1992). Syntax. In N. Blake (Ed.), *The Cambridge history of the English language (Vol. 2): 1066–1476* (pp. 207–408). Cambridge: Cambridge University Press.

Fischer, O. (1997). Iconicity in language and literature: Language innovation and language change. *Neuphilologische Mitteilungen, 98,* 63–87.

Fischer, O. (1999). On the role played by iconicity in grammaticalization processes. In O. Fischer & M. Nänny (Eds.), *Form miming meaning: Iconicity in language and literature* (pp. 345–374). Amsterdam: John Benjamins.

Fischer, O. (2001). The position of the adjective in (Old) English from an iconic perspective. In O. Fischer & M. Nänny (Eds.), *The motivated sign* (pp. 249–276). Amsterdam: John Benjamins.

Fischer, O. (2006). Grammaticalization and iconicity: Two interacting processes. In H. Grabes & W. Viereck (Eds.), *The wider scope of English: Papers in English language and literature from the Bamberg Conference of the International Association of University Professors of English* (pp. 17–42). Frankfurt: Peter Lang.

340 References

Fischer, O. (2010). An iconic, analogical approach to grammaticalization. In C. Jac Conradie, R. Johl, M. Beukes, O. Fischer, & C. Ljungberg (Eds.), *Signergy* (pp. 279–299). Amsterdam: John Benjamins.

Fischer, O., & Nänny, M. (1999). Introduction: Iconicity as a creative force in language use. In M. Nänny & O. Fischer (Eds.), *Form miming meaning* (pp. xv–xxxvii). Amsterdam: John Benjamins.

Fischer, O., Van Kemenade, A., Koopman, W., & Van der Wurff, W. (2000). *The syntax of Early English*. Cambridge: Cambridge University Press.

Fisiak, J. (1968). *A short grammar of Middle English*. Warsaw: Państwowe Wydawnictwo Naukowe.

Fitzpatrick, D. (1994). *Oceans of consolation: Personal accounts of Irish migration to Australia*. Ithaca: Cornell University Press.

Forby, R. (1830). *The vocabulary of East-Anglia: An attempt to record the vulgar tongue of the twin sister counties Norfolk and Suffolk, as it existed in the last twenty years*. London: J. B. Nichols and Son.

Forsström, G. (1948). *The verb 'to be' in Middle English: A survey of forms*. Lund: C. W. K. Gleerup.

Fries, C. C. (1940). *American English grammar: The grammatical structure of present-day American English with especial reference to social differences or class dialects*. New York: Appleton-Century-Crofts.

Gardani, F. (2016). Allogenous exaptation. In M. Norde & F. Van de Velde (Eds.), *Exaptation and language change* (pp. 227–260). Amsterdam: John Benjamins.

Givón, T. (1976). Topic, pronoun and grammatical agreement. In C. N. Li (Ed.), *Subject and topic* (pp. 149–188). New York: Academic Press.

Givón, T. (1985). Iconicity, isomorphism and non-arbitrary coding in syntax. In J. Haiman (Ed.), *Iconicity in syntax* (pp. 187–220). Amsterdam: John Benjamins.

Givón, T. (1991). The evolution of dependent clause morpho-syntax in Biblical Hebrew. In E. C. Traugott & B. Heine (Eds.), *Approaches to grammaticalization (Vol. 2): Focus on types of grammatical markers* (pp. 257–310). Amsterdam: John Benjamins.

Givón, T. (1995). Isomorphism in the grammatical code: Cognitive and biological considerations. In R. Simone (Ed.), *Iconicity in language* (pp. 47–76). Amsterdam: John Benjamins.

Godfrey, E., & Tagliamonte, S. (1999). Another piece for the verbal -*s* story: Evidence from Devon in the Southwest of England. *Language Variation and Change, 11,* 87–121.

Görlach, M. (1987). Colonial lag? The alleged conservative character of American English and other 'colonial' varieties. *English World-Wide, 8,* 41–60.

References   341

Gould, S. J., & Urba, E. S. (1982). Exaptation—A missing term in the science of form. *Paleobiology, 8,* 4–15.

Greenberg, J. H. (1966). Some universals of grammar with particular reference to the order of meaningful elements. In J. H. Greenberg (Ed.), *Universals of language* (pp. 73–113). Cambridge, MA: MIT Press.

Greenberg, J. H. (1978). How does a language acquire gender markers? In J. H. Greenberg, C. A. Ferguson, & E. A. Moravcsik (Eds.), *Universals of human language (Vol. 3): Word structure* (pp. 47–82). Stanford: Stanford University Press.

Greenberg, J. H. (1991). The last stages of grammatical elements: Contractive and expansive desemanticization. In E. C. Traugott & B. Heine (Eds.), *Approaches to grammaticalization (Vol. 1): Theoretical and methodological issues* (pp. 301–314). Amsterdam: John Benjamins.

Greene, R. (2010). *Language, ideology and identity in rural eastern Kentucky* (Doctoral dissertation). Stanford University, Palo Alto.

Grimshaw, J. (1991). *Extended projection* (Unpublished manuscript). Brandeis University, Waltham, MA.

Grzegorek, M. (1984). *Thematization in English and Polish: A study in word order.* Poznan: UAM.

Hackenberg, R. G. (1973). *Appalachian English: A sociolinguistic study* (Doctoral dissertation). Georgetown University, Georgetown, DC.

Haiman, J. (1980). The iconicity of grammar: Isomorphism and motivation. *Language, 56,* 515–540.

Haiman, J. (1983). Iconic and economic motivation. *Language, 59,* 781–819.

Haiman, J. (1985). Introduction. In J. Haiman (Ed.), *Iconicity in syntax: Proceedings of a symposium on iconicity in syntax, Stanford, June 24–6, 1983* (pp. 1–10). Amsterdam: John Benjamins.

Halle, M., & Marantz, A. (1993). Distributed morphology and the pieces of inflection. In K. Hale & J. Keyser (Eds.), *The view from Building 20* (pp. 111–176). Cambridge, MA: MIT Press.

Halliday, M. (1994). *An introduction to functional grammar.* London: E. J. Arnold.

Halliday, M. A. K., & Hasan, R. (1976). *Cohesion in English.* London: Longman.

Hamp, E. (1975–1976). Miscellanea Celtica I, II, III, IV. *Studia Celtica, 10–11,* 54–73.

Hankamer, J., & Mikkelsen, L. (2002). A morphological analysis of definite nouns in Danish. *Journal of Germanic Linguistics, 14,* 137–175.

Hannay, M. (1985). *English existentials in functional grammar.* Dordrecht: Foris.

342 References

Harris, J. (1993). The grammar of Irish English. In J. Milroy & L. Milroy (Eds.), *Real English: The grammar of English dialects in the British Isles* (pp. 139–186). London: Longman.

Harris, A. C., & Campbell, L. (1995). *Historical syntax in cross-linguistic perspective*. Cambridge: Cambridge University Press.

Haspelmath, M. (2008). Frequency versus iconicity in explaining grammatical asymmetries. *Cognitive Linguistics, 19*, 1–33.

Hay, J., & Schreier, D. (2004). Reversing the trajectory of language change: Subject-verb agreement with *be* in New Zealand. *Language Variation and Change, 16*, 209–235.

Hazen, K. (2000). Subject-verb concord in a postinsular dialect: The gradual persistence of dialect patterning. *Journal of English Linguistics, 28*, 127–144.

Heard, N. (1970). *Wool: East Anglia's golden fleece*. Lavenham: Dalton.

Heim, I. (1982). *The semantics of definite and indefinite noun phrases* (Doctoral dissertation). University of Massachusetts, Amherst, MA.

Heine, B. (2003). On degrammaticalization. In B. J. Blake & K. Burridge (Eds.), *Historical linguistics 2001: Selected papers from the 15th International Conference on Historical Linguistics, Melbourne, 13–17 August 2001* (pp. 163–180). Amsterdam: John Benjamins.

Hendery, R. (2016). Untangling synchronic and diachronic variation: Verb agreement in Palmerston English. *Australian Journal of Linguistics, 36*, 429–450.

Henry, P. L. (1958). A linguistic survey of Ireland: Preliminary report. *Lochlann, 1*, 49–208.

Henry, A. (1995). *Belfast English and Standard English: Dialect variation and parameter setting*. Oxford: Oxford University Press.

Herring, S. C. (1991). The grammaticalization of rhetorical questions in Tamil. In E. Traugott & B. Heine (Eds.), *Approaches to grammaticalization (Vol. 1) Theoretical and methodological issues* (pp. 253–284). Amsterdam: John Benjamins.

Hilton, K. (2016). Nonstandard agreement in Standard English: The social perception of agreement variation under existential there. *University of Pennsylvania Working Papers in Linguistics, 22*, 61–70.

Hock, H. (1986). *Principles of historical linguistics*. Berlin: Mouton de Gruyter.

Hogg, R. M. (1992a). *A grammar of Old English (Vol. 1): Phonology*. Oxford: Blackwell.

Hogg, R. M. (1992b). Phonology and morphology. In R. M. Hogg (Ed.), *The Cambridge history of the English language (Vol. I): The beginnings to 1066* (pp. 67–167). Cambridge: Cambridge University Press.

Hogg, R. M. (2012). *An introduction to Old English* (2nd ed.). Edinburgh: Edinburgh University Press.

Holm, J. (1991). The Atlantic Creoles and the languages of the ex-slave recordings. In G. Bailey, N. Maynor, & P. Cukor-Avila (Eds.), *The emergence of Black English: Text and commentary* (pp. 231–248). Amsterdam: John Benjamins.

Holmqvist, E. (1922). *On the history of the English present inflections particularly -t and -s*. Heidelberg: Carl Winter.

Hopper, P. J. (1991). On some principles of grammaticization. In E. C. Traugott & B. Heine (Eds.), *Approaches to grammaticalization (Vol. I): Theoretical and methodological issues* (pp. 17–36). Amsterdam: John Benjamins.

Hopper, P. J., & Traugott, E. C. (2003). *Grammaticalization* (2nd ed.). Cambridge: Cambridge University Press.

Huddleston, R., & Pullum, G. K. (2002). *The Cambridge grammar of the English language*. Cambridge: Cambridge University Press.

Hume, A. (1878). *Remarks on the Irish dialect of the English language*. Liverpool: T. Brakell.

Ihalainen, O. (1987). Towards a grammar of the Somerset dialect: A case study of the language of J. M. In L. Kahlas-Tarka (Ed.), *Neophilologica Fennica* (Modern Language Society 100 years) (pp. 71–86). Helsinki: Société néophilologique.

Ihalainen, O. (1994). The dialects of England since 1776. In R. Burchfield (Ed.), *The Cambridge history of the English language (Vol. V): English language in Britain and overseas: Origins and development* (pp. 197–274). Cambridge: Cambridge University Press.

Irvine, J. T. (2001). "Style" as distinctiveness: The culture and ideology of linguistic differentiation. In P. Eckert & J. R. Rickford (Eds.), *Style and sociolinguistic variation* (pp. 21–43). Cambridge: Cambridge University Press.

Irvine, J., & Gal, S. (2000). Language ideology and linguistic differentiation. In P. V. Kroskrity (Ed.), *Regimes of language: Ideologies, polities, and identities* (pp. 35–84). Santa Fe: School of American Research Press.

Ito, R., & Tagliamonte, S. (2003). Well weird, right dodgy, very strange, really cool. *Language in Society, 32,* 257–279.

Janda, R. D. (2001). Beyond "pathways" and "unidirectionality": On the discontinuity of transmission and the counterability of grammaticalization. *Language Sciences, 23,* 265–340.

Jang, Y. (1997). Minimal feature-movement. *Journal of Linguistics, 33,* 311–325.

Jankowski, B. L., & Tagliamonte, S. A. (2017). A lost Canadian dialect: The Ottawa Valley 1975–2013. In T. Säily, A. Nurmi, M. Palander-Collin, &

A. Auer (Eds.), *Historical linguistics: A Festschrift for Terttu Nevalainen on the occasion of her 65th birthday* (pp. 239–274). Amsterdam: John Benjamins.

Jantos, S. (2009). *Agreement in educated Jamaican English: A corpus investigation of ICE-Jamaica* (Doctoral dissertation). Albert-Ludwigs-Universität, Freiburg.

Jantos, S. (2010). Agreement in educated Jamaican English: A corpus-based study of spoken usage in ICE-Jamaica. In H. Dorgeloh & A. Wanner (Eds.), *Syntactic variation and genre* (pp. 305–332). Berlin: Mouton de Gruyter.

Jenkins, L. (1975). *The English existential.* Tübingen: Max Niemeyer.

Jenkins, J. (2011). Accommodating (to) ELF in the international university. *Journal of Pragmatics, 43,* 926–936.

Jenset, G. B. (2010). *A corpus based study on the evolution of* there*: Statistical analysis and cognitive interpretation* (Doctoral dissertation). University of Bergen, Bergen.

Jespersen, O. (1924). *The philosophy of grammar.* Chicago: University of Chicago Press.

Jespersen, O. (1954). *A modern English grammar on historical principles.* London: Allen and Unwin.

Jespersen, O. (1969). *Analytic syntax.* New York: Holt, Rinehart and Winston.

Joby, C. (2014). Third-person singular zero in the Norfolk dialect: A re-assessment. *Folia Linguistica, 35,* 135–172.

Joby, C. (2015). *The Dutch language in Britain (1550–1702): A social history of the use of Dutch in Early Modern Britain.* Leiden: E. J. Brill.

Joby, C. (2017). Regional variation in Early Modern English: The case of the third-person present tense singular verb ending in Norfolk correspondence. *Journal of English Linguistics, 45,* 338–366.

José, B. (2007). Appalachian English in Southern Indiana? The evidence from verbal *-s. Language Variation and Change, 19,* 249–280.

Joseph, B. D. (2004). Rescuing traditional (historical) linguistics from grammaticalization 'theory'. In O. Fischer, M. Norde, & H. Peridon (Eds.), *Up and down the cline* (pp. 44–71). Amsterdam: John Benjamins.

Joseph, B. D. (2005). How accommodating of change is grammaticalization? The case of "lateral shifts". *Logos and Language, 6,* 1–7.

Joseph, B. D. (2014). What counts as (an instance of) grammaticalization? *Folia Linguistica, 48,* 361–383.

Joseph, B. D. (2016). Being exacting about exapting: An exaptation omnibus. In F. Van de Velde & M. Norde (Eds.), *Exaptation and language change* (pp. 27–55). Amsterdam: John Benjamins.

References **345**

Jucker, A. H. (1997). The discourse marker *well* in the history of English. *English Language and Linguistics, 1,* 91–110.

Khan, A. (2007). *A sociolinguistic study of Birmingham English: Language variation and change in a multi-ethnic British community* (Doctoral dissertation). University of Lancaster, Lancaster.

Kingston, M. (2000). *Dialects in danger: Rural dialect attrition in the East Anglian county of Suffolk* (MA dissertation). University of Essex, Colchester.

Kirk, J. (1991). *Northern Ireland Transcribed Corpus of Speech (Vol. 1) (with S. West and S. Gibson): Textfile.* Colchester: Economic and Social Research Council Data Archive, University of Essex, Colchester.

Klemola, J. (1996). *Non-standard periphrastic DO: A study in variation and change* (Doctoral dissertation). University of Essex, Colchester.

Klemola, J. (2000). The origins of the Northern Subject Rule: A case of early contact? In T. Hildegard (Ed.), *Celtic Englishes II* (pp. 329–346). Heidelberg: Winter.

Klemola, J. (2006). *Was/were variation in traditional dialects of England.* Paper presented at the International Conference of English Historical Linguistics 14, University of Bergamo, Italy.

Kökeritz, H. (1932). *The phonology of the Suffolk dialect.* Uppsala: Aktibolag.

Koopman, H., & Sportiche, D. (1991). The position of subjects. *Lingua, 85,* 211–258.

Kortmann, B. (1999). Iconicity, typology and cognition. In M. Nänny & O. Fischer (Eds.), *Form miming meaning* (pp. 375–392). Amsterdam: John Benjamins.

Kortmann, B., & Wagner, S. (2005). The Freiburg Dialect Project and Corpus. In B. Kortmann, T. Herrman, L. Pietsch, & S. Wagner (Eds.), *A comparative grammar of British English dialects: Agreement, gender, relative clauses* (pp. 1–20). Berlin: Mouton de Gruyter.

Kortmann, B., Schneider, E. W., Burridge, K., Mesthrie, R., & Upton, C. (Eds.). (2004). *A handbook of varieties of English.* Berlin: Mouton de Gruyter.

Kranich, S. (2008). Subjective progressives in seventeenth and eighteenth century English: Secondary grammaticalization as a process of objectification. In M. Gotti, M. Dossena, & R. Dury (Eds.), *English historical linguistics 2006 (Vol. I): Syntax and morphology* (pp. 241–256). Amsterdam: John Benjamins.

Kranich, S. (2010). Grammaticalization, subjectification and objectification. In K. Stathi, E. Gehweiler, & E. König (Eds.), *Grammaticalization: Current views and issues* (pp. 101–122). Amsterdam: John Benjamins.

346 References

Kratzer, A. (1995). Stage-level and individual-level predicates. In G. N. Carlson & F. J. Pelletier (Eds.), *The generic book* (pp. 125–175). Chicago: University of Chicago Press.

Krejci, B., & Hilton, K. (2015). *Agreement variation under existential* there. Paper presented at the Annual Corpus Lunch, Stanford University, Stanford.

Kroch, A. (1989). Function and grammar in the history of English: Periphrastic 'do'. In R. Fasold (Ed.), *Language change and variation* (pp. 133–172). Amsterdam: John Benjamins.

Kuryłowicz, J. (1949). La nature des proces dits 'analogiques'. *Acta Linguistica, 5,* 121–138.

Kuryłowicz, J. (1976). *Esquisses linguistiques* (Vol. 2, pp. 38–54). Munich: Fink [Original work published in Kuryłowicz, J. (1965). The evolution of grammatical categories. *Diogenes, 13,* 55–71.]

Kytö, M. (1993). Third-person present singular verb inflection in Early British and American English. *Language Variation and Change, 5,* 113–139.

Labov, W. (1969). Contraction, deletion and inherent variability of the English copula. *Language, 48,* 773–818.

Labov, W. (1972). *Language in the inner city: Studies in the Black English vernacular.* Philadelphia: University of Pennsylvania Press.

Labov, W. (1989). The child as linguistic historian. *Language Variation and Change, 1,* 85–97.

Labov, W. (1998). Co-existent systems in African-American Vernacular English. In S. Mufwene, J. Rickford, G. Bailey, & J. Baugh (Eds.), *African American English: Structure, history and use* (pp. 110–153). London: Routledge.

Labov, W., Cohen, P., Robins, C., & Lewis, J. (1968). *A study of the non-standard English of Negro and Puerto Rican speakers in New York City: Cooperative research report 3288* (Vols. I–II). Philadelphia, PA: U.S. Regional Survey (Linguistics Laboratory, University of Philadelphia).

Laing, M., & Lass, R. (2008–2013). *A linguistic atlas of Early Middle English 1150–1325* (Version 2.1). Retrieved May 2019 from http://www.lel.ed.ac.uk/ihd/laeme2/laeme2.html.

Lakoff, R. (1973). Language and woman's place. *Language in Society, 2,* 45–80.

Lange, C. (2012). *The syntax of Indian English.* Amsterdam: John Benjamins.

Larsson, K. (1988). *Den plural verbböjninge i äldre svenska.* Uppsala: Institutionen för Nordiska Språk vid Uppsala Universitet.

Lass, R. (1990). How to do things with junk: Exaptation in language evolution. *Journal of Linguistics, 26,* 79–102.

References 347

Lass, R. (1992). Phonology and morphology. In N. Blake (Ed.), *The Cambridge history of the English language (Vol. 3): 1476–1776* (pp. 23–155). Cambridge: Cambridge University Press.

Lass, R. (1997). *Historical linguistics and language change.* Cambridge: Cambridge University Press.

Leemann, A., Kolly, M.-J., & Britain, D. (2018). The English Dialects App: The creation of a crowdsourced dialect corpus. *Ampersand, 5,* 1–17.

Lehmann, C. (1988). On the function of agreement. In M. Barlow & C. A. Ferguson (Eds.), *Agreement in natural language: Approaches, theories and descriptions* (pp. 55–65). Stanford: Center for the Study of Language and Information.

Levey, S. (2006). Tense variation in preadolescent narratives. *Journal of English Linguistics, 34,* 126–152.

Levey, S. (2007). *The next generation: Aspects of grammatical variation in the speech of some London preadolescents* (Doctoral dissertation). Queen Mary University of London, London.

Levon, E., Maegaard, M., & Pharao, N. (2017). Introduction: Tracing the origin of /s/ variation. *Linguistics, 55,* 979–992.

Longobardi, G. (1994). Reference and proper names. *Linguistic Inquiry, 25,* 609–665.

Lorenz, K. (1978). *Vergleichende Verhaltensforschung: Grundlagen der Ethologie.* Wien: Springer.

Lyons, J. (1975). Deixis as the source of reference. In E. L. Keenan (Ed.), *Formal semantics of natural language* (pp. 61–83). Cambridge: Cambridge University Press.

Lyons, C. (1999). *Definiteness.* Cambridge: Cambridge University Press.

Macafee, C. (1980). *Nonstandard Scots grammar* (Unpublished typescript).

Malcolm, I. (1996). Observations on variability in the verb phrase in Aboriginal English. *Australian Journal of Linguistics, 16,* 145–165.

Mallinson, C., & Wolfram, W. (2002). Dialect accommodation in a bi-ethnic mountain enclave community: More evidence on the development of African American English. *Language in Society, 31,* 743–775.

Mańczak, W. (1958). Tendences générales des changements analogiques. *Lingua, 7,* 298–325 and 387–420.

Mańczak, W. (1980). Laws of analogy. In J. Fisiak (Ed.), *Historical morphology* (pp. 283–288). Berlin: Mouton de Gruyter.

Martínez Insua, A. E. (2004). *Existential there-constructions in contemporary British English: A corpus driven analysis of their use in speech and writing.* Munich: Lincom Europa.

348   References

Martínez Insua, A. E. (2013). There-constructions as a choice for coherence in the recent history of English. In L. Fontaine, T. Bartlett, & G. O'Grady (Eds.), *Systemic functional linguistics: Exploring choice* (pp. 207–225). Cambridge: Cambridge University Press.

Martínez Insua, A. E., & Palacios Martínez, I. (2003). A corpus-based approach to non-concord in present-day English existential *there*-constructions. *English Studies, 84,* 262–283.

McCafferty, K. (2003). The Northern Subject Rule in Ulster: How Scots, how English? *Language Variation and Change, 15,* 105–139.

McCafferty, K. (2004). '[T]hunder storms is very dangese in this country they come in less than a minnits notice …': The Northern Subject Rule in Southern Irish English. *English World-Wide, 25,* 51–79.

McCormick, K. (1989). *English and Afrikaans in district six: A sociolinguistic study* (Doctoral dissertation). University of Cape Town, Cape Town.

McIntosh, A. (1989). Present indicative plural forms in the later Middle English of the North Midlands. In A. McIntosh, M. L. Samuels, & M. Laing (Eds.), *Middle English dialectology: Essays on some principles and problems* (pp. 116–122). Aberdeen: Aberdeen University Press. [This paper appeared in 1983 in D. Gray & E. G. Stanley (Eds.), *Middle English studies: Presented to Norman Davis on his seventieth birthday* (pp. 235–244). Oxford: Oxford University Press.]

McMahon, A. M. S. (1994). *Understanding language change.* Cambridge: Cambridge University Press.

Meechan, M., & Foley, M. (1994). On resolving disagreement: Linguistic theory and variation—*There's* bridges. *Language Variation and Change, 6,* 63–85.

Meillet, A. (1912). L'évolution des formes grammaticales. Scientia (Rivista di Scienza) 12, No. 26, 6. In *Linguistique historique et linguistique générale* (pp. 130–148). Paris: Librairie Ancienne Honoré Champion.

Melchers, G. (2004). English spoken in Orkney and Shetland: Morphology, syntax and lexicon. In B. Kortmann & E. W. Schneider (with K. Burridge, R. Mesthrie & C. Upton) (Eds.), *A handbook of varieties of English (Vol. 2): Morphology and syntax* (pp. 34–47). Berlin: Mouton de Gruyter.

Melchers, G., & Sundkvist, P. (2010). Shetland and Orkney. In D. Schreier, P. Trudgill, E. W. Schneider, & J. P. Williams (Eds.), *The lesser-known varieties of English* (pp. 17–34). Cambridge: Cambridge University Press.

Middle English Dictionary. (2011–2014). University of Michigan. Retrieved May 2019 from https://quod.lib.umich.edu/cgi/m/mec/med-idx?egs=all&id=MED20505&type=id.

Milroy, J. (1981). *Regional accents of English: Belfast.* Belfast: Blackstaff Press.

References 349

Milroy, J., & Milroy, L. (1985). Linguistic change social network and speaker innovation. *Journal of Linguistics, 21,* 339–384.

Milsark, G. (1974). *Existential sentences in English* (Doctoral dissertation). Massachusetts Institute of Technology, Cambridge, MA.

Milsark, G. (1977). Toward an explanation of certain peculiarities of the existential construction in English. *Linguistic Analysis, 3,* 1–29.

Mitchell, B., & Robinson, F. C. (2012). *A guide to Old English* (8th ed.). Oxford: Blackwell.

Mithun, M. (1984). The evolution of noun incorporation. *Language, 60,* 847–894.

Mithun, M. (1999). *The languages of native North America.* Cambridge: Cambridge University Press.

Mithun, M. (2003). Pronouns and agreement: The information status of pronominal affixes. *Transactions of the Philological Society, 101,* 235–278.

Mittelstaedt, J., & Parrot, J. (2002). *A distributed morphology account of weren't levelling.* Paper presented at New Ways of Analyzing Variation 31, Stanford University, U.S.

Montgomery, M. (1989). Exploring the roots of Appalachian English. *English World-Wide, 10,* 227–278.

Montgomery, M. (1994). The evolution of verb concord in Scots. In A. Fenton & D. McDonald (Eds.), *Studies in Scots and Gaelic: Proceedings of the Third International Conference on the Languages of Scotland* (pp. 81–95). Edinburgh: Canongate.

Montgomery, M. (1997). Making transatlantic connections between varieties of English: The case of the plural verbal *-s. Journal of English Linguistics, 25,* 122–141.

Montgomery, M. (1998). In the Appalachians they speak like Shakespeare. In L. Bauer & P. Trudgill (Eds.), *Language myths* (pp. 66–76). London: Penguin Books.

Montgomery, M. (1999). Sierra Leone Settler English: Another exported variety of African American English. *English World-Wide, 20,* 1–34.

Montgomery, M., & Fuller, J. (1996). What was verbal *-s* in 19th-century African American English? In E. W. Schneider (Ed.), *Focus on the USA* (pp. 211–230). Amsterdam: John Benjamins.

Montgomery, M., & Hall, J. (2004). *Dictionary of Smoky Mountain English.* Knoxville: University of Tennessee Press.

Montgomery, M., Fuller, J., & De Marse, S. (1993). 'The Black Men has wives and Sweet harts [and third person plural *-s*] Jest like the white men':

350 References

Evidence for verbal -*s* from written documents on 19th-century African American Speech. *Language Variation and Change, 5,* 335–337.

Moore, C. (2002). Writing good Southerne: Local and supralocal norms in the Plumpton letter collection. *Language Variation and Change, 14,* 1–17.

Moore, E. (2003). *Learning style and identity: A sociolinguistic analysis of a Bolton high school* (Doctoral dissertation). University of Manchester, Manchester.

Moore, E. (2011). Interaction between social category and social practice: Explaining *was/were* variation. *Language Variation and Change, 22,* 347–371.

Moore, E., & Podesva, R. J. (2009). Style, indexicality and the social meaning of tag questions. *Language in Society, 38,* 447–485.

Mossé, F. (1952). *A handbook of Middle English.* Baltimore, MD: John Hopkins University Press.

Mufwene, S. S. (1996). The founder principle in creole genesis. *Diachronica, 13,* 83–134.

Murray, J. (1873). *The dialect of the Southern Counties of Scotland: Its pronunciation, grammar and historical relations.* London: Asher.

Mustanoja, T. F. (1960). *A Middle English syntax (Part I): Parts of speech.* Helsinki: Société Néophilologique.

Myhill, J., & Harris, W. (1986). The use of the verbal -*s* inflection in BEV. In D. Sankoff (Ed.), *Diversity and diachrony: Papers from the Twelfth Annual Conference on New Ways of Analyzing Variation* (pp. 25–32). Amsterdam: John Benjamins.

Narrog, H. (2007). Exaptation, grammaticalization, and reanalysis. *California Linguistic Notes, 23,* 1–27.

Narrog, H. (2012). Textual uses of modality and mood in subordinate clauses as part of *speech-act orientation.* In L. Brems, L. Ghesquière, & F. Van de Velde (Eds.), *Intersections of intersubjectivity* (pp. 29–52). Amsterdam: John Benjamins.

Narrog, H. (2015). (Inter)subjectification and its limits in secondary grammaticalization. *Language Sciences, 47,* 148–160.

Nevalainen, T. (2006). Vernacular universals? The case of plural *was* in Early Modern English. In T. Nevalainen, J. Klemola, & M. Laitinen (Eds.), *Types of variation: Diachronic, dialectal and typological* (pp. 351–369). Amsterdam: John Benjamins.

Nevalainen, T., & Raumolin-Brunberg, H. (2000). The third-person singular -(E)S and -(E)TH revisited: The morphophonemic hypothesis. In C.

Dalton-Puffer & N. Ritt (Eds.), *Words: Structure, meaning and function: A Festschrift for Dieter Kastovsky* (pp. 235–248). Berlin: Mouton de Gruyter.

Nevalainen, T., & Raumolin-Brunberg, H. (2003). *Historical sociolinguistics: Language change in Tudor and Stuart England*. Harlow: Pearson Education.

Nevalainen, T., Raumolin-Brunberg, H., & Trudgill, P. (2001). Chapters in the social history of East Anglian English: The case of the third-person singular. In J. Fisiak & P. Trudgill (Eds.), *East Anglian English* (pp. 187–204). Woodbridge: Boydell and Brewer.

Newmeyer, F. J. (1992). Iconicity and generative grammar. *Language, 68,* 756–796.

Norde, M. (2001). Deflexion as a counterdirectional factor in grammatical change. *Language Sciences, 23,* 231–264.

Norde, M. (2002). The final stages of grammaticalization: Affixhood and beyond. In I. Wischer & G. Diewald (Eds.), *New reflections on grammaticalization* (pp. 45–65). Amsterdam: John Benjamins.

Norde, M., & Van de Velde, F. (Eds.). (2016). *Exaptation and language change.* Amsterdam: John Benjamins.

Nurmio, S. (2017). Collective nouns in Welsh: A noun category or a plural allomorph. *Transactions of the Philological Society, 115,* 58–78.

Ojanen, A.-L. (n.d. a). *Past tense forms of the verb BE in the dialect of Cambridgeshire* (Unpublished manuscript).

Ojanen, A.-L. (n.d. b). *Past-tense negative forms of the verb BE in the dialect of Cambridgeshire* (Unpublished manuscript).

Orton, H., & Dieth, E. (1962–1971). *Survey of English Dialects.* Leeds: E. J. Arnold.

Orton, H., & Halliday, W. J. (1962). *Survey of English Dialects (B): The basic material (Vols. 1.1 and 1.2): The six Northern counties and the Isle of Man.* Leeds: E. J. Arnold.

Orton, H., & Tilling, P. M. (1971). *Survey of English Dialects (B): The basic material (Vols. 3.1 and 3.3): The East Midland counties and East Anglia.* Leeds: E. J. Arnold.

Orton, H., & Wakelin, M. F. (1967). *Survey of English Dialects (B): The basic material (Vol. 4.2): The Southern counties.* Leeds: E. J. Arnold.

Ouhalla, J. (1991). *Functional categories and parametric variation.* London: Routledge.

Parrott, J. K. (2007). Distributed morphological mechanisms of Smith Island *weren't* leveling. *University of Pennsylvania Working Papers in Linguistics, 13,* 295–308.

352 References

Peirce, C. S. (1931–1958). *Collected papers of Charles Sanders Peirce* (Vols. 1–8). Cambridge, MA: Harvard University Press. [Hartshorne, C., & Weiss, P. (Eds.) 1931–1935 (Vols. 1–6); Burks, A. W. (Ed.) 1958 (Vols. 7–8)].

Peitsara, K. (1988). On existential sentences in the dialect of Suffolk. *Neuphilologische Mitteilungen, 1,* 72–99.

Peitsara, K. (2002). Verbal -*s* in Devonshire: The Helsinki dialect corpus evidence. In H. Raumolin-Brunberg & T. Nevalainen (Eds.), *Variation past and present: VARIENG studies on English for Terttu Nevalainen* (pp. 211–230). Helsinki: Société néophilologique.

Pérez-Guerra, J. (1999). *Historical English syntax: A statistical corpus-based study on the organisation of Early Modern English sentences.* München: Lincom.

Petyt, K. M. (1985). *Dialect and accent in industrial West Yorkshire.* Amsterdam: John Benjamins.

Pfenninger, S. E. (2009). *Grammaticalization paths of English and high German existential constructions.* Bern: Peter Lang.

Pichler, H. (2018). *From complexity to uniformity, via (contact-induced) grammaticalization: Tracing the evolution of the London question tag 'system'.* Paper presented at the Discourse-Pragmatic Variation and Change Conference 4, University of Helsinki, Helsinki.

Piercy, C. (2010). *One /a/ or two? The phonetics, phonology and sociolinguistics of change in the TRAP and BATH vowels in the Southwest of England* (Doctoral dissertation). University of Essex, Colchester.

Pietsch, L. (2005). *"Some do and some doesn't":* Verbal concord variation in the north of the British Isles. In B. Kortmann, T. Herrman, L. Pietsch, & S. Wagner (Eds.), *A comparative grammar of British English dialects: Agreement, gender, relative clauses* (pp. 125–210). Berlin: Mouton de Gruyter.

Podesva, R. J. (2011). The California vowel shift and gay identity. *American Speech, 86,* 32–51.

Polanyi, L. (1989). *Telling the American story: A structural and cultural analysis of conversational story telling.* Cambridge, MA: MIT Press.

Pollock, J.-Y. (1989). Verb movement, universal grammar, and the structure of IP. *Linguistic Inquiry, 20,* 365–424.

Poplack, S., & Tagliamonte, S. (1989). There's no tense like the present: Verbal -*s* inflection in Early Black English. *Language Variation and Change, 1,* 47–84.

Poplack, S., & Tagliamonte, S. (1991). African American English in the diaspora: Evidence from old-line Nova Scotians. *Language Variation and Change, 3,* 301–339.

References 353

Poplack, S., & Tagliamonte, S. (2001). *African American English in the diaspora: Tense and aspect*. Malden, MA: Blackwell.

Poplack, S., & Tagliamonte, S. (2004). Back to the present: Verbal -s in the African American English diaspora. In R. Hickey (Ed.), *Legacies of colonial English: The study of transported dialects* (pp. 203–223). Cambridge: Cambridge University Press.

Potter, R. (2018). *A variationist multilocality study of unstressed vowels and verbal -s marking in the peripheral dialect of East Suffolk* (Doctoral dissertation). University of Essex, Colchester.

Prince, E. F. (1985). Fancy syntax and 'shared knowledge'. *Journal of Pragmatics, 9,* 65–81.

Prince, E. F. (1992). The ZPG letter: Subjects, definiteness and information-status. In W. C. Mann & S. A. Thompson (Eds.), *Discourse description: Diverse linguistic analyses of a fund-raising text* (pp. 295–326). Amsterdam: John Benjamins.

Pyles, T., & Algeo, J. (2005). *The origins and development of the English language* (5th ed.). Boston: Thomson Wadsworth.

Quirk, R., Greenbaum, S., Leech, G., & Svartvik, J. (1985). *A comprehensive grammar of the English language*. London: Longman.

Ramat, A. G. (1995). Iconicity in grammaticalization processes. In R. Simone (Ed.), *Iconicity in language* (pp. 119–139). Amsterdam: John Benjamins.

Ramat, A. G. (1998). Testing the boundaries of grammaticalization. In A. G. Ramat & P. J. Hopper (Eds.), *The limits of grammaticalization* (pp. 107–127). Amsterdam: John Benjamins.

Ramchand, G. (1996). Two subject positions in Scottish Gaelic: The syntax-semantics interface. *Natural Language Semantics, 4,* 165–191.

Raumolin-Brunberg, H. (1996). Apparent time. In T. Nevalainen & H. Raumolin-Brunberg (Eds.), *Sociolinguistics and language history: Studies based on the Corpus of Early English Correspondence* (pp. 93–109). Amsterdam: Rodopi.

Reaser, J. (2010). Bahamian English. In D. Schreier, P. Trudgill, E. W. Schneider, & J. Williams (Eds.), *The lesser-known varieties of English* (pp. 158–170). Cambridge: Cambridge University Press.

Richards, H. (2010). Preterite *be*: A new perspective? *English World-Wide, 31,* 62–81.

Rickford, J. R. (1998). The creole origins of African American Vernacular English: Evidence from copula absence. In S. S. Mufwene, J. R. Rickford,

G. Bailey, & J. Bough (Eds.), *African American English: Structure, history and usage* (pp. 154–200). London: Routledge.

Rizzi, L. (1990). *Relativized minimality*. Cambridge, MA: MIT Press.

Rodríguez Ledesma, M. N. (2013). The Northern Subject Rule in first-person singular contexts in fourteenth-fifteenth-century Scots. *Folia Linguistica Historica, 34,* 149–172.

Rodríguez Ledesma, M. N. (2017). The Northern Subject Rule in the Breadalbane Collection. *English Studies, 98,* 802–824.

Rodríguez Louro, C., & Ritz, M.-E. (2014). Stories down under: Tense variation at the heart of Australian English narratives. *Australian Journal of Linguistics, 34,* 549–565.

Rohdenburg, G. (1996). Cognitive complexity and increased grammatical explicitness in English. *Cognitive Linguistics, 7,* 149–182.

Rosen, A. (2014). *Grammatical variation and change in Jersey English.* Amsterdam: John Benjamins.

Ross, A. S. C. (1934). A theory of emendation. *Speculum, 9,* 179–189.

Ross, J. R. (1967). *Constraints on variables in syntax* (Doctoral dissertation). Massachusetts Institute of Technology, Cambridge, MA.

Rupp, L. (2003). *The syntax of imperatives in English and Germanic: Word order variation in the minimalist framework.* Basingstoke: Palgrave Macmillan.

Sadler, L. (2003). Coordination and asymmetric agreement in Welsh. In M. Butt & T. Holloway King (Eds.), *Nominals: Inside and out* (pp. 85–118). Stanford: CSLI Publications.

Samuels, M. L. (1989). The great Scandinavian belt. In A. McIntosh, M. L. Samuels, & M. Laing (Eds.), *Middle English dialectology: Essays on some principles and problems* (pp. 106–115). Aberdeen: Aberdeen University Press.

Sapir, E. (1933). La réalité psychologique des phonèmes. *Journal de Psychologie Normaleet Pathologique, 30,* 247–265. [English version published in 1949 as The psychological reality of phonemes. In D. G. Mandelbaum (Ed.), *Selected writings of Edward Sapir in language, culture and personality* (pp. 46–60). Oakland, CA: University of California Press.]

Schendl, H. (1996). Text types and code-switching in medieval and Early Modern English. *Vienna English Working Papers, 5,* 50–62.

Schiffrin, D. (1981). Tense variation in narrative. *Language, 57,* 45–62.

Schiffrin, D. (1994). *Approaches to discourse.* Oxford: Blackwell.

Schilling-Estes, N. (2002). On the nature of isolated and post-isolated dialects: Innovation, variation and differentiation. *Journal of Sociolinguistics, 6,* 64–85.

Schilling-Estes, N. (2004). Constructing ethnicity in interaction. *Journal of Sociolinguistics, 8*, 163–195.

Schilling-Estes, N. ([2008] 2013). Investigating stylistic variation. In J. Chambers, P. Trudgill, & N. Schilling-Estes (Eds.), *Handbook of language variation and change* (2nd ed., pp. 327–349). Oxford: Blackwell.

Schilling-Estes, N., & Wolfram, W. (1994). Convergent explanation and alternative regularization patterns: *Were/weren't* levelling in a vernacular English variety. *Language Variation and Change, 6*, 273–302.

Schilling-Estes, N., & Wolfram, W. (1999). Alternative models of dialect death: Dissipation vs. contraction. *Language, 75*, 486–521.

Schilling-Estes, N., & Zimmerman, L. (2000). *On the progress of morphological change:* Was/weren't *leveling in Smith Island English.* Paper presented at the Linguistic Society of America Annual Meeting, Chicago, IL.

Schneider, E. W. (1983). The origin of the verbal *-s* in Black English. *American Speech, 58*, 99–113.

Schneider, E. W. (2003). The dynamics of New Englishes: From identity construction to dialect birth. *Language, 79*, 233–281.

Schneider, E. W., & Montgomery, M. (2001). On the trail of early nonstandard grammar: An electronic corpus of Southern U.S. antebellum overseers' letters. *American Speech, 76*, 388–410.

Schreier, D. (2002a). *Terra incognita* in the Anglophone world: Tristan da Cunha, South Atlantic Ocean. *English Word-Wide, 23*, 1–29.

Schreier, D. (2002b). Past *be* in Tristan da Cunha: The rise and fall of categoricality in language change. *American Speech, 77*, 70–99.

Schreier, D. (2003). Tracing the history of dialect transportation on post-colonial English: The case of 3rd person singular zero on Tristan da Cunha. *Folia Linguistica Historica, XXIII*, 115–131.

Schreier, D. (2008). *St Helenian English: Origins, evolution and variation.* Amsterdam: John Benjamins.

Schreier, D. (2010a). Tristan da Cunha English. In D. Schreier, P. Trudgill, E. W. Schneider, & J. Williams (Eds.), *The lesser-known varieties of English* (pp. 245–260). Cambridge: Cambridge University Press.

Schreier, D. (2010b). St Helenian English. In D. Schreier, P. Trudgill, E. W. Schneider, & J. Williams (Eds.), *The lesser-known varieties of English* (pp. 224–244). Cambridge: Cambridge University Press.

Schütze, C. (1997). *INFL in child and adult language: Agreement, case and licensing* (Doctoral dissertation). Massachusetts Institute of Technology, Cambridge, MA.

Schütze, C. (1999). English expletive constructions are not infected. *Linguistic Inquiry, 30,* 467–484.

Seidlhofer, B. (2004). Research perspectives on teaching English as a lingua franca. *Annual Review of Applied Linguistics, 24,* 209–239.

Seiler, H. (1995). Iconicity between indicativity and predicativity. In R. Simone (Ed.), *Iconicity in language* (pp. 141–151). Amsterdam: John Benjamins.

Sheppard, M. (2006). *Madonna—Loves: Gay speech in Newfoundland, Canada* (Unpublished Course Paper). Memorial University of Newfoundland, St John's.

Shorrocks, G. (1980). *A grammar of the dialect of Farnsworth and District (Greater Manchester, formerly Lancashire)* (Doctoral dissertation). University of Sheffield, Sheffield.

Shorrocks, G. (1999). *A grammar of the dialect of the Bolton area (Part II): Morphology and syntax.* Frankfurt: Peter Lang.

Shuy, R., Wolfram, W., & Riley, W. (1967). *Linguistic correlates of social stratification in Detroit speech* (USOE Final Report, 6-1347).

Siewierska, A. (1999). From anaphoric pronoun to grammatical agreement marker: Why objects don't make it. *Folia Linguistica, 33,* 225–251.

Silverstein, M. (1979). Language structure and linguistic ideology. In P. R. Clyne, W. F. Hanks, & C. L. Hofbauer (Eds.), *The elements: A parasession on linguistic units and levels* (pp. 193–247). Chicago: Chicago Linguistic Society.

Silverstein, M. (1994). "Relative motivation" in denotational and indexical sound symbolism of Wasco-Wishram Chinookan. In L. Hinton, J. Nichols, & J. J. Ohala (Eds.), *Sound symbolism* (pp. 40–60). Cambridge: Cambridge University Press.

Singler, J. V. (1997). The configuration of Liberia's Englishes. *World Englishes, 16,* 205–231.

Smallwood, C. (1997). Dis-agreement in Canadian English existentials. In *Proceedings from the 1997 annual conference of the Canadian Linguistic Association* (pp. 227–238). Calgary: University of Calgary.

Smirnova, E. (2015). When secondary grammaticalization starts: A look from the constructional perspective. *Language Sciences, 47,* 215–228.

Smith, J. (2000). *Synchrony and diachrony in the evolution of English: Evidence from Scotland* (Doctoral dissertation). University of York, York.

Smith, J., & Tagliamonte, S. (1998). 'We were *all thegither, I think we* was *all thegither*': *Was* regularization in Buckie English. *World Englishes, 17,* 105–126.

References 357

Sobin, N. (1997). Agreement, default rules and grammatical viruses. *Linguistic Inquiry, 28,* 318–343.

Sonesson, G. (1997). The ecological foundations of iconicity. In I. Rauch & G. F. Carr (Eds.), *Semiotics around the world: Synthesis in diversity. Proceedings of the Fifth International Congress of IASS, Berkeley, June 12–18, 1994* (pp. 739–774). Berlin: Mouton de Gruyter.

Sperling, C. (1896). *A short history of the borough of Sudbury in the county of Suffolk compiled from materials collected by W. H. Hudson.* Marten: Sudbury.

Spurling, J. (2004). *Traditional feature loss in Ipswich: Dialect attrition in the East Anglian county of Suffolk* (BA dissertation). University of Essex, Colchester.

Stein, D. (1986). Old English Northumbrian verb inflection revisited. In D. Kastovsky & A. Szwedek (Eds.), *Linguistics across historical and geographical boundaries (Vol. 1): Linguistic theory and historical linguistics* (pp. 637–650). Berlin: Mouton de Gruyter.

Stein, D. (1987). At the crossroads of philology, linguistics and semiotics: Notes on the replacement of *th* by *s* in the third person singular in English. *English Studies, 5,* 406–431.

Strang, B. M. H. (1970). *A history of English.* London: Methuen.

Sudbury, A. (2001). Falkland Island English: A southern hemisphere variety? *English World-Wide, 22,* 55–80.

Sweet, H. (1871). *King Alfred's West Saxon version of Gregory's pastoral care.* Early English Text Society. London: Trübner.

Szmrecsanyi, B., & Kortmann, B. (2009a). Vernacular universals and anglover-sals in a typological perspective. In M. Filppula, J. Klemola, & H. Paulasto (Eds.), *Vernacular universals and language contacts: Evidence from varieties of English and beyond* (pp. 33–53). London: Routledge.

Szmrecsanyi, B., & Kortmann, B. (2009b). The morphosyntax of varieties of English worldwide: A quantitative perspective. *Lingua, 119,* 1643–1663.

Szmrecsanyi, B., & Kortmann, B. (2009c). Between simplification and com-plexification: Non-standard varieties of English around the world. In G. Sampson, D. Gil, & P. Trudgill (Eds.), *Language complexity as an evolving variable* (pp. 64–79). Oxford: Oxford University Press.

Tagliamonte, S. (1998). *Was/were* variation across the generations: View from the city of York. *Language Variation and Change, 10,* 153–192.

Tagliamonte, S. A. (2009). There *was* universals, then there *weren't*: A com-parative sociolinguistic perspective on 'default singulars'. In M. Filppula, J. Klemola, & H. Paulasto (Eds.), *Vernacular universals and language contacts:*

358 References

Evidence from varieties of English and beyond (pp. 103–129). London: Routledge.

Tagliamonte, S. A. (2013). Comparative sociolinguistics. In J. K. Chambers & N. Schilling (Eds.), *Handbook of language variation and change* (2nd ed., pp. 128–156). Oxford: Wiley-Blackwell.

Tagliamonte, S. A., & D'Arcy, A. (2007). Frequency and variation in the community grammar: Tracking a new change through the generations. *Language Variation and Change, 19,* 119–217.

Tagliamonte, S., & Poplack, S. (1993). The zero-marked verb: Testing the creole hypothesis. *Journal of Pidgin and Creole Languages, 8,* 171–206.

Tagliamonte, S. A., & Roeder, R. (2009). Variation in the English definite article: Socio-historical linguistics in t'speech community. *Journal of Sociolinguistics, 13,* 435–471.

Tagliamonte, S., & Smith, J. (1999). Analogical levelling in Samaná English: The case of *was* and *were*. *Journal of English Linguistics, 27,* 8–26.

Tagliamonte, S., & Smith, J. (2000). Old *was*, new ecology: Viewing English through the sociolinguistic filter. In S. Poplack (Ed.), *The English history of African American English* (pp. 141–171). Oxford: Blackwell.

Thomason, S. G., & Kaufman, T. (1988). *Language contact, creolization and genetic linguistics*. Berkeley: University of California.

Thompson, S. A., & Koide, Y. (1987). Iconicity and 'indirect objects' in English. *Journal of Pragmatics, 11,* 399–406.

Tortora, C. (1997). *The syntax and semantics of the weak locative* (Doctoral dissertation). University of Delaware, Newark, DE.

Tortora, C. (2006). The case of Appalachian expletive *they*. *American Speech, 81,* 266–296.

Tortora, C., & Den Dikken, M. (2010). Subject agreement variation: Support for the configurational approach. *Lingua, 120,* 1089–1108.

Trask, R. L. (1996). *Historical linguistics*. London: E. J. Arnold.

Traugott, E. C. (1982). From propositional to textual and expressive meanings: Some semantic-pragmatic aspects of grammaticalization. In W. P. Lehmann & Y. Malkiel (Eds.), *Perspectives on historical linguistics* (pp. 245–271). Amsterdam: John Benjamins.

Traugott, E. C. (1992). Syntax. In R. Hogg (Ed.), *The Cambridge history of the English language (Vol. 1): The beginnings to 1066* (pp. 168–289). Cambridge: Cambridge University Press.

Traugott, E. C. (1995). Subjectification in grammaticalization. In D. Stein & S. Wright (Eds.), *Subjectivity and subjectivisation in language* (pp. 31–54). Cambridge: Cambridge University Press.

References   **359**

Traugott, E. C. (2001). Zeroing in on multifunctionality and style. In P. Eckert & J. R. Rickford (Eds.), *Style and sociolinguistic variation* (pp. 127–136). Cambridge: Cambridge University Press.

Traugott, E. C. (2002). From etymology to historical pragmatics. In D. Minkova & R. Stockwell (Eds.), *Studies in the history of the English language* (pp. 19–49). Berlin: Mouton de Gruyter.

Traugott, E. C. (2003). From subjectification to intersubjectification. In R. Hickey (Ed.), *Motives for language change* (pp. 124–139). Cambridge: Cambridge University Press.

Traugott, E. C. (2004). Exaptation and grammaticalization. In M. Akimoto (Ed.), *Linguistic studies based on corpora* (pp. 133–156). Tokyo: Hituzi Syobo Publishing.

Traugott, E. C. (2010). (Inter)subjectivity and (inter)subjectification: A reassessment. In H. Cuyckens, K. Davidse, & L. Vandelanotte (Eds.), *Subjectification, intersubjectification and grammaticalization* (pp. 29–70). Berlin: Mouton de Gruyter.

Traugott, E. C., & Dasher, R. B. (2002). *Regularity in semantic change.* Cambridge: Cambridge University Press.

Travis, L. M. (1984). *Parameters and effects of word order variation* (Doctoral dissertation). Massachusetts Institute of Technology, Cambridge, MA.

Trüb, R. (2006). Nonstandard verbal paradigms in earlier white southern American English. *American Speech, 81,* 250–265.

Trudgill, P. (1974). *The social differentiation of English in Norwich.* Cambridge: Cambridge University Press.

Trudgill, P. (1986). *Dialects in contact.* Oxford: Blackwell.

Trudgill, P. (1989). Contact and isolation in linguistic change. In L. Breivik & E. Jahr (Eds.), *Language change: Contributions to the study of its causes* (pp. 227–238). Berlin: Mouton de Gruyter.

Trudgill, P. (1992). Dialect typology and social structure. In E. H. Jahr (Ed.), *Language contact: Theoretical and empirical structures* (pp. 195–212). Berlin: Mouton de Gruyter.

Trudgill, P. (1996). Language contact and inherent variability: The absence of hypercorrection in East Anglian present-tense verb forms. In J. Klemola, M. Kytö, & M. Risannen (Eds.), *Speech past and present: Studies in English dialectology in memory of Ossi Ihalainen* (pp. 412–425). Frankfurt: Peter Lang.

Trudgill, P. (1998). Third person singular zero: African-American English, East Anglian dialects and Spanish persecution in the Low Countries. *Folia Linguistica Historica, 18,* 139–148.

360 References

Trudgill, P. (2001). Modern East Anglia as a dialect area. In J. Fisiak & P. Trudgill (Eds.), *East Anglian English* (pp. 1–12). Woodbridge: Boydell and Brewer.

Trudgill, P. (2008). English dialect "defaults singulars", *was* versus *were*, Verner's law, and Germanic dialects. *Journal of English Linguistics, 36,* 341–353.

Trudgill, P. (2009). Vernacular universals and the sociolinguistic typology of English dialects. In M. Filppula, J. Klemola, & H. Paulasto (Eds.), *Vernacular universals and language contacts: Evidence from varieties of English and beyond* (pp. 304–322). London: Routledge.

Trudgill, P. (2013). The role of Dutch in the development of East Anglian English. *Taal en Tongval, 65,* 11–22.

Van Herk, G., & Childs, B. (2015). Active retirees: The persistence of obsolescent features. In R. Torres Cacoullos, N. Dion, & A. Lapierre (Eds.), *Linguistic variation: Confronting fact and theory* (pp. 193–207). London: Routledge.

Van Herk, G., & Walker, J. A. (2005). S marks the spot? Regional variation and early African American correspondence. *Language Variation and Change, 17,* 113–131.

Van Herk, G., Childs, B., & Thorburn, J. (2009). Identity marking and affiliation in an urbanizing Newfoundland community. In W. Cichocki (Ed.), *Papers from the 31st Annual Meeting of the Atlantic Province Linguistic Association* (pp. 85–94). Fredericton: University of New Brunswick.

Van Kemenade, A. (2009). Discourse relations and word order change. In R. Hinterhölzl & S. Petrova (Eds.), *Information structure and language change* (pp. 91–120). Berlin: Mouton de Gruyter.

Van Kemenade, A., & Los, B. (2006). Discourse adverbs and clausal syntax in the history of English. In A. van Kemenade & B. Los (Eds.), *The handbook of the history of English* (pp. 224–248). London: Blackwell.

Vasko, A.-L. (2009). Zero suffix with the third-person singular of the simple present. In A.-L. Vasko (Ed.), *Studies in variation, contacts and change in English (Vol. 4): Cambridgeshire dialect grammar.* Retrieved January 2018 from http://www.helsinki.fi/varieng/journal/volumes/04.

Vasko, A.-L. (2010). Past tense BE: Old and new variants. In B. Heselwood & C. Upton (Eds.), *Proceedings of methods XIII: Papers from the Thirteenth International Conference on Methods in Dialectology, 2008* (pp. 289–298). Frankfurt: Peter Lang.

Vermandere, D., & Meul, C. (2016). How functionless is junk and how useful is exaptation? Probing the -I/ESC- morpheme. In F. Van de Velde & M.

Norde (Eds.), *Exaptation and language change* (pp. 261–285). Amsterdam: John Benjamins.

Vincent, N. (1995). Exaptation and grammaticalization. In H. Andersen (Ed.), *Historical linguistics 1993: Selected Papers from the 11th International Conference on Historical Linguistics, Los Angeles, 16–20 August 1993* (pp. 433–448). Amsterdam: John Benjamins.

Visser, F. Th. (1970). *An historical syntax of the English language (Part one): Syntactical units with one verb* (2nd impression). Leiden: E. J. Brill.

Von Mengden, F. (2016). Functional changes and (meta-)linguistic evolution. In M. Norde & F. Van de Velde (Eds.), *Exaptation and language change* (pp. 121–162). Amsterdam: John Benjamins.

Wakelin, M. F. (1972). *English dialects: An introduction.* London: Athlone Press.

Wakelin, M. F. (1977). *English dialects: An introduction* (2nd Rev. ed.). London: Athlone Press.

Walker, J. (2000). *Present accounted for: Prosody and aspect in Early African American English* (Doctoral dissertation). University of Ottawa.

Walker, J. (2007). "There's bears back there": Plural existentials and vernacular universals in (Quebec) English. *English World-Wide, 28,* 147–166.

Walker, J. (2013). *Subject-verb agreement in English existentials: A cross-community comparison.* Invited paper presented at the University of Bern, Switzerland.

Walker, J. (2014). Contrasting patterns of agreement in three communities. In N. Dion, A. Lapierre, & R. Torres Cacoullos (Eds.), *Linguistic variation: Confronting fact and theory* (pp. 7–21). London: Routledge.

Walker, J. (2015). On the syntax-prosody interface in African American English. In J. Bloomquist, L. J. Green, & S. L. Lanehart (Eds.), *The Oxford handbook of African American language* (pp. 387–402). Oxford: Oxford University Press.

Walker, J., & Meyerhoff, M. (2015). Bequia English. In J. Williams, E. W. Schneider, D. Schreier, & P. Trudgill (Eds.), *Further studies in the lesser-known varieties of English* (pp. 128–143). Cambridge: Cambridge University Press.

Walker, J., & Van Herk, G. (2003). "We labors under a great deal of disadvantiges": Verbal *-s* in Early African American English. In S. Burelle & S. Somesfalean (Eds.), *Proceedings of the 2002 Annual Conference of the Canadian Linguistics Association* (pp. 365–377). Montreal: Canadian Linguistic Association.

Wall, A., & Octavio de Toledo y Huerta, A. S. (2016). Exploring and recycling: Topichood and the evolution of Ibero-romance articles. In M. Norde & F. Van de Velde (Eds.), *Exaptation and language change* (pp. 341–376). Amsterdam: John Benjamins.

Watermeyer, S. (1996). Afrikaans English. In V. de Klerk (Ed.), *Focus on South Africa* (pp. 99–124). Amsterdam: John Benjamins.

Wee, L. (2004). Singapore English: Morphology and syntax. In B. Kortmann & E. W. Schneider (with K. Burridge, R. Mesthrie & C. Upton) (Eds.), *A handbook of varieties of English (Vol. 2): Morphology and syntax* (pp. 1058–1072). Berlin: Mouton de Gruyter.

Wee, L., & Ansaldo, U. (2004). Nouns and noun phrases. In L. Lim (Ed.), *Singapore English: A grammatical description* (pp. 57–74). Amsterdam: John Benjamins.

Wescott, R. (1971). Linguistic iconism. *Language, 47,* 416–428.

Williams, K. (2007). *Ethnic identity and Past be configuration in the Lumbee Community of Baltimore, Maryland.* Paper presented at New Ways of Analyzing Variation 36, University of Pennsylvania, U.S.

Willis, D. (2016). Exaptation and degrammaticalization within an acquisition-based model of abductive reanalysis. In F. Van de Velde & M. Norde (Eds.), *Exaptation and language change* (pp. 197–225). Amsterdam: John Benjamins.

Wilson, S., & Mesthrie, R. (2004). St. Helena English: Morphology and syntax. In B. Kortmann & E. W. Schneider (with K. Burridge, R. Mesthrie & C. Upton) (Eds.), *A handbook of varieties of English (Vol. 2): Morphology and syntax* (pp. 1006–1015). Berlin: Mouton de Gruyter.

Wolfram, W. (1974). The relationship of Southern White Speech to Vernacular Black English. *Language, 50,* 498–527.

Wolfram, W. (2004). The grammar of urban African American Vernacular English. In B. Kortmann & E. W. Schneider (with K. Burridge, R. Mesthrie & C. Upton) (Eds.), *Handbook of varieties of English (Vol. 2): Morphology and syntax* (pp. 111–132). Berlin: Mouton de Gruyter.

Wolfram, W., & Christian, D. (1976). *Appalachian speech.* Arlington: Center for Applied Linguistics.

Wolfram, W., & Schilling-Estes, N. (2003a). Language change in "conservative" dialects: The case of past tense *be* in southern enclave communities. *American Speech, 78,* 208–227.

Wolfram, W., & Schilling-Estes, N. (2003b). Parallel development and alternative restructuring: The case of *weren't* intensification. In D. Britain & J.

Cheshire (Eds.), *Social dialectology: In honour of Peter Trudgill* (pp. 131–154). Amsterdam: John Benjamins.

Wolfram, W., & Schilling-Estes, N. (2005). Remnant dialects in the coastal United States. In R. Hickey (Ed.), *Legacies of colonial English: Studies in transported dialects* (pp. 172–202). Cambridge: Cambridge University Press.

Wolfram, W., & Sellers, J. (1999). Ethnolinguistic marking of past *be* in Lumbee Vernacular English. *Journal of English Linguistics, 27*, 94–114.

Wolfram, W., & Thomas, E. (2002). *The development of African American English*. Oxford: Blackwell.

Wolfson, N. (1979). The conversational historical present alternation. *Language, 55*, 168–182.

Woolard, K. (2008). Why *dat* now? Linguistic-anthropological solutions to the explanation of sociolinguistic icons and change. *Journal of Sociolinguistics, 12*, 432–452.

Wright, J. (1892). *A grammar of the dialect of Windhill in the West Riding of Yorkshire*. London: Trübner.

Wright, J. (1905). *English dialect grammar*. Oxford: Clarendon Press.

Wright, L. (2001). Third-person singular present-tense -*s*, -*th*, and zero, 1575–1648. *American Speech, 76*, 236–258.

Wright, L. (2002). Third person plural present tense markers in London prisoners' depositions, 1562–1623. *American Speech, 77*, 242–263.

Wright, L. (2003). Eight grammatical features of southern United States speech present in early modern London prison narratives. In S. Nagle & S. Sanders (Eds.), *English in the Southern United States* (pp. 36–63). Cambridge: Cambridge University Press.

Wright, L. (2015). Some more on the history of present-tense -*s*, do and zero: West Oxfordshire, 1837. *Journal of Historical Sociolinguistics, 1*, 111–130.

Zanuttini, R., & Bernstein, J. B. (2011). Micro-comparative syntax in English verbal agreement. In S. Lima, K. Mullin, & B. Smith (Eds.), *NELS 39: Proceedings of the 39th Annual Meeting of the North East Linguistic Society* (Vol. 2, pp. 839–854). Amherst: GSLA, University of Massachusetts.

Zwicky, A., & Pullum, G. (1983). Clitization vs. inflection: English *n't*. *Language, 59*, 502–513.

Index

A

Accessibility Theory 66, 67
adjacency 5, 40–42, 45, 51, 55, 70, 197, 270
African American Vernacular English (AAVE) 12, 13, 15, 72, 97, 107, 129, 130, 133, 137–141, 155, 167, 193, 199, 322
Afrikaans 39, 145, 147, 174
agreement 1, 3–7, 12, 13, 25, 26, 34, 35, 49, 51, 56–66, 68, 69, 71, 72, 77, 88, 89, 130, 137, 139, 141, 147–153, 166, 179, 188, 189, 195, 204–207, 212, 237–241, 245, 246, 248, 251–253, 255, 261, 262, 264, 267–272, 274, 275, 283, 284, 293–295, 297, 298, 322, 323, 325
ain't 187, 189, 212, 217, 219, 223

Alabama 27, 81, 102, 105, 167, 181, 185, 211, 215, 256
analogical levelling 31, 166, 177, 179–182, 211, 213, 214
anaphoric agreement 34, 35, 64, 99, 150–152
Appalachia 27, 81, 102–104, 167, 302
aspect 4, 37, 73–75, 108, 166, 241, 295, 308

B

Belfast 3, 27, 47, 58–61, 81, 83
Bequia 129, 296, 305
Bolton 102, 166, 174, 194, 195, 218, 224, 259
British National Corpus (BNC) 175, 245, 290, 307

© The Editor(s) (if applicable) and The Author(s), under exclusive licence to Springer Nature Limited 2019
L. Rupp and D. Britain, *Linguistic Perspectives on a Variable English Morpheme*, https://doi.org/10.1057/978-1-349-72803-9

366   Index

Buckie 3, 27, 82, 166, 177, 178, 197, 199, 205–208, 210, 211, 213, 222, 268

C

Cambridgeshire 134, 136, 144, 166, 173, 190–192, 201, 212, 224
Canada 8, 27, 55, 73, 138, 167, 197, 199, 221, 253, 259, 261, 263
Combinatorial Variability 205, 207–210
constraint hierarchy 198, 200–202, 269, 270, 296, 324
Construction Grammar 9, 62
contraction 256, 261, 270, 272, 282, 304, 309
Corpus of Early English Correspondence (CEEC) 33, 142, 144, 170–172, 175

D

decategorialisation 37
definite article reduction 88
determiner type 261–263, 296–298
Devon 26, 40, 54, 71, 73–75, 81, 89, 97, 108, 138
diagrammatic iconicity 9–11, 26, 85, 88, 89, 96, 147, 148, 166, 179, 292, 293, 306, 322, 323, 326
dialect obsolescence 55
dialectology 3
Discourse-based theory of agreement 64
discourse-pragmatics 5, 12, 69, 299, 300, 324–327
discourse properties 41, 49, 50, 57, 61, 64, 69–71, 150

distance 10, 11, 39, 41, 65, 68, 70, 92, 103, 141, 207, 248, 261, 264, 270, 271, 303, 310
Distributed Morphology (DM) 188, 189
DP-hypothesis 265–267, 303
drag 86, 87, 90, 96, 322, 327

E

Early Modern English 32, 33, 97, 102, 171, 179, 276
East Anglia 13, 33, 130, 131, 133–136, 140–144, 146, 150, 156, 171, 175, 190, 191, 200, 204, 212, 304, 322, 323
East Anglian Subject Rule (EASR) 13, 130, 135–137, 150, 153– 155, 166, 177, 196, 200–202, 204, 212, 323, 325, 327
East Midlands 26, 32, 42, 44, 169, 173, 190
English as a Lingua Franca (ELF) 130, 141, 149, 322
exaptation 7, 8, 15, 26, 34, 36–39, 78, 83, 85, 88, 99, 100, 166, 210, 214–218, 322
Existential *there* sentences 2, 3, 8, 13, 72, 103, 171, 172, 185, 221, 237–239, 241–245, 247, 249–251, 253, 256, 258–260, 264, 270, 271, 273, 278, 282, 290, 291, 295, 296, 299–301, 305, 306

F

Falkland Islands 27, 108, 167, 168, 261, 271, 294

Fens 143–145, 166, 168, 186, 190–193, 199–202, 204, 211–214, 223–225, 301
Following Complement Constraint 90, 110, 322, 326
founder principle 199
Freiburg English Dialect Corpus (FRED) 52, 180, 301
functional grammar 3, 5, 60, 237, 242
functional shift 6–8, 10, 11, 14, 15, 26, 34, 50, 72, 83, 87, 88, 91, 99, 150, 166, 214, 241, 277, 292, 322, 323
fused form 189, 324

G

generative syntax 4, 51, 205, 208, 237, 260, 261, 264
Ghana 148
grammatical agreement 35, 100, 149–154
grammaticalisation 5, 7, 8, 10, 34, 35, 37, 38, 69, 90, 93, 215, 240, 241, 252, 260, 273, 274, 276–280, 282, 284–289, 292, 293, 295, 299, 300, 305, 306, 308, 309, 324

H

habitual 4, 73–75, 77, 87–89, 95, 107, 108, 136, 137, 155
hypercorrection 72, 155
hypoanalysis 216

I

iconicity 9, 11, 12, 14, 15, 26, 50, 69, 85, 91–94, 96, 110, 111, 196, 210, 219, 292, 326
iconicity hypothesis 10, 26, 88, 111, 241, 252, 274, 292
iconic motivation 9, 11, 12, 89, 91, 93–95, 147, 189, 214, 218, 326
identity 4, 5, 25, 56, 64, 68, 72, 87–89, 96, 110, 186, 193, 209, 219, 244, 322, 326, 327
identity construction 72, 88
identity marker 96, 322
innit 224
in't 217, 219, 220, 223
intersubjectivity 287, 289, 307
Ipswich 135, 136, 143
isolation 144, 166, 177, 299
isomorphism 9–11, 88, 89, 92, 111, 147, 179, 213, 240, 293, 306

L

language contact 141, 142, 144–147, 149, 155, 198, 264, 322
language variation and change (LVC) 3, 12–14, 238, 274, 300
layering 4, 90, 91, 198, 214, 280, 292, 322
levelling 1, 31, 37, 51, 97, 98, 109, 145, 146, 166, 172–187, 189–194, 197, 198, 200–202, 210, 211, 213, 214, 218, 222–225, 257, 301, 323
Lexical-functional grammar 60

368   Index

lexical unit 187, 295
Liberia 138, 199
Linguistic Atlas of Early Middle English (LAEME) 31, 42, 48, 53
Linguistic Atlas of the Middle and South Atlantic States 184
locative inversion 253, 254
locative *there* 239, 241, 276, 279, 283, 292
London 27, 30, 32, 33, 79, 101, 102, 109, 131, 142, 149, 166, 171, 175, 180, 192, 193, 195, 201, 202, 211, 212, 224, 302, 309
Lumbee 193, 197

M

Middle English (ME) 1, 2, 28–33, 40–42, 44–47, 53, 54, 63, 69, 76, 89, 97, 98, 108, 109, 111, 131, 144, 168–171, 178, 196, 211, 221, 253, 254, 275, 276
Minimalist Program 187, 205, 246

N

narrative 4, 6, 9, 71, 72, 75, 78–85, 89–91, 96, 109, 137, 198, 326
negative allomorphs 187
Newcastle Electronic Corpus of Tyneside English (NECTE) 54, 62, 82, 180
Newcastle-upon-Tyne 81
Newfoundland 8, 14, 27, 70, 73, 76, 77, 82, 86–90, 96, 110, 167, 327
new information 65, 91, 240, 242, 244, 254, 274, 278, 291, 293–295, 324, 326

New Zealand 3, 27, 167, 254, 255, 261, 263, 271, 297–299
Northern Ireland 52, 193, 198
Northern Subject Rule (NSR) 4, 5, 13, 25, 32, 39–47, 50–52, 54–57, 61–64, 66, 67, 69–72, 75, 76, 82, 85, 89, 91, 95, 99, 102–108, 111, 135, 138, 139, 141, 148, 150, 151, 154, 166, 169, 171, 172, 174, 177, 178, 180–182, 196–201, 204, 207, 208, 210, 212–214, 221, 224, 322–327
Northumbrian 28–30, 42–44, 46, 53, 97, 98, 101, 106
Norwich 129, 134, 135, 140, 142, 143, 146, 173, 322
Nova Scotia 129, 138, 167, 199, 221, 222, 259, 261

O

Ocracoke 27, 50, 71, 104, 167, 183–187, 190, 192, 197–199, 223, 225, 301
Old English (OE) 3, 9, 25, 28–30, 41, 43, 44, 46, 47, 49, 61, 63, 88, 97, 105, 108, 111, 140, 211, 221, 225, 251–253, 274–276, 280, 286, 306, 308
Ontario 253
Ottawa 27, 55, 167, 197, 259, 261, 262

P

Palmerston Island 167
past BE 2, 3, 6–8, 11, 50, 55, 88, 91, 102, 104, 136, 154, 165,

166, 168, 169, 171, 172,
174–176, 178–186, 192–203,
206, 207, 210–215, 218, 220,
221, 223–226, 257, 259, 272,
280, 295, 302, 304, 323–326
Petty Harbour 76, 86
polarity 4, 6, 11, 91, 166, 167, 177,
183, 185, 186, 200, 204, 211,
213, 215–219, 225, 302, 303,
323, 326
predictability hierarchy 5, 68, 69
presentational marker 72
presentative signal 240, 241, 273,
274, 293–295, 309
proximity effect 40, 42, 54, 55, 60,
63, 69–71, 100, 106, 178, 224

Q

Quebec 259, 263, 271, 272, 296,
305
quotatives 82, 84

R

Reading 8, 10, 14, 27, 85, 89, 90,
96, 105, 110, 166, 190, 197,
217, 220, 243, 248–250, 291,
293, 298, 303, 322
reallocation 145, 177, 193, 211,
214, 215, 217, 220
reanalysis 7, 8, 28, 35, 37, 215–217,
277–281, 284, 289, 292, 305,
306, 308
regrammaticalisation 26, 39, 69, 78,
83, 88, 322
reorganisation 185, 223

Republic of Ireland 221
restructuring 15, 84, 186, 223
Rocky Mountains 167, 256, 258

S

Samaná 106, 129, 130, 138, 199,
222
secondary grammaticalisation 8, 274,
284, 285, 288, 289, 292, 298,
308
Shetland Islands 259
simplification 142, 146, 168
Singapore 106
Smith Island 27, 167, 185, 188, 197
South Armagh 81, 102, 166, 198
Southern England 186, 202, 323
Southwest of England 72, 74, 102,
108, 132, 146, 173, 193, 223
stance 88, 217–219, 278, 287, 305
Standard English 1, 2, 25, 26, 44,
61, 62, 72, 74, 80, 86, 98,
108, 151, 154, 165, 167, 174,
180, 183, 185, 188, 205, 208,
237, 245, 299, 302
St Helena 81, 129, 145, 146
Strangers 142–144
subjectification 70, 274, 278, 281,
288, 290, 307
subject-verb agreement 1, 6, 12,
34, 35, 56, 57, 62, 64, 69,
102, 137, 139, 141, 155, 204,
212, 237, 239, 241, 245, 255,
260–262, 269–272, 283, 284,
295, 300, 302
Suffolk 134–136, 143, 144, 173,
191, 200, 259, 302, 304, 309

370 Index

Survey of English Dialects (SED) 3,
  51, 97, 98, 102, 131, 132, 134,
  168, 173–175, 184, 194, 257
Sydney 202, 203, 212, 256

tag-questions 91, 194, 195, 215,
  217–219, 225
textual meaning 286, 287, 290, 299
topic manager 290
Toronto 259, 263, 296, 305
Tristan da Cunha (TdCE) 3, 129,
  130, 145, 146, 167, 182, 211,
  215, 322
Tyneside 27, 54, 103, 166, 180
Type-of-Subject effect 40, 46, 47, 54,
  63, 67, 70, 71, 106, 224

underspecification 206, 208
unidirectionality 38, 286

verb agreement paradigm 189
verbal –s 2–8, 10, 12–15, 25–27, 30,
  32, 34, 39, 40, 42, 46, 50, 52–
  55, 57–64, 69–78, 80, 82, 83,
  85, 86, 88, 90, 91, 94–97, 99,
  100, 102–110, 129, 137–139,
  141, 148–150, 155, 165, 166,
  179, 181, 182, 196, 197, 199,
  200, 204, 205, 207, 210, 218,

  221, 224, 237–241, 251–265,
  267, 269–274, 280, 282, 284,
  292–294, 298, 299, 301, 303,
  306, 307, 321–327
verbal zero 2, 3, 13, 33, 97, 129–131,
  133–137, 139–147, 149, 154,
  155, 166, 196, 200, 204, 212,
  225, 259, 322–324
Verb Second 283
vernacular culture index 86
vernacularity 85
vernacular verb constraint 86, 90

was-generalisation 172, 173, 176,
  181–183, 185, 211, 213–215
was levelling 224
was/weren't 6, 11, 91, 165, 167, 176,
  177, 185, 186, 189–193, 196,
  200, 204, 212, 214–217, 219,
  222, 301, 326
Welsh 46, 59, 92, 101, 106, 111,
  151, 152, 270
were-generalisation 172, 173, 175,
  176, 184, 190
were levelling 175, 176, 194, 224
West Midlands 32, 48, 169, 170, 176
West-Saxon concord 44

York 88, 194, 195, 197, 198, 211,
  214, 253, 256–258, 263, 271

CPSIA information can be obtained
at www.ICGtesting.com
Printed in the USA
LVHW081824140619
621265LV00008B/226/P